That's the Way
It Was

That's the Way It Was

The Life and Times of Standish Curtis Hulse

July 10, 1906 - February 21, 1997

Compiled & Edited by
JENNIFER HULSE WATTS

Wattsup Publications
1094 Locust St.
Willits, CA 95490
wattsup@gmail.com

Printed by

GORHAM PRINTING

Centralia, Washington USA

ISBN: 978-0-9969097-0-9

Printed in the United States of America

First Edition

I dedicate this book to the memory of my father,
Standish Curtis Hulse,
who inspired me in so many ways.

CONTENTS

PART THREE: 309
WHEN MY SHIP COMES IN 309

Family Tree

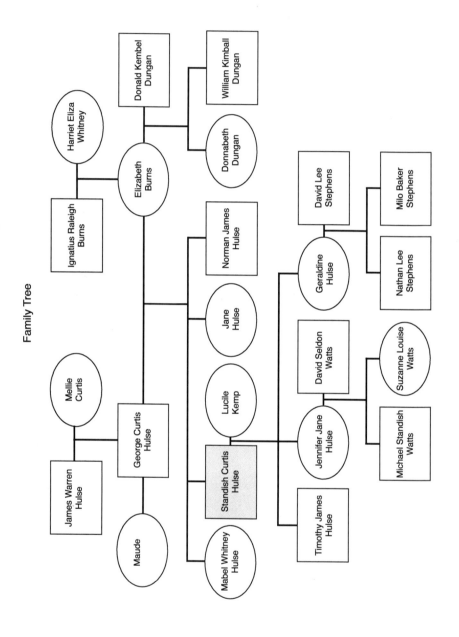

Preface

WHEN MY FATHER WAS IN HIS LATE SIXTIES he sat down at his old Underwood typewriter and began writing down memories of his childhood in San Jose. He could see the vast changes that had taken place in his lifetime and he felt there was value in recording them.

In spite of being self-taught, Dad was an excellent writer who could bring a sunset to life or tell a colorful tale that would stay in your mind like a photograph. He enjoyed writing and the volume of letters he wrote to his mother, and his wife, Lu, over the years is a testament to his love of words. He liked to read and especially enjoyed poetry and delighted in the metaphor, which colors his writings so beautifully.

The book is in three parts; his youth; his journeys; and his married life. He grew up in San Jose but after tragedy occurred, he went off to find adventure. He then returned home and tried to settle down, but became discontent so he set off once more. During his years at sea and his time in the Army, he came to manhood. He enjoyed meeting new people, trying new things, learning new skills and feeling capable and competent. After he returned home, he married and then dedicated himself to his marriage and his family, using his skills and experiences to be a successful husband, father and provider. This is the story of that journey.

This book, while a biography of Dad, is also a history of the 20th Century, with his life spanning it from 1906 to 1997. When he used to tell me stories of his youth, he often ended with the phrase, "That's the way it was." Hence the title of this book.

The reader will find some racial slurs in the text. I have left them in as they reflect his speech, often without any intention of causing offense.

As I have been writing this book I have followed Dad from San Jose to New York City, from Portland, Oregon, to Antofagasta, Chile. I have been with him on shipwrecks and in foxholes, through storm and calm, from jungles to opera houses. I have studied the times and the places and come to a much greater understanding of the man, Stan Hulse.

Dad was an idea man, a dreamer – he was always thinking, observing, questioning. He was opinionated at times and was a stimulating conversationalist. He appreciated life because he had lived it. Where many feel uncomfortable with the sea, he loved it. He was comfortable living on that edge. He grabbed hold of life and enjoyed the ride to the fullest.

I hope you, the reader, will enjoy taking this ride with him.

~*Jenny Watts*
2016

A little girl
A little boy
A big dog
Sitting on the curb in the dusk,
watching darkness gently usher out the day.
They sit talking of the days to come
and of the noble things that they are to do.
Their world is one apart from ours.
Only the dog seems to understand.

Stan

PART ONE:

Coming of Age

Chapter 1. Early Childhood

My FATHER WAS TIMEKEEPER on a dredging project down in Georgia. It was a job he had taken sometime after my sister Mabel was born in San Francisco, June 28, 1903. It was a rough life that didn't suit the little family, so he decided to leave it and head back out West. On the way, they stopped to visit his parents in Mt. Vernon, Ohio, and have the family doctor take care of the expectant mother. They were staying with my father's aunt, Abby Kinney, when Dr. Lee delivered the baby, July 10, 1906, who was later to be christened Standish Curtis Hulse, and it was in her home that I was born.

My father, George Curtis Hulse, was born August 3, 1876, in St. Louis, Missouri, and he grew up in that bustling city. He was the oldest child born to James Warren Hulse and Mellie Curtis. When he was six years old, his sister, Mabel, was born, but she died very young, leaving George the only child. His father, James, was himself an only child, and he had inherited quite a fortune – enough that he never really had to work. So George was raised up in considerable wealth and comfort.

In his youth he spent some time hunting and fishing with his father. He never learned a trade or profession but took up photography and was later to make a living as a photographer and photo finisher. He was a gentle person, well read and of nice appearance. He sported a mustache, was of medium build and stood six feet tall.

At the age of 26, he met Elizabeth Burns in Chicago, where they were both visiting. He had no job at the time, but she was taken in by his dashing manner. She was 19 years old and was a small woman who stood five feet and three-quarters of an inch tall. She dressed fashionably and always wore a hat and gloves when she went out. After a whirlwind courtship of two weeks, they were married August 19, 1902, at St. Mark's Episcopal Church, Chicago, with Rev. William White Wilson, rector presiding.

After I was born, our family of four came west by train to San Jose, California, where my mother's family was well established. We moved into a house on North 6th Street. There my father built a darkroom, and established himself as a photographer. Photography had graduated from the daguerreotype[1] and come into the reach of many with photographic film. He was called upon to photograph the usual weddings and funerals, and often the dearly departed resting in splendor in his or her satin-lined casket. Those pictures were sent back to the old country to show how nicely so-and-so had been laid away.

On March 23, 1908, my younger sister, Jane, was born. My very first recollection is of watching a Fourth of July fireworks display while seated at her feet in her perambulator in 1909. I guess I was about 3 years old.

About the same time I took a pair of scissors and sheared off my knuckle. I was looking at the blood coming out and my mother saw it and was quite excited, wondering what to do. They decided it wasn't necessary to have it sewn, but it left me quite a scar all my life.

Our house on North 6th Street had running water, which was something at that time, and we had a stove that was fired by wood. We had lamps in those days, kerosene lamps. The kerosene was delivered to our house in 5-gallon cans, and we would fill up the lamps with the kerosene, and that was our light.

I learned an early lesson while pushing a wooden box across a long porch outside our house. As I pushed one end of the box, the other end flew up and whacked me a terrible blow just under my chin. My, but it hurt! That was over 60 years ago and I still feel the

---

1 The daguerreotype was a photographic process where the image was made directly on the silvered surface; it is very fragile and can be rubbed off with a finger.

The house Standish was born in, Mt. Vernon, Ohio, July 10, 1906.

Baby Standish

Standish, 1908.

Jane, 1910.

Standish in Indian suit, 1909.

Mother, Mabel, Standish and Jane, March 1910.

4

hurt and the pain and remember being gathered into the loving arms of my mother. The big sobs that came from the very depths of my being gradually subsided as she comforted me, while we rocked gently in the old rocker. I never pushed a box that way again.

About 1910, we moved to a two-story frame house at Tenth and Empire Streets in San Jose. The house was on the northeast corner and had a beautiful white picket fence along the street. In back of the house, at the rear of the property, stood the tankhouse. That's what we called the enclosed space on the ground floor of the structure that supported a large wooden tank that held the water supply for the house. Above this tank stood the windmill, which pumped the water from the well into the tank. The height of the tank determined the water pressure coming into the house.

My father was a commercial photographer by then, so he set up his darkroom in the tankhouse. He went around taking pictures and brought them home to develop them into prints. That was all quite new in those days. The Brownie Kodak, an inexpensive box camera, was just coming into vogue, and my father also processed the new picture film being made by Eastman that was fast becoming a craze. A year or so later, photo finishing left little time for photography, and he set up a laboratory in a suite on the second floor of a building on First Street and Post, in downtown San Jose. My mother supplied the money to set him up in this enterprise. My father did a nice business "photo finishing" until he sold the business, Hulse Service, in 1930.

About 1914, he became associated with A.R. Tower. Tower had a motorcycle and traveled up and down the state opening accounts in drugstores and news vendor shops where people could leave their Kodak film for processing by Hulse Service. The box camera was coming into its own and snapshots were the thing. Most of the accounts mailed the films in for processing, but some would send them in by stage: automobile stages served many of the cities up and down the state in those days. He made frequent trips to the Post Office and stage depot where the films were picked up. They were processed the same day and sped on their way as quickly as possible.

In 1916, his booming business required a larger plant and he moved into the entire upper floor of the Clayton Building at 36 West Santa Clara Street, between Market and First Street, where he "installed the most modern and complete plant in the west." His workmanship became known as exceptional and at one time, he conducted the biggest photo finishing business in California, serving some 250 stores in California, Oregon, Nevada, Idaho, Washington and Arizona. [2]

Sometimes Jane and I went to work with Father. The booming of the big fire bell atop the firehouse on Market Street was cause for great excitement. When the bell rang, we rushed to the window of the shop, craning our necks in anticipation. After a short, breathless wait, around the corner came the Fire Chief in his red, rubber-tired buggy. Dressed in his blue suit and military cap, he leaned somewhat forward holding the reins of his speeding horse straight out in front of him.

Moments later, around the corner came the fire engine, smoke billowing from its boiler! On a high seat, the red helmeted driver, whip in hand and clutching the reins would urge the plunging steeds onwards. Clinging to the rear were a couple of helmeted firemen, one furiously clanging a big shining bell. The boiler too, was beautifully polished and glistened in the sunlight. The acrid smoke and the noise of the speeding engine frightened the horses, and the drivers along the way often had to get down and quiet their teams. The prudent drivers, who had heard the bell at a distance, would be standing at the head of their horse teams in order to quiet them as the engine roared by. It was exciting to see the scared and sometimes rearing horses as the engine passed. It wasn't until later that they added a big hook-and-ladder that would sweep around the corner with a great roar of its gasoline engine. It had two drivers, one in front to drive the vehicle and one on the rear to pilot the long ladders around the corners, otherwise they would never have been able to make the turns.

One afternoon, while we were living at Tenth and Empire Streets, our little white pet dog went mad. Jane and I were playing in the yard when, hearing our screams, my father rushed out of the tankhouse to see what was the matter. There he found us being confronted by a viscous, snarling dog that was foaming at the mouth. Up until then, he had been our pet. Dad herded us into the house and it seemed like hours that we were stuck inside wondering what was what. I still remember hearing the roar of the shotgun blast that sent the poor beast to dog heaven.

Mabel, my older sister, attended a school across the street. Poor Mabel. Someone had tried on her sunbonnet and as a result, Mom

---

2 Quote from the *San Jose Evening News*, December 13, 1916, vol. 67, issue 142, page 8.

found lice in her beautiful head of long chestnut hair. Only one thing to do – shave her head. As a precaution, Mom had all of our heads shaved. Mabel, Jane and I were as bald as billiard balls. Mabel had quite a time going back to school without any hair, but it was quite the thing to do. Many of the kids had their heads shaved.

We often walked a few doors up Empire Street where delicious smells came from the little "Mom and Pop" shop there. They had a big copper kettle near the front door in which they made delicious taffy candy that you could buy for a penny. I think maybe my sweet tooth started there.

Stan and Jane with their heads shaved due to lice.

A few blocks north of our home was the old Chinatown at 5th and Jackson Streets. It was a little settlement of mostly shacks and small buildings. I don't recall any street lighting and almost no side-walks, only wooden boardwalks. The settlement was surrounded by a high barbed wire fence, and at the threat of a Tong War,[3] the wooden

---

3 Tongs were Chinese gangs that ran highly profitable gambling houses, brothels, opium dens, and slave trade enterprises in Chinatown. Tong Wars were turf battles concerning criminal enterprises.

gates would be closed to keep out the feared Tong hatchet men. Those wars, originating in San Francisco or one of the other large Chinatowns in the state, would present the danger of hatchet men paying a visit on the local members of a rival Tong.

Daily the Chinamen, with their long, black queues, would pass our house carrying long poles over their shoulders from which were suspended bamboo tubs at each end, much like a wine barrel that had been cut in half. In those tubs were carried produce, fresh fish, eggs, pottery, big brown earthen urns of soy from China, live chickens, etc. to the many Chinese cooks in the greater houses about the city. The fish in the tubs were alive, and if a customer wanted only a half, the Chinaman would deftly fillet the live fish, without disturbing the vital organs, and pop the remaining half back into the water to be delivered live to the next customer. The tubs of swimming fish were fascinating.

They often carried shrimp, fresh clams and oysters in the bamboo tubs swinging from the ends of their poles. The Chinese at that time were still digging clams and oysters from the oyster beds that they tended on the tidelands of the bay. The beds covered up to several acres each and were enclosed by fences made of thin poles stuck into the sand to keep the oysters in and their natural enemies out. The Chinese did a big business in this popular food. I can remember my father bringing home an oyster loaf — a loaf of milk bread hollowed out and stuffed with succulent oysters. It was good. The Oyster Loaf was a well-known San Jose restaurant, and that was a specialty there. It did a good business, too. It was very popular.

Up until that time, there was no large municipal sewer system. San Jose had just started one downtown, but all of the residences still had septic tanks. It wasn't long before the oyster beds became polluted and by the late teens, the bay oyster and clam days were over.

There were many cane chairs in use, and the Chinese did a big business manufacturing and repairing the wicker work. They used to pass the house bearing huge loads of these chairs — what today would be a pick-up load — tied into enormous bundles at each end of their jinn-poles. They also sold Chinaware and earthenware pottery, large and small, and did a big business in laundry.

Sometimes we'd walk to Chinatown for dinner. My dad would carry me most of the way on his shoulders, but not in wet weather. There were no sidewalks in front of most of the shops, and in the winter the muddy streets were all but impassable. There was one little

8

restaurant that was run by a Chinaman who had worked for my great-grandfather, J. R. Whitney, at the old family home at Tenth and San Carlos Streets. With his little wrinkled face beaming and his head bobbing, he greeted us as though we were royalty. He took such pleasure in watching us enjoy his wonderful dishes!

He had a funny little native restaurant and he ushered us upstairs to a room that had a balcony extending over the wooden sidewalk. Here we dined in view of the kitchen that was also on the second floor. In the summer the tables on this balcony were always full. They were low, round tables and the patrons sat on low stools. When you sat down, the waiter brought a big pot of steaming tea and little white china cups. When the tea arrived a little was poured into the tiny cups, which looked like small bowls, and swirled about and tossed onto the floor, as was the custom. A wise sanitary measure, I am sure.

The place was lighted by a gaslight, and since there was not a fork in the place, we had to use chopsticks and Chinese spoons. This was no problem, for my mother had lived in the Orient for ten years and had taught us how to use chopsticks. My mother did bring forks in her handbag for us kids, which we would have to resort to before the meal was over. The only patrons I recall seeing besides ourselves were Chinese, and we created somewhat of a stir when we showed up. It was as though we had stepped into another world.

We sometimes had hot dishes delivered to the house. In the evening, by appointment, a Chinaman would come trotting up to the door with insulated boxes slung from ends of the inevitable pole, and in these boxes were various delicious Chinese dishes, steaming hot. I came to love Chinese food from an early age.

I remember one summer afternoon when I was about five years old. Jane, Mabel, Mother and I were sitting on the lawn in the back yard. The warm sunshine filtered through the trees and the summer breeze carried the spicy fragrance of the pepper trees through the air. We were listening to Mother read poems by Edward Lear from the *Book of Nonsense*. It was one of my favorite books and I especially enjoyed the silly cartoons that went with the poems.

Suddenly, the earth began to shake beneath us, which was an awful feeling. We all ran to Mother's arms. Jane started crying and we held tight together watching the house and the trees sway and creak around us. I didn't know what was happening, and was terribly frightened, but Mother kept holding us for what seemed like an eternity.

Finally the earth quit shaking but by that time we were all crying.

We ran into the house to find several dishes and vases shattered on the floor, and the pantry a mess, but the house itself suffered no major damage. Then we joined the neighbors outside who were all talking at once, describing their experiences of the earthquake. It was the first one I ever felt.[4]

Stan and Jane on porch at 10th Street house, 1910.

Mother's comment: "The chest, which is unduly prominent, can be accounted for by the fact that he is posing with his new necktie of which he is exceedingly proud."

Chapter 2. Villa Avenue

IN 1912, OUR FAMILY MOVED to the corner of Villa Avenue and Myrtle Avenue in San Jose. My parents purchased the house with money from the estate of my mother's grandfather, John Roswell Whitney. It

---

4 July 1, 1911: Earthquake today at 2 p.m. caused minor damage and considerable fright among the people. It was centered near Coyote in Santa Clara County. It did considerable damage at Lick Observatory where the large telescope was moved ¾ of an inch.

was the home of Judge Brady, and we lived there until 1915. The lot was beautifully planted. Mrs. Brady enjoyed cultivating her garden and she had a vast collection of flowers and over 50 trees on the property. It was a big lot, over a quarter of an acre. We had a fig tree and lemon trees, cherry trees and peach trees, magnolias and a number of eucalyptus trees. There was a big rabbit pen with about 50 rabbits.

The house itself was beautiful. It was a spacious place, built around 1880, and typical of the better homes of its day. It was the kind of house suitable for entertaining in the gay formality of the 1890s. It had three stories and a full basement. There were servants' quarters on the third floor, and the first floor was raised high enough to allow windows in the basement, in which there were living quarters for the gardener who took care of a big coal-fired furnace. There were storage rooms in the basement and an old disused electric generating plant that had been superseded by the central power plant. This was one of the first places in the valley to have electric lights. The generator was a single cylinder engine run by gasoline, and a bank of glass jars filled with electrolyte served as the storage batteries. Since this was a somewhat tenuous source of light, every room had its own gas fixture and gas was our principle source of light. The hall, the living room and parlor, and the dining room had ornate chandeliers equipped for both gas and electricity. This was in contrast to our neighbor, Theuerkauf, who relied mostly on kerosene lamps until they wired their house for electricity. We also used kerosene lamps to augment the other lighting. The frequent power failures made it advisable to have an alternate system of lighting.

Up the stairs from the garden was a large front porch. Double doors, with heavy brass hardware and etched glass, opened into a large entry hall. Inside the front doors stood an ornate hat rack and an umbrella holder, and nearby, a table held a silver tray in which calling cards were placed. My mother received visitors on the first and second Wednesdays of the month.

Off the entry was the double parlor, where I used to love to lie on the thick green carpet and listen to my mother play the piano. She had studied piano since childhood and at the time of her marriage, was considering the concert stage. She had a beautiful "touch," and my eyes would fill with tears, I was so moved by the loveliness of the music. She used to say that she "strummed" the piano, and she spent many hours there playing music by her favorite composers, Grieg and Nevin.

11

A set of sliding doors could be used to reduce the size of the double parlor room in order to make it more suitable for an intimate gathering. I remember Christmas morning there. They kept the parlor door closed until Dad had lighted all the candles on the big Christmas tree. The candles were about five inches tall and as thick as your finger and they burned for quite a while. When he gave a signal, the

9 Villa Avenue, San Jose.

folding doors to the parlor were opened, and the lighted candles on the Christmas tree shone forth to our great delight and squeals of joy. We watched the tree until we had our fill, and then Dad went about the task of blowing out the candles one by one before we got down to the business of the day.

One Christmas, my mother helped me write this letter to Santa Claus:

> *Dear Santa Claus,*
> *Please send me a stove – and I want a "choo choo"*
> *– a kitchen and a little velocipede.*
> *Send to 9 Villa Avenue for Christmas to*
> *Standish Hulse*

Standish with his choo-choo.

Next to the living room was the billiard room, one wall of which was lined with books. A large porch went out from either the billiard room or the parlor. Another door off the hall was to the dining room. It had high wainscoted[5] walls with a plate rail.[6] Another door led through a passage to the kitchen pantry area.

The stairway to the second floor, with its heavy balustrade and fancy newel, had the typical landing halfway up.[7] On the second floor were the family bedrooms and above them three bedrooms for the servants, though we never had more than two at one time: a cook and a housemaid. There was also an upstairs sitting room complete with fireplace and a large upstairs porch where we kids liked to sleep on warm summer nights.

We were just settling in to our new house in the spring of 1912, when one of the great disasters of the 20th century occurred. It was late afternoon, May 6, 1912, just before dark, when two men hurried down the middle of the street. Each carried a bundle of newspapers under his arm and was bawling "EXTRA, EXTRA." They stopped now and then to press a paper into the hands of an eager buyer with the speed and dexterity that only a professional news vendor could achieve. My dad rushed out and for five cents we got the news of the

---

5 Wood paneling on the lower part of the walls of a room.

6 A rail or narrow shelf fixed along a wall above the wainscot to hold plates, especially for ornament or display.

7 A balustrade is a row of repeating small posts that support the upper rail of a railing. The newel is the post at the foot of the staircase.

sinking of the *Titanic*. The shocking headline under the six-inch high EXTRA: "Titanic Sinks, Hundreds Perish," brought us the news of one of the greatest marine disasters in history. The paper was full of pictures of the palatial craft, the greatest ship that had ever sailed, and it was hard to believe that it had been lost. The paper contained the long black-bordered columns of those who had perished.

Each weekday morning, my father left the house to go to work. He walked one short block to The Alameda where he caught the streetcar into downtown San Jose. Mother stayed home with her growing family and the servants. The day was punctuated with the many delivery men that plied their wares through the streets of San Jose.

Early in the morning, before breakfast, our milkman, "Peg-leg" Adams, arrived. He had lost his foot in the war, the Spanish-American War, and had a wooden peg strapped to the stump. He rolled up in his old rickety wagon with several big dairy cans of milk in the back, and Jane and I were sent out with a lard pail, a standard utensil in those days, to get the milk. He measured out the desired amount and poured it into our pail. We took the milk inside and poured it into flat pans for the cream to rise. Much of what we ate had cream in it or on it. Flies were a real problem, but I never saw anything thrown out because a little fly got into it. You just scooped the fly out. If we didn't meet "Peg-leg" at his wagon, he'd laboriously clamber down, and I can remember well the bump, bump, bump of his wooden leg on the concrete walk as he lumbered along to the kitchen door. If we ran out of milk, one of us kids was sent to his place for it. We hated to go, as his cows were in a small dirty barnyard that smelled to high heaven, and the flies just swarmed about the premises, but no sickness was ever traced to the milk that I can remember.

We got daily mail deliveries. The postman drove a low wagon equipped with a box-like cab. It had a low rear step that enabled him to reach into the compartments in which the letters had been sorted. It didn't have a regular seat on it. It had a little side bench that he could perch on and then a big bin in front of him, in which all the letters were placed in various piles. He sorted the letters as he rode along, and when he got to a particular address where he wanted to stop, he'd say, "Whoa," as he descended the step, and the horse would stop while he was delivering the mail, and wait till he got back.

The horse knew the route perfectly and made his way along the street, stopping and starting the length of the block to keep abreast of the postman as he went from house to house to drop off the mail. The postman zigzagged from side to side across the street, and if he stopped to chat with somebody for a while, the horse would stop and patiently wait. The horse did the whole route without being instructed except possibly to "Git up" a little when the postman wanted him to hurry. It was blocks before the driver had to touch the reins.

The bread wagon came by every other day. In back of the driver's seat was a big box-like compartment filled with bread. None of it was wrapped and most of it was French style or hard crust type. This horse knew the route as well as his master and stopped at the regular customers without command. As they rounded the corner Mr. O'Keefe, the driver, reached back and grabbed a long loaf of bread and swatted the horse across the rump with it. The horse trotted on around the corner and stopped, without a command, at the next house on the route.

Once a week the fish wagon came by, I believe it was on Friday. It was a little wagon with a big box on the back, and the back end of the box would lift up and make an awning. Inside he had a number of fish, with ice thrown on top of them. We heard him a block away as he announced his coming with a blast on his "fish horn," an oversized version of the horns we use on New Year's Eve, and the cry of "Fish, fish! Fresh fish!" throughout the neighborhood. Our cook, Signorina, went running out to select a fish for dinner, and the peddler cut any size fish she wanted and weighed, trimmed and scaled it ready for the pan.

Signorina was just about as wide as she was tall. Mom described her as Sra. Four-by-four. The only cooking she knew was her native Italian style, using more onions and garlic in the short time that she was there than had been used by our household in years. She spoke little English and my mother couldn't speak her language, and she was unable to Americanize her style in any degree. The meals she prepared were sumptuous to say the least. She loved cooking and she cooked and cooked. The house and the family reeked of garlic, so after several months of delicious meals heavy with pasta, Mom let her go. Signorina was replaced by Nora, an Irish girl just over from the old sod. Nora was a gem and stayed with us until a reversal in the family fortunes necessitated her departure.

Another character was Joe Savio, the vegetable man. He was jolly and roly-poly, an Italian from the old country who came over as a young man. He had a truck farm out on the edge of town. Since he had to take his products to town to market them, he loaded up with his best produce and peddled it in the better neighborhoods. Twice a week he stopped at our house, driving his team of two fine bays pulling a big green wagon, to supply us with fresh vegetables.

He'd pull his team up to our gate, and he and our cook would take care of restocking the produce. It was great fun for us kids to climb all over his wagon inspecting his wares. Joe would always give us a carrot or even a banana. Years later while drinking some of his homemade wine – it was during Prohibition – Joe confessed that all those little gifts to the neighborhood kids found their way onto the produce bill sooner or later.

Joe's route brought him to our house about midday. Our place was the last place on his route, and after leaving us he drove around the corner to where a big elm tree grew. There he ate his lunch and drank a big jug of red wine and took a nap in the cool shade. I can still see roly-poly Joe with his bowler hat pulled over his face, propped against the tree trunk, the now almost empty jug at hand, taking his siesta. I have never seen a more florid face. To give him credit, the produce market did open in the wee small hours, and you had to be there early to get the best fruits and vegetables.

His wagon route prospered and he bought more land. His family worked hard in the fields, and then came an unexpected boost: Prohibition. Joe started selling some of his "foot juice" to his friends. His wife and girls used to trod the grapes barefoot to press out the wine just as they did in the old country, Italy. When word got around, Joe found that he had a host of friends, and he did make good wine. But that's another story . . .

In the fall, the wine grapes came in on railroad cars – like coal cars – pulled by big steam engines. People went down to the rail yard and loaded their wagons full of grapes and took them home to make grape juice out of them. The grape juice fermented and became wine and that was that. Lots of people made their own wine. It filled a need, I guess.

Most of the houses in the neighborhood had chicken yards. There was no garbage collection, and anything edible was eaten by either the dogs, the cats, chickens or goats. The few tin cans were thrown into a pit in the back yard, and all the bottles and worn-out clothing, papers, pans, etc. were collected by the "rags, bottles and sacks" man. He was a junk dealer who would buy most anything. You could hear him coming way down the road as he'd holler, sometimes even through a megaphone, "Rags, bottles, sacks," repeated and repeated as his old nag plodded slowly down the street. He'd stop at the house and you could take out even a bottle and sell it to him and maybe get as much as a nickel for it. Old sacks brought prices; old rags brought prices; and he would buy copper, iron or other metals and even old pots. Most any old bric-a-brac you had around the house you could sell to him. It was kind of a windfall for us kids to collect a few bottles and sell them to the "rags, bottles and sacks" man when he came along. He'd give us a nickel and we'd take it down to the store and get a whole bag of candy. His rickety wagon with its gaunt horse was the last of the horse-drawn vehicles to depart the scene.

Coal used to be delivered to the house in sacks. We'd get ten or twenty sacks of coal at a time. The coal men were all covered with coal dust, and they'd come up to the house in their wagon and carry the coal down into the basement and into our coal bin where we'd have to shovel it out, scoop by scoop to feed the furnace.

I almost forgot about Mr. Roberts. He used to deliver kerosene, gasoline and coal oil for our room heaters in five-gallon cans. He drove a nice team that he was very proud of, and he kept his red and black wagon shined and polished. He and his family lived down the street from us and, as the years went by, the families became good friends. During the flu epidemic in 1918, his son Gordon died and we went to his funeral. The coffin was set up by the front window in the living room, and the mourners filed past to pay their respects to "Pinky," as he was called.

The most impressive teams that came by the house were those drawing the brewery wagons. They were matched teams of heavy draft horses. Some were black, gray or dappled, others were sorrel or chestnut, and always especially matched. They were beautiful horses and they pulled the long brewery wagons. The principle feature of the brewery wagon was two long racks on which were stacked barrels of beer. They used to deliver the kegs of beer to the many German immigrants who lived on Villa Avenue.

Some of the families, when they got their beer, would make a little bit of a celebration of opening the keg. They had a bung starter, a big mallet for removing the bung (or stopper) of the cask. The keg would be set on the floor, and the master of the house would tap on

17

either side of the bung until it popped out. Immediately he'd stick the spigot into the bung hole and knock it into place with the mallet. The first beer to be drawn off would be just full of foam and we kids used to love to sit around and sip that foam. The adults were quite amenable to having us eat the foam, which was usually a lot of air, and got a big kick out of our delight at the foaming beer.

The beer was brought over from the brewery, The Fredericksberg Brewery, on Santa Clara Street near Hester Avenue. One time Mother and Father took me for a walk, and they stopped in for a glass of beer. They sat me up on the bar next to a big bowl of pretzels and let me sip the foam off their glasses. Pretzels and beer!

In the summer we went camping at Long Bridge out of Saratoga. Originally a wooden bridge that crossed over Saratoga Creek, it was the longest bridge in the county when it was built. But in 1902, the wooden bridge was replaced by a two-lane stone span, and near the bridge was a campground. We stayed there two or four weeks, I don't remember, on those camping trips, setting up a big tent next to a picnic table. There was a pond down the hill where we swam in the warm summer afternoons.

My mother always brought along a clothes basket. One day she opened the basket to take out some clothes, and there was a big snake in there. It was just resting in a nice warm place, so she pulled the snake out and that was the end of the snake. She didn't like snakes.

While we were up there camping, a forest fire burned over the crest of the hill to the south of Saratoga. The fire came up to the top of the hill, and we could see it from our camp. We thought we might have to go, but we didn't. They put the fire out and we saw the men come down the road after it was all out.

The road back down to Saratoga was quite steep, so to drive down the hill you had to tie a log to the back of the car for a brake. You could always find something up there to use to slow the car going down the hill.

Chapter 3. Her Majesty, Grandma Harry

WE OFTEN HAD VISITORS come to the house to see my mother. There was one I will always remember. She rolled up in front of our house in a beautiful buggy pulled by two fine horses: a Hansom Cab. The driver sat on a high seat behind the cab, which was all enclosed for privacy as well as the weather. It had a little window on each side, and I saw her peeking out through the window, and I wondered who had come to visit us. When she stepped out of the cab, she didn't just come to the house. It was more that she arrived. She swept out of the cab with a certain majesty, adjusted her feather boa, which wrapped around her neck and trailed almost to the ground, and with her face wreathed in smiles, she swept across the sidewalk and up the walkway and mounted the stairs to the front porch with a flourish. With outstretched arms, she greeted her family. Her assurance, her poise, her sense of complete command was something majestic.

My mother greeted her, and we were introduced to Grandmother Harriet, who told us to call her Grandma Harry. She was a short woman, like my mother, only a little over five feet tall, with a medium build. She was flamboyantly dressed with a big wide-brimmed, picture hat, with resplendent ostrich plumes set atop her luxuriant red hair, a color that was helped along with a henna rinse, with somewhat startling results – a "secret" that was quite obvious. Her complexion was very fair, of which she was proud. She was always careful to avoid the direct sun and while riding in an open carriage or taking a stroll, usually carried a parasol. A beautiful diamond cross, hanging from a gold chain around her neck rested on her ample bosom. Her flowing gown of dark green velvet was hemmed with a narrow band of soft brown fur. Though she had on long kid gloves that covered her arms above the elbow, the fingers of the glove were tucked into the sleeves at the wrist, exposing her fingers sparkling with rings. No, no one ever upstaged Hattie!

In those days a lady was never seen in public without gloves, and I can remember that she had a pair for every costume. Many of them were of kid, white, black, green, brown, etc. Then there were lace ones and knitted ones, most all of them long enough to come well above the elbow. Her hats were really something. I remember some of them: big, wide-brimmed creations adorned with ostrich or egret plumes; sometimes swathed in flowing veils and held in place with ornate, jeweled hat pins. She had a beautiful collection of jewels, many of which came to my mother when Harriet died. But alas, all of them found their way into the pawn broker's hands during the lean years.

Harriet was the daughter of John Roswell Whitney, who we called Grandpa, and Harriet Almira Baldwin, nicknamed Golly, who were married September 30, 1850, in Jonesville, Michigan. Their first child, Horatio, was born in January 1852, and on March 8th of that year, they set off for California in a covered wagon. They traveled to Council Bluffs, Iowa, from where they set off across the plains. It was a wet and cold journey over almost impassable, muddy roads. They probably used oxen because they could get by on less graze than horses, and due to the size of the migration that year, with over 50,000 people making the crossing, feed was a serious problem.

It was at Fort Hall, Idaho, that Horatio, who was endowed with an abundance of golden blond hair, was "kidnapped" by the Indians. The Indians mixed with the settlers as the wagons were stretched out over several miles around the Fort. They were mostly looking for handouts, for it was here that the emigrants cut their supplies to the minimum to lighten their loads for the desert crossing ahead. Horatio was asleep under a wagon when one of the squaws was so intrigued with this golden-haired baby that, when no one was looking, she picked him up and rode off. Horatio was missed very quickly and a short ride overtook the culprit and the babe was restored to loving arms.

On July 4th the Whitneys arrived in Salt Lake and sixty-five days later they arrived at Bidwell's Ferry, Butte County, California. The next day they reached their destination, Marysville, on September 8th, six months to the day from their departure.

Harriet Eliza was born in San Francisco about 1860. She was an only daughter, a sister, Mary, having died in infancy in 1857. She had two brothers, Horatio and Ellard Beans Whitney, who was born in San Francisco in 1862. Golly had at least two other babies that died at birth and a son, Edgar, who died young, a frail, sickly child. Horatio died in Geneva, Switzerland, August 4, 1884.

As the daughter of the house, Harriet grew up completely spoiled. She had a quick temper to match her red hair, but was not one to carry a grudge. She grew into an impetuous, vain and fun-loving young lady who loved clothes, good times, and people and had a great sense of humor. On occasion, she was quite generous, like the time she gave a taxi driver a new car because she liked him! – an act that really caused the tongues to wag. It was after Grandpa's death. Harriet was in San Francisco one evening and decided to take a taxi home to San Jose. The taxi driver was "so nice" and his cab was getting old, so she made him a present of a brand new automobile! A Pierce Arrow, no less![8]

While in her teens she traveled a good deal with her mother and brother Ellard. They spent considerable time in Europe where Harriet became quite a linguist. She spoke German, French, Italian and Spanish. Later in Japan, she learned Japanese. I know nothing of her formal education but that she was an omnivorous reader. She had an inquiring mind and even read the Encyclopedia Britannica from A to Z. She sang and worked hard training her voice. My mother, who learned to accompany her on the piano while in Yokohama, said that Harry had a very good voice but made no pretense at its being great. Harriet loved music, and was a great opera-goer.

Harriet married Ignatius Raleigh Burns, an importer of crockery, glassware, lamps, etc., when she was about twenty, and they lived in San Francisco where their daughter, Elizabeth, was born, January 15, 1882. Harriet's brother Ellard was a business associate of Mr. Burns at the time of Ellard's death in 1887, and he was twenty-six when he died.

Mr. Burns was a New York socialite. He was descended from Otway Burns, captain of the *Snap Dragon*, and a famous privateer in the War of 1812. There is a magnificent monument to his memory in Burnsville, North Carolina, a town that was named after him. After I.R. Burns's divorce from Harriet, he married Bessie Afong of the very wealthy Hawaiian-Chinese family, in 1899. The couple lived in New York where he was a stockbroker and sold insurance. They made many leisurely trips around the world before settling in San Diego where he died in 1941. They had no children. After he died, she moved to San Francisco to be near her family.[9]

After her separation from Mr. Burns, Harriet came back to her father's house at Tenth and San Carlos Streets in San Jose. It was a large wooden house that had been manufactured in the East and shipped around the Horn, a prefab of its time, big but not pretentious. San Jose was a bustling town then of about 15,000 people.

Grandpa also had another place, a vineyard and orchard about

8 The San Francisco Call, Friday, June 26, 1908, pages 1 and 3.

9 Clarice B. Taylor's "Tales about Hawaii: The Story of the Afong Family." Clarice Taylor, a columnist for the *Honolulu Star-Bulletin*, wrote this series of articles, which appeared daily during the summer of 1960.

two miles north of Los Gatos, and it was there that he built his own private art gallery, an account of which appeared in the *San Jose Mercury* in 1892, entitled, "The Fine Art Gallery of J. R. Whitney. Some Valuable Paintings. Souvenirs of Travels Over the World." He had made his fortune as a commission merchant in San Francisco in the 1860s. He bought and sold goods of all kinds, from silver ore to kerosene, for the commissions. He is listed in the Directory of San Jose, 1878 by Castle & Wright as "Capitalist."

During this time, the only social group that Golly belonged to was the Ladies Benevolent Society, which concerned itself with the orphans and destitute aged. It was to this life that gay, fun-loving Harriet found herself committed when she returned home.

Finding herself somewhat socially *de trop*[10] because of her recent separation, Harriet decided to move to the Orient. She sailed from San Francisco, March 22, 1890, with her eight-year-old daughter, Elizabeth (Bessie). They were accompanied on the voyage by her mother and father, Golly and Grandpa.

They arrived in Yokohama, Japan, where Golly helped Harriet set up housekeeping. Grandpa gave her a generous allowance. It was enough to provide ample servants, the best tutors for Bessie and lovely living quarters. That she enjoyed this life is attested to by the fact that she remained there for ten years.

Grandpa went on to Hong Kong, Canton and on around the world. He went to India, Arabia, through the Suez Canal, visited the Great Pyramids of Egypt; then to Jerusalem thence to Bulgaria, Vienna, Berlin, Copenhagen, London and on to Boston and across the continent via the Great Lakes arriving home July 15th, 1890.

Golly stayed in Yokohama until the middle of August and brought home with her a beautiful Japanese girl about the same age as Bessie. Misa Seki grew up in the Whitney household and later she and Bessie became lifelong friends.

Yokohama had a foreign settlement that was one of the most delightfully gay places of the Gay Nineties. It was a refueling port for many of the ships of foreign navies and the officers seemed much more concerned with social engagements than naval maneuvers. Harriet being young, good looking, beautifully dressed, and a delightful companion, added to the fact that she was an accomplished linguist,

---

10 Meaning: not wanted or needed

made her very much in demand at the almost continuous round of social functions. It was a life of teas, balls, concerts, receptions both ashore and afloat, parties and all the social whirl of the Gay Nineties. There was something doing every night, and the household never came to before noon. The servants preserved absolute quiet until Harriet awakened. "Night was a time for fun! Why waste it sleeping?"

Bessie never attended a public school. Harriet enjoyed teaching her daughter and also saw to it that she had the best tutors. For example, a French woman would spend an hour or more every day drilling Bessie in French. It was the international language being used at the time, and Harriet saw to it that her daughter was letter perfect. Bessie was also required to spend long hours at the piano and, as a result, became a very fine pianist. When she returned to this country she was almost persuaded to go on the concert stage.

Bessie and her mother were waited on hand and foot. They had help with their bathing, their dressing, even with brushing their hair. Bessie used to tell of the struggle that she and a couple of giggling Japanese maids used to have getting Harriet into her hourglass figure corsets, the latest thing from Paris. When they went anywhere there was always a group of *jinrikisha*[11] men at the gate to whisk them through the colorful streets. It was in this setting that Bessie grew to womanhood: servants for everything, studies and clothes the only problems, and social functions the order of the day. She had almost no childhood playmates her own age, and she accompanied her mother to most of the social functions.

There was never a man about the house for there were no secrets in the settlement. The servants knew everything and discussed everything among themselves, and all the news passed from servant to employer. The extent that the servants knew the problems of a particular household was manifest by the fact that if a hostess happened to have an inferior chafing dish and you had just gotten an elegant one you would find it in use at your hostess's table, she not having an idea in the world where it came from. The next morning it would be in its customary place. No harm done. You might well be the beneficiary the next time if your house-boy felt that your table needed upgrading. It was a transparent society with few secrets and lots of gossip.

---

11 A small, two-wheeled carriage drawn by one or two persons. A *jinrikisha* was also Misa's dowry when she came from Japan. It is now in a museum in St. Paul, MN.

Harriet was able to keep Bessie looking like a little girl (she was only 4 ft. 11 inches tall) for quite some time. But over the years Bessie learned to play the piano beautifully, and people began to notice that little Bessie was indeed becoming a lovely young lady. And so it was, the gay young divorcee had a real problem – a grown-up daughter. The corsets, the henna, the massages, the fashions could not alter the fact that Harriet was "fortyish." The ideal was over; she was past her prime. Harriet packed her wardrobe into some sixteen trunks and returned home to the States in 1901, moving in with her parents once again.

Grandpa's was a far different world than Yokohama. The household ran on schedule, a certain menu for each day of the week, the only changes being due to season. The meal hours were punctual and the monotony of the menu was in sharp contrast to the delicious fare of the Orient. (Bessie did say that the great amount of fish in the Japanese diet did get tiresome.) By now they were spending most of their time at "the ranch" near Los Gatos, Grandpa absorbed in his art gallery and the rest of the family pretty bored.

Grandpa had no use at all for social functions, and Misa used to tell of the time that Grandpa was away and Harriet, who had just returned from Japan, decided to throw a party out at the ranch. After the guests had departed, Misa and Bessie took brooms and erased all the telltale buggy tracks, and Grandpa never knew how much his hospitality had been enjoyed. There was also a story that Grandpa got religion one time and stood up at a Baptist meeting and confessed his sins. He went one better: he named names and places, which added nothing to his popularity, no doubt.

This colorless atmosphere was not for Harriet. She wanted the bright lights, the nightclubs, the theater, dancing and living it up. One thing she liked to do most was to spend money. She did keep one foot on home plate, as it were, but New York, Chicago and San Francisco were of much greater interest, and she spent as little time as possible at home.

This flare of Harriet's for the good life worried Grandpa, and he therefore fashioned his will to provide her with ample funds during her lifetime, leaving the bulk of his estate to be divided among his grandchildren and great-grandchildren.

About this time, my mother, Bessie, who was an accomplished pianist, was planning to go to Europe to accompany a singer on a tour. But she met George Hulse in Chicago, and they got married a couple of weeks later in that city on August 19, 1902.

In 1903, the Whitneys traveled to Europe. Golly was taken ill on arrival in Ireland, September 1903, and she died there February 3, 1904. They were in Londonderry, Ireland, at the time, and she was buried in the Londonderry City Cemetery. J.R. went on to Paris, France, where his daughter, Hattie, joined him. Then he died at the Hotel Rivoli on October 5, 1905. At his request, he was cremated at Père Lachaise Cemetery – the famous cemetery – then his ashes were taken by Hattie to Londonderry, Ireland, where he was buried "in and at" the foot of the grave of his beloved Harriet.

His was a large estate consisting in part of business property in San Francisco, some of which was on Market Street and some on Clay Street; some business property in San Jose as well as a number of rentals. In addition, there was the ranch out near Los Gatos with a full bearing orchard and vineyard that was one of the largest in the state. His business partner had been T. Ellard Beans, president of the San Jose Bank, and Mr. Whitney probably had an interest in the bank as well. His estate was appraised at $23,299.

When Harriet heard the terms of her father's will, she was furious. She wanted cash. She wanted to live as the daughter of a wealthy Californian should live: traveling about the capitals of Europe enjoying the gay life. H.B.M. Miller, her father's attorney had drawn the will. Years later, when I talked with him, he told me how he had tried desperately to persuade Harriet to abide by her father's wishes, but she was adamant. She would not go along and if H.B.M. would not petition the court to set aside the will, she would find someone who would. She then persuaded her nephew, Ellard, to go along with the liquidation of the estate. She also persuaded my mother, Bessie, after many tearful talks, to agree. The probate court denied the petition and an appeal was made to a higher court. Foreseeing a lengthy court battle, the judge ordered all of the furnishings of the Whitney ranch home, as well as the entire contents of the Whitney's private museum, put in storage in a San Francisco "fireproof" warehouse for safekeeping.

It was nearing the first of April, the spring after her father's death, before the court's order to board up the ranch and the museum and move the contents into storage was executed. On April 18, 1906, the 'quake struck and the Great Fire of 1906 left 497 blocks of the heart of San Francisco in blackened rubble.

As the smoke cleared over the rubble that was San Francisco, there was left but ashes of so many hopes and dreams, and amid the ashes was the lifetime collection of J. R. Whitney, pioneer, scholar, financier and world traveler. They included paintings, etchings, books, porcelains, objets d'art and mementos that he and Golly had collected over a lifetime, from their trip West in a covered wagon to their many travels around the world.

But Harriet had plenty of money and continued to travel and live the good life. On one of her trips to Europe, she met William W. Wilson of Jamaica, B.W.I. on the return voyage. After she said good-bye to us on that day in 1912, she went east to join Wilson and marry him. It was a happy marriage for her. She was very active socially and founded the Girl Guides Association on the island. She lived in Jamaica until she died in Kingston on September 16, 1916, and she is buried there.

Chapter 4. 1913

WINTER CAME ON AND WITH IT THE RAINS. After a heavy rain, the creeks of San Jose flooded, and the logs washed down with branches and all sorts of wood. We enjoyed watching the men who stood up on the bridges and speared the wood for firewood. That was the way a lot of people got their wood, and it was quite a scene as they speared the wood and hauled it up onto the bridge.

Alviso and the area where the San Jose Airport is now were all underwater in the winter. The creeks and rivers all flooded when it rained. The streets were not paved and were full of chuckholes that became mud puddles in rainy weather. There were no curbs and gutters, just shallow ditches along the side of the road that filled with water and were wet until the dry season.

After a rain, the puddles became a fine place to sail boats – just a piece of wood fitted with a paper sail, but it made us happy. Some of the puddles were pretty big too, and a mishap would result in wet and muddy feet, much to our mother's annoyance.

Some days visitors would come by in their horse-drawn carriages. Sometimes Uncle Needham, who was our Godfather, drove over in his buggy and parked his horse over by the side door then went inside to visit my folks. Our next-door neighbor, Fred Theuerkauf, had a very handsome team of light grey ponies. He waved to us kids, whip in hand as he took off at a fast trot in his shining surrey with the fringed top, the wheels flashing in the sun. Poor Mr. Theuerkauf died of pneumonia after washing his surrey one cold rainy day. The family moved out to Sunnyvale where his son had a big dairy ranch.

Jane and Stan in 1912.

Into his house came our new neighbors, Roy and Peggy Walter.

Roy and Peggy had no children of their own and all but adopted Jane and me. Roy used to spin 'tall tales' and we kids loved it. He peopled his barn with a whole menagerie of strange and exotic beasts, and we delighted in the wondrous tales Roy told. The imaginary collection of animals became quite real, and we peeked around corners of the barn and in the dark recesses under the house forever seeking a glimpse of the elusive creatures. There too, the savage Indians lurked, unseen, in the darkness. On my seventh birthday, July 10, 1913, I received a special note from him:

1913, July 7th

Dear Standish: -

I have just been thinking that next Thursday is our birthday, yours and mine, and like a good pardner, I wanted to write you a letter, to remind you of it, and recall the many pleasant hours we have spent together in the past. And I trust that the future will give us further association, and greater opportunities to enjoy the social companionship which exists among men of our type; for you must recall that we were bold and valiant frontiersmen, ready at the beck of a hand to respond to the supplication of beauty in distress, or to assault with irresistible ardor the cruel and bloodthirsty savage who ranged the plains between our home and Santa Clara.

How pleasant are those memories. I can recall now, how, with battle ax in hand, you dashed to the rescue, and mowed down whole ranks from among those hordes of swarthy, bloodthirsty, yelling fiends, cleaving a way for me to follow until together, we had overcome practically insurmountable difficulties, had won in the face of overwhelming odds, and had at last won to their innermost retreats, released their perishing prisoners, and carried away with us their priceless treasures.

Those treasures, which we concealed in our secret hiding places, I know you have guarded well. Before long, I will come to you, and together we will count them over, and plan other and more brilliant incursions into the country of our hereditary enemies. Disclose our secrets to no one, but be ready when the moon is at its full, at the hour of midnight, to meet me at our old trysting[12] place. I will have our rope ladder placed so that you may leave your home by stealth, in the dead of night, when all others are sleeping. Then we will assail our Indian foes, who are planning our downfall, when they are resting in fancied security, thereby adding to the glory of our cause, and increasing the brilliancy of our careers.

What news is there along the frontier? What news have you of our collection of wild animals, which we keep, and allow no one to see? Our cat, is it as fierce as ever? Our trained snake, do you keep it well concealed in its old quarters? Our wild buffalo, panther, lion and trained elephant, what of them?

When you have time, write me fully regarding them all, and also let me know if you will be ready on the appointed night to go in quest of honorable adventures. I feel that I have been resting too long, leaving to you the guard over the frontier.

I offer you congratulations for your approaching birthday and trust that you will convey to your honored parents and esteemed sisters expressions of my sincere regard. Guard well our secrets, however, and when the proper time has come, we will

---

12 A meeting place, a rendezvous.

*cleave our way to glory, and emblazon our names on the pages
of history in glittering letters that will never fade.*
Your comrade in danger,
Roy Walter

He was my first hero, and I shall remember him always.

In the summer, they dammed Guadalupe Creek at Julian Street, and a boating pond about a half mile long resulted. The creek was just a few blocks from our house, but the dam was about a mile away. Some Sundays we took an outing to the pond and watched all the boats moving to and fro along the creek. The ladies in their big hats, holding their dainty parasols, looked gay and pretty sitting in the boats, while the straw-hatted young men in their shirt sleeves with their bright, fancy sleeve bands plied the oars. At the dam itself, there were a number of swimmers and along the banks an occasional fisherman.

On nice days, a waffle man used to come by with a two-wheel pushcart. It was fitted with a glass-sided box and a kerosene stove. He rang a hand-held dinner bell as he came down the street shouting, "Waffles, hot waffles, hot waffles." We'd run out to his wagon and stand around the cart as he cooked the waffles. Then he'd sprinkle them with powdered sugar and serve them hot – my, but they were good!

Once in a great while, an organ grinder passed through the neighborhood. His little monkey, either atop the organ or perched on the organ grinder's shoulder, doffed his little hat and passed a tin cup for our pennies.

The ice man, too, was a welcome sight. He gave us kids chips of ice as he cut the big blocks into pieces that would fit into our icebox. He used to put straw hats on his horses' heads on hot days. They looked so funny with their ears sticking up through slits in the hats.

Another wagon that was at the corner of First and Santa Clara Streets for years was the popcorn wagon. It was a glass-enclosed affair and a man stood inside with a big round popper in which he popped bushels of popcorn. The popper was going most of the time and he'd fill it up and let the popped corn pop out of the popper down into a big pile underneath. He'd put a little melted butter and salt on it and sell it at 5¢ a bag in a striped bag. Those 5¢ bags were bigger than the 25¢ bags you get at present.

About that time we got our first street lights. One was hung at each intersection. They were of the electric arc type.[13] It was great for us kids and added a new dimension to our games, as we all loved to play outdoors in the evenings until bedtime.

At that time The Alameda, the main thoroughfare that was a block from our home, was not surfaced. There were two streetcar tracks in the middle, on either side of which was the roadway, dusty in the summer, muddy in the winter, making it difficult for the ladies with their long skirts to make their way through the mud to board the cars. The car barns, or streetcar garages, were next to the brewery, and the streetcars were drawn by horses at first, pulling the cars along the rails. That only lasted a short while, then they turned to electric-powered streetcars with overhead wires, which went to Santa Clara and out to San Jose.

The streetcar had a long pole, called a trolley pole, attached to its roof that would touch the overhead electric wires. Back at the power-house, big steam engines turned huge generators to produce the electricity needed to operate the streetcars, which were also called trolley cars. There were yellow ones, which were local cars, that went out to about 21st Street or even further and also went to Santa Clara. And there were red ones that went all the way to Palo Alto.

My mother liked to ride those cars and one night I guess she felt housebound; anyway she took me for a ride on the streetcar. We rode to the end of the line in East San Jose where we bought some chewing gum. The motorman changed the trolley from front to rear and with a clang, clang of the bell we were on our way home. She had to pay another nickel for the return trip all the way back to Santa Clara, but children under twelve were free. We sat on the "dummy," the seats on each end of the car that were in the open, one on each side of the space occupied by the motorman. Besides the dummy seats, there was an enclosed center section, but it was nice to ride out in the open air. It was quite an outing.

The cars were so slow that a good sprinter could overtake them unless the car had a long downgrade pull, then it rocked and bounced along making it necessary to hang on. Every once in a while, the trol-

---

13 Arc lights were one of the first electric light sources and were widely used for street lighting. An electric spark in the air between two conductors produced a dazzlingly bright light that lit up a large area.

ley jumped off the power line and a shower of sparks flashed in the overhead wires. The conductor had to dismount and rearrange the trolley on the line.

In those days, the conductor made change out of a coin changer on a belt at his waist. He rang up the fare by a tug on an overhead cord leading to a counter that rang a bell each time it was pulled. This system later gave way to the one-man operator who had a coin box into which you dropped your fare.

We sometimes took the big Red Cars out to Saratoga. The ride across the valley and a mile and a half up through the wooded canyon brought us to Congress Springs, the mineral springs that gave Saratoga its name, after Saratoga Springs in New York. We took along a picnic lunch, and spent the day at the picnic grounds where we were allowed to take off our shoes and go wading in the creek. A band usually played an afternoon concert.

Sometimes we took the Red Car to Alum Rock Park on the eastern side of the valley, and on busy days they hooked on a trailer – an open car with seats clear across – to take the picnickers out to the park. At the park there was a menagerie with several dens in which lived some bears. They also had wolves, coyotes, foxes and other animals as well as a big bird collection.

The highlight of a trip to Alum Rock Park was a swim in the big heated indoor pool with its steep slide. The pool was heated by natural hot springs. We were never ready to get out of the water, and Mom had to "put her foot down" to get us out.

Luna Park was another amusement spot. It was at the end of the Red Car line on North 13th Street and was designed as an entertainment destination for the trolley cars. We hopped on the trolley car and it took us right to the entrance of the park. Besides its Ferris wheel and merry-go-round it had a roller coaster. A ride on it was a real thriller. There were carnival concessions and a "Tunnel of Love" where you took a boat into a darkened tunnel. I liked the scary ride but the real purpose of the tunnel was lost on me. We'd take along a picnic and just go spend the day watching boxing matches and entertainers and enjoying the rides.

In the spring and early summer, the right of way along the interurban car tracks was a solid strip of golden California poppies. The railroad tracks went through the valley and out to Palo Alto. And when they had poppies in poppy time, both sides of the tracks would be just miles and miles of these doggone things. They were very pretty. They were wonderful. The seed had been sown when the roadways were first put in and poppies were everywhere throughout the valley. They were wonderful.

Spring and summer passed happily and when fall arrived and school began, my mother decided to keep me home one more year to play with Jane. She thought that we should begin school together when Jane turned six.

That fall a memorable event happened on October 10, 1913, with the blasting of the last barrier in the Panama Canal that connected the waters of the Atlantic and the Pacific Oceans. The blast was set off by throwing an electrical switch at the White House, and to celebrate the occasion, every factory whistle and train whistle and all the school, fire and church bells sounded off to their fullest. The air fairly buzzed with the noise, the like of which was never before heard. By contrast, a couple of jets taking off today would drown out what we thought was a terrific din. Some of the neighbors added their bit by stepping out into their yards and firing off their shotguns. All very exciting to us kids. And thus was marked the opening of the Panama Canal, a passage with which I would become quite familiar.

My brother Norman was born on November 6, 1913, and we were thrilled to have a baby brother. I still remember the rows of diapers drying on the lines in the backyard. Norman was about six years younger than Jane. There was a gap largely because my mother and father didn't get along too well and then they patched things up, as it were, and then when my brother died they kind of gave it up.

When Norman was about a year old, Mabel, Jane, Norman and I were christened in the Trinity Church on Second Street.[14] I remember to this day getting splashed with holy water and me in my new suit of clothes too! Norman cried loud enough for both of us. Misa Seki and Edith Needham were our Godmothers. Dwight Needham was one of the Godfathers and I don't recall any other, but it was quite a function.

My mother was completely enchanted with baby Norman. When he was less than a year old, she wrote this letter to her mother in Jamaica:

Mabel is nearly as tall as I am – just think of it. She does well in all studies but arithmetic which she abhors. Can spell

---

14 The Trinity Episcopal Church on North Second St. at St. John in San Jose.

almost any word whether she has seen it or not. She is pretty good with the Baby but Standish is better – takes care of him like a little grandmother. It's so funny. All the children think there never was anything quite like Baby, and really he is the dearest, sweetest thing that ever lived. Just coos and talks all the time unless hungry – when he screws up his face and howls, then stops, looks round to see if anyone is paying attention, and if not, howls again – then if you speak, he goes "hum, hum" "hum, hum" – scolding – until

he gets dinner, takes a few swallows and stops and scolds a little more, then eats, and scolds both at the same time until he begins to be "assuaged" when he will look up and laugh —

At night he wakes up and "talks" to me & smiles and goes off to sleep with never a cry. Any time one catches his eye he smiles, then laughs. Even strangers, he looks at them intently first, then smiles and ends by laughing aloud and captivating them.

I never enjoyed or adored anything so much in my life as I do that adorable youngster. He is so sweet and so soft and cuddly and everything lovely. I'm a perfect fool over him. You'd just think him great I

Mabel and Norman, 1915.

know, even though you aren't baby crazy as I am. He's more interesting than Stan because he's more intelligent, really seems to understand things – and notices so much. He can pat-a-cake. Had two lower teeth before he was four months old and they do look cunning.

He is really a pretty baby – better than pretty because intelligent looking, and his beautiful little soul seems to shine thro' his eyes which are very large and blue.

Jane is an awfully sweet kid – big-hearted, impulsive, quick-tempered and remarkably bright. A woman in this neighborhood who is a college woman, Mrs. Owen, an authority on

Norman, 1915.

economics, etc., who numbers profs. and other "head-lights" among her intimates, told several people "that she had never seen a child that she considered so remarkable or that had such possibilities for good as Jane – that she was the only child she had ever seen that she would like to bring up." I felt properly complimented and honored when it came to me. Jane though is great.

Stan is a love – just the tender-est, most chivalrous, willing & loyal little chap going. He adores Jane and Baby and says of Mabel that "poor kid she can't help it if she's horrid, 'cause she got into the habit of it when she was little and can't get out of it, but I guess when she gets bigger she'll be alright 'cause nobody'll like her."

He's the philosopher. The other day George barked his shin and said "Ow" and Stan said, "Well you got hurt but not injured – there are lots of things in this world that hurt you but don't injure you." He's awfully funny. He and George went up to Mr. Adet's (of Yokohama) ranch for the week-end a few weeks ago, and he told Mr. A. that "when he got big he was going to be a farmer 'cause it was cheaper. You raise your own fruit & vege-tables, and you don't have to have so many clothes."

A dear little girl of three comes here to play sometimes. She is devoted to a doll minus eyes, "sans everything" in fact, and after watching her the first day she came here, he came to me and said "Honey, I'm going to marry Florence Tower when I get big 'cause she's so good to her doll that I know she'd be good to her children." He's a cure.[15]

You see there is to be no race-suicide in my family – am already training them for their family that is to be, thereby making good citizens – national prosperity – "Eugenics"[16] is

---

15 The meaning of "He's a cure" is "he's a a rollicking, funny, queer, sharp fellow." Source: "The little Londoner" by Richard Kron, 1907.

16 Eugenics is the belief and practice which aims at improving the genetic quality of the human population.

to become second nature if I can make it.

Stan always keeps himself clean so he will have nice clean children. We talk freely on all subjects they are interested in. Therefore, they have no morbid curiosity. And let this be written down by St. P. in the Big Book, I have never told them any kind of a lie, never taken refuge in a subterfuge, or broken a promise to any of them. That makes for absolute confidence in me. If I don't know about what they ask me, I tell them I don't know, but will find out; and I do find out (make it my business to do so) then tell them.

George often says that Stan is a dandy fine little chap and that he only wishes poor Mabel was half as good or as pleasant. Stan has that same sweet smile he had when a baby. Mabel, poor kid, isn't bad, just supremely selfish. Never wants to put herself out one instant to give anyone else a few minutes pleasure. She will run errands, on the other hand, most willingly. And lie, gee whizz she can lie faster than a horse can trot. She's a funny combination to which I sometimes think that the Lord, and sometimes that the Devil, holds the key. She has charming manners – company manners – but growls around like an old bear at home.

Chapter 5. Around the Neighborhood

A NUMBER OF OUR NEIGHBORS were from the Old World. On the next street, their backyard abutting our backyard, lived a family who had just emigrated from Europe. They built a large round oven of brick and adobe in which they baked large, round loaves of bread. I think the best bread that I ever tasted was the nice warm bread from their kiln. The flour was especially selected by the housewife, not for its ease of handling but solely for its baking qualities, and that made the big difference in their bread. On baking day, now and then, they sent over a loaf just as a friendly gesture. It was a nice place to live.

We kids especially loved the two big cherry trees on the front lawn. When the fruit ripened in early summer, we always ended up with tummy-aches from eating too many of the delicious, ripe fruit. Santa Clara Valley was a paradise for orchards of all kinds, and we had fresh fruit for much of the year. We also had a chicken yard, as did many of our neighbors, so we always had fresh eggs. We also kept rabbits and a couple of goats that the hired man took care of. In the vacant lots throughout the neighborhood, which were more numerous than the houses, cows were often staked out to pasture.

The many delivery men continued to make their rounds, but for other supplies, we went to the old Hester Market, about three blocks down The Alameda. It was so different from today's supermarkets. It would be called a little store today, but then it was quite adequate to serve that whole district.

The canned goods occupied only a small shelf space: there were mainly canned fruits, tomatoes, peas and corn, usually one brand of each. There were very few packaged products. The roasted coffee was scooped from a big bag, weighed and then ground. The delightful smell of the fresh ground coffee beans filled the store. Molasses was still sold by the pint and poured into the customer's demijohn.[17]

Cheese was always cut from a cheese wheel or round, either with a big knife or a cheese wheel cutter – a circular board with a cleaver-like knife attached to it. The grocer would put a round of cheese in the cutter and, by manipulating a lever, turn the cheese to position it, then pull down the huge knife and cut off a wedge of the approximate weight desired.

That was only one of the many new inventions that was just coming about. Up until that time, a boiled ham would be cut with a big butcher knife. About that time the store acquired a cutter that actually had a revolving blade, and it would slice the boiled ham in any thickness desired.

Soda crackers were packed in big barrels, and if you wanted soda crackers, he took a paper sack over to the barrel and he would take out as many dozen soda crackers as you wanted. They were sold by the pound. There was no such thing as packages of soda crackers. Sugar did not come in packages in those days. It came out of a sack, as a rule, that was dumped into a bin and again scooped out into paper sacks and sold by the pound.

Rolled oats, a principal breakfast food, were scooped from a big burlap bag. Bacon was by the piece, never sliced; potatoes usually by the sack; cookies came in large boxes and you purchased as many as you wished. Pickles and olives were in big barrels. Corned beef was kept in a barrel of brine. Newspapers were often used to wrap such things as smoked salmon, dried herring or dried cod fish. Lima beans

---

17 A demijohn is a large narrow-necked bottle usually enclosed in wickerwork.

and lentils, white and red beans, and rice were all in bins. We used to buy dried corn, and sometimes they'd grind the corn for us, and we'd use the corn for chicken feed. Tea and spices were either in bins or large ornate tins from the Orient.

Kerosene was an important item, and the shops often had a gallon can that had a spout. In order to keep the contents from spilling, the grocer skewered a small potato on the spout.

The grocer had a big basket of fresh hens' eggs but did not carry fresh milk. The dairy store down the street carried milk, cream, buttermilk, cottage cheese and eggs, while the bakery took care of the bread, etc., not the grocer.

Canning supplies were an essential item. You could buy paraffin and rubber seals for Mason jars. There was a jar with a heavy glass top that was held fast by a stiff wire that was snapped in place, which was much in use at the time. Many used one-quart tin cans similar to today's one-quart paint cans. And then there were jelly glasses of various sizes as well as different sized Mason jars.

There were two or three kinds of hand soap, none of them wrapped separately. Large blocks of yellow laundry soap were used for washing clothes. The housewife shaved off a cupful and put it in the clothes boiler – a large oblong tub that was put on top of the stove. In this way the clothes were boiled on top of the stove and gave credence to the line in the song, "Who threw the overalls in Mrs. Murphy's chowder?"

Blueing was used widely in home laundry and was sold in bulk. It came in little balls about the size of a marble, and the laundress would tie a half dozen in a cloth, making a blueing bag. This was swished about in the rinse water a moment or two until the desired blueness was obtained. So the laundry department consisted of a supply of yellow soap, a box of blueing balls and a barrel of starch. Dresses, shirts, bed sheets, etc. had to be starched before being ironed as it made ironing much easier.

When we lived on Villa Avenue, the cook and the maid used to do the washing. One day a week was set aside for washing. After the clothes were boiled, they were taken out and scrubbed on a washboard. Then they were carried out into the backyard and put on long lines with clothespins to dry in the sun. After they were dry, they were brought in, and the next day was a big spree of ironing for several hours. The maid would be tied up with the chore of ironing all the table cloths, the sheets, the towels and clothes. It was quite a chore to get the laundry out – usually a two-day project.

When we were rewarded with a nickel, we'd walk to Hester Store and get a big ice cream cone. Or we'd spend our nickel on a bag of candy, carefully selecting such goodies as jawbreakers, nigger babies, or gumdrops. And there were candy bananas, chocolate-coated marshmallow cigars, licorice pipes, just to name a few. A five-cent bag would hold a lot of delights.

In the same block with Hester Market, just across The Alameda from Hester School, was a shopping district that consisted of a butcher shop, a barber shop, a wood and coal yard, a shoe repair shop, a dairy store, a bakery and a couple of other small businesses.

In back of the stores was a big barn that housed the horses that pulled the wagons for the businesses. One night the barn burned and all of the horses perished. I still remember the awful feeling of disaster when, in the morning, I looked upon the charred remains of the barn and the smoldering bales of hay and saw the horses being carried out. It was quite a tragedy for the market to burn up. It was closed for a while, then the grocery store was able to open up again and we bought our groceries there once more.

Hoboes used to stop at our house asking for food. My mother never turned them away, and after a time, they became a real pest. Our fence had been marked, indicating that it was a soft touch, and when the marking was removed, things settled back to normal. The hobo of that day would split wood for an hour to pay for his meal, if the housewife insisted, or sometimes spade a patch in the vegetable garden. As kids, we were always somewhat afraid of them, with their mysterious bundles slung across their backs. They were a group of floaters that occupied camps in the bushes along the railroad tracks. When the camps would get too big, the sheriff would send a squad of deputies to break up the camp and send them on their way.

We had a young man, a forlorn figure, who stayed with us for a while. Fred Walgren did odd jobs about the place. He had his quarters in the garage. We kids liked Fred and he played with us a good deal, but Fred was saving his money to get together a grub stake so he could go prospecting. It made no difference to Fred that his dream was a half-century too late. One day he brought home a donkey in preparation. We had a lot of fun riding it for several days while Fred got together the rest of his things. The big day arrived, and Fred loaded the donkey with all the provisions and gear. As he piled the stuff on, Fred's high spirits were in no way shared by the donkey, and its ears kept getting lower and lower as they lay back against his neck.

About this time Fred was ready to go, but the donkey wasn't. A tug on the halter rope only set the donkey in reverse. Finally, in desperation, Fred whacked it across the flank with a stick. This brought results. The donkey bucked and kicked out with both hind legs at the same time, then amid much snorting and braying, took off along the picket fence, scraping the gunny sacks against the pickets. Immediately there was a shower of beans and canned goods as the pickets ripped open the sacks. The load now being completely top-sided, swung under the donkey and its kicking and bucking strewed it over quite an area.

It was several days before Fred was re-provisioned and his pack saddle mended, and this time he did get started only to return, sans donkey and gear, about a week later. Fred later left to seek his fortune and we never again heard of him.

Here's something I wrote about Fred:

And then there was Fred . . .

And then there was Fred . . .

Fred was our handyman, who lived above the garage. We were very fond . . .

"Hello, kids," he greeted us.

"Hi, Fred!" Jane called.

"Hi," I said.

"Well, now . . ." He stopped and lit his pipe, took a few puffs to see that it was lit, then resumed: "Well, now . . ."

"Well, now . . ."

He stopped and stared. We turned – a man with two heads was coming down the street.

Jane and I hopped on our scooters, which we had made by nailing roller skates onto the ends of boards, and we rode back and forth on our sidewalk. We were lucky to have one of the few concrete sidewalks in the neighborhood. When we first moved there, it was the only house in the neighborhood that had a concrete sidewalk with curb and gutter. Since we lived on the corner, it wrapped around two sides of the house and gave us quite a nice course to ride on with our wheeled toys.

But in the summer of 1914, the calm of our quiet neighborhood was shattered by a man with a bundle of papers under his arm, crying

"Extra, Extra, WarExtra!" As the great conflagration of World War I began to inflame Europe, there arose a great deal of bitterness against the Germans. At home in San Jose, some of the people wouldn't even speak to their German neighbors – those kind people who had provided them with fresh bread for so many years.

News of the sinking of the *Lusitania* by U-boats came in the same shocking way as the war had, in May 1915. Again the pictures of the beautiful luxury liner brought the war closer, and I became aware that there were such things as Germans who were fast becoming "Huns."

Chapter 6. The Circus

WELL DO I REMEMBER my eighth birthday. The pair of new skates was wonderful, but the best was yet to come. Tomorrow would be the circus day and we would all go to the circus.

My mother had kissed me good night, and I could hear her softly playing the piano in the parlor below. Sleepily, I lay there thinking about the posters on the fences and power poles that told of the daring trapeze artists, and the big poster of lions and tigers and elephants and other wild animals that covered the side of Watkins's barn. I went over every detail in my mind. There was Buffalo Bill with his silver beard and long mustache flowing in the wind as he rode with his six-guns blazing, and now I was riding beside him in hot pursuit of a band of painted savages. Tomorrow I would see him in person and see his buffalo gun. The lion jumping through the flaming hoop seemed to get bigger and bigger as he leaped straight at me. Then there were all the tigers and the monkeys and the elephants and . . . I was asleep.

It was just before dawn. The still of the night had given way to the strange sounds coming from the street, which had awakened me. It was a moment or two before I realized that it was the sound of wagons – big, heavy wagons – lots of them – rolling down Villa Avenue. Jane, Mabel and I hopped out of bed and hung out the window to watch the animals come up the street. The creaking of the harness, the muffled noise of horses' hooves, the crunch of the ironclad wheels, the jingling of the wagons, the occasional shout of the drivers and now and then a pistol-like report as a long whip cracked just over

41

the backs of the straining horses. It was not a big noise but it was impressive and in the predawn darkness, it filled my heart with excitement.

Peering through the open window into the darkness, I was met with a strange sight indeed: a long line of big wagons pulled by teams of horses. The wagons were shrouded in heavy canvas. We knew that under the canvas were beautifully gilded cages housing lions and tigers, monkeys, rhinos – all the jungle animals – even a big glass-enclosed cage full of snakes – anacondas and boa constrictors.

Beside some of the wagons walked men carrying lanterns to light the way. The thin feeble light in the predawn darkness gave a weird effect so unlike the glittering circus parade later on that day, with its bands, its calliope,[18] its prancing horses in gay trappings.

Strange noises came from the shrouded wagons: the roar of a lion or the snarls of the big jungle cats gave us a big thrill. A break in the line of wagons was filled with a string of camels each led by a rope attached to a halter. Behind them rolled another wagon that was pulled by a huge elephant led by a man with a short stick. Following this wagon was a string of six more elephants each holding on to the tail of the one in front. Then came three giraffes whose heads were almost up to my window. There was a team of zebras pulling a light wagon. They looked like mules that had been decorated with paint. It was turning light by the time the last of the wagons had passed. I don't know how long the procession lasted, but what seemed like a countless number of wagons rolled by on Villa Avenue on their way from the railroad siding a few blocks away to The Alameda and the big hay field that later became the Singletary Tract.

We could hardly wait to eat breakfast in our eagerness to go watch the huge canvas tents go up. The elephants seemed to know just what to do as they tugged and pulled on ropes and suddenly, as if

---

18 The steam calliope is also known as a steam organ. Circus calliopes were mounted on a carved, painted and gilded wagon pulled by horses.

by magic, the huge circus tent stood before us.

Some of the older kids in the neighborhood earned tickets to the show by carrying water to the animals. The elephants especially used a lot of water, sometimes filling their trunk and squirting it over themselves, and sometimes on the boys who brought the water! There was great excitement when the big circus parade marched through town. At the head of the parade rode a man on horseback wearing a tall hat and announcing with a megaphone, "Hold your horses, here come the elephants." Such excitement!

The star of the show was Buffalo Bill Cody. He had a large white mustache and a pointed beard. His silver hair down to his shoulders and an ornate buckskin jacket made him a very colorful figure as he rode around the circus ring on a beautiful horse, waving to the cheering crowd. He was the last of the great buffalo hunters. The four-hour show had Indian war dances, an "attack" on a stagecoach, trick riders, bronco riding, ropers and sharp shooters as well as many wild animals. It was a theatrical spectacle called the Wild West Show and people came from all over the county to see it, many of them in horse drawn carriages; most of them by streetcar and a few by automobile.

Then the circus packed up and moved out of town, a train of 52 boxcars transporting the show across America to the next lucky town.

Chapter 7. Changing Times

It was while living on Villa Avenue that we got our first automobile. In fact, we had two of them. The garage at the rear of the property had at one time been for horses and carriages, but had been converted and now housed two automobiles. One was a big Franklin touring car and the other was a runabout called a Little.

The Franklin was a big, beautiful automobile painted a soft, dove grey with black leather upholstery. It had all the accessories: head lights, running lights, horn, crank, windshield frame and supports, door handles, etc., all shining brass.

The two big head lamps were fueled by a big, beautiful, brass carbide generator that was mounted on the running board. Gas was generated by allowing a controlled amount of water to percolate through carbide crystals. It didn't pay to be caught too far from home after dark without an extra supply of carbide on hand. In addition to the carbide lamps, there was a pair of kerosene running lights on either side at the base of the windshield. They cast a feeble ray at best.

A few years later, the carbide generator was replaced by a changeable cylinder of gas called Presto Lite. Now instead of having to wait for the carbide gas to be generated, all we had to do was to turn on a valve at the tank and light the burners in the head lamps and "Presto," we had lights. That was much better than having to wait five minutes or so for the old generator to do its stuff. Now and again the supply of gas in the tank would be exhausted before we got home, and the lights would fail. It was not serious because at the speed of ten or fifteen miles per hour, it made little difference whether we had our big but feeble head lights on or not.

George Hulse with one of his automobiles.

The Franklin also had a large brass horn. A flexible brass tube ran from the horn to a rubber bulb mounted on the door on the driver's side. A vigorous squeeze of the bulb would yield a decided "honk." A horn really "honked" in those days.

Tires were a big problem. Flats were the order of the day and a trip of any distance was more than likely to produce a flat. The demountable rim had not yet been introduced and punctures happened all too often. Tire irons would be brought out and the tire pried from the rim and repairs made to the tube. Then we had the task of getting the tire back onto the rim and reinflating it with a hand pump. On a hot day this could be a mean task. It was enough to ruin an otherwise nice day. All the males in the party, and sometimes the ladies, would pump for a brief time. In the case of a blowout, there was a boot that was sometimes laced over the ruptured casing to serve as an emergency measure until a new casing could be had.

One day we got a windshield for the Franklin whose upper half would swing out to allow the breeze to blow on our faces on a hot day. And next we got a fabric top. It wasn't until later that side curtains, which fastened to the fabric top, came along and we were able to travel in the rain. The curtains were fitted with isinglass panels that let in some light.[19] It was all very crude but it was the forerunner of the glassed-in auto body of today.

There were no gas stations, and running out of gasoline was a serious affair. It was not unusual to see a team of horses towing a car back to town. We bought our gas from the grocery store in five-gallon cans, and later we had a rack on the running board that held two five-gallon cans, which added considerably to our driving range.

On a nice day, Dad liked to take us out for a drive. He put on his white linen duster that swept almost to the floor, then set a cap on his head, sometimes with the visor turned to the back, put on a pair of big goggles and then pulled on a pair of gauntlets that reached almost to his elbows. Then he was ready to start the engine. He primed the engine with raw gasoline through petcocks in the top of the cylinders, and then stepped to the front of the car and took hold of the big brass-handled crank that stuck out in front. With luck, after several attempts, the engine came to life with a terrific roar – frightening the first time we heard it – and then he dashed for the controls to nurse the engine into a continued cacophony that was the signal for us to pile in.

Many people were injured cranking cars of this period when the engine "kicked" and the crank spun backwards. My father's cousin, Curtis Ringwalt, was killed cranking a car when it kicked and he fell backward and hit his head, fatally injuring him.

That event involved a very strange episode. My mother was upstairs when she heard the telephone ringing. We were the first to have

---

19 Thin transparent sheets of mica called "isinglass" were used for windows in early automobiles and sometimes trains.

a telephone on Villa Avenue. I think our number was 1273. The phone was on a small table in the downstairs hall. She started down the stairs and was startled to see a man standing on the stair landing. She let out a cry, then realized that the man she saw was Curtis. She proceeded down the stairs and as she went forward, the figure was no longer there. Amazed, she was brought back to reality by the ringing of the phone. She answered it and it was Western Union phoning a message that Curtis had been killed. The household had heard her cry on the stairs and had hurried to see what had happened, and she had mentioned the name Curtis even before picking up the phone.

The women dressed in the same linen dusters, gauntlets and goggles, their hats tightly secured by a colorful veil tied under the chin that all but concealed their faces, and for good cause, too, because the car did not yet have a windshield! Then off we went, bumping along at ten or fifteen miles an hour, scaring chickens and horses and their drivers half to death. When they saw us coming, some of the drivers leaped from their rigs and grabbed their horse's bridle to steady the terrified animal until we roared past.

On the outskirts of town, practically every house had its flock of chickens, many of them feeding along the side of the dirt road. One of the great mysteries of the time was, why did the chicken invariably run to the other side of the road when it saw a car bearing down upon it? When Dad squeezed on the big black rubber bulb to blow the horn, the chickens squawked and scattered, but now and then one failed to make it across our path and the feathers would fly.

Everywhere dogs dashed out, barking and snapping at the wheels, and people in the fields looked up and waved to us as we chugged past. On an outing up Steven's Creek, the road wound along the creek bank and now and then dipped into the creek to follow along the opposite bank for a ways. There were several crossings but no bridges.

There were only a couple of ranch houses along the whole stretch of the road, and we stopped almost any place we chose for our picnic. We kids played in the creek, catching frogs and waterdogs and every now and then turtles, while Dad made a fire and put on a pot of coffee. We could spend the day without being disturbed.

The other car we had was a Little. It was called a Runabout. It was much smaller than the Franklin. It had a single bench seat wide enough for two and under the seat was the engine. To start it, Dad inserted a crank into a hole in the side of the box that held the seat,

46

and cranked away until the engine began to chug and bang. The seat was rather high and the steering post much longer than those of today. The throttle and spark controls were two levers extending from the steering column just under the steering wheel. We hadn't yet seen the foot throttle, changeable inflated tires, windshield wipers or electric lights.

But changes were coming rapidly. They started to pave The Alameda, which, up until then, had been a wide, unpaved road with a double rail for the electric cars. Our house was a short block from The Alameda, and Jane and I were fascinated by all the noise and commotion. The roadway was first plowed up by big plows that were almost the same as the plows used by farmers, only a little larger and heavier. We watched team after team of horses and mules bring in sand and gravel from Coyote Creek in wagons drawn by teams of two or four horses. All of the wagons had to be loaded by men with shovels and even the drivers would turn to with their shovels and help with the loading.

Teams also pulled the grading equipment, known as "Fresno scrapers." The teamsters continually bawled at their teams, "Gee" or "Haw," as they pulled on the reins or lashed the animals across the rump. The scrapers scooped up the earth and deposited it where it was needed, or it was hauled away.

Some of the dump wagons were the newfangled type. They had a trap door bottom, and a pull on a lever let the doors fly open spilling the load. But many were the old-fashioned kind that had two-by-four slats in the bottom of a box-like bed. The two-by-fours would have to be pried up through the sand or gravel in order to let the contents spill through the resulting hole. It was a slow, hard job.

After the grading, there were huge steam rollers that shuffled back and forth belching big puffs of steam as they packed down the gravel bed. The din of those steam engines, clanking and chugging noisily over the newly spread gravel, kept us wide-eyed.

We watched as the workmen poured the concrete, which was mixed right on the job and poured in place. The concrete mixer, a machine with a big revolving drum, was brought in and the men shoveled in the sand and gravel and poured in sacks of cement. The mixture was then dumped into wheelbarrows and trundled into place where they poured it into forms on the ground, smoothed it off, and poured water over it. They did this for about a month, section by section. It went awfully slowly.

We spent many hours standing by the side of the road, out of harm's way, watching the activity. It was almost like a circus. Slowly, The Alameda had two wide strips of pavement, one on each side of the streetcar tracks. The dust and the chuck-holes disappeared beneath the beautiful hard surface. Then the sidewalks were laid, so that in the wet weather you could walk to the streetcar without wading through mud puddles.

It took weeks to pave what can now be done in a matter of hours. And so were erased the bare footprints of the padres along the Mission Trail.

The gas lamps along The Alameda gave way to electric lights and the lamp lighter with his short ladder and lighted taper, who used to drive up in his buggy at dusk and blow them out in the morning, became history. The Alameda became the pride of the city. As the paved streets grew more numerous, the horses gave way to an ever increasing number of automobiles.

Several automobiles showed up in our neighborhood. As Charlie Polhemus rode past in his big Winton, speeding at 15 or 20 mph, the dogs rushed out yipping and barking and snapping at the wheels as they bounced over the chuck holes and mud puddles. Charlie paid them scant attention, while the dog owners watched their pets in horror as they raced dangerously close to the speeding wheels. We always knew Charlie was going by from the roar of the motor and the chorus of barks and yelps. All of this was quite a din in those days but today would hardly be noticed as a noise.

Charlie, who lived down at the end of the street, was working on a biplane. I don't remember that he ever got it into the air, but it was the first aeroplane that I ever saw.

Our neighbor across the street, Mr. Clark, bought a brand new automobile. It had a drive-chain from the engine to the back wheels, not unlike a bicycle chain, only bigger. Several of the more prominent ladies who lived along The Alameda were seen in their new electric cars, driving down the newly paved road. These conveyances were either shiny black or grey. They were nicely upholstered and carpeted and the one bench seat was sometimes curved in a modified crescent so that it could accommodate four people. They were the first car bodies enclosed with glass windows that extended clear around. They had curtains, and the ladies looked elegant as the little cars hummed along almost silently. One was Mrs. T. Ellard Beans, wife of the bank president, and another was the wife of Doctor Gerlach.

One day Mr. Clark had the whole neighborhood buzzing. He had contacted one of the Senter boys, a mile away, by wireless. It was the first time that anyone on the block saw people communicating by wireless. All he had was a telegraph machine and an aerial high in the tree behind his house. Of course, it was in code and I couldn't understand it, but it wasn't many years later that we heard Pop Harold's voice come over the air on our crystal set. The loudspeaker hadn't put in an appearance yet and we had to wear headphones, but that was the beginning. All of this in a distance of just a couple of miles!

Mr. Clark also had the first motorcycle in the neighborhood. Its roar would wake up everyone on the street. Would wonders never cease?

Mr. Hyde had a Stanley Steamer. It was not a noisy car, but it was a big car. If you wanted to really go someplace, you got in one of those. But if you just wanted a little short ride, you would probably use a smaller car.

Villa Avenue was still unpaved. A few of the many vacant lots had new houses on them and most of the cows had disappeared. The modern world was coming to San Jose.

Chapter 8. A Visit from Granddad

THAT WINTER GRANDDAD, James Warren Hulse, came to visit. He was a large man, well mannered and kindly. "He was a dear," Mother used to say of him. He told us the most wonderful Indian stories. In the telling, there was often confusion as to just who was the hero. Granddad, I don't believe, ever fought an Indian but I imagined him a great Indian fighter, right along with Buffalo Bill and all the rest. He was very proud that he was a direct descendent of Daniel Boone and gave me a book entitled *Scouting with Daniel Boone*, in which he traced on the flyleaf, his forbearers.[20] I still have the book dated "Jany 1915."

J.W. Hulse was a rich man's son. He was born Nov. 20, 1843, in Weston, Missouri. "At that time Weston was the farthest 'west town' in the United States," he told me. "It was located on the Missouri River and was surrounded by uninhabited woodlands. There wasn't a

---

20 The lineage from Daniel Boone to J.W. Hulse is transcribed on the flyleaf, the inside front cover, of the book.

James Warren Hulse with Jane, Mabel, Norman and Stan.

single bridge across the Missouri River, and there were very few ferries operating. The only roads were old Indian trails, not wide or straight enough for a wagon. They wound through the forest land, just wide enough for a horse and rider.

"My father, George Tuthill Hulse, came to Weston in 1840. At that time it was hardly a dot on the map, with only 300 people living there. He met my mother, Mary B. Warner, in 1842. She had been married to Alphonzo Van Bibber who had died suddenly, and my father was administering his estate. So they got married in July of that year and started a family. They had three children: George Warner, who died as an infant, myself, and my little sister, Emma, who died young. My father, George, became a cashier for the Weston Branch of the Mechanics' Bank, and he was a justice of the peace there also."

"So what was Weston like when you were a little boy?" I asked.

"Weston was a riverfront boom town. By the time I was about your age, there were 4,000 or 5,000 people living there. Steamboats came upriver and unloaded supplies for Fort Leavenworth and for shipments west on the Oregon Trail. The people going west needed provisions to go across the prairie, and so that's what a lot of people did in Weston – they equipped the pioneers before they crossed the waters of the muddy Missouri. All day long you'd hear the whistles of packet steamers loaded with local produce, whiskey, tobacco and hemp. Why, Weston was a bustling little town in those days."

"Daddy says that you're related to Daniel Boone!"

"That's right. It's down through my mother's side. She's the great-granddaughter of Daniel Boone. Daniel had a son named Jesse; then Jesse had a daughter named Minerva who married Captain Wynkoop Warner and they had my mother, Mary B. Warner. So that makes you a direct descendent of the great Daniel Boone."

Granddad then went over to his trunk and pulled out a beautiful, gold-headed walking stick. "Wow, what's that?" I asked him with my eyes bulging.

"Have you ever heard of Ben Holladay?" he asked me. I shook my head, and he went on. "Weston was the hometown of Ben Holladay. He arrived there in 1838, set up a small tavern and started several business ventures. He was a man who made money from everything he touched. Well, he could see the potential for supplying the pioneers with equipment and provisions, and he also saw that he could make a lot of money by carrying the mail across the Wild West to California and Oregon. He operated supply trains for the U.S. Army during the Mexican War, and he started a distillery in Weston in 1856, making some of the best bourbon whiskey in the country. And you've probably heard of Buffalo Bill."

"I saw Buffalo Bill riding a beautiful horse at the circus last summer!" I shouted.

"Yep, he was a mighty good rider. One of the best. He rode for the Pony Express when he was 15. Then Ben Holladay gave him a job shooting buffalo to feed railroad workers. That's how he got the name Buffalo Bill."

"He was the best buffalo hunter that ever lived!"

"One of Ben's business partners was my Uncle Ted. He was my mother's brother, Theodore F. Warner, and they lived right next door to us in Weston. My father was also good friends with Ben Holladay, and in 1858, after Ben had made a lot of money, he gave my father this gold-headed walking stick as a gift.[21] You can see here that it's inscribed with 'George T. Hulse from Ben Holladay 1858.' "

---

21 This cane was given to the Wells Fargo History Museum in San Francisco in 1979, by Stan Hulse. It was moved to their Phoenix Museum in 2005.

Daniel Boone Ancestry

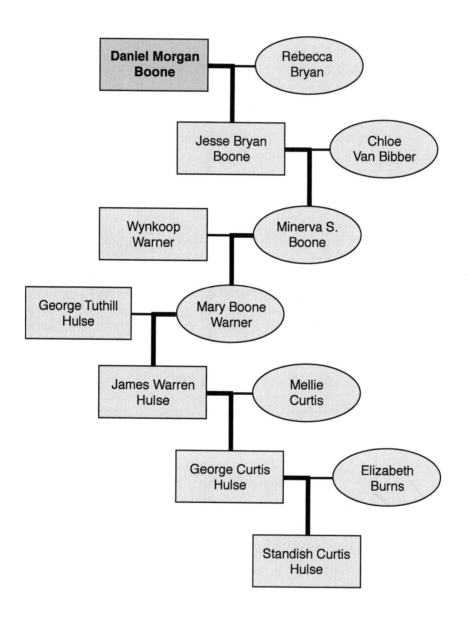

"Is that real gold?"

"Yes, the veins in the quartz are real gold from California."

"Was your father rich too?"

"Yes, he made quite a fortune. You see, Weston was a thriving city in the 1850s. It was second only to St. Louis in state population. And since Dad had been there from the beginning, as it were, his fortune had grown along with the town. He was a good banker and very honest. Everybody respected him. Then a chain of disasters struck that caused Weston to decline as fast as it grew. The first was a fire in 1855, when most of the downtown business district was destroyed including Ben Holladay's International Hotel. That was a terrible thing. The second was a change in the river channel during the flood of 1858. It shifted the river about two miles away from Weston, completely destroying the port. The third was the Civil War, which caused a great division over slavery issues in our town."

"Did you have slaves?"

"There were lots of slaves in Weston. Many people brought a few slaves with them. And the slaves did all the hard work farming and raising tobacco. We had three slaves when I was growing up. But my father was not in favor of slavery, as most people around Weston were. Missouri was a slave state and Kansas Territory, right across the river, was attracting a lot of people who were against slavery. There was hand-to-hand fighting on the streets of Weston every day over the slavery issue.

"So when the war broke out, and his Union sentiments were pretty unpopular in Weston, we moved to St. Louis. He became cashier of the main branch of the Mechanics' Bank and worked there until he was 70 years old."

He got up again and walked stiffly over to his trunk and took out a large photograph and brought it over to show me. "Now here's a picture of my father, your dad, me and Grandma in Mt. Vernon, Ohio."

"Look at his long beard," I said pointing to the old man in the photograph.

"Yes, that's your great-grandpa, George Tuthill Hulse. They used to call him 'Billy-goat' Hulse on account of that beard."

"He looks really old."

"Yes, let's see, that picture was taken in about 1893. My father was 84 years old when he died in 1894. He had a stroke four years before he died that paralyzed him and made him an invalid. That's why he's

George Curtis Hulse, George Tuthill Hulse, Mellie Curtis Hulse and
James Warren Hulse, 1893, in Mt. Vernon, Ohio.

in that wheelchair. Grandma and I took care of him in Mt. Vernon
until he died.

"Then about 1900, we moved to Montana, and set up housekeeping in a small cabin near Gardiner. I became a gold prospector and
filed some twenty gold claims. After a time, Grandma Mellie had her
fill of that kind of life and moved back to Mt. Vernon where her sister lives. I stayed on doing some hard rock mining for gold, but I
haven't hit the big one yet!"

"Mommy says she was up there once."

"Yes, that's right. After she and your father got married, they
spent their honeymoon with me in my cabin near Yellowstone. That
winter the snows covered the cabin. We melted snow in a five gallon
can on the back of the stove to get water. They had a wonderful fall
and part of the winter, but as the snows continued to pile up, they
decided to leave for San Francisco."

"I guess you really love the outdoors."

"Yes, fishing and hunting and gold mining are what I enjoy the most. And baking bread! How would you like to help me bake some bread today?" he asked.

"Yes siree," I answered.

Granddad was a great cook and a charming host. He stayed for several months, and one of the things we all remembered was the wonderful bread that he baked. It was delicious! He'd only let us eat one loaf while it was hot out of the oven – my, but it was good! He kneaded the dough, let it rise in the heated kitchen, then stoked up the fire to just the right heat and then popped the loaves into the oven to bake. He enjoyed the eager reception his baking always got.

He was well-read and charming. He loved his Masonry and was a Knights Templar, 33rd degree. In the spring, Granddad returned to Montana and his mining claims. We all missed him, but I think my mother missed him the most. She loved the big man dearly.

A year later he wrote to me from the Park Hotel in Livingston, Montana, not far from Gardiner:

May 19, 1916

Dear Stan,

It is a stormy day. The mountains are covered deep with snow & the foothills have a heavy coat too. Won't be able to get up to the mine for a month with a wagon. Am going to Gardiner in a day or two & then to a ranch where I often visit during the summer. Am feeling pretty well tho my knees are lame most of the time & I guess you could outrun me.

How is your garden coming on? is it vegetables or flowers? Write to Gardiner.

Love for all from
Granddad

Rheumatism finally drove him from his claims and he came back to San Jose where he rejoined Mellie in 1918. They lived on North Thirteenth Street until he died, December 9, 1919, at the age of 76.

Mellie, my grandmother, who we called "Dan" – short for "Dan-ma" – sold the claims after his death, which enabled her to live comfortably to the end of her days.

Chapter 9. Fire on Villa Avenue

ONE FALL MORNING IN 1914, Jane and I set off to school. We walked up Villa Avenue past two vacant lots to The Alameda. Passing several old pepper trees, whose fragrance filled the morning air, we chased some chickens that were feeding alongside the road. Almost everyone around had chickens, and they roamed about in the daytime and were brought in at night.

On that beautiful morning, Mr. O'Keefe, the bread man, was just making his rounds in his bread wagon. We waved to him as they trotted by.

It was only two short blocks down The Alameda to Hester School, the new Hester School. The old school was a two-story frame building painted yellow. A big bell in the belfry atop the roof summoned the pupils to school. But it had been torn down the summer before, and a new concrete and stucco building opened its doors to us in September. Jane and I reluctantly attended. My mother had kept me home because, as she said, "Jane and Stan got along so well together, I didn't like to separate them." Jane was 20 months younger than I and we were inseparable playmates. So it was that I was eight before I first saw the halls of learning.

It wasn't long before I had my first fist fight with a kid called Jelly Face: he had a big birthmark on one side of his face. In those days lots of kids had nicknames like Slim, Peg-leg, Gimpy and many others.

The principal got wind of our fight and we were pretty scared when we were called into his office. "Pop" Trace was a stern but just man. He stood for no foolishness and fighting was strictly against the rules. We stood there shaking as he cited our infraction. The big leather strap hung on a hook on the wall behind his desk, and we knew that a spanking with it was the usual punishment. But after a long lecture and some severe looks, we were spared, and never again did I face Pop Trace and his strap. After that, Jelly Face and I became good friends.

I was a little old for the coloring and paste up of first grade, but passed the time quite agreeably looking out of the window and dreaming – yes, I became a dreamer. In June 1915, I was advanced to the second grade and I was getting along all right when, one day in mid-December, I was looking out the window dreaming, and curiously watched a column of smoke climbing straight up in the morning sky. After a few minutes, the column grew and then I realized it was a house afire. Though the trees hid our home from school, three blocks away, the ominous black column, now growing to alarming proportions, had to be our house.

Fear clutched my heart as I watched a lone fire engine clang past the school. I sat there and waited and waited watching the black smoke fill the sky. After what seemed an eternity, the principal came to the classroom door and called me into the corridor. My sister, Jane, was already there and he marched us down to his office. He was very kindly as he told us not to be afraid, but he had received word that our house, at #9 Villa Avenue, was on fire and that a member of the family would soon come after us.

It seemed like forever before my father showed up, and we piled into the auto and in moments we were staring at a flaming heap of rubble from which two chimneys stood starkly naked. The lone fire engine crew joined the spectators. We were out of the city limits, and they did not have enough hose to reach a distant hydrant.

In the street were a few pieces of furniture – one, I remember, was our billiard table, its cracked marble top sagging into the gutter. The College of Pacific was located just three blocks north of our house and some college boys passing by had risked their lives to pull the billiard table from the fire.

In the ashes lay most of the mementos and memorabilia of my Mother's ten years in Japan before she was married. Those were irreplaceable things, but the billiard table, that had been "saved."

According to the newspaper, "Mr. Hulse had left home after having an early breakfast. Later in the morning, his wife was preparing breakfast and heard a strange crackling sound. This was at first believed to be made by the water pipes, but later she sent one of the servant girls upstairs to investigate, and the fire was discovered in the room over the kitchen.

"Neighbors were attracted, and a considerable amount of furniture was rescued. The house was a fine two-story structure and an attraction to the neighborhood. It was partly covered by insurance."[22]

We lost all our personal things: albums, clothes, and keepsakes. After the house burned, Mrs. Pierce invited us to stay at her house on

---

22 San Jose Mercury News, December 17, 1915, Vol LXXXIX, Issue 170, Page 1.

the corner of Villa Avenue and The Alameda. Mr. Pierce owned the lumber mill, and they had the most beautiful wood paneling in that house. The next day we went downtown to get some clothing: all we had was what we were wearing. Only the chimneys were left standing from the beautiful house that had been our home.

The house probably caught fire due to faulty wiring. It was one of the first houses in San Jose to have electricity, and Judge Brady had installed a home generating plant even before San Jose had an electric utility company. The fire had started up in the attic somehow, probably from the wiring.

Chapter 10. More Changes

AFTER THE FIRE, WE MOVED to a place on Third Street near the tracks while the folks hunted for a new home. It was a comfortable place in a nice neighborhood where some of the old families of San Jose lived. The two-story house had a barn in the backyard where we used to play. Here we stayed until March of the next year, 1916. That spring, summer and fall came and went, and somehow I did not go back to school. It was only a "temporary" stay so Jane and I stayed home, but it lasted fourteen months.

We had a telephone there. It was a desk set, with a mouthpiece on a short post, mounted on a round base. The receiver hung on a hook just below the mouthpiece where it was lifted up or down. When we picked it up we automatically got the operator, who would say, "Number, please." She knew everybody and you could talk to her like a friend. You could often get your party by asking for them by name. "I want to speak to Mrs. So and So." "Okay," and they'd ring her for you. There were not many subscribers in those days.

That summer we took the train up to see the Panama-Pacific International Exposition in San Francisco. It was the 1915 World's Fair and it was wonderful. The exposition was a celebration of the completion of the Panama Canal, and it also commemorated the 400th anniversary of the discovery of the Pacific Ocean by the explorer, Balboa. It was a big boost for the city which, only nine years before, had been devastated by the 1906 earthquake and fire.

I especially loved the Tower of Jewels. It was a very tall tower that had thousands of colored glass "jewels" that decorated it. They shimmered in the sunlight, and at night a searchlight shined on them and they sparkled like a fairy castle. There was also a nightly fireworks display that was quite spectacular.

I remember a giant Underwood typewriter that they had there. It was so big that people could stand on the keys, and every day they would type out the day's news headlines. The men jumping up and down on the keys to make the words appear seemed to act like cats jumping around on a hot tin roof.

Another big thing that I remember was the San Jose Tower. It was a tall iron tower

Tower of Jewels

at the intersection of Santa Clara and Market Streets in San Jose, the main intersection of the city, that reached 200 feet into the air. The "powerful arc lights on top of the tower shed a soft radiance over the city and could be seen from the surrounding foothills." [23]

Then one day, on December 3, 1915, it just fell down Market Street. It didn't have any excuse, it just fell. It hurt one man's hand, that was all. It might have killed horses and everything else.

On the corner of First and Santa Clara Street was the First National Bank. That was the tallest building in town, ten stories high. Then there was another bank building about two blocks down on First Street that was about eight stories high.

After a while, things got busy at First and Santa Clara and there was a STOP sign, and when it was turned around it would be a GO sign. In the busy time, a man would come out and set up this post, and he'd turn it to GO or STOP. It was the first one in San Jose.

My grandmother had moved to Jamaica in 1910, after she married

---

23 "Ten Years in Paradise," page 61.

William Wilson. She sent me a nice letter that Christmas.

> *1915, Dec. 29, Jamaica, B.W.I.*
>
> *My Dearest Standish,*
> *I thank you so much for your beautiful photo. I am very proud to have a grandson with so sweet and clean and brave a face. If you were British you would soon be a Scout master. We have heaps of Scouts here and Billie is the Patron of St. Aloysius Troop: they wear Khaki, blue neckerchiefs and carry a blue banner with "Be Prepared" in gilt and a gilt fleur-de-lis, etc. They are Catholic boys but he is not a Catholic, altho he is great friends with the nuns and priests and manages His Lordship the Bishop's papers for him. I wish you all lived here so I could see you. I miss you all very, very much. Soon I will send you my photo that you may see how a Not-Indian looks. Be very good to your Grandma and little Mother and obey them and your Father always. I know by your face that you will. Fond love, dearest boy and remember, I am looking forward to your being a fine grand man. "Banzai."[24]*
>
> *Your loving Grandma,*
> *Harry*

Chapter 11. Topside

IN SPRING OF 1916, we moved out to Topside, a 30 acre apricot and prune orchard at the end of Wardell Road off the Saratoga-Cupertino Road near Saratoga. The family gave it the name Topside because the house was situated on top of a knoll. We had a wonderful year there. At Topside, Norman was very badly burned playing with fire, and it was months before he recovered enough to walk: a trying time for the family.

That fall I started back to school. I was ten years old and hadn't completed the second grade. So Mom got us a pony cart and off we went to school. It was the Lincoln School, a mile away, at the corner of Prospect Avenue and Saratoga-Cupertino Road. We were not the only equestrians, so our pony cart was not unusual, but the darn pony

---

24 "Banzai" is a Japanese cheer that translates as "Long life!" or "Hurrah!"

was balky and slow so after a few days, we started walking, cutting through the orchards to save a few steps.

Lincoln School was an old-fashioned, two-room school house. We had three teachers there. One teacher took the first, second and third grades, and that was in a separate building. Then in the main building, we had the fourth, fifth and sixth grades in one room, and the seventh and eighth grades, which the principal taught, in the other room. By spring I was too big for the second grade, so I sat with the third graders.

Topside in Saratoga

In those days the whole Santa Clara Valley was orchards, all the way from Saratoga across the valley. The orchards were all owned and operated by the people who lived on them. There were mostly prunes and apricots, but there were a few pears down by the bay and a few walnuts also.

Along about the first of April, they held a Blossom Festival each year in Saratoga. That was a big, merry time. The valley was just a sea of blossoms, and people came from all over San Jose out to Saratoga to enjoy the day. As many as 10,000 people gathered in the natural amphitheater adjacent to the old Saratoga Inn, and there was a speaker and sometimes a parade. It was rather a joyous moment, when the fruit trees in bloom created a carpet of white stretching across the valley floor.

I remember lying in the grass in the orchards under the trees when they were in blossom, listening to the bees. My, the bees – there were so many bees in those days, the orchards were just full of bees. I loved to lie on the green grass and watch the bees in the blossoms. They really did make a buzzing sound as they visited the millions of blossoms, their sweet fragrance wafting through the breeze. There

Barn at Topside.

were snakes, too, but they didn't bother you, and there were a lot of rabbits and quail, which I used to hunt. But the place has all changed; my, it has changed. There are no rabbits, no quail. All those things are gone.

On May 1st we had a May Day celebration in Saratoga. In those days it was a pretty big affair. The streetcars brought people out from San Jose, and they gathered in a campground right outside of town. They put up May poles and some of us went one way and some of us went the other way, until finally we wound up the ribbons. It was a lot of fun.

That summer I became a farm boy. We had a cow on the ranch; in fact we had two cows, at one time. That's where I learned to milk when I was only about ten. We had two horses to plow the fields. To feed the horses, you climbed up on the loft in the barn and with a big fork, pitched down some hay into the trough, and then gave them a ration of oats. The horses pulled a sidehill plow along the hillsides. It had a hinged blade so you could plow in either direction. Then they pulled a spring-tooth harrow to break up the big chunks. This harrow was a big wide farm implement, a heavy frame with maybe 20 iron teeth for cultivating the soil and every farm had one.

We had chickens and rabbits too, and I had a gun and I hunted for squirrels. Jane and I fed the chickens from the big sacks of chicken feed, and gathered the eggs. My father killed the chickens for food. He chopped off their heads, and sometimes one ran around the yard without its head. And we skinned and dressed the rabbits. You had to eat them because there were so many of them. So we had rabbit frequently and chicken. The butcher came by twice a week and that took care of the meat. Emma was the cook out at Topside, and she had a child, as I remember.

When the apricots ripened I learned how to cut the 'cots and set them out on drying trays. The trays were about three feet wide and about six feet long, and we set the 'cot halves out all over the trays. About 20 trays went into a big cabinet, and the sulfur went in a container in the bottom. We left them in there overnight with the sulfur burning to expose the fruit to the fumes, and that killed all the bugs and kept the 'cots orange as they dried. Then we took them out and put the trays in the sun to let them dry. That's the way we made dried apricots. My, they were delicious.

Then when the prunes were ready, we picked the prunes. To prepare them for drying, we filled a big strainer with a couple of boxes of prunes, and dipped it in a tank of lye for a few seconds and then pulled it out. It cracked the skins so that the prunes dried faster. We washed them off a little, but we weren't worried about the lye. I just loved those sweet prunes. We had wonderful summers out there. We only lived there about two years, but I loved it.

Apricots on drying trays.

In the summer we'd take the prunes into town in the wagon. It would take most of the day. We'd pass by old lady Winchester's house. Always something going on there. She was crazy, you know.

When we moved up to Topside, the water system was ancient. Down the hill from the house was the well, and up in back of the house was the tank house. Our water pressure depended on the tank to give us gravity pressure. Dad bought a new pressure pump that pumped the water up from the well. It went into the tank, if you wanted, or it pumped the water right up into the house. This was a new thing, because it kept pressure on the water the whole time, and you had water any time you wanted.

So we had indoor running water, just cold water that is, due to the new pressure pump. For hot water, we put a big tea kettle on the stove. The tea kettles were big in those days. To take a bath, you had to heat water on the stove, in the early days. Then we got a gas water heater. When Dad turned that on, it made quite a noise. In fact it roared, but then you could take a bath. So the new water system pumped the water up to the house and into the water heater and we had hot running water! I knew it both ways: with and without the modern system.

We had a telephone out at Topside, but it was an eight-party phone. You had to take off the receiver and listen. When you got a chance, you broke in and said, "I want to use the phone now." And maybe they'd hang up, or they might tell you to go ahead. The phone was generally busy with that many people on one line.

In the fall, I was promoted to the fourth grade in the main building. The school house had a belfry, and it was quite an honor to be called upon to ring the bell. The lucky one would start the bell to rocking with a few tentative pulls on the stout rope, and then with a mighty pull, the big bell would thunder out, sounding the end of the day. I was a happy kid when it was my turn to ring the school bell.

They had a privy out there and if you wanted to use it, that's where you went, to the doggone privy. That year the privies were converted to chemical toilets: a foul-smelling arrangement, but it did help to keep down the flies.

Saratoga was only about a block long in those days. There was one main store on the corner of Saratoga Avenue and Saratoga-Sunnyvale Road, then there was a block of stores on the right hand side and about two or three stores on the left-hand side, and a horse-shoe shop on the corner and that was all there was in town. An old green bus came from San Jose through Cupertino and out to Saratoga twice a day. It was a long, rough ride.

We lived out there when they paved the Saratoga-Sunnyvale Road. Before that it was just a dirt road. They were paving the main roads in those days, but they couldn't pour a hill. They didn't know how. So in Saratoga, the main street was all laid in brick, and you came off the cement and hit the brick as you turned up Saratoga Ave.

A guy named Parson lived in the place up above us on Wardell Road. He got a new Ford. It was very exciting. We had a Mitchell, a large, fashionable touring car, and a Ford.

When I was only about ten, they took me to the dentist, to Dr. Cirton in San Jose. He had a drill that was operated by electricity. It went up to the ceiling, went across and came down, and he had this thing like a trolley that he pulled around. He was very pleased with this drill and it was very new and great stuff. I was a victim. I think he drilled either 11 or 13 teeth that day and damn near killed me. Oh, I suppose there was Novocain, but there was a lot of pain, and it ground away so slowly and painfully. I had 15 fillings, and I went home a wreck and went to bed. I think I stayed in bed two days. Oh, he really fixed me up.

After the New Year, Mom and Dad and Norman took a trip back east. They stopped in Mount Vernon, Ohio, to visit his mother's relatives and Great Aunt Abby on their way to New York. Mabel, who was 13 at that time, wrote them this letter:

to G.C. Hulse, c/o Mrs. A. Kinney,
122 East High St., Mount Vernon, Ohio
1917, February 4
Dear Daddy:—
　　Thank you very much for the bead purse. I think it is so pretty. I hope you are enjoying the trip. You bring N. and Mamma home pretty soon. I had a fine time at the Vendome the other night.[25] I did not go to bed until two. Everything is allright at Topside. Mr. Grant came and varnished the floors. I hope you like New York.

Love From
Mabel

---

25 The Vendome Hotel, built in 1888, was a first-class hotel in San Jose.

Chapter 12. Jamaica

THEY HADN'T BEEN HOME LONG when Mom decided to take Norman to Jamaica with her to settle her mother's estate.

Her mother, Harriet Burns, had met William Wilson, a wealthy Jamaican businessman, on board a ship coming back from Europe. He enticed her into joining him in Jamaica, in February 1910. They were married in Massachusetts, November 8, 1909, then they went to Kingston, Jamaica, and lived there in grand style for several years.

With her charming manner, she endeared herself to the people of the island. She loved animals and was active in the local S.P.A.J.,[26] and she was a prime mover in the local Girl Guides Association. She was very patriotic and, along with Wilson, was active in recruiting Jamaican men into the Great War. "She also interested herself in the way of providing comforts for the men, and her words of good cheer to them were at all times appreciated." Her last public appearance was at a big war anniversary demonstration on August 4, 1916, before she contracted a serious illness from which she died on September 12, 1916. "The funeral cortege . . . was a large one." [27]

William Wilson persuaded my mother to come to Jamaica to finalize her mother's affairs. Early in 1917, she and Norman sailed for Jamaica, and Jane, Mabel and I stayed home with Dad at Topside. Wilson showed her a grand time and, when she was ready to return home, he invited her to bring the rest of her children to visit for as long as they cared to.

I was getting along pretty well in the fourth grade when my mother decided to take all four of us kids to Jamaica. That November we sailed from San Francisco aboard the SS *Newport* for the Panama Canal and eventually on to Jamaica. We had a wonderful trip through the Panama Canal. It was the first of many times that I sailed through the Canal.

We stayed for almost a year. It was a delightful time. We first stayed at the Myrtle Bank Hotel, where our family was lodged in a lovely suite while construction of Willie's mansion was completed.

---

26 Society for the Protection of Animals in Jamaica.

27 Quotes are from Obituary of Mrs. William Wilson: Jamaican Family Search Genealogy Research Library, "Who's Who in Jamaica 1916," Obituaries, Mrs. William Wilson.

In Mazatlán: Mother in back row, right center, with Stan; Mabel, Norman and Jane in front, right side.

Myrtle Bank Hotel, Kingston, Jamaica, B.W.I.

Rockfort, Jamaica, 1918.

Wilson had made his money in St. Pierre, Martinique, undoubtedly by growing sugar cane and turning it into rum. When Mt. Pelée, the volcano on the island, became active in 1902, he boarded a ship leaving the island. As they sailed away, the volcano erupted pouring a cloud of flaming gas on the city of St. Pierre, killing everyone except one prisoner who was in an underground prison. From there he moved to Jamaica where he had a large "farm" or perhaps a "plantation." I don't remember what he grew on his land but he had fifteen employees.

He built a beautiful home out at Rockfort, near Kingston. It was right on the waterfront with steps leading down to the beach. In front were spacious grounds with a beautiful garden that gave way to a race course and cricket field complete with stands for spectators. Any prowler that was unaware of our secret weapon was due for a surprise, for if they stumbled upon one of the peacocks that roamed the place, they could be half scared out of their wits by the banshee cry of the startled bird. A signal to investigate . . .

We had horses to ride and a buggy with a coachman. A retinue of fifteen servants catered to our wants. There was a big ballroom whose ceiling was 24 feet high, to make dancing in the tropics more comfortable.

Besides the main guest room, each of us kids had a separate bedroom. My mother had a bedroom in the same wing as ours while Uncle Willie, as we called our host, had a master suite. All in all, it was quite a mansion. He tried to persuade my mother to become permanent mistress of it. But she and my father had not yet come to the end of the line.

Jane and I spent a great deal of time in the water. We swam whenever we had a chance. One time we swam out to where a ship was anchored and the captain invited us aboard for lunch. We also joined the native kids diving for coins that were tossed overboard.

Once, a group of us went over to Port Royal, which guarded the harbor entrance. It was out on the tip of a long tongue of sand called "The Palisades." The place was a ruins, and in the clear water we could see some of the remains of the buildings that had sunk to the bottom of the bay in a terrible earthquake in 1907. The wrecks of some of the thirteen ships, which had been lost along the shore when the earthquake had darkened the lighthouse, lay resting among the rocks.

When I returned to Jamaica in 1962 with our family, a road had been built out to the old fort and some of the ruins had been partially restored. There was a partly sunken powder magazine that I remember exploring on my first visit and a sign on a restored brick wall still bearing the legend: "You who tread his footprints remember his glory." It is a tribute to Lord Horatio Nelson, for whom my great, great-grandfather, Horatio Nelson Baldwin, was named.

While we were in Jamaica, my father was taking care of the ranch at Topside. He missed his family very much and wrote this letter to Jane and me:

1917, December 16

To my dear little kiddies, Bill and Freckles -

Greetings, how are you bugs? Do you know Daddy thinks you are nothing more or less than plain frauds. Here you have been away for seven whole weeks and neither of you have written Daddy a letter, Jane did send me a very pretty post card, but I want letters telling me what you do from day to day.

Mama wrote me that you were going in wading and swimming, and that you liked it very much. It must be lots of fun if the water is warm enough and I expect that way down there it is.

Well another week and Christmas comes. Daddy is wondering what you will do about a Christmas tree, maybe you will have a banana tree instead of a redwood, wouldn't that be a funny sort of a tree, just think after the presents were all distributed you could sit around and eat the bananas. Have you seen any monkeys yet? The other morning when I was going to town, just beyond the school a coyote trotted out of the orchard and across the road when he stopped and watched the machine. That is the first one I have seen around here.

The little chickens have grown until you can hardly tell them from the old ones. I wish you were here to get under the barn and look for their nest; they are hiding the eggs. Emma found one nest about a month ago with sixteen eggs, but since then we have not found a single one.

Now write me a nice letter and tell me all about your Christmas, which I hope will be a very happy one.

Daddy

Uncle Willie had a big Pierce-Arrow touring car in which we took many trips about the island. His chauffeur, Morgan, was an excellent driver, and the roads were all macadam (made of broken stone) and kept in first class shape by convict labor. Uncle Willie was constantly directing Morgan to hurry it up. When it rained, there would be puddles in the road. I can still remember how Willie would laugh as some poor pedestrian, usually with a huge load balanced on her head, walking along the side of the road, would be drenched when the car hit one of the puddles and splashed all over these "niggers." He would let out a hearty laugh, "Ha, ha, ha!" He got a big kick out of it. I guess that was one of the reasons my mother decided he wasn't the man for her. He wasn't a mean man, but he did like his jokes. In that time and place, it was funny. The natives had not yet learned that a speeding car would splash a puddle, and their surprise was something to see. We had one of the very few cars. Everybody walked where they wanted to go. In those days, Jamaica was very, very small, it was really a jungle. There were people there, but not like there are today.

I remember another incident when my mother was riding horseback along a road. A car came along, frightening the horse, and it threw her heavily to the side of the road. A very polite Englishman came up to her and graciously inquired, "May I assist, Madam?" before extending a hand to help her to her feet. A true gentleman, taking no liberties.

Dad wrote this letter to Norman in Kingston, Jamaica:

1918, Sunday Jan. 29 Topside
Daddy's Baby Boy,
    What did you want to fall in the water for? You must be
very careful cause you might turn into a big fish. I has not got
any chew gum but here is a nickle so you can buy some and
please chew one piece for me.
        With lots of love and kissing from
                    Your
                    "Far away Daddy"

In March, my mother sent him a letter in reply:

Norman's letter taken as dictated:

Dear Daddy to send me a letter and I want him to send me some

70

Christmas presents from Mimi's store.[28] *I guess that's about all.*
I want him to send me some Japanese books. I'm going to send
him some "flower-loves."

Norman

I remember a big party that we had. There were cases and cases of soda pop. There was one drink called "cola" different from our Coke but very good. It was all iced in big laundry tubs and the servants poured continually. The big ballroom, with the doors to the veranda flung wide, was filled with music from a lovely orchestra. The guests were in their finest, sparkling with the family jewels, each hoping to make an impression or at least keep from being totally eclipsed. My mother, a petite person who wore clothes beautifully, was dressed in a stunning black gown and sporting some of her mother's beautiful jewels. She was lovely, and Uncle Willie was very proud of her.

All this was before air conditioning. We had many electric fans, but the sea breeze through the many open doors to the veranda was delightful. We slept under mosquito netting canopies but other than that, we learned to tolerate the pests. Scorpions were a bit of a problem. We were at a party at a neighbor's when one of the darn things fell from the ceiling right onto the shoulder of one of the ladies on the dance floor. Fortunately, someone brushed it away before it stung her. We had a number of lizards that occupied the house with us. They liked to stay up near or on the ceilings where they lived on mosquitos. They bothered no one and were just part of the scene.

We used to go visiting at a number of houses. There was a big place where a Japanese or Chinese family lived, and we used to go over there for the tennis matches. There was a guy named Chickie who was about five years older than I. He was a friend of the family, and whenever we had dances or parties, he was always there. I liked him and I met up with him again years later.

While living in Jamaica, it was decided that we kids should have a governess. She was a mousy individual and Morgan, the chauffeur, would go into town and bring her out to Rockfort. About the time she was to arrive, Jane and I would be swimming so far off the end of the pier that we always managed to lose at least half an hour before she could coax us to get our books open.

---

28 Misa Seki, who we called Mimi, married Geo. Okamoto and they had a gift shop called "The Mikado" in San Jose.

1918, April 14, Sunday
from Dad at "Topside"

Shame on you young man, the very idea of your only hav-ing caught seven fish since you have been living right next door to their home. Try spitting on your bait, that is what the niggers do down south, and they claim it gets results every time.

I have just come in from the chicken yard, went down to kill a mongrel dog. It was not a very large dog and was racing round as fast as it could so it took five shots to do the job. I managed to hit him three of the first four times, but not in a place that stopped his running. Used a new 35 calibre automatic that shoots like lightning.

I told Mama to tell you that I had a new roadster. It was a Mitchell and would make around seventy miles an hour, but it used so much gas and oil that I have disposed of it. You would have enjoyed gliding over the roads as I did sometimes, but if you had been with me, any of you, I should not have felt like taking the chances that anyone does to ride so fast.

I was very glad to hear from Mama that you are doing nicely at school. Don't be afraid to practice writing, writing is one of the very important things in business. Many people who want to employ help have them apply for the position by letter, and when a letter comes that is poorly written they throw it aside without further consideration. So you see it is necessary for you to be able to write a good hand.

I am also glad you are doing lots of swimming, I know you like it and it's fine for you. How long can you swim now without resting?

Daddy.

These were war years and my mother was a very patriotic person. We were at the motion picture theatre one evening, sitting in the owner's box. Willie owned both of the theatres in Kingston at the time. After playing "God Save the King" the orchestra broke into "The Star Spangled Banner." The beat, however, was to ragtime. My mother, in high dudgeon, stood up, strode to the orchestra pit and stopped the music. She laid down the law, told the orchestra leader that if he was to play it at all, it was to be played correctly. After which it was, too.

Months slipped by. We were having a wonderful time and Willie wanted to make the arrangement permanent. But my mother decided we should be with our father and so, after six months in Jamaica, we said good-bye and sailed for New York on the SS *Carrillo*. As we approached New York, we sailed into submarine infested waters. The U-boats were blockading New York. Somehow we got through though eleven ships were sunk that night.[29]

The New York water front was a teeming mass of horse-drawn drays, carts and wagons of every description; their drivers bawling at their teams and at one another in a din like Babel. Our party, my mother, we four youngsters, and two servants — two young black women that my mother brought back with us — attracted no little attention. The Jamaicans were awestruck and showed it as they struggled with our baggage that included a big parrot cage, in which Laurita kept a constant clamor. The noise, the smells, the litter of the fresh horse manure that covered the place, made the day memorable. We finally emerged from the jumble and with the help of two taxis made our way uptown.

My mother found a flat near Central Park where we stayed for a month. We had a great time doing New York. At the old Hippodrome, we saw Houdini and Al Jolson and attended the Metropolitan Opera. Jane and I spent a lot of time in Central Park, playing and having a lovely time. In those days, it was a very civilized place; a lot of nursemaids with their perambulators and well-dressed charges made up much of the crowd.

We were residents of New York City for six weeks, then we took the train to Mt. Vernon, Ohio, my birthplace, where we spent a week or so visiting the relatives. We met my father's aunts and cousins: Aunt Julia Ringwalt and Aunt Abby Kinney and their families. Then we came home by train to San Jose, and our fairy tale-like voyage was over. It was the middle of 1918.

My father came down to meet us at the train, looking a bit seedy. Norman was pretty well healed up from the burns he had sustained at Topside, before our trip to Jamaica. Dad greeted us as we got off the train, but he didn't take us home to Topside. He had sold the ranch, and moved into town. He bought a place at 1310 The Alameda on the corner of Villa Avenue, just one block from our old house that had burned down.

---

29 According to Ellis Island Archives, they arrived in New York on May 9, 1918.

Chapter 13. Home Again

IT WAS A LOVELY PLACE, a big old-fashioned house. It had four or five bedrooms, servants' quarters and a big kitchen. Our household at that time consisted of Mother and Father, us four kids, Jeanette Morgan (a foster child from a broken home whose parents we knew very well), Mary the cook and Gwendolyn the maid, the two colored girls from Jamaica, and Morgan the chauffeur. Why? No one knows!

Armistice Day Parade, 1918.

Back to Hester School: I tried the fifth grade. About two days later I was back in fourth grade. It was too easy so I was sent to a private school along with Jane and Mabel. We weren't in any "grade." They taught us excellent manners: drawing room presence. We could dance and converse very well, but we couldn't spell or cypher[30] and my penmanship was weird to say the least. Washburn School worked on us for a while but it was a losing battle from the start.[31]

The Great War had been ongoing during these years and I, as a child of 12, was only vaguely aware of it. But when the war ended and the Armistice was signed on November 11, 1918, "the eleventh hour of the eleventh day of the eleventh month" in 1918, the "War to End All Wars" was over. A big parade marched down the main street of San Jose: soldiers and artillery guns, women in long white dresses, just hundreds of people marched, and everywhere there were flags. San Jose and the thousands of towns and cities from coast to coast went wild. It was a day of celebration, a day to be glad you were an American.

Granddad had moved to San Jose in 1918, while we were gone, and he rejoined Mellie there. They were living on North Thirteenth Street at that time.

Christmas came and went, and in January my mother was operated on for her appendix. She was very much afraid that she would not survive the operation, so she left this note:

1919, January 27
"I wrote this the morning I was operated on for appendicitis
& "etc."

Monday
My Babies —
    Remember always that I love you adoringly – not one better than another, all just the same only you each appeal differently – that's all. My love and thoughts go with you to Eternity —
                    God bless you
                    Your Mother.

---

30 Archaic: to do arithmetic.

31 "Ten Years in Paradise," p.61: the Washburn school, conducted by Mr. & Mrs. Washburn, is a commodious structure where pupils are prepared to enter college.

During this operation, she actually died. She said she was in a tunnel-shaped area, with a very bright light that she was moving toward. It represented peace and comfort and she was moving toward the light. Then she heard a voice behind her, and it was Dr. Bullock's voice saying, "Bessie you can't go. You can't leave the children." Reluctantly she turned around and went back to Dr. Bullock.[32]

Summer came, and one of the things we loved to do was to take the train over to Santa Cruz. You could take the steam train from San Francisco all the way to Santa Cruz in those days. It went from San Jose out to Los Gatos and through the mountains to Santa Cruz. If it rained, there were curtains that we hung up on the hooks that would keep the rain out. They were made of cloth and they had windows in them that were made from isinglass, so you could still look out the windows. Santa Cruz was just a beach in those days, as far as I was concerned.

There was a place there at Seabright where we liked to stay. It was a long, sandy beach between the boardwalk and Santa Cruz harbor. We were there on my birthday, July 10, 1919, and I received this birthday greeting:

Outside of envelope:

1919, July 10
"Towards the long-wanted bicycle.
from
Jane, Mabel & Me."
    "We were at Seabright"
Inside letter:

My dear Stan,
    That you may be healthy, happy and prosperous on the anniversary of this day is ever the loving wish of
Grand dad
    San Jose
    July 10, 1919

Enclosed is a check drawn on the St. Louis Union Bank to Stan C. Hulse for $2.50, signed J. W. Hulse.

---

32 This story was told to me by Bill Dungan who remembered his mother telling him about the time she died.

In the fall, Jane and I went over to San Jose Normal Training School,[33] which was part of the San Jose School system. We were taught by student teachers in a massive two-story gray structure near Seventh Street. Somehow I managed to be promoted out of the sixth grade and into the seventh.

It was while living on The Alameda that Otty Oberowski helped me build my first radio in 1920. He was studying radio and working on one, and he decided he'd build me one, because he liked me and "if he got the things he could do it." So we worked on it together, and when it was done, we could hear a guy named Senter, down at the corner, who used to broadcast. Up until that time no one had radios, but as time went by, there were gradually more and more stations that we could pick up. So that was my first radio.

Then my dad got interested in radio and in March he opened a radio shop. It was one of the first radio stores in California. The radio shop was in addition to the photo shop. He just fixed up the front of the store as a radio store. He had a counter where you could leave your film, and in the back of the store we made the prints. That was in 1920, and I was about 14. I worked for my dad at that time. I used to ride my bicycle delivering the packages of photos in Santa Clara, in East San Jose, in South San Jose, in North San Jose. I rode all around on my bike. I guess I rode about 15 miles a day. His shop was located at 53 South First Street. He had a young boy taking care of radios in there and I used to help with the radios, but I was mostly in delivery.

Radios, in those days, were big things. They were delivered to the store in big crates that stood about four feet high. It took two men to carry one. It was like a piece of furniture, nothing like the radios we have now.

Chapter 14. Norman

SHORTLY AFTER MY 14TH BIRTHDAY, a terrible thing happened that was to completely change the course of my life and that of our family. Mabel was 17 at that time, Jane was 12 and Norman was 6 ½ years old.

Grandmother Dan and Granddad had been living on North Thirteenth Street since he left the mines in Montana in 1918. But after

_____

33 San Jose Normal Training School later became San Jose State College.

Radios being delivered to Hulse Radio Service

Granddad died on December 9, 1919, at the age of 76, she came to live with us. She was 75 years old, but still a strong-willed woman. She had put some of her belongings down in the basement for safe-keeping, so she kept it locked most of the time. There was also a storeroom down in the basement where we kept things like you would in a garage.

July 11, 1920, was a Sunday and that day Norman begged Mother to take him around to visit everyone he knew. So she did. Among others, they went to visit the Okamotos.[34] Misa Seki had married a man named Geo. S. Okamoto and they had three children, Fuji, June and Yukio. Fuji was about my age and our families were good friends. The Okamotos were living at 326 North 21st St. in Japan Town in San Jose at that time.

Monday, July 12th dawned warm and beautiful. The calmness of the summer's day did not warn us that this would be a day that would change our lives forever.

There was a general bustle around the kitchen that morning. The fragrant aroma of tea and freshly made biscuits filled the air as Alice placed them on the table. Alice Burke had come back with us from Jamaica and served as the maid and cook around the place. At 24 years old, she was already a widow and part of the family, as it were. She was colored and had come to America to start a new life here. Jane and I sat eating our cereal at the kitchen table. She was going to visit her girl friend and I was going to work with Mom and Dad.

"Can't you hurry up?" Dad said to Mom, "I have to get to the shop. It's going to be real busy today."

"Yes, I'm coming," she answered, as she pinned her sun bonnet to her hair. She was wearing a fashionable long-bodied, calf-length dress with high heels that elevated her "five-foot and three-quarters of an inch" to almost 5 ft. 4 in.

They hurried out the door to catch the streetcar to work. It ran down the middle of The Alameda, right in front of our house. This trolley line took them right down to Market Street where they got off just a block from the office, Hulse Service, at

---

34 This information came from Mari Takaichi Lee, daughter of Fuji Okamoto Takaichi.

53 South First Street. The two-story brick building faced the beautiful St. James Park across Market Street. It was a lovely place to take an afternoon nap, lying on the grass under the trees. But on that day, there was no time for naps.

Dad must have told to me to fill up the gasoline tank of the automobile before I left for work, because I had a can of gasoline, about half full, which I had taken to put down in the storeroom. But the door was locked, and Grandmother had the key, so I left it at the top of the stairs leading down to the basement and forgot about it. But I just remember how it got there. I hopped on my bicycle and rode down The Alameda to join my folks at work.

It was my job, at 14 years old, to make the deliveries and pickups. When I arrived at the shop, I checked the bin that held the finished photos, pulled out the packets, put them in my bag, and threw it over my shoulder. "I'm off to make deliveries," I called as I headed for the door. "Stop at the Post Office and buy some stamps," my dad called after me. "Okay," I said, as I went out the door.

I hopped on my bicycle, and headed up Market Street making deliveries while Mom and Dad ran the store. I went around to all the pharmacies and picked up the rolls of film to be developed, and delivered the finished photographs. We had a very busy operation there. At that time it was the largest photo finishing business in California. Since it was shortly after the Fourth of July there were many photographs to be developed that week.

Mom worked at the counter helping customers who came into the shop. Her polite but efficient manner kept the front counter running smoothly. The Brownie camera was the most popular box camera of the day. It was mass-produced by the millions, and was quite durable and inexpensive. Adults as well as children just loved taking photographs and it made for a lively photofinishing business!

Dad was busy overseeing the photofinishing, ordering paper and chemicals, setting up new distribution points and sometimes even working in the darkroom, which he loved to do.

A young woman named Maude worked with us, doing a little bit of everything. She was tall and thin with extremely long, black, curly hair that she usually kept tied up in a bun on the back of her head. Donald Dungan, a recent Stanford graduate, was boarding with us and working for my father at the photography shop.

We probably had lunch at the shop. Mom would have brought us some food packed in a basket by our cook, since it was too busy to go out for lunch.

Meanwhile, Mabel and Grandmother were at home with Norman. Norman was a darling boy, blond and beautiful. He was playful and happy and the "apple of my Mother's eye." It's not that she didn't love us all, but Norman was the baby and everyone just adored him. My father took lots of photographs of him and he was a favored child. But he got into trouble at times. He seemed to enjoy playing with fire and had burned himself badly when we lived at Topside. But he had healed up while we were in Jamaica and was a happy, healthy boy once again.

After lunch, Grandmother had probably gone to her room to take a nap, and Mabel, at 17, might have been curled up in a chair in the parlor reading a good book in the warm afternoon. She was awakened from her reverie when she heard a loud explosion outside the house followed by an awful scream that would follow her down through the decades of her life. Her heart was pounding as she jumped to her feet. "What was that noise? Where is Norman?" she thought as she ran outside to see what had happened. When she came around the corner, what she saw filled her with horror. She froze in her steps, not knowing what to do, then she called out frantically for Grandmother and Alice, and ran for the phone.

When we got the call, Mabel said, with her voice trembling, "Come home quick! Norman has been burned." So we knew it was bad. We caught the next streetcar and we were home in about fifteen minutes. We jumped off the car and ran across the roadway to the house. Storming in through the front door, we could hear Norman's cries and rushed into the parlor where Alice had laid him on the couch. And there he was, just scorched. The acrid smell of burnt skin and singed hair filled the room, along with his desperate cries of pain. The sight of his face made my stomach crawl up into my throat. He was a sad sight to see.

Mom ran to his side, wanting to hug his poor little body, but afraid to touch him. His blond hair was scorched and his clothes were stuck to his burnt skin. She started crying uncontrollably. Dad picked up the telephone and called Dr. Bullock, then he started asking questions, looking for someone to blame for the terrible accident: "Where was Mabel when this happened? She was supposed to be watching him! How did this happen?"

It seemed that Norman was playing with firecrackers, probably left over from the Fourth of July. Mabel was supposed to be watching him, but she hadn't been watching him well enough. He had found the can of gasoline at the top of the basement steps, lit a firecracker and dropped it into the can of gasoline. It must have made a terrible explosion and he was horribly burned.

Soon Dr. Bullock arrived. He examined poor Norman, put cold compresses on his burns, but he couldn't save him, and he died about seven o'clock that evening.

Mom went into her room and cried and cried for hours. It seemed that her grief would never end. That was a bad time.[35]

Well, my mother never recovered. You might have known my mother, but you never really knew her because she never was the same. She was a long, long time coming out of that. So that was a terrible thing because it left a scar on everyone. Why hadn't I put the stuff away? Well I couldn't. My grandmother had the key so she was the responsible person. But my sister was responsible because she was taking care of him and she had not taken care of him at that time, so it was one of those things. My mother was looking for

---

35 This piece was written by Jenny Watts incorporating bits of information that Stan told of the event.

someone to blame, because she was out working and it happened, and there was no one really. It was a bad, bad thing. My sister Mabel came in for the bulk of the blame. My grandmother had locked the cellar to keep her things in there, so I couldn't put the gasoline away. That was another appalling thing against Grandma. And the fact that Mabel was in charge of him at the time, that was bad for Mabel.

Then there was Donald Dungan. He was living with us at the time and he was very attentive to Mom. He took my mother out and drove her around Santa Clara Valley and spent a good deal of time with her. My father let him off work to do that, and he took over looking out for my mother. She called him "Pal-O-Mine", and they became close friends. He had finished Stanford and had been boarding with us for about six months. He was 12 years younger than my mother, but he took care of her at that time. My father took to sleeping in another room of the house, but that was more or less an ordinary occasion in those days.

Then she took up spiritualism, and got very much involved. She was trying to communicate with Norman. She just wanted to know if he was all right. They tried all kinds of interesting things. I saw a table go up the stairs one time. When you're in a position like that and see all these things happening, you can believe in them, there's no doubt about it. And there was no reason to see that little table go up the stairs – it's just one of those things. It would make a believer out of anyone!

There was a lot of knocking. Several of them would sit around a table, and it would bounce up A, B, C, D then it would stop. Next it would be A, B, C, D, E, F, G. So D.G. would be the initials of somebody, or something like that. And a lot of that happened around the place. I saw enough of the "supernatural" to decide that it was not good to play with. Just not good, that was all. A Swedish lady finally convinced her that she had gotten through and that Norman was all right. But she was a long, long time coming out of that.

Our household broke up after his death. My mother and father decided to get a divorce, and that's when we moved from The Alameda over to Martin Avenue. It was Mabel and Jane, and my mother and I, and Donald came along. He wasn't living with my mother then, he just came along. We had a couple of servants over there and a cook, so we kids never suffered if we wanted something to eat because there was somebody there to feed us. I was out of school for a long while.

Chapter 15. Teenage Years

IN MAY OF 1921, MY MOTHER left Dad for good. Don and my mother married and moved from San Jose to 26th Avenue, San Francisco in May 1921. I was 14, and I went to live with my grandmother, Dan, who had a very comfortable little house out on University Avenue in San Jose. She bought additional land behind her house where she tended a lovely rose garden.

My grandmother, Mellie Curtis Hulse, was born in 1844, in Vermont, one of four children, three daughters and a son. Her father, Mark Curtis, moved the family to Mt. Vernon, Ohio, where he became a well-known merchant in the dry goods business, and the head of a prominent Mt. Vernon family. In 1869, the family moved to St. Louis, where he was involved with the manufacture of cooking and heating stoves. There she met James Warren Hulse, and they were married in 1874.

They made their home with his parents in St. Louis. It was there that they had two children, George Curtis Hulse, born August 3, 1876, and a daughter, Mabel, born in 1881, who died as an infant in late 1882. It seems that they continued to live with his parents, and in the late 1880s, they all moved to Mt. Vernon together. After James' mother died, in 1884, they took care of his father until he died in 1894.

Mellie was an extremely proud person, proud of her descendency from the Mayflower Pilgrims, tracing her lineage back to Myles Standish. She could follow the line directly back through her father, Mark Curtis. His great-grandmother was Abigail Standish, who was the great-granddaughter of Myles Standish.

After his father died, James

Mellie Curtis Hulse, c.1925.

Miles Standish Ancestry

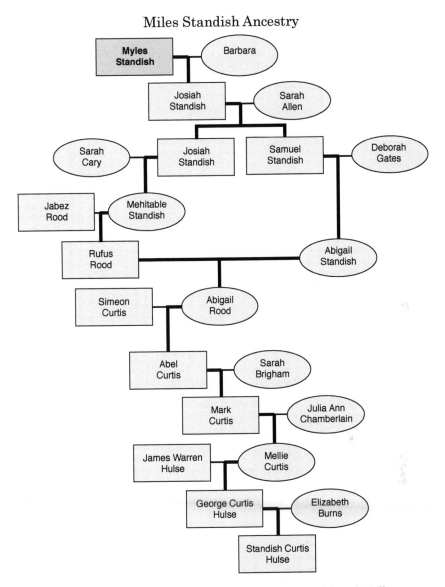

and Mellie moved to Montana, near Gardiner, outside of Yellowstone National Park, where he filed a number of gold claims. In 1899 he was one of the owners of the Park View Mining Company that owned 11 claims on Crevasse Mountain. Mellie tired of the life there after a while and moved back to Mt. Vernon. Then in 1918, she moved to San Jose to be near her son, George, and her grandchildren.

In her home on University Avenue, she often had "ladies to tea" and she served cake or a dessert that was simply wonderful. She never told anyone her recipes and her cooking was done behind closed doors. When she died in 1930, at the age of 86, her wonderful secrets went with her to the grave. She had a small group of bridge players who she entertained regularly and she enjoyed reasonably good health until her death.

Not long after he left my mother, my father married Maude who had worked at the shop for him and was some 20 years younger than he was. G.C. (my dad), Maude and I lived on University Avenue with my grandmother and they put up a tent for me in the backyard where I was very happy to be. It was a special camp tent and I lived for a year in that while my dad bought the place next door. The house burned down, very fortunately, the night he bought it. Very fortunately, because he built a house there that we liked. He didn't have to wreck the old house that was there. I lived with them and worked with them for three years.

After I had worked for my dad awhile, I got promoted, more or less, and Dad gave me an interest in the business. He used to keep a record of how much I earned and how much went to the business. He left the business entirely in my hands for several months when he took a long vacation. He was very busy. He had a woman that he was very much interested in, and he went off with her, I don't know, three months maybe six months. I can't remember her name, but she was very nice.

Maude stayed around and lived at the house, and we just kept the business going while he was gone. I pretty well ran the business at that time, and Maude did the finishing work on the pictures. She had one or two girls helping her on that end, and I had a radio guy who came in and worked on the radios, which were just coming into their own in 1921. Then finally G.C. came back and joined the parade, and we cried and made up and everything was all right.

In September 1921, my mother and Don moved to Adeline Dr., Burlingame.

no date, Monday nite. 9 p.m.
Dearest Mom,
    How are you and the rest of the family? I am O.K.
    I would have been down Sunday but we went house hunting so being unable to be in both places at the same time, I was un-

86

able to get down to Burlingame. Now you understand.

We had a pretty good day today and got the work out in good time. I am down at the shop now watching a tank of packs. I have met a bunch of fellows that I used to know and they all seem glad to see me, which is very gratifying. Jane has no friends apparently, except a Jewess who's father has a "cut rate" shoe "parlor" on Market St.

Saturday nite I went to see the "Merchant of Venice" at S.J.H.S. [San Jose High School] and it was very good. Frank S. and Mintha were in it and it was put over well.

The new set is a wonder. A man eating next door was a violinist and he came over and asked who was playing the violin and seemed greatly surprised when he found it was over the radio. It ought to sell like hell.

Maude is very nice to me, so is Dan and so is Dad. Jane does not have much to say but she is not as unpleasant as she might be.

Dan worries about my sleeping outdoors and was going to buy me a wardrobe trunk to keep my clothes in but I persuaded her not to. She is queer. Well I am going home so good night.

Lots of love,

Stan

P.S. See you this weekend? If I can make it.

I tried to get into San Jose High School, but they wouldn't let me in with no credentials. I went over to Santa Clara High, talked to the head man and he said he'd give me a chance. That was in late fall 1921.

Dear Mom,

Yesterday Dad phoned to prof. Leland at the S.J. High, and asked him if I was to take an exam in the near future or not. Dad told him what I had been doing and Leland asked who had been teaching me.

Then right away he said I didn't have a chance to get in and I had better go to some school till June. Then he said if Dad wanted he could give me an exam but there wasn't any use because I would never pass. So you see he did all he could to throw a wet blanket on my prospect of going into High.

I went home and got cleaned up and went over to Santa Clara High and told Prof. Thomson that I had been through the eighth grade work at a private school and I wanted to enter his

school in Feb. and I wanted to know what I was to do about it
and all he said was to come over on the 3rd and register and he
would take me in.

    *I didn't even have to tell him what I had done, who my
teacher was or anything.*

    *When he said just come over and register on the 3rd I could
of kissed him I was so happy, especially after what Leland had
said and it was sure a great relief, believe me.*

    Well I will see you Friday night, Dearest.

        Love from

          A Happy Kid – Stan

So he said all right, I'll put you in class, you bring me your graduation papers. He called me several times for them, but I never got around to getting them, since I didn't have them.

At last I was in High School. I did all right that first half-year, but blew it the second year, became hard to manage, became persona non grata when I turned in a fire alarm to see if the newly installed gadget would really work. It did.

I met Freddy Franck in high school as a freshman at Santa Clara. He was just about my age, and we belonged to a group of kids. We became good friends and I'd go over to see him or he'd come over to my house and we'd shoot the breeze or play cards or something. We kept up the contact over the years. Yes, I guess he was my oldest friend while he was still alive.

I stayed at Santa Clara High School for about a year and a half. I used to like to go down to Adolph's to practice boxing.

Wednesday   *(Written on Hulse Kodak Finishing Service paper)*
Dear Mother,

    I just had time to write to you so I thought I would write.

    *Maud is petting the parrot's back and fighting with it. She
sure has it tamed.*

    *Every once in a while I go around the corner and have some
of those Chinese noodles to eat.*

    *Last night I went down the road to Adolph's and put the
gloves on with a new Kid and gave him a black eye. He never
touched me hard enough to hurt. We only had one two-minute
round so I did not get time to finish him.*

    *Tell Jane that the Kids at school ask where she is all the
time.*

Well, I am running out of ammunition so I will have to stop writing.

Love, Stan.

Spring 1922

Dear Mom,

I'm awful sorry you are feeling rotten. I am as good as they make 'em.

School is dandy and I am getting along pretty well.

I am taking Community Civics, Com. Arithmetic, General Science, and English. I keep pretty busy taking care of these subjects so I don't get much time to write.

Friday a boy that weighs about 130 and is about a half-a-head taller than I, said something about a girl, that I didn't like. We were right in the assembly hall when he said it. I was so dog-gone mad that I hit him right in the jaw. To make a long story short, he apologized and I made some hit with the girl. Well I hope you will be better by the time you get this.

Love, Stan.

That summer I signed up for C.M.T.C., Citizen's Military Training Camp in Monterey. I had just turned 16 and I decided I wanted to join the Army. So I was inoculated for C.M.T.C. and the next summer, in 1923, I went in for a short stint.

In September 1922, Mom and Don moved to 400 Primrose Road, Burlingame where Donnabeth was born on June 23, 1923. They made up her name taking Donna from Donald and Beth from Elizabeth.

In December I joined the DeMolay, the young men's branch of the Masons. My Granddad belonged to the Knights Templar, a Christian fraternal organization that is part of the Masons. So I joined up, but it never really took with me.

1923, Feb. 1, 4:30 p.m. Friday, Santa Clara, Calif.

Dear Mom,

How are you, and the girls and Don. I'm fine and dandy.

Last week I did not come down because I slept so late Saturday morning.

I had a swell time at the "Soaks" dance. I took Iris and she thought I was slow because I didn't even put my arm around her.

89

Tonight I am going to Hermione Butti's house and tomor-
row night I am going to a party at a girl's house. So I guess I
won't see you this week-end.
 I'm having a swell time at school and am getting along
pretty good with my studies as well as the girls. I'm glad that
I'm not quitting in Feb.
 Maude and Dad have been getting along pretty well so far.
 The men haven't finished working on the house yet. They
are painting some of the rooms now.
 I am running out of things to say, so I'll have to quit saying.
    Say hello to everybody.
     Love
     Stan.

 P.S. I wrote one letter and didn't mail it. I am writing this in
the S.C.P.O.
    Your flirting Son (So they say!)
    Stan

So then we moved into the new house, which was next door to
my grandmother's house on University Avenue in San Jose. It was a
modest, two-story house with three bedrooms upstairs, and downstairs was a dining room, a living room, a bedroom, a bath and a
kitchen. The three of us moved in there and then Mabel came down
and joined the party. My sister Jane had moved up to Burlingame at
that time to live with Mom and Don.

no date (written on Hulse Kodak Finishing Service paper)
Dearest,
 I received your letter tonight, and I want to tell you that last
week after Dad talked to me I started to work hard. You may
not believe me, but it is the truth.
 By the time you see me I will be studying hard, and getting
someplace. This last week I did much better and it pleased me a
great deal.
 Well, I haven't much to say for myself.
    Love to Jane and yourself,
     Stan.

Dear Mom,   *1923, April 23*
 How are you dear? and the rest of the folks.

I'm finer than frogs hair and am tickled pink. Today I got my report and it is the first report that I enjoyed showing. The others were no fun presenting, but this one is the best yet. This is the way it goes:

Algebra	*2+*	*and I raised my last 4 to a 2 – that's good.*
Ancient History	*2+*	*nothing mean about that*
Mod. & Med. History	*2*	*was 3 last time.*
		She is the teacher I have a hard time getting along with
Physical Ed	*2*	
Com Arith	*2 -*	

If you don't think this is an improvement you will never see one.

Dad gave me $5.00 for this report.
Hot Dog ! ! ! !
I guess Jane is thrilled to the core over the invite to the next Soaks dance. Doc thinks she's all right.
I am not sure of the date: either the 5th or the 12th; probably the 12th; let you know later. Saturday Doc and I and "Sheik" Alderman went up to the Liberty Hall Skating Rink. We had more darn fun than I can tell. We also had a lot of thrilling spills and collisions. I am still recovering from some of them.
I am going up there again some time. It's lots different from skating on the sidewalk and it's a lot more fun.
Sunday Frank and Jack, a kid that's going to camp with us, he is a good kid, and myself went to the show.
I have seen a lot of Frank lately and we have made a lot of plans for this summer.
Well, it's getting late and I can't keep my eyes open any longer. So here's hoping this letter finds you in the best of health and spirits.
Give my love to the girls and say hello to Don for me. I don't think he cares about sharing my love.
Love, Stan

P.S. R.S.V.P.

I did fairly well for a time. Recall an A in History under a young prof. named Ed Hoagg. Later – much later – he was a fellow Lion in Burlingame.

1923, April 25 from Burlingame
to Mr. Standish Hulse, P.O. Box 1309, San Jose, Cal.
Tuesday, 6:30 p.m.

Stan, old dear! I am really delighted over your report –
always knew you could do it if you only would! Now that you
have done so well you will have to keep up the good work.

I am the only invalid in the family and I weigh only 117 or
so, therefore hardly expect to pass out immediately.

Glad Daddy appreciated your work to the tune of $5.00.

Jane is very pleased at being asked by Doc ("he has such
pretty brown eyes") – let her know the exact date so she can get
properly marcelled.[36]

D & I drove down to S.J. Sat. I expected to find you here on
our return and was disappointed. However, Mabel says you
were fixing up the car – that's good work.

Glad you enjoyed the rink – ice is good enough and hard
enough for me.

Jane is going for a hike (Sat. to Sun.) with the Sparks Gym
bunch this weekend. Mabel is going out with Don R. to a dance.

If you want a "nice quiet time" come down – or rather up –
always want you.

I am glad you and Frank are seeing more of each other – I
like him!

Who are you taking to the dance? Mabel says you looked "so
nice" in your new togs. I told her to wait until she saw you in
your "lid!" Was glad to hear from you as well as to see the fine
report!

Excuse scrawl – this leaves me in fine health and spirits
soaring—

Lovingly dear,
Mom

All send salutations.

But discontent kept creeping in. I liked some aspects of school, and I liked my job. During most of my school years I had a job of sorts: delivery boy after school and Saturdays for several markets in San Jose. I worked for my dad and learned the photofinishing business. I had very little time for sports, though in my Freshman year at Santa Clara High, I did make the track team in 1923.

---

36 Also called marcel wave, a hairstyle characterized by repeated regular waves, popular in the 1920s.

Santa Clara High School track team, 1923. Stan, left front.

1923, July 6

Stan dear—

Enclosed find a check, the girls send $5.00 for your birthday with love and good wishes for a jolly time. We talked it over and decided you would rather have the money to spend on your trip than to have ties and socks!

Have a happy time & remember I am always loving you and am very proud of you.

Careful how you souvenir! Call at Gen'l. Delivery S. Cruz P.O. on your birthday!

> *Heaps of love*
>> *Your*
>>> *Mother.*

Chapter 16: C.M.T.C.

THE END OF JULY 1923, I joined the Army for the first time, at the U.S. Army Summer Training Camp, Del Monte, Monterey. It was known as the C.M.T.C., the Citizen's Military Training Camp and I was 17.

August 2

    We waited around after we arrived Thursday until the afternoon then we were examined. I had a four and a half inch chest expansion. Not so bad, eh. My hearing and sight were both normal. In other words, I was O.K. generally.

    Friday we spent in getting our equipment in shape and Sunday I went to P.G. [Pacific Grove] and Monterey. Met some girls and they are good kids too.

    Monday we started to drill and we drilled almost ten hours getting ready for General John James Pershing. The next day I had K.P. for fifteen hours shining pots and pans getting ready for Black-Jack. Believe me I was a tired woman. The next day we turned out at four-thirty to get all shined up for the review. We ate at 5 a.m. then we went down to the polo field where the review was held, and where we drill, and we drilled until about 9:30 then the cannons at the gate started to fire salutes for five minutes for Black-Jack. The next step was to be reviewed. He took his post and we went through the manual-of-arms for his benefit. Then the thirtieth infantry marched off first but made a kinda punk showing. Our battalion was in the center of the C.M.T.C. Companies. We made a swell showing as we marched past the General at platoon front. After a good hike we were finally massed around the old Black-Jack and he gave us a swell talk. I was just a little bit away from him and he seems like a good scout. Then we marched back to our company street and pretty soon he came up and told us what a good line we had held then he beat it and the cannon started firing again.

My mother wrote to me about once a week.

1923, August 7th

    Two dandy letters from you. They are newsy and very well-written in spite of fatigue.

    I can imagine you were tired – it seems that the Army works you to a fare-the-well! Awfully glad you saw Pershing – he's a Jim-Dandy! You must have been quite thrilled. Nice of him to take the trouble to compliment you chaps. Just maybe you weren't chesty, eh? He reminds me (from his Pattie Weeklie pictures) of Dad when I first knew him. Dad was mighty good-looking I tell you.

    Your Colonel must be nice. Good for you hon! Four and a half inches isn't so puny, no need to worry just yet . . .

Which reminds me of the President [Harding]. Too bad he died. I guess he was a nice man, clean and kind. A Buckeye like yourself!

Being in the army I suppose you will have all sorts of special "turn-outs" (don't know what to call them – probably not exercises) on account of his passing. Hope to get down but as I wrote – may not.

Donnabeth is awake and I am jiggling her so excuse scrawl if you can't read it at all . . .

Are you enjoying the training and would you like to be in for life? . . .

Stan at C.M.T.C., 1922.

Wouldn't mind another jaunt down there myself, would you?

You must have lots of fun. I'll doll up like a chicken, put Donnabeth on the floor, leave Don at the gate and drive to see you and get a rise out of the youngsters and then have them say, "shucks the old hen" – time flies and with it youth and beauty but we have compensations such as you and knowing how darned little we really know! Really, joking aside, when the girls arrive there is apt to be a stampede.

Donnabeth really is getting darling; laughs and crows and at times howls – but is always interesting. You will probably be her slave this winter, but I'm glad you're coming – did not want to insist on poor Daddy's account (you were like a straw to a drowning man to him) you understand; and I think that you have had a good and restraining influence on him. Had you come down when we all did, I think he would have gone plumb to the devil!

I am sure Donnabeth joins me in love, hugs and kisses! . . . Take care of yourself and have all kinds of fun.

> *Aff'y*
> *Mom.*

Stan and Donnabeth, 1926.

August 6

Today we went out on the range. Frank and I both shot a forty-five out of a possible fifty at two hundred yards. That's pretty good shooting.

About the Girls coming down on the eighteenth, I don't think I will have much time off because we have a parade on that date and besides we have to give demonstrations of this and that most all day.

Last nite I was M.P. until 10:30 and believe me it was some job because I had to enforce a bunch of new regulations and all the other M.P.'s quit at 9:00 p.m. Then too, I had to stop all busses and machines to see if the fellows had on regulation suits. If not, I sent them back and made them change before they could go out of the post.

Saturday I was in charge of five fellows to take them around town and keep them out of trouble. That was a great job too.

Yesterday afternoon we went out in a motor boat, about fifteen of us, with a Wop and tried to fish, but all of us got sick and fed the fish, but four. I was one that didn't.

Tomorrow I go out for machine-gun fire. I will probably have to do some hard work shooting those darn guns.

For a while this afternoon we had instruction in mortars and one-pounders. We may have to shoot them. I don't know.

August 10

Last nite I was in charge of quarters, and it was some job. I had to keep all the fellows quiet after nine o'clock and that is just about the time they get in from the show and swimming parties. I also had to see that all the lights were out at ten-thirty, then I had to take bed check and report the missing. Tomorrow after-

noon we are going to have a special class in machine-gun fire. The class consists of twenty-five fellows and we have fifty thousand rounds of ammunition to shoot. This represents about $3,500 worth of shells that we are to shoot tomorrow afternoon. It won't last long because we can shoot about five hundred rounds in a minute without hurrying and we will have four guns in action.

Yesterday we had to hike about two miles to witness a demonstration the thirtieth infantry was carrying on. The most interesting part of the whole thing was the 75 mm guns in action. They shot about $2000 worth of shells in about 30 minutes. The next most interesting was a gas attack which they pulled on us. We did not know it was coming and it enveloped us in a thick, white, harmless, fog. It was so thick that we could not see the men next to us, we couldn't even see the ground, but we flopped down and in that way we managed to get a little air. It was very hard to breathe through, and it scared some of the fellows. The officers got quite a kick out of it. When we got back we were a dirty bunch, believe me.

1923, August 14
dearest –

Your two dandy letters of 6th & 10th to answer; we enjoyed them very very much!

Well rather, that is "pretty good shooting" – you and Frank will be sharp-shooters yet! . . .

This M.P. business is great stuff and I bet you had your hands more than full. It must have been fun just the same and when you took the boys into town & stopped machines etc. I just know that chest expansion measured some 5½ to 6½ inches.

I think the K.P. work fine training for you. When you move into your mansion you can come over at dinner time & prepare spuds – I wouldn't want you to miss Camp or to forget your training – or can't you look a potato in the eye? . . .

Putting your family to sleep in quarters must be equal to quieting Donnabeth – worse, because you can't give them "drops" like D. gets!

Judging by all you have to do, you will have to take the Rest-Cure when you get mustered out.

Do you think you'd like it for a life-work?

What an appalling amount of money is spent on teaching people to kill. If it could only be spent in helping them to live well, how wonderful it would be. But me, poor mortals aren't

97

ready for that yet and until we are "Don't tread on me" should be our motto backed up by airplanes of all kinds! "Them's my sentiments."

The gas attack must have been weird and scary.

Your letters are well-written and worded and interesting . . .

All send best. Be glad to see you but know you are enjoying life. I am getting better & better.

Love, Mom.

Stan (center) at Crissy Field, San Francisco, 1923.

That fall I went up to Burlingame to live with my mother. I had a little house of my own in the rear of my mother's home. I entered Burlingame High, though they hounded me for months for my former school records. I stayed there for a year then I quit and went to sea. I just decided to go to sea.

In April 1924, I went over to Avon, near Vallejo, and signed up to go to sea. I told my teacher that I got a job with the black gang[37] on board an old Associated Oil Tanker. She cried. She had been encouraging me to write.

Chapter 17: To Sea in a Sieve

I WENT TO THE ASSOCIATED OIL PLACE, where I met the big shot and told him what I wanted to do, and he said he'd send me up to Avon. So I went up to Avon and signed on the SS *Newport* as a wiper. It had a

---

37 The black gang is the part of a ship's crew that works in the engine room. They were called 'black' because of the soot and coal dust that was thick in the air in the fire room/engine room.

crew of about 25 men. I had a pretty lousy job as a wiper. It was the lowest job in the business and the business had all gone to hell. The unions were just about broken; there was no union. You worked out of a company-run hall. It was a lousy job and the food on board the ships was very, very rough. We had eggs every day but boy, those eggs were pretty strong, pretty old. But we ate them. I stayed on there for about six weeks or so sailing up and down the coast.

On July 16, 1924, I signed on another ship, the SS *William F. Herrin*. I was still a wiper, spending most of my shift in the engine room. We sailed all the way up to the Columbia River, to Portland.

1924, July 20, Sunday
Dear Mom,

How is everything? I hope your back is better.

I haven't been sea-sick yet, but this morning I had to do a two hour watch 6-8 before breakfast and I got sick from an empty stomach, but I stood my watch.

My job is cleaning up the gratings around the engine; you know the top layer of grates! My Station is the Dynamo Room. I have three dynamos and an ice machine to keep clean. I have to keep the floor clean and dry all the time. It is a steel floor that is always greasy and oily. When I finish with my station I go down below and clean the engine. When there is nothing to clean I find something to do, like going over all the hand railings with emery cloth or something like that.

I am using the top of the stationary box for a desk because there is a big card game going on on the table next to my bunk. In our room there is a fellow with some East Indian blood, one with some negro blood and one with some Greek in him, there is also a Dutchman fireman that came on yesterday, and the kid and myself. Most every nationality is on board.

Last night we were in Avon; we are going back tonight. It was warm and I got up at about 10 p.m. to get a little something to eat and I found five bed bugs on me. The Greek said that he estimated there were about 5 thousand in the bunks. I believe him.

They feed us pretty well, 3 squares a day and a night lunch. We have steaks and chops, bread and butter, fruit and salad, and dessert. Sunday we have chicken or maybe it's seagull.

The boat is larger than the Newport was and about 40 men in the crew. She does 9-10 miles an hour, taking about 8-9 hours to load or about 18 hours to unload and load.

My job is pretty darn hot. I perspire very freely, so much so, in fact, that my upper is wet the next morning after drying all night. While I am working there is a steady stream running off my nose. But all told, it's not so worse.

> *Love to the family.*
> *Hope this finds you well.*
> *Love, Stan*

1924, August 10
Dear Mom,

I got yours of the 6th and was glad to get it.

Now to answer some of your questions. The hotel was O.K. and I got back to the boat all right. The Phonograph goes most of the time; it sure sounds good, too. One of the fellows bought some new records, three of them.

I'll bet Donnabeth is cute but was sorry to hear she missed the Phonograph.

As for being able to paddle my own canoe, I am getting along with colors flying.

Now that I am Chief Wiper with two men under me, I like the Job more than ever. To be on less than three weeks and go up a peg isn't half bad.

So far I have been taking up firing, oiling and watertending. Three good jobs in the engine department. I can do some of the fireman's duties and have been learning how to tend water. I also am learning how to handle the pumps to load and discharge cargo. The Watertender is teaching me about pipe fittings, pump packing, gasket making, etc.

Most every nite from around 6 to 8, I study oiling. The Oiler teaches me how to change the dynamos and keep them from getting hot, to make out the log book and to oil and take care of the engine.

It seems to me that I am doing more jobs, that have responsibility attached to them, in one day than I have done in the whole of my career. I am getting along so well that I feel like staying with the ship until the end of the year, at the end of which time I will have gained enough knowledge so that I can handle my part of the engine room.

The First Asst. and I have talked quite a lot and he says even if I don't stick with the ship, most of the things I learn I can use any place on shore. I am sure gaining a lot of information aboard, and I think it is worthwhile.

The 1st asst. has taken an interest in me and in putting me wise to a great many things. He offered to help any time. I think I can get more out of a half year here than I can get out of school. That is with everybody pulling for me.

Think it over and let me know what you think about it. I'll do what you think is the best. Well, so much for that.

I put in 1½ hours overtime last nite and then helped the oiler. We went ashore this morning and did the town – very exciting. We got some ice cream and came back to the ship for lunch.

When we were tying up at Avon, the Oiler, who takes care of the exhaust valves and the log book, had to oil the engine, so I took the exhaust valves and controlled them without making a mistake. I had to keep the log too and it kept me pretty well on the jump because each move we made I had to work the valves, take the time, and tell what move it was. Some times we made three or four moves a minute.

Well, we will be leaving for Avon in a few minutes so will have to step on it if I want to get this off. Hope you can read it.

Wish everyone the best of luck and hope you get rested. Take care of yourself and don't do any work.

Lots of Love, Dear,
Stan.

1924, Saturday, August 24
Stan dearie —
. . . Any old time you want to come home, why come along. I fully expect you for the Feb. semester. If you don't go through High I am sure you will regret it later. I shall be very very sorry – it means as much socially anyhow – unless one knows certain things one is socially, that is to say, "conversationally" lost! . . .

Love, dear honey, always
Mom.

Dad also encouraged me to go back to school.

1924, August 21
Dear Stan,
Had your dandy letter a few days ago, and will answer at more length before long. Am writing this to answer your question as to what it would be best for you to do. As you seem to be much interested in your work and feel that you are learning something of value, I can not logically make any objections to your going on with it until the first of the year. But if you do,

101

boy, make up your mind to dig in and work like Hell when you go back to High. No late hour weekdays, try to get as much out of your books as you are now trying to get out of your engine room training. You have at intervals proved to us that you can do fine work "when you want to," and believe old dad, if you do not go further with your elementary education you will regret it all of your later life. The time is here (you have passed your eighteenth birthday) when you must begin to work out some of your own problems.

> Love and aloha
> Dad

Then I got a job as an oiler on the same ship. But before I got that job, I stood a watch as fireman on board, because I was pretty well interested in everything that went on down below. Our ship just went up and down the coast: Monterey to San Pedro and up to Oregon. I was hoping always to get on one that went over to Australia, but I never got there. I stayed on there about three months.

1924, Aug. 31
Extra !! Extra !!
Dear Mom,
    Today is Sunday and we are about half way between Pedro and S. F. It's a rotten day too.
    . . . Well, having had two wipers quit under me I must be some slave driver, but no more! I quit my job wiping today (Now don't get excited) to sign on as oiler. Hot, bow - wow !!
    Who said I couldn't get along on my own? I can, because now I am one of the Petty Officers. Get clean sheets every week, eat better, nice room with just two in it (me and my partner, a navy boy.) And everything else.
    My watch will be from 4-8 morn. and night.
    The 1st asked me if I could handle it and I said I could, so today being pay day, I went up to the Captain and got my pay and signed off. Then stepped around the table and the first said, "Sign on as oiler," so I did. I felt weak but got by.
    Not bad, eh? Here 3 weeks and Chief Wiper 3 weeks more and Oiler. A raise of $15.00. I'll be Chief engineer soon, maybe.
    Here is some of my $70 that I got this month. You can put it in the bank, spend it, or do any thing else you like with it.
    I start my new job 4-8 tomorrow nite. Stay around doing nothing on Sunday, except wash my clothes, write some letters

and play checkers. Very hard to do, like fun it is . . .

Yesterday at Port Costa taking on fuel-oil, one of the valves got stuck and when the settlers were full they could not turn the darn thing off, and the oil overflowed through an overflow pipe onto the nice white poop-deck. The wind caught it and sprayed it all over the white paint and everything else, and before they got the valve closed there was about three inches of oil all over the white deck. This had to be cleaned off. The wipers (myself and two others) had to help the sailors clean up. We worked all afternoon at it and then quit. The sailors worked until late last nite and started again for a few hours this morning. Such is life. This caused a great deal of excitement and a lot of extra work.

Hope you are O.K. in every way. Lots of Love Dear, to all.

Your Loving Son
Stan

1924, September 6
Hip, hip, hooray! Tiger!!!

Stan honey – bully for you – such good news, I am "dee-lighted"; so is everyone. Of course I had to casually spice the news! Mrs. B. says "that is great – best thing in the world for you. You'd get along anywhere because nobody could help liking you etc. etc." (was quite eulogistic).

When I phoned for meat I told Mr. Geary and he sounded much pleased, said "That beats High School any time!" . . .

You certainly had moral courage my love (to sign off and on again, Flinnigan Flannagan) it took the best kind of courage too dear!

Doesn't it give you a fine feeling to know that you can & have made good? So many people just flounder around – are drift-wood on a sea of ineffectuality.

The clean sheets & state-room appeal to me most strongly! And it is nice that you are in with a lad! Also the raise is fine!

Thank you dear heart for the offer of your money – I couldn't take it honey, but I want to keep it for you.

. . . Donnabeth is charming – getting naughty, spunky 'n everything! Hope you will pay us a flying visit one of these days or nights!

Much love dear – always – & my best thoughts go with you.
Mom.

As an oiler, my job was to oil the ship's machinery – to oil and clean the moving parts of the engine. You had to swipe your hand across the machinery as it went around and if you didn't time it just right, you'd lose your hand!

1924, September 8
Dear Mom,
    . . . This morning we had the cold water to the condenser running through the fire pump. The fire pump stopped, "busted." No water in the condenser. Steam running under pressure in the tubes turned the water to steam around them. Another pump is started and things get hotter. The place is filled with steam. Lots of excitement. I am sent up to crack the back-pressure valve over the condenser. We expected it to blow up but nothing gave way. Why didn't it get cool? – pump's going. Some fellow notices down below that the sea valve is closed so he spins it open. The pump pumps cold sea water into the hot steam in the condenser and all this time I am adjusting this valve. When water and steam hit the gratings under me shook – so did everything else. I got away from it but it didn't blow up. It didn't miss by much. It was just luck that it didn't.
    Well I am here and now know how to handle a similar circumstance.
    The engineer was on the dock but there were three water-tenders, two oilers, two wipers and a fireman below. When the pressure went up in the condenser they all had jobs elsewhere and booked up a cooler and quieter climate, with the exception of the "kid," the watertender who caused it all by not doing the right thing at the right time, and myself!
    I was as cool as a cucumber and never thought about myself until the cold water hit the steam and then all I did was to get back from the condenser to start a pump that would take off the water now going into the hot-well. It wasn't as romantic as it sounds. I was just doing what I was supposed to do. I'll tell you about it some time when I am home. That's all of that for the present.
    My first watch as oiler I took her out of Pedro O.K . . . We picked up an oiler in Pedro the same time I went oiling and he got fired today so the kid and I are doing 6 hours on and 6 off until the new one arrives. The fellow that got bounced claims to have sailed for 18 years and I am a better oiler than he is. The 1st said so. By the way, I am Chief Oiler. I give the others their

oil and rags, etc. We have less than two gallons to go 4 hours on.
Well I won't get any sleep today. I'll have to make the 4
hours that I got last night do for today . . .
Hope I will see you all soon, dear. I miss you.
Lots & lots of love, dearest – Stan.

1924, September 10
We salute thee O Chief O!
My dear Dear you have a truly, heartfeltly thankful Mother
– I shan't be sorry when you get on shore again in spite of the
fact that your work is good for you in many ways. Don will ex-
plain your letter to me – and, you can fill in details later!
I can understand this much though, you just missed being
scalded to death. It is only because your mind & heart are so
filled with kindliness towards all that nothing was able to harm
you; like Don, you attract the good. I am proud to think that, in
spite of the awfulness of the situation, you thought only of what
it was up to you to do – that shows "entrails" (prettier word
than "guts," also more elegant & refined & I wouldn't be uncouth
for worlds) the kind that took the Boys "Over the Top" old dear.
Even the fool "kid" must be O.K. bring him home some time – if
you care to . . .
Love always
Mom.
I'm f.l.g. (fine, lovely, grand), back 'n everything.

We were coming down the upper bay towards San Francisco. We'd been up to Martinez where we unloaded. The first engineer had the watch and we were steaming full ahead when the telegraph bell sounded for emergency "Full speed astern." A quick look and no engineer. He had gone topside for another drink. Well, it could only mean that we were running into something. I looked around and there was nobody there but me. So I just stepped over and I pulled the engine astern. It was a big damn engine, and a hell of a big lever. There were a couple of levers you had to push. I just put my foot against the side of the thing and I pulled the lever, and I happened to hit it about right, because I had been used to doing the oiling and all. I had gotten used to the rhythm of the ship. I just got it on the right rhythm and pulled it over and it just went "psew," like that. It was running full astern, then pretty soon the chief engineer came rushing down the ladder, but by that time it was all astern. Then pretty soon we got the word "stop" and then "go" so we had missed what we were heading for. That was my first experience with the throttle of a ship. What a hellofa mess if the timing had not been right!

No, they didn't thank me for that. They don't thank anybody on a ship. Lucky I didn't get fired! Pretty rough ship. They killed 89 men on the ship before I came on. There was a lot of gas on the ship and they used to get gassed, and one time they had a bad fire on board. So it was a bad ship, but I finally got off.

My first shipwreck was when I was working as an oiler on the SS *Herrin*, Associated Oil Tanker. It was on the Columbia River going up to Portland and we went over the sandbar at the mouth of the Columbia River, and a big wave hit the ship and it went down, it landed on the sand. It didn't break a hole in it but it bent the bottom badly. So we left Portland and came on down to San Francisco and went into dry dock in San Francisco and they fixed the bottom of it. That was my first experience with a shipwreck.

When we went into dry dock, on October 20th, I lost my job there. They put somebody else on, and I came home and Mom was glad to see me. She was living in Burlingame on Primrose Avenue and she convinced me to try school again. I struggled for a year, and finished out the term, but it didn't take, whatever I was doing, it didn't take. So I quit at the end of the term and went back to San Jose and went to work for my father. It was 1925, and I turned 19 that summer. He wanted me to come and live and work with him, so I did.

That pretty much covers my formal schooling. I next entered the "school of hard knocks" where the learning process really began.

Come with me into the hills.
Climb their sloping sides.
Lay down upon the grass.
Gaze out over the valley that we have just left.
Look at the little manmade houses,
how small they are.
The people are hardly visible.
Look out across the valley and see the hills
on the other side rising majestically in the background.
Fill your lungs with the cool air
and you find yourself enjoying the fruit of living.

Stan

PART TWO:

The School of Hard Knocks

Chapter 1: Restless

"YOU KEEP WHISTLING ALL THE TIME you're down there. If you're whistling, I know you're not drinking, so you just keep whistling."

That was Joe talking, Joe Savio. Joe had been our vegetable man when we lived on Villa Avenue and had since retired. But he hadn't stopped making his own wine. That evening we were sitting around the table sharing a bottle of his best Dago Red, and playing Pinochle with him. He wouldn't charge us anything for the wine, but we had to play Pinochle in order to drink with him. As long as we sat there playing Pinochle, he'd keep bringing the wine out of the cellar, and once in a while he'd send one of us boys down to fill the bottle again. But he made sure we didn't take a nip while we were down there by telling us to whistle until we got back. So we'd go over and have a few drinks of wine with Joe and play cards for a couple of hours, and we got a lot of fun out of it. That was during Prohibition and it was part of my early introduction into wine drinking.

It was in those years that I met some fellows who became lifelong friends of mine. In January 1926, I joined a fraternity, ΒΦΣ, Beta Phi Sigma. It was not a college fraternity, it was a secondary fraternity, a high school fraternity. That's where I met Curly. His real name was Lawrence Hausam. Curly had an older brother and he and I were fraternity brothers. Curly joined the fraternity a little later, then his brother got married and that's the last I saw of his brother. But I saw Curly up until he died. In fact, he came to visit me when we were up at Lake Pillsbury in 1968.

I had met Freddy Franck in high school as a freshman at Santa Clara. He was just about my age and we became good friends. He was Jewish, with a dark complexion and dark brown, short-cut hair. He was a bit of a comedian, but always told his jokes with a straight face. He liked to have fun, and we had a lot of good times together. He lived with his parents in a big old house in San Jose. We went to dances and shows and sometimes didn't get much sleep. But we had a lot of fun. So it was Fred and Curly and I, and we fooled around together for several years.

I met John Bruce when he was going to college at San Jose State Teachers College. He and Jim Chesnutt were both going to San Jose State. Freddy went to State for a while then he wound up at Stanford. I guess I knew all of those guys up until they died, many long years later.

After I left Burlingame High School, in June 1925, I worked with my dad at Hulse Radio Service for about four years. The business was located at 293 South First Street, San Jose. He had moved it there in September 1924. I worked very hard in those years and got along pretty well with Dad and Maude. We had only one point of disagreement and that was his drinking. I loved my dad but his drinking annoyed and hurt me, and his conduct would fill me with resentment. We never knew when he'd be in his cups. He wasn't so much of an alcoholic – he just didn't give a damn. Maude and I ran the business whenever he'd have a lapse. It was well-organized and all we had to do was to maintain the service. He carried the load most of the time but occasionally Maude and I would find ourselves alone – Dad had taken a few days or weeks off.

I tried to get Dad to go fishing at Big Basin with me one weekend in July 1926, but he was too tired so we didn't go. He seemed a very old man at that time, though he was only fifty. I thought that if he got out more he wouldn't be so tired, but he didn't see that end of it.

In September of that year, I took at trip with Freddy up to the Sierras. We fooled around Fallen Leaf Lake and Lake Almanor, did some fishing and had a great time.

Stan at Echo Lake (left) and Freddie Franck
(above) on camping trip.

Fallen Leaf Lake

Dearest Mom,

    Ever since we left you we have been moving, at least most of the time. The first nite out we stopped in Stockton and took my girl friend & one other to a dance at Lockford about 15 miles from Stockton. I had a very good time & I like the girl a lot.

    We left Stockton about 12:30 Sunday and got to Chico at 4:30, ate and started to Chester where we slept in the car all nite. The next morning we went to Lake Almanor about 10 miles away and made camp. We stayed there that nite and then came down to Feather River where we camped over nite and then started for Fallen Leaf Lake. We ate at Truckee after going thru the most beautiful forest I have ever seen. It sure took the cake.

    It's been cold as the deuce up this way and last evening it was 30°F, so drained the radiator of the car to keep it from freezing. To-nite it's almost 40°F so its quite warm, almost.

    The fishing is the bunk. I have seen, but that's all, some wonderful fish. Some of them have been 18 to 20 inches long. I caught one about 12 inches long so have at least had a taste of them.

    Well tomorrow I think we will be on our way out of here – it's too darn cold. We have hiked quite a lot and are feeling fine. I've done the cooking and it's been a great success so far.

    Well the hour is late & the light is poor so will say good-nite.

    Lots & lots of love & the best of luck.

    Your son, Stan

We came back to San Jose, and I worked with my dad for about two years straight without a vacation. On my 21st birthday he gave me this birthday card:

Birthday Greetings to my Son
A happy birthday to you my Son,
Not only this day but every one;
May all your cherished dreams come true,
And life bring real success to you.

[signed] G.C.H.

And a card from my mother came with this poem:

This is a wonderful day for you,
And a day to make wonderful wishes too:
So I wish you everything under the sun
The heart could wish for at twenty-one!

"Mom"

On July 10, 1927, when I turned 21, I came into some money – I came into a thousand dollars. I took the money and bought a new Nash Roadster. I was living pretty high then because I had a car and could drive around.

Sometimes I'd drive up to San Francisco with a friend of mine named Ford, and we'd visit this family who had a daughter who was an awfully nice girl. The mother and father would put on parties for us, and there was always plenty to drink. I guess we went to two or three of them, maybe more, and we had some pretty good times.

The Nash Roadster was a pretty fast car. It would go 60-70 mph. During the winter I spent my time and money and one day I lost the car. They came and repossessed it. I had spent a thousand dollars on it, but that didn't buy it. The money had come from my grandmother, Harriet Whitney, and I blew it. It just came and went. Easy come, easy go.

I worked hard and played hard at that time. I fell in love with June Kernan, a little red head. I couldn't do enough for this little goddess. I put her on a pedestal and never noticed her feet. But it was a stormy, fighting, frustrating affair. Neither of us was good for the other. She

112

did influence me for the good because she wouldn't drink, so I couldn't drink when I was with her. When we would fall out, I'd go my way. I saw her off and on for several years, but our lives took different directions.

I knew all the better bootleggers in those days. I had some wild times over at Capitola, and in San Francisco at Aladdin's. One place had a key, FRANKLIN 1212, for gin. I drank a lot on weekends but managed to avoid trouble. Since all the best people drank, I had plenty of company.

I remember one wild party at Almaden schoolhouse, rented for the occasion by a sorority at San Jose State. I took Ursula Howard, and it turned into a brawl. It got rough and out of hand. They had

June Kernan, 1928.

jack-o-lanterns, big pumpkins for decorations. Most everyone spent the better part of the evening outside in the parked cars drinking, etc. It was fun when one of the guests returned to the dance floor to take a big pumpkin and push it down over a victim's head. Before long all the decorations found similar use and pumpkins and everything else were soon flying about. I left by a window, neglecting to open the same before going through – Oh, it was a great party!!

Then there was the old "Who, Who" House with the cop so drunk he was going to shoot a bottle off a spare tire. The spare tire was carried on a rack at the rear over the bumper. He was standing to the rear of the car, and had he fired, he would have surely broken up a very busy couple, oblivious to the real threat to their lives –

In the summer of 1928, I finally took a vacation and went up north, went up through Willits, crossed over through Eureka to Redding and came back to San Jose. It's been over 50 years since we made that trip and my, the country's changed. When we were going up Highway 101, we got stuck out in the country and we didn't have a place to stay. So we stopped on the road and stayed overnight. I don't

Jane and Stan about 1928.

suppose you can do that now, traffic and all. But in those days, you could stay all night and not see anybody.

During those years I was working real hard for my dad. But I started to feel restless because I could see what was happening. I was a little guy and I was growing up, and getting into the business and I was going to be stuck right there. I wouldn't be able to go any place.

So I told my dad, "I want to take some time off. I want to go and see what's happening before I marry and settle down. I want to go out and see something of the world before I become just another guy that gets married in town and settles down here. San Jose is not enough."

He knew I had been to sea and he said he understood. So he said, "All right you can go."

When I went he tore up all the agreements that we had. I had thought at the time that I owned half the business. The business had been bought by my mother. It was all her money that had gone into the business to make it. She had inherited money all her life and had houses and everything, and he hadn't inherited a dime. When I got back, he just gave me $50 and said good-bye. So that ended my career in the business.

I went up to Atherton, where my mother was living at that time, and I was quite ill. I came down with the flu and for about six weeks I was in pretty bad shape. I had gotten extra tired working and that was one of the reasons I wanted to get out and see something. I told her about how Dad had let me go and she got quite upset about it.

"He can't do that!" she said.

And I said, "Well, he did it."

So my mother went down and talked to my father and told him, "Look, Stan has a portion of the business here and you've taken it all away from him."

"Yea, because he's gone and he's not interested."

"Well, he's living with me and he is interested in it."

Dad decided he wasn't going to pay me and I was through and that was that.

So she went to an attorney, a nice guy in San Jose, and she told him about it and he said to sue him. So my mother had me bring suit in my name and sue him for an accounting – that was all it was. It wasn't a suit against him, as it were, it was just an accounting. My mother testified, and he managed to stall the thing for a year or more. When the suit finally went to court, son of a gun, if his damned attorney didn't start to make the thing a personal affair. And that was bad. So I won the suit, and the judge found that he owed me about $3500 bucks. In those days that was pretty good money. I think $10,000 was a retirement figure.

He had actually lied about my position working for him. I remember he said I had never owned any part of the business and I was just working, that was all. Well, I had a record of my payments in the business and that held me in good stead. So when I got through and won the case, I said the hell with it, and I didn't try to collect anything from him. I never collected a dime from him. To hell with it. I just let it go.

I didn't see him until 1939, over ten years later. A long time. I saw him again just after we were married, and once when Tim and Jenny were little, before Geri was born, and then he died. That was that. He always felt that I had hurt him. That was the way he felt about it, nothing I could do. The girls, Mabel and Jane, knew what the thing was and they never blamed me. They just figured the old man had done me dirt.

When my grandmother Dan died in 1930, she left me a little bit of these and those, I don't remember what they were, but I never got what she left me. However, that coffee urn came down to me later. After my father died, Maude inherited it and her new husband had no use for it, so she gave it to me. It's a silver coffee urn with *Mellie Curtis from Father and Mother* inscribed on it and the inside is porcelain. It's quite a good-looking thing. On the bottom it says *June 13, 1868.*

Chapter 2: Pescadero & La Honda: 1930

DURING THAT TIME, I STAYED with my mother part of the time in Atherton, until I met this fellow, Emery Bloomquist. He lived up in the Santa Cruz mountains over by La Honda with his mother. Emery and I started looking for something to do, and he and I decided to buy a little ranch. We went over to see his uncle who owned the ranch. He was an old fellow in his late eighties, and he was pretty well crippled up. He sold us the ranch, but it wasn't worth anything. It was ten acres just staked out with a little cabin on it.

So we bought the ten acres early in 1930. We lived up there in the house and we decided to open a chicken ranch. First of all, we bought about 500 baby chicks. We put them in the car and drove over to my mother's place in Atherton and went in and had something to eat before we went over the hill. When we came out, by golly, we found that I hadn't allowed enough air in, and the chickens were dying from lack of air; they'd used up the air. So my mother helped me open up the cartons. We worked on them for about an hour and got them breathing pretty well. We lost about 50 of them I guess. So it wasn't real bad but it shook me up.

We took them on over to the ranch near Pescadero. We let the chickens out to run in this very nice chicken yard that we had built for them. As time went by, we had some trouble with the roosters and the chicks because the little roosters would get after the little chicks. So finally, when we were able to tell which were which, we got most of the little roosters and killed them for fryers.

One time we raised some ducks from duck eggs. I had a chicken sitting on them and the hen got tired of sitting on them and up and left, just before they hatched. You see, they take quite a bit longer to hatch than chicken eggs. So I had four or five eggs, and I couldn't do anything with them. So I put three of them in the oven, because we had a wood stove and it threw out a certain amount of heat. I kept them there for about three days and one of the eggs hatched and out of it crawled this small duck. I kept it alive in a box and I was the only person it had ever seen, and the doggone duck thought I was Mama. Every place I went that duck would go. I'd get up in the morning and the duck would be there cheeping away. I'd feed it, and when I washed dishes it would swim around in the dish water and the duck was just totally my bird. Then one day, I went to work and the duck was used to walking between my feet and it got between the calf's feet and the calf stepped on it, and that was the end of the duck.

I got a job working on the La Honda Road. It was a little trail through the mountains and if there was any rain you couldn't possibly get over it. So the County decided to build a road into the mill and into the park.[38] We worked on one half of it all one summer and on the other half of it the next year. I worked for a guy up there who, when you stopped to light a cigarette, you could only light it and then you picked up your shovel and started shoveling. You didn't waste any time smoking. That was the only break you got. We worked for about four and a half a day. That was pretty good money for those days, that was pretty good pay. I used a shovel and an ax and different hand tools. It was pretty hard work clearing away the stumps, boulders, brush and trees. Once we had the roadway cleared they used a horse-drawn grader to smooth out the road.

1930, May 7, Pescadero
My Dearest Mom—

I just had to write and tell you how much I've been thinking about you and how I love you. I can't help but think of that song "Mother o' Mine" and the way you have stood by me. Sweetheart, I love you so, so much.

Well I'm sorry that I didn't get over the week before Lent to help you move but E. & I had a little work to finish up before going to work. Oh yes! We are working. E. & I have landed jobs.

The chickens take care of themselves during the day while E. & I work on the new road from La Honda. We get up at 6 a.m. and feed the chicks and make breakfast & put up our lunches and leave for work at 7:15 then we go over the grade and work. E. has been building fence from the top of the grade this way, while I have been laboring down on the other side of the grade.

The first couple of days I was sure all in after the first few hours but I am hardening up so that I feel pretty good at quitting time – at least half alive.

The job is pretty hard. We (that is the gang of five I work with) have been clearing the right of way for the shovel. We fell trees, cut brush, blast stumps, and split wood. The other day we

---

38 San Mateo County's Memorial Park is located in Loma Mar and is operated by the San Mateo County Department of Parks.

117

split wood all day and believe me it was some job. I got plenty of
blisters.

Today I loaded blasts that we drilled yesterday and had
them all set to shoot at about 11:30 this A.M. One had 150 sticks
under it and another had over 200.[39] These we set off with a
battery and they sure lifted things but they were beautiful shots
at that. We shot a lot of small ones with fuse and had good luck.
Tomorrow will finish up most of the blasting tho.

Well dear, I'll tell you all about it as soon as I see you, but
the money question is temporarily taken care of with this job. I
like it too.

   Lots of love dearest, Your loving son.
        Stan.

We built a bridge up there. We had a concrete mixer and we poured cement into the darn thing and gravel and sand and mixed our own concrete and built the bridge across the creek. That was quite an event.

One time I almost got hit by a tree. They were snaking out some trees and they hooked a chain on one end, on the butt end to pull them out. And that time the butt went into the ground and the tree swung around and caught me. Instead of throwing me down the bank, it threw me up the bank, so I went up about ten feet in the air and I landed right on the bank. It just boosted me up in the air.

One day we were working on the road and we were cutting big logs and one of the fellows was leaning over holding the wedge and watching somebody pound down on it. Well, a chip of the steel came off the wedge and flew into his eye. It stuck in it and I could see the purple right down the side of his eye. There was nothing to do for it. I took him to the ranch that was near the job, and from there somebody took him over to San Mateo Hospital where they took out his eye.

Things were going pretty well, then Emery got a job with a floor company on the bay side. So he went back over the mountains and left me with the ranch. I went to work for a company building a subdivision, for a month or more. They were doing a lot of logging up there and I helped them with the logging. I drove a team around for most of the day hauling the stumps and snaking logs that were cut up

---

39 Sticks of dynamite.

and getting them out of the roadways for the subdivision. The rest of the time I was on one end of a crosscut saw making some of the larger logs smaller. They paid me about $10 a day and that was big money for driving a team. That was a very interesting job.

There were a couple of brothers that had a place near me there. They were the Blomquist brothers, part of the large Blomquist clan. I worked for them in the mill for a while, and I was very good friends with them. We drank a lot of beer in those days, made a lot of home brew. I went down there one night consuming this beer and they filled a bottle with Epsom salt in the beer and I drank it. It didn't taste very good but it was something to drink. It sure worked on me!

In Pescadero, at that time, the main street had a grocery store, a post office and a few other stores – that was all. It was just a block long. There were a few people who had ranches around the area. About once a month they had a 'special' down at the high school in Pescadero and all the townspeople would come to a dance. When they had a party, everybody in town came. There were about a hundred people at those parties all told. Then at midnight they closed the dance off and had a big dinner. And they had some dinners down there – oh, gee. We used to sit around there, and it would be light by the time we got home in the morning. We had a great time at those dances.

One of the guys had a girl – I forget her name – and she was quite enamored of me and in fact when I left the place, I'll be darned if she didn't show up over in San Carlos at my mother's one day. She was just a mountain kid and it was one thing in the mountains but to be a mountain kid in town is something else. I finally got rid of her and that was that.

The end of that summer the work ran out. About that time there was a fire in the creek bed south of Loma Mar. Everybody went over to fight the fire. I got over there and they decided to put me to work watching the fire, after it was out. One night the fire started to break out, and I stayed on the fire and fought it until about midnight. The guy who was with me left and went down to Pescadero and got a dozen or twenty more men, and they came on up, but I had managed to get the thing under control by myself. It was a hell of a fight.

119

1930, September 10, Butano Creek   *Wednesday p.m.*
Dearest Mom,

I'm just dropping a line to let you know where I am and how come.

Monday morning when I got to Loma-Mar, the pump hadn't been installed so that tied things up at the dam, so I was laid off until they had a job for me. Just after I got the news, and before I could get started back, Albert Bloomquist came along and wanted fire fighters so I stepped into his car and left for the scene of action, which proved to be the hillside about a mile above the end of the road on the Butano Creek.

We got our tools and hiked up the trail to the fire and went to work making a clearing clear around the fire. There were about 35 of us and we had the trail around it before noon. After that we just watched and about four p.m. we quit for the day with the fire under control. Then Albert and I and the other Bloomquist brothers went to Pescadero where I saw Burt Werder, the warden, and asked him for a job watching the fire until it's out, and here I am, a fire guard. (What next?) If it doesn't rain, I may have to stay in these parts for a couple of weeks yet. But I may leave Saturday nite.

Well, to get back to my story – After I got the job, which is thirteen miles by road from the ranch, I decided to come over and stay on the creek so I got some grub and came over. Tuesday, about noon, a woman came up to the fire and asked questions, which I answered, and I told her that I was going to camp on the creek all week, so she said that I could use her cabin (I knew she would before she said it) because no one would be there all week and I might as well.

Here I am in a very nice cabin – fireplace, phonograph, electric stove, shower, and what have you – also a good bed. It would have been a darned cold camp up here so I am very lucky to be so nicely billeted. The woman's name is Rochex. Niz lady!

Tuesday morning I came on the scene of action and found who I was to work with. He is a very nice fellow who lives on a ranch about six miles from here. He has lived in these parts for years and is interesting to talk to – he's fifty-three years old.

He and I are the only ones on the job so we just walk around the fire-trail and see that all is O.K. then we go down to the creek and make coffee and eat lunch and talk and then go around the fire again and explore the country that is burnt over – about a square mile on the side of a very steep hill – then back to our camp and so to our lodgings. All of which makes it a very nice job.

The country up where the fire started is in a ten-thousand acre tract of timber that runs over toward Boulder Creek and Big Basin. The fire didn't do very much damage – it just burned the brush and down timber and leaf mold, etc. that has been piling up for years without damaging the redwoods to any extent.

At night, four fellows guard, but by day there are just the two of us and we both like it up there fine.

Well, it's getting late so will say good-nite, but wish you were here – you'd like the house fine, and too, it's too big for one man. Oh well, why kick about that.

Just lots of Love,
Stan.

1930, Sept. 14, Butano Creek   Sunday
Dearest Mom,

Well dear, I'm still at my latest occupation.

Today was Sunday and some of the cabin owners were in for the day but most have left. It's rather lonely up here with so many cabins empty and no one to talk to at night. I was up on the hill all day so didn't get a chance to talk to any of those that did come in at that.

Well it's nice and cozy in here this evening. I have a fire in the fireplace and it feels very comfortable and pleasant too. Wait till I poke it up a bit. There, that's better.

To get back . . . Things are getting very quiet on the hill and the trees are not falling like they were a few days ago. You see the territory covered by the fire was virgin forest and there were a number of pines in it that were ripe. These pines burn at the base and within three or four days become so weakened that they fall. Being very large trees, some seven or eight feet through at the base, when they go they do a lot of damage. For instance, the day before yesterday one particularly large one fell and carried ten others with it. I happened to be standing watching it when it started to fall and, as it was not falling toward me, I stood and watched it go. The havoc and terrible loud crashing noise in so quiet a place put me in mind of the "crack of doom." It really was something to watch and hear.

The Rochexes haven't been out this week so I haven't become any better acquainted with my kind hosts. But I do enjoy their cabin.

The fire warden was up yesterday and wants us to stay un-
til the fire is out, which I hope will be by the last of the week. It's
hard to tell because there are spots inside the line that have
dried up since the fire swept over and these catch fire and these
in turn dry out old logs and they burn, so this may keep up until
the rain starts or until a heavy fog puts it all out.

This makes the end of seven days that I've put in up here
and if only there were some people around it would be a picnic,
only Harry and he wears very well but he is far from being a
crowd.

I've played most of the records that are here, and there's a
very large stack too. But they should put in a radio, it's so much
work getting up and changing records and cranking the darned
thing all the time.

Did I tell you there was a shower in the bathroom? Oh, yes!
and hot water too. All the comforts of a first class hotel.

Well sweetheart, I must get my beauty sleep and besides this
letter seems to sound sleepy, so I'm going to turn in.
> *Always*
> *Your loving son*
> *Stan*

I stayed in a house up there for 21 nights during the fire. The fire broke out one of those nights. The wind came up and blew it and it just started to burn. I stayed and fought it and it never got away.

1930, September, Butano Creek

> *Tuesday nite*

Dearest Mom,

I have more time to myself in the evenings so I am using it
most profitably – writing to you.

Well, everything was going along nicely up on the hill until
yesterday. The first thing was a spark flew across the trail on
top of the ridge and set leaves on fire. We got a trail around it
O.K. and went down to the creek some two miles from the fire to
our camp and had lunch, then we went back up to the top and
stayed until 4:30 or so and started down for the last round of
the day. When we got to the far corner, the fire that had been
smoldering in a little draw, had jumped the trail and started up
the side of the canyon with a roar.

Well, Harry and I got to the top of it and checked it by
scratching a trail in front of it. By this time it was getting dusk

122

and we couldn't possibly trail the thing so Harry beat it, while there was still light enough to see his way out, for help. Well, I stayed until about 9:00 p.m. all by myself with no light, food, or water before anyone came. I held her too. I just stayed right at the top of the blaze and when it would flare up from the sparks across the little check line we had made, I'd make my way to it through the smoke and brush and put it out. I held it, but I sure sweat plenty. When the crew came on, all they had to do was trail it and it was all over.

But the funny part was this: when Harry got down to the road, he found the two fellows that guard at nite just starting up. He told them what had happened but being out of breath and excited when he told it, things sounded pretty bad. So they got in their car and went back to Pescadero to get help and Harry went on home.

I had told Harry that I could hold it and about five men could trail it when he left me, but when he sent the two to town, he didn't say anything about how many men were needed. These fellows roused the town and about thirty came out to fight the new fire that had broken out – Yes, it was a new fire that was going to burn the whole canyon by the time the news got spread around.

They called Burt Werder in Redwood [City] and wanted him to come right up. He had just gotten in off the San Gregorio fire after all day and nite and was all in, so came up the first thing this A.M. with ten men from Redwood City to fight this big fire.

Well, the crew that came on last nite had the trail made and were leaving in less than an hour. So Burt W. was surprised to find things so quiet, and as there was nothing to do, he had the crew he brought over back-fire all the bad places so that now the whole area inside of the trail is just about clean, so there won't be any more episodes like this one. For which I am duly thankful.

Gee! This was long-winded. Hope it makes sense.

Will say "adios," with much love to all. Good nite dearest.

Stan.

1930, October 1st, Wednesday
Dearest Mom,

Fred and I went to the dance Sat. nite and we had a very good time. There was a girl there who is the daughter of Harry, the fellow on the fire with me. She told me that Harry thought I was so very nice and how much he liked me and ended all by *saying that she felt the same way about me. Her mother was there and kept looking me over. After I took the girl to supper, she told me that her mother thought I was O.K. and suggested that she have me over some time. As we were sitting in the dance hall she tried to talk, and get me to talk seriously and to tell her things. You know, the kind of things a girl likes to hear. But not me. She's nice – yes, a very nice kid but she hasn't that certain something so I just kidded her a little and let it go at that.*

Monday A.M. I went to work down by the shovel directing traffic and then Frank sent me up to the dump. That's me, Dump-man.

I'm working about three miles from the shovel which is taking the bank off the road and thereby widening it. The bank being rocky, they are hauling this up to the road where I worked this spring to use it to rock the road with.

My job is to direct the dumping and spread the load over twelve feet while it is dumping. They only haul about fifty loads a day so it is a very easy job. I wish I had a nice easy-chair, then I'd have a soft job. Ho! Ho!

Something must be wrong with the shovel because no trucks have been up for an hour. (It broke down for an hour and a half.)

This week the weather has been punk – everything grey – beautiful but sad.

Oh yes, there is a bootlegger that wants to rent the place for $250.00 per mo. for a few months to make up a batch of alke [40] *but I don't think I'll rent to him because I might get into trouble and a few shekels isn't everything in this man's world. . . .*

At one time I had a place on the river up there and some guys came along and wanted to rent it. So I rented the place to them and they made bootleg in there. It was during the bootlegging days.

I remember one day I drove up to the place and went in, looked around and left. I got in the car and just started down the road, and I think three cars came along, and the guy I was with said to me, "Geez, I think those are Feds." And sure enough, we went up the road and turned around and came back and the cars were parked

---

40 "Alke" is short for alcohol.

124

there. And the Feds went in, and they knocked it over and took the guys. So I just missed that one. Just missed.

On the way home one night I picked up a nail so I had to change the tire to be ready to go to work the next day. I took the tube out of the spare and put it in the casing and then put that back on the car. It was almost dark before I was finished so I didn't get my supper cooked until quite late.

I was tired and dirty from working on the road all day, and was washing up at the pump outside the barn before I went in for the evening. Everything was quiet except for the sound of the water spilling into the basin while I cleaned the dirt and sweat from my face and hands. As I splashed the cold water on my face, I felt something looking at me. I looked around and there was a big mountain lion about 50 or 60 feet away just looking at me out of the brush.

It was a beautiful animal, with a sleek body that was more than three feet long. I was fairly quiet and all by myself, and he just stood there for the longest time staring at me. It made me feel quite uncomfortable since I didn't have a gun with me and he seemed in no hurry to clear out. So I walked over to the house and up the stairs and went inside to get a gun. But when I returned, he had disappeared.

I was up there not quite a year. Late in October 1930, I left La Honda and headed down to Carmel to look for a job down there.

Chapter 3: Bumming Around

It was the midst of the Depression and there were no jobs to be had anywhere. I had a little money saved up from my work on the fire, so I decided to go exploring. I took the bus down to Carmel and spent about a week looking around.

1930, October 22
Dearest Mom,
   Just a line to let you know I'm O.K. The bus got me here without the least bit of trouble. So far I haven't found a thing to do with the exception of a small gardener's job for one hour.
   I'm staying at the Sutton Place for five a week – have an attic room which is much nicer than it sounds.
   This is a beautiful little place but it is dead as far as business is concerned. The tourist trade hasn't come along as yet and

125

every one is crying their eyes out. In the last few weeks there have been several business failures, and in a town of this size, that's a lot.

I haven't gone native yet and don't think I will. More likely I'll pull out when my week is up. You can't live on views etc. you know.

Lots of good looking cars and women but the women are as hard to get acquainted with as cars are to get. But I can look anyway!

The next day ——

Yesterday afternoon I met a man named Jack something or other who used to be in San Jose and who was an Elk. He and I have been together ever since and are both in about the same financial condition so have had many things in common. He's a nice chap and we may find something to do yet. He has a nice roadster so we've been riding around enjoying the scenery and each other's company. Last nite we had supper in Pacific Grove and it was a very nice one too – only fifty cents.

My eats cost less than a dollar per day. This was accomplished by shopping around after paying 25¢ for a bowl of soup my first nite here. Last nite we went to the show here and saw a good picture after which we had a cup of hot cocoa. Then to bed. He has gone to Monterey this afternoon to see about a job in the local theater and may get me one too. It's just a thought tho.

The weather here is beautiful or lovely or both. But it is far from being the place to work in – so much nicer to just poke around and talk and look than work.

Jack and I spent a couple of hours out on a point overlooking the ocean this morning and enjoyed ourselves thoroughly.

Well, dearest, I send my love to you and the family and am sorry we can't all be down here having a wonderful time.

Lots and lots of love to you dearest.
Stan.

Chapter 4: Chili Bean Ranch

AFTER CHRISTMAS, JOHNNY BRUCE and I went down to Almaden and spent some time at Ben Peckham's place. Ben was an attorney in San Jose and a friend to the Japanese-American community. During World War II, he protected Japanese property by transferring it into

Stan at the Chili Bean Ranch   Stan and John Bruce, 1931

his name and holding it in trust for them until they returned from the internment camps. So he was a friend of our family because of our close relationship with Mimi and her family.

Ben just enjoyed having us up there, as far as that was concerned. Peckham used to come up about once a week, maybe every two weeks, to see us. He always brought some food along, so we always had food. Ben and I did a little hunting and fooled around. He had a couple of horses up there. They didn't have any saddles but we used to ride around. It was just a time for us to rest up and take it easy.

Johnny and I were not close friends but I knew Johnny when he was in College. I had met him at one of the fraternity houses. I remember meeting Johnny in front of the post office in San Jose and he asked me about going to sea, because I had sailed on a tanker, on that first trip. I told him about working on a ship, and he was always going to do it, but he never did.

We stayed up there for a month or so, and we drank quite a good deal. That was kind of too bad, but we drank and got pretty tight. Johnny Bruce described it in a letter he wrote for my 77th birthday.

Una Vispera del Ano Nuevo al Rancho
del Rio Frijole Chile

Remember Stan?

That eve so long, long ago that ushered in the dismal decade of the 'Thirties. Can it be possible that more than half a century has gone by? It can, and it has.

The Eve of 1930.[41]

For me, and doubtless for you, that was a most extraordinary New Year's Eve, and thus vividly memorable. Not that it introduced such a depressing decade, both economically and spiritually. We were young and hardly so prescient that we could foresee the lean years coming, or even bother a hoot about the morrows ahead on a night acceptably given over to abandon, a night of unbridled revelry.

We had gone quail hunting in the afternoon – rather, you had. I had tagged along as a sort of Labrador pointer. We flushed a covey and quick blasts issued from the double barrels. Two birds dropped like feathered rocks among the mesquite.

We had had quail on toast for breakfast once, but this was a special occasion calling for special fare. And so, while the revelers down in the more civilized places guzzled on bathtub gin made passable by ginger ale and nibbled at cold chicken cacciatore and pasta, we relaxed over copious aperitifs of cognac and dined elegantly on quail on toast (or expected to). It would be a nice touch to say we had a gob of chili beans as a salute to the place, but that was served in a way. Our salutes to the evening, if not the place, soon made us full of beans.

A word about this aperitif, a multipurpose drink that did brave duty as an appetizer, an after-dinner liqueur, a midnight toast, or in the chatterful wait for the bells as an increasingly gracious refill that kept the spirits from waning and the waning year from dragging. Ben Peckham's Rare Old Cognac. You and Ben and I were its only known connoisseurs.

Its rarity was such that no sophisticated palate could possibly mistake it for, if I may impute a relationship, a distant French cousin. Its distinctive flavor undoubtedly de-

---

41 His recollection was off by a year. It was New Year's Eve 1930, according to Stan's letters.

rived from the fact that it was native to the Chili Bean River Ranch, a circumstance that dictated its method of production and imparted its unique quality. Ben Peckham's Rare Old Cognac was concocted, not distilled. Still, it was easier to get past the glottis (after the initial, anesthetizing slug) than any of the famous brands of Half Moon Bay Scotch. They all bore skillfully counterfeited labels. I remember tossing off a wee drop of White Horse – and spewing it out. I felt certain it had not come right from the horse's mouth.

Back to Ben's beverage. Old–? Well, not by the standards of today's cultivated taste and competitive market. Spirits spend years aging in oak barrels. Ben's cognac never saw the inside of a barrel, or even a keg. The jug we tippled from that night had probably been filled a month earlier, perhaps two months. And that, for that time, would be the equivalent of today's 12-year-old Johnnie Walker Black Label or, in the cognac line, Remy Martin or Napoleon Brandy.

Remember, this was Prohibition, one of the eras of legislated paranoia that periodically afflict America. It predated synthetics and instants, for the only aging granted beer and wine was the journey from the fermentation vat to the speakeasy. Once the drippings from a still filled a wooden tub, caramel coloring was stirred in, and the batch then siphoned into bottles and rushed off to a thirsty market, peddled as fine old charcoal-filtered Kentucky bourbon. Into the next tub might be swirled some smoky essence: ah, Chivas Regal!

You might ask – well, not you, but someone who did not swill his way through that innocently inebriated era: but wouldn't they know it was all a fake, all rotgut? The answer, of course, is simple: how? These were for the most part people who had never before drunk an alcoholic beverage, and many would likely not have done so then, had they not been forbidden to. Therefore, how would a person who had never sipped a dram know that Scotch really did not taste like paint thinner? (Though he guzzled the stuff himself, no painter would dare use it as a thinner – it would eat through the woodwork.)

By the standards of that day, then, Ben's cognac was indeed old, if not aged. And so was his Dago Red, to use the vernacular of the time for red wine, usually chianti. In the cabin we found several cases of dusty, cobwebby bottles. (Cabin? We called it that, despite the fair-sized kitchen; a living room with an upright piano hauled up the two-mile mountain trail by twelve men and six horses; a bedroom; a screened porch with comfortable chairs and daybeds.) Near the cabin was a small building with a tack-and-tool room, and a bathroom with shower. A half-dozen horses grazed the 47 acres and had to be rounded up when we wanted to ride.

Dinner was a little late – not the fault of the wood-burning range, but the odd behavior of our appetite. It stubbornly resisted stimulation and required an inordinate number of aperitifs. If not a stimulating effect as an appetizer, they did produce a staggering effect, which became noticeable during our trips out to the clearing for biological purposes, simultaneously taking lingering 1929 looks at the stars and remarking on their infinitude and glister (thanks, Mr. Shakespeare!).

I acted as sommelier, dusting off and uncorking a bottle of vintage Dago Red, while Stan served up as chef what he had brought down as huntsman. We were fortunate the aperitifs had at last done their job, for the oven's appetite apparently had needed no artificial stimulant. The plump quail, well beyond well-done, sat shriveled and forlorn, each in the center of a slab of well beyond well-browned toast. We glanced at each other, then at the quail, and reached in unison for the Dago Red. The quail, so petite on the fields of toast, seemed far too great a delicacy for an urban ranchero's taste, looking as they did like roast chickadees.

Dinner was over in no time.

Stan consulted his watch and said, "Only twenty minutes of '29 left."

We filled our glasses and went outside.

It was a night of scintillant beauty, just cold enough to be bracing (we felt wonderfully braced) and so clear we could see a thousand light years away. The sky appeared perforated by a billion pins.

After a spell in the openness of the clearing to gaze at the heavens away from the artificial illumination below, we walked beyond the front of the cabin and stood on the rim of the hill, at this point a bulge with wooded precipitous ravine on the right that provided a course for winter downpours and Ben, a place name: the Chili Bean River. Our sight was not restricted to miles. Progress had not yet coined the word smog and we gazed at the cluster of stars that was San Jose, a prune-and-apricot center in the outer fringe of cosmopolitan San Francisco's exurbia, where 25,000 satisfied souls still clung to the indolent, worryless life of the old mission days, though the brown-robed padres had long since gone. Through binoculars we could dimly make out the modern-day landmark and the pride of the town, the First National Bank's towering skyscraper – ten stories high!

The lights of San Jose shone 25 or 30 miles away, by Maxwell or Peerless roadster; half that by the old crow's flight (unless the old crow had been dipping into Old Crow). A good 40 miles or more farther we could plainly see the galaxies of the East Bay, distance bestowing a twinkle.

We knew that as the new year drew nearer the revelry grew louder in these brightly sparkling places. We saw, we listened, we heard nothing. Nothing of the joyous din, that is. Only the sight reached us; none of the noise. A bit unearthly, yet decibels from the silent world of the deaf; in this eerie stillness we could still hear the small scurrying and rustling and death-struggle sounds of the nocturnal wild: a raccoon or a pack rat, an owl up on the ridge, the choked-off squeak of a field mouse.

Stan stepped over to the kitchen window to look at his watch in the yellow glow of the kerosene lamp within.

"Seconds away..." He raised his glass. "Good-by to old '29."

"R.I.P."

We solemnly finished off the drinks. Before I could shout a welcome to the new year, the stillness was shattered by a blast that made my right eardrum vibrate. Stan had fired a scatter of bird shot into the night from a short-barreled sort of shotgun pistol that Ben used to control the snake population. We whooped and hollered and scared hell out of the prowling little predatory creatures. Then we stumbled back into the kitchen and offered an equally solemn toast, then a few jolly ones, to 1930.

I awoke slowly, wondering what had happened and why I had not gone to bed, only to discover I was in bed, fully clothed except for shoes, one nearby, the other over by the door. It was daylight, too daylight.

I picked my way to the screened porch with great care, out of consideration for my head. Stan was snuggled in a daybed, sound asleep (rather, silent asleep), his sloughed-off clothes indicating his zigzag progress toward bed. On his head, at an angle so rakish it hid half his face, rested a cowboy hat.

Thanks, guy, for that rich memory.

My letters to Mom painted a rather different picture.

1930, December 31, Wednesday
Dearest Mom –

Just a line to let you know I'm up at the Chili Bean Ranch and am well and enjoying myself.

Woke up this A.M. to greet a real old-fashioned rain. It is still raining and doing a good job of it too.

John and I got breakfast together and it was a good one indeed. We had fried quail – which I got the day before – and baked beans and canned apricots and fried mush and coffee.

While we were putting the above mentioned groceries away, the horses – five of them – watched us through the door and windows and stood licking their chops – or whatever it is that horses do in such cases.

Time out . . .

John and I studied over a story plot of his so I am continuing this on the first day of a New Year.

It rained all day long yesterday so had to stay in the cabin. We read, talked and ate and finally sat down to a game of chess to while away the evening. Not a very hilarious way to celebrate the eve of a new year but a bit more sane than that spent by many.

Today the rain let up for a while and we took advantage of the opportunity to get out, and played barnyard golf then some golf with the regulation clubs and ball. The cleared patches around the cabin serving as a course. Rules were made to suit our needs and the game was a lot of fun. We played until the rain drove us in and that's where you find me now. We have just lighted a lamp and will soon be making supper after which maybe some more chess.

Sunday ——

Well dearest – Today Ben Peckham came up with his son, a nice fellow about my age, and Jim Chesnutt and a friend of his. The six of us had a dandy time. John and I got the dinner. It was quite a success. Fried fillet, hot biscuits and honey (I made them and they were just delicious, or so everyone said) also green peas and just a few beans Spanish. This was headed by hearts of artichoke salad – some menu for the mountains or any place else for that matter. We lingered long over our empty plates and had a dandy time. The conversation was lively and at times very amusing and clever.

Later we walked down the trail a way with our guests and waved them a good-bye as they disappeared down over a hill some distance below us.

Now we are sitting at the table with two lamps between us. John is reading some letters and making comments from time to time while I am busy trying to answer him and write at the same time. Outside the wind is whistling and howling around the cabin while stretched far below us and out past the mouth of the canyon, at the head of which is our cabin – lies the valley. The town of San Jose looks like a diamond choker set in a black velvet case. With the neon lights as rare rubies in this beautiful necklace. The description is not so hot but the sight is none the less beautiful.

Yesterday I went out hunting and got three quail and one rabbit. So last night we had rabbit, Spanish beans, baked macaroni with tomato, and hot biscuits. Boy! but it was a good meal. We ate until we were stuffed and stuffed some more.

Tomorrow I shall let you know more about the happenings on the Chili Bean and the doings of your wayward son.

Monday, Jan. 5th 1931

This morning we again woke to a dull rainy day. Last night's wind having blown it up.

The kitchen is snug and warm. The tea kettle humming softly on the stove in the corner and the dishes, left from yesterday, washed and put away.

John is plugging away at the typewriter and I'm sitting at the table smoking my pipe. Outside the light rain continues to patter on the roof and trickle down the window pane.

Yesterday Ben mentioned that he knew your grandfather – my great-grandfather – and your mother. Also he recalled the old Tenth Street home.[42] Small world after all. Isn't it?

Ben is really a very fine man with a wonderfully quick, active, and retentive mind. He seems to observe everything – is generous and considerate. He does a lot of listening and adds a word or points out a discrepancy in a nice way and at the right time. I like him very much but am a little in awe of him. That of

---

42 J. R. Whitney owned a home at Tenth and San Carlos Streets, San Jose.

course, is as it should be – the respect of the lesser mind for the greater.

To get back to you and the new house, I guess you are at last becoming settled and finding places for at least most of the things tho it looked like a hopeless task at first. Now that the grand-Billies[43] have left and school has started and the New Year begun, I hope that you get a good rest and take care of yourself. Take things easy for a while at least. Then you will be able to get more out of living when you feel rested. You were pretty tired when I left.

John and I just finished lunch. Had broiled lamb chops and they tasted fine.

The other day while I was out hunting, I left the path and made my way up the side of a hill through sagebrush. When I got to the top I found that I was on another hill than that which I thought I was going up, so I made my way to the bottom of the ravine over a deer trail. There were fresh tracks and, as I made my way on my hands and knees through the brush that was so thick walking was impossible, two deer started up about fifteen feet in front of me and bounded out of sight. One was a beautiful buck having at least three points on his antlers.

Well, I finally made my way down to the bottom where I knew the going would be easier. There was a little trickle of water flowing down over the moss-covered rocks into little crystal clear pools. Each pool was more beautiful than the one below it as I made my way upward. It gave me a queer feeling to look at them and know that possibly I was the only man who had ever looked on these beautiful works of nature - myself and countless deer and wild animals. The sight more than compensated for the well-over-an-hour hard climb through the brush that was all but impenetrable. Soon I had reached the top and came out on the top of Bald Mountain. As I stepped out of the brush two large flocks of quail that were feeding right at the edge took to the air and dove into the brush some distance away making a startling din in the absolutely quiet atmosphere.

It was getting quite late and looked like it was about to rain so I took the trail down the mountain and hurried back to the cabin. I no sooner reached it than the shower broke. Again I had played in luck.

---

43 This refers to Don's parents, William and Martha Dungan.

I stopped writing to take advantage of the hour or so lull in the rain and got some air and exercise chasing a golf ball through the mud.

Awhile before supper I made some very fine nut bread which I am now eating and enjoying tho I am as full as a tick. You know how nut bread is. Each bite calls for another and another ad infinitum.

The night is another stormy one and the warmth in here is in sharp contrast to the cold, windy rain outside.

If the storm doesn't clear up and let me outside, this "note" will have to be bound in volume form. I think sheep skin binding would be quite the thing don't you or maybe banana skin!

While I was filling the lamps today I cracked the bowl of one of them and it looked like our bright lights would be reduced by half. But being a person of great resource, I fitted the burner on a mason jar and it is now casting its cheery rays on this little note.

I am beginning to feel sleepy so will lay my writing aside for the night and as you see, my thoughts are oftenest with you and of you. Good nite dearest of Moms.

Saturday P.M.

The rain kept up until Wed. when it let up for a while and I got out for a few hours. It was nice to be out in the air again after two and a half days cooped up in the cabin.

Thursday was a beautiful day and it has been thus since. I have been gathering wood and cutting it and shoveling off the trail these nice days and the exercise has pepped me up.

Today I finished the trail and I hope Ben comes up before it rains again and sees how nice it looks. This afternoon John and I holy-stoned[44] the kitchen floor and cleaned house so now everything is nice and clean and comfortable.

Speaking of our lamps, I was rummaging around among some cans and found two mantels for a Coleman lamp that was up here. I fitted them on the lamp and since we have six or eight gallons of gas up here we are enjoying the bright light very much.

Last nite I set a trap beside my bed out on the sleeping porch for the mice, then blew out the candle, and no sooner settled

---

44 To scrub or scour with a piece of soft sandstone.

down than Bang! Number One. I got up and reset it. Got back in bed and in about five minutes another mouse bit the dust. Well I reset it again and the same thing happened. After that the bait was gone so I got to sleep without any further interruptions. However there were no nuts stored in my shoes this morning as there usually were.

Jim and a couple fellows came up today so I am sending this back by them.

Well dearest, this brings my love to you and the family.
Your Loving Son,
Stan.

1931, January 15, Thursday
My Dearest Mom,

It was a real treat to hear your voice this afternoon. But it wasn't half as good as seeing you would have been.

I was sorry to hear you had been having trouble with that nasty back – and it is a nasty back when it goes ker-plunk – of yours. I hope that now it is okay though. I think it must come from nerves and the best thing for nerves is rest. So again I say. Get all you can. . .

Fred came up Monday. We had a good time. He and I played golf and pitched horseshoes. At night the three of us play cards or checkers or chess.

This A. M. he and I hiked up to Bald Mountain where the horses graze and brought back two of them. We saddled up and went down the trail to where the car was parked and rode into Robertsville where we bought about sixty pounds of grub. I phoned you from there. Then we turned around and came back to where the horses were tied. Fred left for home and John and I split the load and tied the grub to our saddles and made our way back to the cabin. We arrived at a little after five p.m.

To give you a better idea of the location of the cabin: You take the Almaden Road from San Jose. About six miles out you come to Robertsville, which is a junction. At this place there is a general store and there was also a bar on the other corner of the side road. There was a water-trough in front of the store in the horse-and-buggy era. This has since been replaced by gas pumps, however.

As the story comes to me, in the days before Prohibition this water-trough afforded the proper excuse to stop and water the horses. In this way the trip to the mines was inevitably broken for a rest period. The bar did a flourishing business and the

136

*place became famous in a modest way. But to call a place after
its only bar, even in those times, was a bit too much. So it was
named after the owner of the general store, a Mr. Roberts. The
bar has since been closed and the place turned into a dwelling.*

*After leaving Robertsville you turn off the Almaden road a
few miles out. You are now on the Guadalupe Road. This brings
you out past the Guadalupe mines [45] and ends a few miles further on. At the end of this road is where we left the horses and
where the trail begins which leads to the cabin. This trail is a
little over two miles from the cabin to the road and for the most
part it is almost straight up and down. Again, I'm glad I am not
a horse, when I think of them toiling up the steep climb with
some individual kicking them in the slats to force them to
greater speed.*

Saturday P. M.

*John and I got to talking last nite and I didn't finish my let-
ter but I'll tell you about today.*

*This A. M. we had a late breakfast and then decided to hike
over to the old Almaden Mines. They are about four miles over
the hills from here but we thought that it was only a couple of
miles. We started out at about eleven o'clock and hiked over. We
first came to the old diggings but decided not to waste much
time exploring them. Then we climbed over the mountain to the
old town. What a place!*

*Looking down on the town you can see the ruins of at least
fifty buildings strung out over the hillside and scattered over the
floor of the canyon. In the principle section of the town is the old
company store. It is a long brick building with iron shutters
over doors and windows. The roof has long since fallen in and
now nothing is left but the four walls with the shutters hanging
at the empty openings. We explored this place at length and
found a great many bottles that once contained Scotch or champagne, among the ruins.*

*Next we made our way across the old stage road that
wound through the town down to the Hacienda de Almaden and
on out to San Jose. Some two hundred feet from the store stands
the old school house. It is in very good condition, being intact as*

---

45 During the California Gold Rush period, the New Almaden Quicksilver Mines just
south of the city were the largest mercury mines in North America. The mines were
highly important, since mercury was used to extract gold from ore.

far as roof and walls are concerned but badly in need of repairs before classes start again.

In one of the rooms there is an old piano, one of those that was flat, long and large. In its day I'll bet it was the grandest thing in miles. However today it is shy a couple of legs, many strings and a keyboard. Aside from the rust and the aforementioned losses, also a few others that I failed to mention, it too is in good condition.

The schoolhouse itself is a large building having four large rooms. It was a surprise to see such an imposing structure in such a seemingly little town. However, in its day the town must have had a rather large population.

We made our way from house to house or rather from ruin to ruin. Some had had fine gardens with picket fences around them. In some of these gardens were little paths and beds bordered with red bricks forming attractive designs. Today the gardens are weed-grown and the bricks are moss-covered. The fences have disappeared but for a stake here or a post there. However the bricks still form the outline of paths and flower beds. The wood rats have taken possession of the houses and the coyote walks unmolested through the streets.

It seems hard to believe that here people once lived, loved and died, felt life at its best, drained the bitter cup of grief, in fact here has been run the gamut of human emotions. But today all that is but a memory. The decaying ruins bearing silent testimony to the fact.

Below us and toward the Hacienda still stands the tall brick smoke stack towering sixty feet or more amid the ruins of what used to be a mill.

It was beginning to get late and, as my appetite was overcoming my curiosity, we decided it wise to start home. We got back about five p.m., hungry as a couple of bears and not a little weary. However supper has raised/revived our spirits and the day has held much of interest.

When we got back and got a fire started we began to look for wood ticks. John found five while I doubled that with a count of ten. Even now I keep thinking that I feel one crawling on me, but I'm almost sure that I got them all. (my mistake)

Last nite for supper I made some of the best biscuits. Tea biscuits. They were a joy to any cook's heart. I made them like any biscuit is made but added a tablespoonful of sugar to the dough. Then when they were in the pan I greased the tops with butter and sprinkled a little sugar on them. To this I added a bit of cinnamon sprinkled over the sugar. Well there were only four left out of two large heaping cupfuls of flour. There wouldn't have been any left but that we were too full to eat any more.

We sure eat up here if we don't do anything else!

You asked if I didn't get lonesome up here. Sometimes, Yes. Right now I'd like to be home with you and the family. But this is a queer world. It seems there is always something we would rather be doing or someplace we would rather be.

A tick just fell out of my hair onto this paper — X marks the spot he landed. His last landing was on top of the stove. That made eleven. Not a bad harvest at that. Now John and I feel all creepy again. He swears his hair is full of them and that he won't be able to sleep tonite. Ticks or no I'll sleep like a log.

The weather has been beautiful all week so expect Ben up in the A. M. That means a big feed at noon and a way of mailing this letter.

Well sweetheart, I'm going to bed now so say good-night. Again my thoughts are with you and yours.

Good night dearest Mom.

Stan

Wednesday, January 21
Dearest Mom,

It has started to rain again, so I am taking this opportunity to tell you more about the life up here.

No one came up Sunday so, of course, I couldn't send any mail out. It was a nice day too. We had a big pot of beans ready to feed our guests. John and I have had a nice time eating them all by ourselves. There is still enough left for one more meal. But I don't think that we will miss them when they are gone.

It seems I have wandered quite away from the Chili Bean. The Chili Bean River, as you may have guessed, is nothing more than a joke. It is a dry gully that lies just below the cabin and even in the wettest weather carries no water. But all mountain cabins should, for romance sake, have a river at the door. We have ours too, The Chili Bean!

Friday Night
Well dearest — Something interrupted me on Wednesday while I was dashing off a few lines to you and I have just gotten around to the typewriter again. Now that I am back at it, I don't know what to say.

Tonight I cooked a very good meal. We had creamed crab that was really very very good. I baked some patty shells to put it in. Then I baked some potatoes. First I put a little piece of bacon in each one before I baked them and they turned out dandy. Then to top off the menu, we had some hot biscuits. The whole was quite satisfying.

In the trap near my bed, I have now caught fifteen mice. That's quite a number of mice to catch by one's bed, don't you think?

Just before I sat down to write I gave John a surprise. We were playing chess. John is pretty good at the game, too. But tonite, as he was working to checkmate me, I snook in and cornered him. He was quite surprised but I had him. That made up for some of the many times he has beaten me. I may learn the game yet.

The weather seemed to be clearing up tonight. I sure hope it does. It's the bunk to have to stay indoors all day when you are up in the mountains. Then too, if it clears up and is a nice day Sunday, we may have visitors. We both crave news of the outside world, and I want to mail this letter.

Sunday, Jan. 25, 1931
Dearest Mom,

Ben has come up today so am sending off my letters to you. With him came Jim and Don and George Millard. We have had a nice feed and they will be starting home soon.

As soon as you get word of that job or the approximate time that I may be called upon to report for an interview, please let me know. In an emergency, Fred Franck can possibly reach me the quickest of anyone as he knows all about getting up here.

They have brought up some more food so John and I will be able to have quite some feeds this coming week. Ben is sure nice that way. Every time he comes up, he brings as much as he can pack. Few people would do as much.

Well, I have to get back to our guests, so will say goodbye. Again I send my love, dearest, and hope that everything is going just fine and dandy with you.

Your loving son,
Stan

Chapter 5: Looking for Work

IN FEBRUARY, JOHN AND I SHOVED OFF and headed down to Hollister to look for work once more. John had a job with the local newspaper, the *Free Lance*. He had chosen J. Campbell Bruce as his pen name.

1931, March 6, Hollister
Dearest Mom,

Well I have been here for some time and like the place a great deal but to date have found no work.

John has passes to the theater and we see every change of bill. This gives us something to do in the evenings that otherwise would be awfully dull.

Both Sundays we have had dinner with the Suttons and they are a very likable couple. Mr. Sutton is the managing editor of the "Free Lance" and is a good sport. He is a little Englishman and his wife rules the roost much to the delight of certain town gossips. She is big-hearted though and has been very nice to me.

When we go over there we play 500. It is a pretty good game and we have a lot of fun telling how badly we are going to trim each other and if we fail, making excuses.

Last night Mr. and Mrs. Sutton and I went to some amateur fights at the local gym. They were very entertaining and we had a lot of fun. John did not go as he had a date.

This is a dandy little town and I would like very much to find a job here but there are none to be had, or so it seems. There will be work here however as soon as the fruit season opens. I can't wait that long tho so may be home very soon if nothing breaks.

Reporters John Bruce and Jim Chesnutt (middle two), 1930.

The Suttons are coming over tonight to play cards and we expect to have a very pleasant evening.

Well dearest, this is to warn you that I may put in an appearance very shortly and it will be good to see you again too.

Lots of love,
Stan

1931, March 8

Well Stan honey, have you thought my arm sprained or something? I have rather expected you back from day to day – have missed you!

You and John must be nicely located. There are always nice people everywhere, and you seem to find them – it is a happy faculty.

We are jogging along as usual. Don working, Mabel seeking employment in furs, etc. I suggested today that just possibly if she looked less like half a million or so, she might get something. Was she annoyed? Oh no! After the door was shut she stormed around talking to herself, "Not a decent pair of shoes to my name, no clothes," etc. etc. Poor old Mabel. She worked about a week, got "fired" and bought herself an evening dress!

I am studying contract bridge Thursday evenings in one of Sister's classes. She asks about you. Mabel says G.C. always asks about you. We think he misses you but wouldn't admit it.

Billie had his head cut open by one of those very heavy swings which hang from big chains; it was in the school grounds opposite Lock's Drug Store so we were right by the Phys. & Surg. Bldg. & he got sewed up pronto. Was O.K. right after and very proud of his heroism & bandage! Donnabeth is getting along nicely. We have acquired a dog, "Jean": a very nice mutt like old "Bobs"; even Mabel likes her.

There is no news. G.C. & Maude had a fair trip. G.C. was ill from the heat (and I imagine booze) & Maude was sick and the "Saramacca nearly broke in two" – part of the voyage was very rough!

Mabel has been out twice with Vincent and this week-end Augy is having a "party" and M. & V. are going.

Had lovely days & glorious nights lately. How's Hollister? Am scratching this off and hope you can read it.

Love always,
Mom.

P.S. Have a nice time & see that John teaches you the newspaper business so you can become a Mr. Scripps.

We had a lot of fun down in Hollister – a lot of fun with our drinking. Johnny and I were drinking quite a good deal, but not too much, we were not drunks. Johnny was getting along with some girl teacher down there, and he was doing all right for himself. The three of us used to go out nights to lots of dances and whatnot, as young people can always find something to do. We went out to one place, I remember, outside of Hollister. It was a big bootlegging joint and we got a big gallon of this liquor. Somebody tipped me off that the cops were coming and a bunch of us got out of there in a hurry, right through the window, broken glass trailing behind us. When the cops knocked the place over, they arrested anybody who was connected to the place. It was a great big hall and we just got out in time. I didn't have any job, and had I been there, I would have been stuck.

Another place we went to was all covered with the bark of red-wood logs like a log cabin, only it was big – a big dance hall. You'd go in there, and this was Prohibition … oh, my God – everything would show up at this place: bathtub gin, home brew, anything that would pour showed up there in quantity. And the first thing you know, everybody would be staggering around – it'd be a total debauch. One hundred percent. No sober person could stay there, so it only left the drunks and everybody was that way.

And when they headed for home, they'd go off the road, maybe hit a phone pole. Cars didn't go very fast, maybe 25 miles per hour, they just wouldn't go any faster. There wasn't much two-way traffic so the biggest danger was missing a turn, it wasn't somebody running into you. They didn't *all* kill themselves on the way home, but I buried a few friends in those days.

John and I spent a lot of time together at that time. We enjoyed the same things – especially the great out-of-doors. In a letter some years later he recalled:

> *One time we were headed for Big Basin and arrived at the summit above Saratoga just before twilight. The ragged outline of the Mt. Hamilton range across the valley bathed in a suffusion of soft golden color so that it stood out in startling sharpness like a stereoscopic picture, or a rare oil painting by a master. That still sticks in my memory –*

And in mine, also.

Chapter 6: Off to Sea Aboard the SS *Colombia*

IN MAY OF 1931, I FINALLY GOT A JOB. I was hired by the Panama Mail Company as a checker on the *Colombia*, a freighter that traveled back and forth from San Francisco to New York via the Panama Canal. At least it was a job with three square meals a day and a bed to sleep on, and that was something in 1931, in the midst of the Depression.

We sailed out of San Pedro with a full load of cargo on board and enjoyed calm seas as we headed down the coast of Mexico. I was 25 years old.

1931, May 10, Mother's Day
Dearest Mom,

I hope this finds you and all the family in the best of health.

I suppose that you would like to know a little about my new home. Well, I can say this much, I like it better than I thought I would.

The three fellows in my room are about my own age and we all get along very nicely.

This P.M. finds us twenty-four hours out of San Pedro and the sea is as calm as they make them.

We have a full load of cargo on board, in fact, we had to leave some behind, after stowing some of it on deck in L.A.

There are about a hundred and twenty-five men in the crew. 40 odd are Chinese who are the cooks, cabin boys, waiters, etc. for the passengers. They – the Chinamen – are all on our side of the ship. In fact, there are eight on either side of our room and at this time in each room they have a phonograph playing. The most awful noises are all we can hear. But the chinks are sitting in front of the darn machines in a trance. "Beauty is local custom."

The first night out we had the porthole open and about 11:00 p.m. the sea came in and soaked my bunk. I didn't waste much time getting out of bed. I turned the mattress over and borrowed a blanket and in that way managed to put in a rotten nite. The mattress was still damp on the other side.

I am lying on my bunk while I am penning this.

We have a passenger list of about 70 people first-class and a few steerage passengers; also, we have about forty deportees who are aft in the steerage too. There are four women deportees and it is funny to see the men go after them. Tonite they were up on the deck by #5 hatch – that's the rear hatch and the one that I have to check – and were dancing. There were about 10 men to one woman and they felt very flattered at all the attention they were getting. At least they looked as pleased as could be.

The barrage of Chinese music has stopped for a minute but it sounds funny to hear the chinks jabbering away. – It is hard to realize that I am really here and not just dreaming. – Those fellows are a happy lot and don't ask anything but to be left alone. They squat around the companion-way[46] near our door like monkeys, peeling potatoes or eating their bowl of food in real Chinese coolie style.

This job is really quite a job. We have to check all the freight into and out of the hatch that is assigned to us. We keep right on the job as long as our hatch is open while we are in port.

When we are at sea, we have to get up all the bills of lading and tags and company's records to send into the office. For instance, I went to work at nine this A.M. and worked until about 8:00 tonight making duplicate bills for all the cargo to be put off at Cristobal, Canal Zone – twelve copies each. It wasn't such bad work and to tell you the truth, it is better than having nothing to do but lay around your bunk all day. The time passes quickly. There is no one to drive you like a slave while you are plugging along as you will. We get up a little past six in the morning and have breakfast at seven or not at all. Then at nine we do what there is to be done in the office.

Tonite for supper we had roast duck and creamed potatoes and squash and a delicious salad – tomato stuffed with chicken and celery, etc. – homemade bread, nice sand-dabs —you know those thin fish – and ice cream and tea and I guess that's all. Anyway, I'm full. And sleepy.

I'll add a line before I post this in Mazatlán, Wednesday. Good-nite dearest of Moms.

Tuesday night:—
Well dearest, I've been busy the last two days hectographing records of the cargo.[47]

---

46 A staircase leading from a deck to the cabins or area below.

47 The hectograph is a printing process which involves transfer of an original, prepared with special inks, to a gelatin pad pulled tight on a metal frame. After transfer of the image to the inked gelatin surface, copies are made by pressing paper against it.

Last night we didn't get through until about 10:30, but quit at 5:00 this P.M.

Tomorrow we will be in Mazatlán and start to unload about 7:00 a.m. and sail at 2:00 p.m. so am finishing this note tonight. There is nothing much to say but will write again soon.

I still like the job and seem to be catching on – hope so anyway.

Love to all, Thanks again for the loan.
Your loving son,
Stan.

The Chinese crew lived next to us and they played music all night long – Chinese music – and it was a terrible thing. We had about 30 waiters and stewards to take care of the rooms and they were all Orientals and spoke very little English. They couldn't go ashore because they weren't allowed in most places so they played their crazy music all night long and gambled with the dominoes they had – Mahjong it's called – making noise. I guess they were getting about $30 a month and room and board, the same thing many of us were getting, but they got more because they got tips from the passengers. Then after they served their time, they shipped the whole bunch back to China and got another crew. The company kept them a year or two years and then sent them back. They came to make money to send back to their families. They were pretty good eggs.

As freight checker my job was to check all the freight into and out of the hatch assigned to me. When we were in port, I had to work as long as my hatch was open. Then, when we went to sea, I had to get up all the bills of lading to discharge the cargo when we got into port.

We sailed down the coast to Mazatlán. The weather was hot and sticky. Working in the hatch, I would get soaking wet just checking the cargo without even handling the stuff. At night my bunk was hot all night and I tossed and turned in a pool of sweat. The heat was uncomfortable but not unbearable. The lack of sleep was the hardest part because we had to work until ten or eleven every night after we left a port, and then they called us to get up at six the next morning.

1931, May 25
Dearest Mom,

I am sorry that I haven't been able to write more often and tell you more about this trip but we have been so busy that I haven't had time to collect my thoughts and jot them down.

We had to make some two thousand accountables of the freight we have taken on besides our work checking in some twelve thousand bags of coffee and checking out general cargo and flour that occupied the space where the coffee is now stowed.

None of us have been ashore in any of these ports but I hope to be able to go to a show in Panama tonite, if we make the Canal early enough for us to dock.

. . .

Today however we have nothing to do as our work is all up to date so am writing this.

We have had to put in a couple of long shifts so far but the hardest was at Puntarenas where I didn't finish work until three-thirty a.m. I got up for breakfast but didn't have to work the next morning so slept until time to dress for lunch.

To go back a bit, there were three little kids aft in the hospital traveling as kind of second class passengers to Corinto with their folks. The oldest was about six, the next three and a half and the youngest about two. Their mother was a good-looking Spanish woman and the father, an American. When I would come up on deck they would climb all over me and want to be picked up and played with.

They were all good-looking and their mother kept them nice and clean. I had a lot of fun with them and the one about 3½ years old and I got along so well that he didn't want to leave at Corinto and neither did I want him to go. I miss the little fellow a lot.

Corinto [Nicaragua] was the first port where I had a chance to put my foot on the dock, as we checked from the dock there. I got some mangoes and they were good – 6 for five cents. I might have gotten them for less but didn't have the time to argue and beat the price down. It seems that everything is about three times higher when you first ask than what it can be had for if you argue long enough.

Some of the hills along the coast are beautiful and I have seen some lovely sunsets as well. But it seems a checker is not a tourist and is not allowed a great deal of time to enjoy all the beauties of the voyage.

I flirted with a good-looking señorita that came aboard in one of the ports and we both had a lot of fun. I got a lot of fun out of it anyway, because the competition was pretty keen with *four musicians and three checkers and a freight clerk and my-self all trying to get a tumble. Just in fun.*

At Corinto we picked up a few passengers that are going back to the States who have been through the Managua quake.[48] One woman came aboard on a stretcher – she was crushed pretty badly. There are some others who are in bad shape too.

On the dock I talked to some of the Marines that were there at the time and they tell me that it was as bad as it could have possibly been, and it is amazing that anyone came out alive. From some of the pictures I have seen it sure looked terrible.

We all get along very well together and at nite when we are not too tired the storekeeper comes in with something to eat and we have a feed and a rubber of bridge. These little parties are one of the best things that happen on the voyage, but have to be pulled off on the Q.T. [quiet] as the ice cream and cookies are borrowed from the ship's stores and it would be too bad for us if we got caught in the act.

We have very few privileges on board, but it isn't as bad as it might be because the crew is a good bunch taking them as a whole.

Almost every night there is lightning. Sometimes before go-ing to bed I go up on deck for a few minutes and watch it. Some-times there will be some beautiful flashes that light up the whole sky. I love to stand on deck and see the different designs that it makes as it arcs from one cloud to another or flashes down to the water.

While in Puntarenas, it started to rain about eleven p.m. It was a real tropical rain. We ducked for cover and as we were loading into small box cars, the crew that was handling the cargo and I climbed into the nearest one and there I sat: in a box car on a pier, in the dead of night, with rain pouring down and eight Central American natives huddled in beside me for an hour. I couldn't help thinking that it's a funny old world after all.

I have skipped around a good deal, but there has been so much going on that is different and at times I have been so tired when things were happening that it is like trying to recall a dream.

I had a good rest last nite and am feeling fine today.

I send my love to all – Donnabeth and Bill and May and

---

48 Mar. 31, 1931 earthquake and fire destroyed much of the city and killed 2,000 persons.

Don and You. Say hello to anyone that you think would like me
to say hello to them.

> *Lots of love, mother dear, and I think Don is too darn good*
> *the way he got that money for me.*

Love Stan.

We sailed through the Canal to Cuba and up to New York. We always stopped in Cuba. It seems to me that we took a lot of rope out of Cuba to the States but I don't remember what we carried there. Possibly it was fruit from California around to Havana. We used to carry a lot of fruit, canned fruit.

When we stopped in Havana, we often went uptown and had a drink because we had a set sailing schedule. One time we docked in Havana and when we finished the hatches, about five o'clock, we left the ship. They figured for sailing at eight o'clock, so I went uptown for a drink and a look around. I went into a big bar there that was a popular place and I sat on a stool and ordered a drink. While I was waiting for the drink a taxi driver came up to me and he said, *"¡Venido, venido, venido!"* – "Come, come, come!"

So I got in his cab and he drove like the devil down to the dock. I couldn't understand it, but somehow he knew that we were sailing. He rushed me onto the dock and they were just pulling the anchor up. So I walked over and grabbed the gangway and they pulled it up, and I went aboard just like I was working on the dock. No one ever got wise to the fact that I was uptown. I never saw the guy again, but he sure saved my hide. He knew I was remiss and he just grabbed me and "Come on, come on," and took me, or otherwise I would have been left in Havana, of all places, and they would have shipped me back to the States. That was the closest I ever came to being left behind.

1931, June 5, Friday
Dearest Mom,

> *Your letter reached me in Havana. It was quite a surprise and I was sure tickled when I got it. You are always thinking of nice things tho.*

> *Until we left Cristobal we had been working pretty hard but since then things have been much easier.*

> *The trip down was only one thing – work. However, we had one evening in Panama and spent most of it riding around seeing what we could. Some place too.*

But the port of ports is Havana!

I could live in Havana for a long while without wanting to move. It is a beautiful place.

From the sea it looks to be about the size of San Francisco, but still a little smaller than that. There are not nearly so many tall buildings but I believe that you would be surprised at Havana today.

It has all the charm of Panama – the narrow streets, the old buildings – that old world atmosphere – but it is not nearly so dirty, and life seems to be pitched at a different tempo that makes Havana so much more alive.

The three other checkers and I finished work at five o'clock when we were in Havana. We cleaned up and went ashore and hired a car. We drove around the town seeing the sights for an hour and then stopped for dinner. The drive was great.

We had a nice dinner at a café on the plaza across from the Capitol building. We sat under an awning out in front and watched the day turn to nite as we ate.

While we were eating, two little Spanish girls came up to us and in spite of our protests, pinned a rose on our coats. They were so cute – about 6 or 7 yrs. old – we had to pay them or they would not go away. We paid. I don't think I was ever "taken in" as neatly as they took me, but I sure had to laugh at the high-powered salesmanship.

After supper, we took a walk around town, that is the center of it, and strolled down the "prado," I think that's what it's called. It is a long walk down the center of a wide street. The walk is made of marble and there are stone benches on either side where you may sit and rest and watch the flood of people slowly walking up and down. The walk is shaded by a row of trees down each side. It is very beautiful and is also quite the place to see or be seen. At least so it seems.

On our trip around the town on foot, we were stopped many times by men telling us about a particularly fine house with all young girls in it. However, since we weren't interested, I don't know what kind of places they really were.

Some of them, I hear from the fellows, are pretty fancy places. Twice we were stopped by women and one of them sure tried hard to sell us on the idea. We went back to the boat at 9:30 as she sailed at ten. It was a delightful trip ashore and I had a lot of fun. We make New York tomorrow about noon.

The trip from Puerto Colombia to Havana was wonderful. The water was smooth and at night the moonlight on the water

*and the soft night air combined to make a night for romance.
But, woe is me, I had no woman.*

*The traffic in these waters is much heavier and at times we
see as many as five or six boats around us at a time.*

*It is cool in the harbor and I could stand it a little warmer. I
am getting used to the heat and this cool weather is uncomfortable. Oh well!*

Lots of love to all.
Your loving son
Stan.

In 1931, there were quite a number of cars in Havana, but they
were old cars, and there was a lot of poverty in the town. Much of
the town was fairly middle class, however, and you could take a walk
at night, walk around the center of town and it wasn't a bad place to
be. It was kinda nice.

There was a rum joint across the bay from where we used to
dock. It was the Bacardi place and I remember going out there and
having a drink of rum. They had a nice big bar there, and when the
ship came in maybe a hundred people went out there and drank their
rum. But rum was not too good a drink in those days. A lot of people
liked it because it was better than the whiskey they were getting
ashore. It was real stuff, and whiskey could be anything. They sold a
lot of rum to the passengers who took it aboard and tried to smuggle
it into the States because it was Prohibition.

Havana was a frequent tourist stop. The roads were paved and
business was good. It was a popular port and a bustling city, then it
just went to hell when Castro came. But it was awfully good in those
days.

I went by the cemetery and there was a big pile of bones, I remember. They would put somebody in the cemetery for a while. And
if the family didn't keep up the payments, and nobody did, well then
they dug up the bones and put them on the pile. There was a big pile,
higher than this room. It was all people's bones.

1931, June 22, Balboa
Dearest Mom,

*We worked up until sailing time in N.Y., after 12:00 noon, a
little over thirty hours. I was pretty tired but felt no ill effects
from the loss of sleep.*

Well, we are at sea today, and very much at sea, too. Last

151

*night we ran into some large swells and today we have a little
wind to go with them. The result is that this old tub is rolling
and rocking plenty.*

*I am trying to write this while sitting on my bunk and using
a card table for a desk. I have to keep one leg braced to keep me
from falling out onto the deck and the other leg to hook onto a
leg of the table to keep it before me. Such a life!*

*We have been taking it easy yesterday and today, but to-
morrow we make Cartagena [Colombia] where we have a good
deal of cargo to discharge and where we will likely pick up
about 10,000 bags of coffee. We have the space on board for
that but may not get that many.*

*The next day we make Puerto Colombia. Then on to the
Canal arriving in Cristobal, Saturday, where I will expect a
letter from you. I sure hope it's there.*

*The passengers are not much in evidence today, for some
reason. There were several that tried to come up for lunch, but I
hear changed their minds upon entering the dining salon or
shortly thereafter.*

There goes some Chinese music next door! Those boys seem

Canal Zone, Cristobal street scene, 1933.

to never tire of it. I'm quite different tho. They play Mahjong every nite but, as it is for money and strictly a Chinese affair, I haven't been able to learn how the real Mahjong is played.

In our leisure time we play a lot of bridge, but since there are no experts on board, I doubt if my game has improved. How is your contract coming? I hope you enjoy it as much as ever.

Well, dearest, we are on our way to Cristobal and will arrive during the nite. In Puerto Colombia, we had two hours off for lunch and took advantage of the time to go ashore and look around.

Puerto Colombia is the shipping point for the town of Barranquilla, which is some twenty miles from there. The town of Barranquilla is the commercial center for the district and also it is located at a point in the river that contacts the interior of Colombia. The coffee is shipped down to Barranquilla and there by rail down to Puerto Colombia.

The port itself is not much of a place. In fact, it is one of the worst "holes" I have ever seen. There must be about a thousand houses – those little mud places with thatched roofs, painted a faded blue or pink.

There are no sidewalks and the streets are little narrow affairs all cut away from the rain. In fact, they are more like ditches than streets and, as there are no vehicles in the town, there is no need to improve the streets.

There are plenty of dogs and pigs and donkeys and smells and that's about all. No beautiful buildings of any kind but a neat stone church that is very poorly decorated. It has a few religious prints on the walls and wooden benches and some gingerbread around the alter, which is made of wood – a very poor place indeed.

We spent an hour walking around and it was very interesting, but to be stuck there for more that that would be hell.

In Cartagena we did not get ashore but we could see all the old landmarks of the places that played such an important part in the days of the Spanish Main. The old fort and the hill behind the town etc. are all there.

Well, I could write more but have to go back to work now. I am feeling fine and dandy and everything is coming along O.K. Again I hope this finds you well and happy. I have been behaving myself so don't worry about me. Also, I am being careful of my health and limbs which are okeh.

Again I send my love to all and to you, my dearest Mom.

Stan.

When we sailed out of San Francisco, we stopped in Manzanillo, Mexico; Champerico, Guatemala; Amapala, Honduras; La Libertad, El Salvador; and Carrillo and Puntarenas, Costa Rica. We stopped almost every day so we worked like the devil going down. We were busy doing bookwork between ports, making lists for every port we went into. We made books to discharge the cargo and got all the papers ready for the customs people. Then we made out a list and checked it off as the cargo was discharged. We checked in the cargo if we got any, and made up a manifest, so that when we got to Panama, we gave the government a list of all the cargo that was on board ship. That was quite a job. We used to work hard.

1931, August 1
Dearest Mom —
  Well how are you? I hope that this finds you well and in good spirits.
  How are your insides? I hope they are not bothering you.
  You know, I thought we were taking a light load out with us, but by the time we left L.A. we had a full cargo aboard and picked up 5000 bags of garbanzos (a sort of bean) at Mazatlán.
  We have had some tough times in some of the ports. Lots of work.
  I haven't written before because when I had the time I wasn't feeling like myself. It wasn't until we started in on the real work that I felt like anything. Wasn't sick but felt cross and out of sorts. Thinking too much I guess. However, I feel fine and dandy now.
  We are a day out of Panama. Will mail this from Cristobal and then I can answer any letters that are waiting there for me.
  While in San Jose de Guatamala we had to work for twenty-two hours.
  About midnight it started to rain so we had to cover up the hatch. We then started in on a deck cargo of lumber and worked it for about three hours in the rain. I was very uncomfortable standing there all the time counting the boards as they made up the slings.
  We finished working our cargo about five a.m. and then steamed down to Acajutla [El Salvador], which is about three hours run. We were lucky there. It was too rough to work, so we lay at anchor all day without working. We made up our sleep and missed what would have been a hard shift coming so soon after our long one the port before.

Morro Castle, Havana, Cuba.

While in Corinto [Nicaragua]we were treated to a young typhoon that came down on us from out of a clear sky. It was just like a cloud blowing over the place and drenching everything. The wind blew with an awful force and the rain was so thick as to make it impossible to see clearly one end of the ship from the other end.

1931, August 10
My dearest Mom,
    Tho there is nothing to write about I have decided to drop you a line. I have been thinking about you a good deal and since I can't be with you I will have to resort to my rusty – I mean trusty – pen.
    This morning we sighted the tip end of Cuba and will dock in Havana tomorrow where I sure hope to hear news of you. As you know, your dandy letter reached me in Cristobal. I want to thank you again for taking care of things for me.
    The sea is beautiful thru here. The deep blue water, which is of a shade that is impossible to describe, stretches out on all sides. It is calm with a gentle breeze blowing across our decks.
    I stood in the very bow of the ship looking out over this beautiful sea as far as the eye could reach and over the horizon where the white and grey clouds seem to rest on the very water's edge. They are all that divide the beautiful blue dome above from the darker but no less beautiful water.

*The calm tranquility of the scene – only broken by the flying
fish that now and then darted up in front of the bow and sailed
along the top of the water for a way only to dart back down
with a tiny splash – makes one think more of the spiritual side
and lifts one out of the everlasting sameness of life.*

*The very air is so good that it seems hard to fill your lungs
deeply enough.*

*Later this evening I will again go forward and watch the
sunset. If it is like the one last evening it will be beyond description, and it will be. The most gifted pen could not do justice to
the sunsets in these southern waters. I will not try but you must
recall them: each surpassing the last.*

*Perhaps there is a lesson in these very sunsets. Why recall
the past when the present is so beautiful. The past is gone. Today is real.*

I remember one trip I sailed out of Cristobal, which is on the Atlantic side of the Canal, and I got something like the flu, knocked me
cold. The doctor gave me oil to drink, but I was pretty sick for a couple of days. Another time I had heatstroke, and that was pretty rough,
too.

On the *Colombia* there were five checkers, and we worked the
holds when we got into port.[49] I checked the time of loading the hold
and watched everything that went in and out of it, sort of like a policeman. I wore a cap like the officers with a gold band on it. I wasn't
getting any money but I was a big shot. We only got $50 a month for
that kind of a job. It wasn't too good, but it was something.

On the ship we had a little cabin for the checkers. The room was
maybe seven feet wide and long, and the five of us were caged up in
there. It was in a terrible place right next to the engine room, and it
was hot with practically no air in there. We had one little porthole and
when the weather got heavy and the ship was loaded, we had to close
the porthole because the water would wash in. It was just hot, stink-

---

49 Cargo in old freighters was carried in holds - cavernous spaces inside the hull of the
ship, covered with large waterproof hatches in the deck. Masts and booms (cranes) over
the holds allowed the ship to load and unload itself in primitive port facilities. All cargo –
whether bags of coffee, crated goods, etc. – was lifted up and lowered into the holds, one
piece at a time, except for bulk cargos like grain, and ores, which could be loaded directly
into the holds by conveyor belt or bucket crane.

ing hot. There we were down in the tropics with all the heat from the engines, and it was a hell of a place.

I drifted off thinking of happier days spent at Chili Bean Ranch:

Those winter evenings spent before the roaring stove in that homely little cabin in the mountains: reading by candle light, the smell of the wood, the candle wax dripping down the bottle that served as a holder, the shadows on the wall, the patter of rain falling on the roof, the sound of the branches scraping on the shingles. Yes, I can close my eyes and see it all, smell it all, hear it all again. Now I am sweltering in the the heat, the thudding, pounding, banging noise of engines right below, the hissing of steam, the reek of oil, the clang of bells and dripping hot evenings . . .

When we got to New York, we used to stay there from three days to the better part of a week. The *Colombia* was a passenger ship carrying about 125 passengers. In those days, we loaded the ship up with cargo and then let the passengers aboard on the sailing date.

1931, August 18
Dearest of Moms,
 Well here I am in New York.
 This morning I wrote the following letter to you while sitting on top of a barge out in East River. I was waiting for them to unload the damn thing, so made good use of the time.
 Yesterday we finished discharging about four in the afternoon. I went out to the end of the dock and called up "Chickie." I got in touch with him and he asked me to run out and see him. I did, and he is the nicest sort of a person. A real dear. I'll tell you what I can about him.
 He is in the Ford dealer game. In fact sold more cars in N.Y. during 1930-31 season than any of his competitors. For this little accomplishment he has two fine loving cups donated by Henry.
 The present business was founded by Chick and Elliot some four years ago, as I figure it. As you see they have done wonderfully well. When Chick came into the salesroom, I knew the minute I saw him that it was he. He also recognized me and greeted me most heartily. It seemed good to see him, too.
 Thirteen years in the big city have not changed him a great deal. He is not a hard type of man at all. He still has that charming English manner tho, of course, it is not quite so decidedly

English. He is just a natural sort of person. In business he is known as "Chick" and he tells me that that has helped him a great deal in business.

The men working for him seem to like him so much. I don't blame them a bit because the little I saw of him in his office, he impressed me as being a very good executive.

He is very much wrapped up in his work. He likes it and his people like him. All of which has helped him along the road to success. Which road he is traveling in high [gear], taking enough time out to enjoy a little golf and to be with his wife and two fine boys as much as possible.

He is the same lovable chap that you knew thirteen years ago [in Jamaica]. A little heavier, yes! but still the same. He always will be a young person tho he lives to be a hundred.

We went out to Chick's bungalow out on Long Island, where I met his wife. He introduced me as the brother of the girl he almost married. She is a lovely girl; good looking with lovely coloring; not too heavy but nicely upholstered.

Well, we had supper and a young girl came in that lives nearby. She was about 19 or so – a petite little thing with brown hair and eyes. Later, a young couple dropped in and the six of us went out swimming at a wonderful beach. After our swim, we went to a very nice place and danced and ate. Had a most dandy time. Besides the music they had an entertainer who was very clever, sang naughty songs – not too naughty – but very funny. It was great.

We were late getting into this man's town, but as there is little coffee, we didn't have much work while discharging, as the coffee is the only thing we check out here.

We started to load today and will go right after it tomorrow morn until late in the night.

Saturday night, the night we arrived, the new checker and I took the salad maker ashore and went to the Roxy Theater. Saw "Bad Girl" which was entertaining.

The stage show was very beautiful. They gave a few selections from "Samson and Delilah." The scene where Samson pulls down the pillars was very well done – looked almost real. The three of us took a bus ride down Fifth Avenue out past Grant's Tomb. The air felt great and, as it was in the late afternoon, we got back just in time for dinner.

As I sat writing this letter this morning, a Goodyear Blimp flew overhead and out over Manhattan, which is just across the river. We don't see those things as often in the west as they do here. They look very nice and graceful like a sausage flying around over the tops of skyscrapers.

Sunday, John and I went out to Coney Island. It was a lovely day and we had a good time just looking around. It reminded me of what the old Irishman said on the job at La Honda, "A popcorn ball in one hand and a ice cream cone in the other, looking on and watching the crowd have a good time."

Well, it was somewhat like that but we went out to watch the crowd and enjoyed the sights.

Later, we saw George Bancroft in "Ladies Love Brutes." A good show.

We then got something to eat and, as it was early, took in another show, "The Miracle Woman." It was a very good play and the acting was far above the average.

I was interrupted a while ago to chip in on a quart of ice cream with three of the fellows. Now I am back to you.

I miss you so much, dearest, and do so hope you are taking care of your dear self.

It will be dandy to be home again, I can tell you.

Since coming to New York, I have felt like a different person. With the exception of a few days, I felt just fed up with the whole thing. The old ship just kind of got me down. Here I have shaken the kinks out of myself and feel all together different. Besides, on the home voyage I have something to look forward to at the end of the run, and that is you.

I'll say goodnight and send my love to all – May God keep you.

Your loving son.

August 19th

We will work late tonight and sail tomorrow noon.

Am sending some pictures that I had taken out at Coney Island. What do you think of them? Have enjoyed this trip to N.Y. and can see how some people can enjoy living here.

Have a few minutes more so will tell you about seeing a ship bombed. It was an old hull that the government towed out to sea and dropped bombs on. We watched it for a half hour and it was quite some sight. This all happened a day out from N.Y. coming in.

Well, time passes and the Chinese are making an awful din next door so it is hard to think.

Again I send my love,
Stan

1931, August 31st, Balboa, Panama
My dearest Mom,

I received your cable and was quite surprised to get it too. Very glad to hear from you and to know you are well.

We left N.Y. with a light load, most of it for Puerto Colombia and Cartagena. We worked hard in those ports and expected to load a little in the Zone and have a nice easy time of it on the way home. Well, it was a great deal different when we got here. We have almost a full load of freight and have a great deal more booked at some of the other ports.

We will also make Amapala, Honduras, and La Unión, El Salvador, both extra ports. From the looks of things, we will probably be two days late getting home. That's two days less in S.F. as the ship has to sail on time or as soon after as possible.

We have a lot of office work to get up for the cargo taken on here, and it looks like a good workout all the way home. Such is life on the high seas.

I think of you very, very often, and don't like to be away for so long a stretch.

How are "Sister" and all of her's? How are Mabel and her beau "V." getting along? I hope for the best. Say hello to Don and give the kids a kiss for me.

Please take care of yourself, honey.
All my love, Stan.

Chapter 7: Shipwreck of the *Colombia*

WHAM! PAIN SHOT THROUGH MY SHOULDER as I awoke to find myself thrown against the bulkhead next to my bunk. Shouts came from the guys in the other bunks:

"What was that?"

"Holy smoke! I think we've run aground!"

"Let's get outta here!"

I knew at that moment that we were shipwrecked. Fortunately we had the porthole closed because there was water rushing, and I could feel the spray of water and foam washing against the side of the ship. I could hear the hull scraping the rocks underneath us, as it bounded and rebounded seven times before it settled down on the ocean floor. One of the fellows had a light on so I looked at the clock. It was 12:20 a.m.

The ship started to lay over immediately as I climbed out of my bunk. The five of us were all scrambling out of the place, bumping into each other in that tiny cabin. I just grabbed a hat and put it on and rushed out the door. The hallway was fast filling with crewmen.

I ran to the ladder just aft of our cabin and climbed up to the deck above. It was right under the poop deck aft, and there I ran into the steerage passengers who were trying to get out too. There might have been 50 of them from Mexico and Central America. We had picked them up just the day before in Mazatlán, and they were headed back to China. I told them to wait for me because I knew how to open the door and they didn't.

So I rushed up another deck to the hatchway and unbolted the doors, which were all closed up because of the storm. We finally got the bulkhead doors open and the Chinese all rushed up on deck. They were right behind me as I headed over to the lifeboats on the port side. There weren't many boats, only eight of them. We got the guys from steerage spread around in the boats and we started putting the boats over.

I took charge of my lifeboat, and waited until one of the mates who was directing, told us to lower the boat, Number 6 I think it was. So we lowered it down to the water and it hit the water just right and just sailed out, away from the ship. The water wasn't particularly rough. We weren't in any danger. We just rowed out of the way, got out to sea and waited till morning.

We had a couple of sailors come along and they took charge of the boat from there. I think we had about 20 people in our boat, al-

Colombia sinking off Cape Tosca, Mexico, Sept. 13, 1931, taken by Stan.

though some boats had as many as 40. It wasn't real organized as to who went in which boat. We were aft and the people who were aft came in our boat, while the passengers went in the boats up forward. There were plenty of lifeboats for everybody, and by one-thirty in the morning, everybody was off the *Colombia* and into the lifeboats.

We were tossed about in the water for two hours until the seas began to calm. We were pretty close in to shore, but we couldn't land the lifeboats because the waves were breaking and would have wrecked us, so we had to pull out to sea. You don't go near shore when you're in a lifeboat . . . the rocks and all. We sailed around that night as the sea calmed a good deal, and pretty soon, about four o'clock in the morning, we saw a ship coming. Then we knew were saved.

After floating for more than five hours in lifeboats, all were taken aboard by the steamer *San Mateo*, a freighter of the United Fruit Company. Actually I was one of the first men taken aboard after the women and children had been lifted from the other lifeboats. We climbed aboard that ship and we just let the boat go. By six o'clock the last of the eight boats had been reached and its passengers were aboard the fruit liner. The ship was loaded with bananas and we had all the bananas we wanted to eat.

The *Colombia* was way over on her side, and it eventually went down. So we left the *Colombia* where she had driven her prow into the jagged trap of rocks known as Cape Tosca at the southwest tip of the small but rugged Santa Margarita Island, 150 miles north of the tip of Baja California. The *San Mateo* sailed up the coast a ways until nightfall and we put into Magdalena Bay. There was a long beach with nobody on shore. So the ship anchored in the bay and we went ashore and camped in the little cove overnight.

We were to be transferred to her northbound sister ship, the *La Perla*. The *San Mateo* left in the morning, and all day we lay in Magdalena Bay. About 8 p.m. the *La Perla* arrived. It picked us all up and took us north to San Diego. We were glad to be back in the U.S.A.

In San Diego we were picked up by the steamship *H.F. Alexander*. It was a big passenger ship and very fast in those days and it was working on the coast at that time. It sailed from San Diego to San Pedro where it stopped to pick up people, and that night it sailed up to San Francisco.

1931, Monday Sept. 14.
on United Fruit Company stationery
Dearest Mom,
It is now 8:20 p.m. and we have just left the tug "Peacock" that stopped to pick up our captain and mate and chief engineer. Our next stop is Los Angeles where I will mail this to let you know when and how I will be home. Hope you get it in time to be of use in locating me.
Well I am fine and dandy. Have had an experience that had all the thrills that one can imagine in a shipwreck but thank God we were spared any of the horrors.

Everyone lost everything in the way of worldly possessions but consider themselves lucky to have a whole hide – as indeed we are. Think of it! 234 persons taking to the boats in pitch-darkness and not so much as a smashed finger in the lot.
When we left her she was listed over better than thirty degrees but we got all the boats off without accident. I will be seeing you very soon but not too soon for me.

Stan hugging his mother.

My mother came down with the family to see me when the ship came in to San Francisco. She was all dressed up and a newspaper man took a picture of me hugging my mother on the dock. The newspaper clipping said, "Mrs. D. K. Dungan of San Carlos was among the happiest when she greeted her son, Stanley Hulse, checker on the ship." They drove me home hanging on every word as I told them about the shipwreck.

I sold a photograph that I had taken

of the sinking ship, to the *Los Angeles Times*. They paid me $10 for the film and were happy to have the picture.

Then we were laid off work. They only paid us until the time the ship had sunk. So we just got a petty amount of pay, and we didn't get any compensation for clothes or anything. So I stayed at my mother's awhile.

Panama Mail Steamship Company

September 13, 1931

Mr. Standish C. Hulse
Check Clerk
SS COLOMBIA

Dear Sir:

As a matter of record, on account of the SS COLOMBIA being lost, you are detached as Check Clerk without pay or board money, effective with the close of business this date.

Very truly yours

[signature]

GENERAL MANAGER

I was a little hungry that time, because I didn't have any money. I went to San Francisco looking for work down at the docks. I remember eating peanuts one time for lunch, a penny's worth. You could get quite a lot of peanuts for a penny.

Chapter 8. Looking for Work, again

IN OCTOBER, I WAS LOOKING for work again. I went down to Monterey where I got in touch with an old friend, and I was able to stay with him in Pacific Grove for a while. It was a comfortable little place and we had some pleasant evenings playing cards and visiting.

Jobs were a thing of the past and no one seemed to want my services or anyone else's. Once in a while I'd hear about a job and look into it, but nothing ever seemed to pan out.

I went down to Hollister, having heard about a job down there, but nothing materialized there either.

Between looking for jobs, I managed to find a party now and then. Two young ladies showed me around the valley and it was a beautiful ride. Then I took them both to a dance in San Juan Bautista and we had a dandy time. I danced until 2 a.m. without missing a single dance.

John and I and another fellow went to the Pinnacles and that was very interesting. We went through deep caves and explored them for a long while. We climbed up to the top of the canyon and then climbed some of the pinnacles themselves. We had a lot of fun, but came down pretty tired.

1932, February 19, Thursday from Hollister
Dearest Mom,

I arrived in this fair city just before five o'clock after making the trip in five jumps. One to just a block past the house in S.J., then another to a point on the Monterey Road [in San Jose] about five miles out of town; next in an old rattle-trap of a car, that would not go over twenty miles-an-hour, as far as Morgan Hill; then another lift, and a better one, to the junction at San Juan; and then on into town.

I found John and we went to the little house that he has rented. It is located in the rear of another house in which lives the landlord. It is a nice little place of two rooms. It also has a shower and lavatory. In the largest room, which serves as a living room, is a gas stove and a neat little sink and here is where we do our cooking. The other room is the bedroom.

The first night, John and I and the Managing Editor of the Free Lance, the paper that John is on, and his wife went to a dance. We were to act as judges, as the affair was a masked one. Had a good time and met some rather nice people.

Saw Roy Emerson yesterday and went up to the local Elks Club with him last night. Met some of the better citizens there and liked many of them very much.

I have found nothing in the way of a job to date but have been keeping an eye out for anything that may come along and have several people doing the same for me. I have also picked up a few things about news work that I didn't know before.

You may send my mail General Delivery at present, as John has his sent to the paper.

Will say good night to you and send my love.
Your son
Stan.

A month later, I got a letter from John Bruce that convinced me to give Hollister another try.

standish, me biy:
    what the heck, sir! why u no write and let Hollister know you arrived home safely? the female population of this county seat is forlorn. damsels plod down the street with humped shoulders and far-away looks in their eyes, as if they're looking 'way out san benito st. to the bolsa road corner, waitin' for the sailor lad to plod wearily 'round the bend with seaman's bag o'er shoulder.
    here's the new dope: providing you haven't landed the elusive and furtive job as yet. charlie sutton comes through with a spellbinder. he announces that Pewett, boss on the pinnacles trail job, plans to take on two more men by first of the month. and charlie, he says he ask about puttin' on you and the boss, he says o.k. so where there's a promise, there's still hope . . . charlie thinks it's quite sure.....
    the wee hoose is nae the same since ye left, laddie... tha porridge is all burnt, mind ye.... sae i'll be hopin' tae see ye...
                    hello to everyone
                    ~ Spider

So I went back down to Hollister:

1932, March 30, Hollister
Dearest Mom,
    Arrived in Hollister none the worse for wear. Had a nice ride (rides) all the way down. The orchards and fields were beautiful. They seem more so each year, but I suppose it's that my capacity for appreciation increases and not the blossoms themselves.
    The wildflowers, too, seem more beautiful as they tint the otherwise green fields and hills with their lovely color. The white-blossomed orchards with their green and yellow carpets look like a setting in fairy land. The air --- but you know what it is like. I am wandering, so to get back . . .
    The pinnacles job is still up in the air (that's where pinnacles usually are) and so am I.
    To pass the time to best advantage, I spent a few hours of the afternoon out soliciting printing jobs for the printing department. Sold two orders for cards and received the staggering sum of 70 cents, not dollars, for my efforts in

commissions. The results have spurred me on to greater
endeavors and I will canvass the town further tomorrow.
Spent the morning trying to sell some more printing matter
and have made three dollars up until now when I have stopped
to eat lunch.
I send my love to you always,
Stan

I canvassed the town getting orders for printing and got some forty-odd dollars worth, but as I had covered the town, the job gave out almost before I had added anything to my capital. I was working on a ten percent commission, so it didn't amount to much.

Many times I didn't have any money. But very fortunately, Don (Duge[50]) had a job and he kept the job all through the Depression. Whenever I was broke, flat broke, I went home and my mother gave me a dollar or two dollars, something like that. And, boy, I had money. But I was lucky, Duge was lucky, my mother was lucky. We didn't have any money, but we had luck.

After Hollister, I went back to my mother's place and it was there that I got a call to go to San Francisco in May 1932. The boss called and said if I was home, I could go out as the ship was going out that afternoon. So I just hopped on a bus and away I went.

That was the SS *Santa Elisa* and it sailed down the coast, through the Canal and around to New York. I was on that ship for about a year.

Chapter 9. SS *Santa Elisa*

IN MAY 1932, I FINALLY GOT A JOB – as a checker on the SS *Santa Elisa*, with a salary of $45.00 per month. We sailed out of San Francisco, through the Panama Canal and around to New York and Philly. The first time I saw the "Big Ditch" I was very impressed. The "Big Ditch," the Canal, is certainly a wonderful piece of work and a monument to its builders that is probably unsurpassed in all history. The more often I passed through it, the more wonderful the accomplishment seemed. And to think that there were forty or more feet

---

50 Pronounced "Doog"

that we couldn't see under the water!

The interior of Panama was most beautiful. Sometimes it was exceedingly hot, but in November it was cool and comfortable. The trees were in full bloom with their vivid red blossoms and it was lovely. Coming through the Canal one day I got into a conversation with a big coal black nigger who I knew had come from Jamaica after hearing him speak. He had that genteel charm that only the Jamaicans have, and when I told him that I too had been there as a child he just puffed up and smiled in such a way that you would have thought that he was talking to the King himself. Those fellows are so proud of their little island, to have someone say that they found it beautiful is just the same as personal flattery. I left him a while ago thinking of the ships sailing in and out of Port Royal and of the day that he will be aboard one of the incoming ones – if he wins in the Panama lottery, that is. It took me back to the time I spent in Jamaica as a kid with Mom, Jane, Mabel and Norman. But that was another story.

My job as checker wasn't too hard most of the time, though some days it was slow and tiring. One day I worked for 16 hours checking copper. That was a long day.

On my first trip down the coast, I made one mistake. That was a bad one. I gave a couple of sacks of flour to San Jose that were for La Libertad. When I wrote Mom about it she wrote back, "Two sacks of flour dropped off at the wrong place should not wreck the Company even in this depression. If that is the only mistake you make, I shouldn't be surprised if you were made Admiral or some such next voyage."

But nothing more was said about it, and by November, I was promoted to boss checker. I had two new fellows working under me and had to break them in. They were as green as grass, but I figured that under my guiding hand, at least one of them would turn out to be worth his salt. It was new for me to be supervising someone else, and it put me just a step down from being a freight clerk. The new position had some responsibility attached to it, which was just what I had been looking for.

Most of the time the work went along as smooth as silk and we had a good deal of time to ourselves. We all took a hand in whatever there was to be done and, though I got most of the hectograph work, things were much more pleasant than on the *Colombia*. Winter was coffee season and that kept us pretty busy. On the way down from

Grace Line's brochure for the new "*Santa*" Ships

Los Angeles, we made eight ports before Balboa and picked up a good load of coffee.

Shipboard life was pretty good. The food was the best that money could buy in those parts. We had chicken twice a week and duck at least once. There was always something on the menu that tasted good. We even had ice cream and cake and watermelon for dessert. It sure helped the job to eat like we did.

The summer was awfully hot, but the heat seldom bothered me. It did make some of the passengers uncomfortable, but if one doesn't like the heat, he should stay out of the tropics. On the other hand, it could be quite cold in New York and Philly, especially after having just travelled through the tropics.

When we arrived at the harbor in New York that November, it was grey and overcast. It looked like it would snow but it didn't. There was a dull grey fog-like atmosphere and a low sky that made the foot of Manhattan look ghost-like in the distance. The whole thing was a study in grey and it was beautiful. The air was crisp and cold but not that dull cold that freezes the very marrow of your bones. It was quite nice out, though standing out on the dock all day checking, the air lost some of its charm and the warm air of the interior of the ship was pleasant to contemplate.

It was nice having a few passengers aboard. There was a very nice young lady on one trip that it was my pleasure to talk to several evenings after the ship's company had retired. Of course, I had to be very careful who saw me talking to her, so the whole affair had to be carried on with the utmost caution. The night watchman was a good scout and by telling him in advance where I would be, he failed to get around to that spot. All of which was very romantic.

When we arrived in Punteranes, it was closed to the ship's crew, so I was fortunate to get ashore. The Counsel was a Costa Rican and a very nice old fellow. We finished up the papers and then went over to a *cantina* and wet down relations with a whisky and soda, which I paid for. After the drink, I asked how much that would be and was informed that it would cost me $4.75. Well, I thought that I was stuck for sure, but when I took out an American dollar bill, the waiter grabbed it and started to count out a handful of change. He gave me almost two dollars Costa Rican in change, which sounds like a lot but is worth about thirty-five cents. Well, when I got back to the ship, I told the purser that I had bought the old gent a drink, so he put it on the expense account and gave me the price of the drink. Pretty nice fellow.

I met a fellow named Eldon Sterling on the *Colombia* and he sailed on the *Santa Elisa* as well. He was about five years younger than I and at first I had trouble with him, but we came to understand each other. He was a darn good kid and he treated me white while I was aboard the *Santa Elisa*. We became friends and palled around together when we were in New York and Philly.

When we got to New York that August, Sterling and I had a dandy time in the big city and enjoyed our stay at the New Yorker. It was hot and we took so many baths that we both looked a bit pale when it came time to leave. It was my first real bath in months.

I enjoyed the layovers in New York, but I wouldn't live in that town for a lot unless that lot came awfully easy. I didn't like the place. "Thems that like it can have it." I think there's something wrong with anyone who would give up California for New York City.

Another time when we were in New York, I went uptown with Bob, a San Carlos boy, and we shopped around for a while looking for a suit for me. We found one all right and then looked up a couple of male passengers at the Commodore Hotel and had supper with them. They all went to the fight (Walker-smelling) and I went up to the Hotel Astor to meet Sterling and Hoge and our ladies at nine p.m.

The meeting successfully culminated, we took ourselves to the Hollywood Cafe, a sort of nightclub. We got there a little after ten and stayed until around three. They had a good show that was apt to shock those who are easily shocked. There were a lot of scantily attired girls and some who were attired even less. Well, we had a lot of fun dancing and watching the crowd. Jack Sharkey, heavyweight boxing champion at the time, was there and got up and took a bow as did another pug named Johnny Risco.

After the show we had to take the girls home and they lived over in Jersey. We rode on one train after another and then a taxi and at last we got them home. Then we had to find our way back, which we did at last, a little before breakfast. A bit tired, yes, but with a better knowledge of New York and its neighbor state.

One night in Colón, Sterling, Hoge and I took three of the passengers ashore to a nightclub and didn't get back until 6 a.m. – a bit tired but it was worth the candle. I got some sleep on the way through the Canal, so it worked out all right.

Sterling and I worked together a lot and got along well. The work was a bit hard, but I found it very interesting and with lots to do, the days rushed past, and most were too short. It helped to be interested in what I was doing instead of just plugging along, as I had been for the last six months.

That November, we were in New York for Thanksgiving, and I bought myself a heavy, warm overcoat for $20, as my old one looked poorly. It was a big help in that climate.

Sterling and I took in a show in the city, Eddie Cantor in *The Kid from Spain*. A lot of fast and clever cracks: "For every contented cow

Stan checking cargo on the New York waterfront

171

there must be a contented bull." It was very funny in spots.

There was also a Walt Disney cartoon that was the best thing that I had ever seen. I wished that Mom and the kids had been there to enjoy it with me. It was a Mother Goose story, all in color. The scenes were beautiful, just like the pictures in a deluxe edition and so very, very cleverly done.

First there were the two little children, a darling Dutch girl and boy. They were making their way through the woods with its weird trees and startling sounds. They were frightened and the little folk of the wood only added to their terror as they scurried past. Then the sound of music and a cautious peek into a glen. A beautiful scene was before them, a happy company of gnomes. They were all busy at a thousand and one tasks and in making merry. They entertained the children and then the witch appeared on her broom. And what a witch she was! She gave them a ride on the broom and then to the candy house. Then the capture and transformation of the children into bugs; the gnomes to the rescue and the turning of the witch into a rock. It was called *The Witch's Rock*. It had so much color, action, and beauty – it was delightful.

The air was much clearer in the evening than in the morning. Looking across the river toward Manhattan, it too looked like a fairy scene. All the harsh outlines were blotted out by the night and the millions of lights twinkling in the countless windows sparkled like jewels. The distance made everything look so small that it was hard to realize what a huge pile of stone and steel it really was. The river in the foreground, with its silvery sheen and the little boats going up and down, added to the beauty of the picture.

The last night we were in New York that trip, Sterling and I took two girls to the Grand Central Hotel for dinner and dancing. We had a dandy time and the food was delicious. It cost more than I thought it would, but it was a lovely place and we got out without having to wash the dishes.

We sailed down to Philadelphia the 23rd of November. The weather was nice when we got there and Bill and I had a lovely day out at the zoo. But it turned cold the next day. After supper it was below 26 degrees. It was too cold for Sterling, and almost too cold for me, but as it was Saturday night, I decided to go uptown to a dance. It was a long four-block walk to the streetcar line and I almost turned back. The wind was freezing cold as it swept in off the river. I got to the dance and it was a nice place, much better than the places in the west usually are with no wops and the like. I met some very nice girls and one really nice girl who was as pretty as a picture and not a bit conceited. She let me see her home on the streetcar, but she wouldn't have if I had had a car.

It was so darn cold when we got to her house that she asked me in to warm up. Her mother was sitting before the fire and we chatted for a minute and then she excused herself from the room. In a few minutes she called us into the kitchen for coffee and cake. Very likable people. Not members of the four hundred but still not common. I was surprised to find such a nice girl at a public dance. I had a date to call the following night but nothing came of that little romance. It was just as well.

I had a few romances with passengers. In Havana I took a girl ashore and we had a great time. We went to a nightclub and danced until the wee small hours. I had a lot of fun on that trip. Maybe too much, as the captain didn't like the checkers mingling with the passengers. But I liked to have my fun.

In November of 1932, the radio was buzzing with election propaganda. As Mom wrote, "The more one hears about the 'other fellow' the further away from the truth one gets. Anyhow, I am going Roosevelt and I believe Don, Hoover. So his vote cancels mine and vice versa."

Roosevelt won all right, and the Great American Public ran true to form when they elected him. I figured they had changed horses at the wrong time. "We will probably get our beer but at what price?"

There was a lot of money bet on the elections. In fact, gambling was quite popular in the '30s. One night I won $14 at poker, which made nice spending money ashore. Another time I lost my spending money, about $7, in a crap game.

Mom wrote me about one of her neighbors: "The Jack McDonalds went to the Dog Races with the Walshes and Morans, and it developed that J.M. had drawn his salary in advance and all their savings, and betting as high as 50 dollars on a race, lost every cent they had. No money for food, rent or anything. They all came back to Walshes and Mrs. W. fed the crowd, and after self-recrimination and weeping and gnashing of teeth, they all dispersed at 4 a.m."

The Depression years were a hard time, but as long as I had work on the ships, I didn't suffer. Three square meals a day and enough money for a little fun on the side. It also gave me enough to send some home at Christmas.

1932, December 10
Dearest Mom,
I am sending this little bit to help out Santa Claus. I may not get in until the last minute or even as late as the 26th. So please get the kids some little thing and something for yourself and Don. Please have a good time spending it, that is all I ask.
Love, Stan.

1932, December 21
Stan dearest – yours with inclosure came a few days ago, you were over-generous as usual – the best X'mas present in this world will be your presence — (no offense_!)
Hurry home to your always loving
Mother.

One of the things I loved about sailing was a little rough weather. Sailing out of Havana one time, I stood by the rail and watched the whitecaps racing by in an ever changing pattern. When we fell into the trough of a wave the water was on a level with the deck or, if it was a big one, it was above us. It looked like they would break and come tumbling upon us but they never did. At the last moment the ship rose up and the waves rushed astern. Looking up to the top of the wave from below, it was a sparkling whitecap and just below with the sun shining through, the solid water was a beautiful emerald green. Scenes like that were one of the compensations that sea life afforded. There is a thrill when the seas are churning about you in their fruitless effort to beat the ship back. At least I always hoped that her efforts would be fruitless.

Philadelphia was the end of the run. We emptied everything out of the ship then killed the rats and started over again. Sometimes we were there three, four or five days. We started loading in Philadelphia and then went to New York and finished up.

We got into a good storm on the way back from Philly one time. It took us thirty-six hours to make a run that ordinarily took about ten or twelve. The ship was very light because we didn't have any ballast in it and it tossed around like a shell. At one time we were listed over better than thirty degrees. I knew it was way over because I slept pretty much on the wall that night in my bunk. (If it had been the other way I would have slept on the floor.) The next day they straightened it up and we went back to New York. I felt like a real 'salt' because it didn't bother me a bit. I felt no fear or sense of danger at all. In fact, at the height of the thing, I turned in and slept like a log until ten the next morning.

We sailed to New York and finished loading, then just before sailing, the passengers came on board. I remember the passengers waving at everybody on the dock, and some of them were crying. We just looked at them and chuckled because we didn't know anybody.

There were a few quite wealthy people on the *Santa* boats, the big boats. I remember one guy, who had a lot of money, reached in his pocket and pulled out a $20 bill and gave it to me to handle his baggage. Well that was a hell of a lot of dough. Then he got to thinking about it and he said, "Say, I made a mistake. I gave you a $20 bill, I meant to give you a $2 bill." So he gave me a $2 bill instead.

Stan, about 1931.

But the sea racket wasn't what it was cracked up to be. At times I got plumb fed up with it even when everything was going all right. It wasn't the work or the crazy hours but the incomplete life one leads aboard ship that got me down. I know now why sailors get drunk and raise Hell. It's just to blow off steam. Because one's steam pressure sure goes up after a few months of that life.

I was drinking some ice water one day and the first engineer came out of the engine room looking awfully hot so I threw a glass of the ice water on him to cool him off. He didn't seem to like it as he chased me halfway round the ship before he gave up. He sure looked surprised when that water hit him and I got a good laugh. But after that he was out to get his hands on me, the big bum.

By January 1933, my time on the *Santa Elisa* had come to an end. I was sorry to leave the old ship and my many friends aboard. It had a very pleasant atmosphere that was hard to find elsewhere. Sterling and I didn't leave the ship until sailing time. Most everyone in the crew was at the rail to wave good-bye to us. It was a nice send-off. All the mates, the purser, the steward, the crew, Chinese and all, were there. Even the captain smiled fondly down at us. And away she sailed. Out to sea and out of our lives, leaving many pleasant memories that lived on long after she was laid on the scrap heap. When we left the ship it was snowing. The soft white flakes looked so pretty sifting through the air.

Chapter 10. New York City

WE ARRIVED IN NEW YORK a day late owing to the fact that we made an extra port. Sterling and I checked into a room at the Taft Hotel, right off Times Square on Seventh Avenue. Radio City was just behind us and we were in walking distance of a hundred shows. It was a lovely room with bath and twin beds that Mr. Palacios, our new purser, reserved for us after meeting us aboard the *Santa Elisa*. The night we got in I went to the new Radio City Music Hall. It was a wonderful place, beautifully finished and very grand. It was done in the modern style, not the jazz or cubistic style, but with the straight lines and solid colors that were so artistic when properly used. It was colored a rich brown, paneled with bronze.

The stage was so very large and there were nearly five hundred people on it at one time. All the acts were very good and some of the chorus was just lovely. The orchestra was made up of a hundred and ten musicians, and they played the "Orpheus Overture" so beautifully. It was well-received, and you could have heard a pin drop while the first violinist was playing. The picture, starring George Arliss in *The King's Vacation*, was not so very good, but the whole show was the biggest thing I had ever seen. It was cheap at one dollar, and I wished Mom had been there, as she would have enjoyed it as much as I did.

I saw a number of shows there: *Rasputin*, *Whistling in the Dark*, *The Sign Of The Cross*, *State Fair* with Will Rogers, and *Ben Hur*. Some were better than others, but I enjoyed the excitement of the theaters in New York.

The City, however, with its beautiful monuments to man's ingenuity, had so many places that were sordid and unlovely. I watched the little children playing in the streets in the poorer quarters – with their ragged clothes and worn-out shoes. On the shady side of the street it was so very cold, and if the wind was blowing it was too cold to play out of doors so they had to go inside. The squalor in which they lived, with never a sight of those green hills: never to know the joy of tramping about them; never to know the smell of pure mountain air perfumed with pine or redwood; not to know what it is to fish along some stream that comes tumbling down a canyon, with its fern-covered banks and little falls that splash over the moss-grown rocks. And there too, were the parents of these same children selling papers and chestnuts on the cold, wind-swept corners. While above them, shutting out the sun, stood those same monuments proclaiming us the richest country on earth. Yes, we were far from the millennium.

Everywhere there was so much that was sad and ugly, there was no use looking for it. Misery and poverty rear their ugly heads wherever civilization is to be found. My mother commented in a letter:

> *New York is so entirely man-made, the Almighty doesn't seem to be anywhere about or to have had anything to do with it – yet nothing so truly marvelous could have been conceived within man's tiny brain-cells unless they were the mediums through which came divine-infinite ideas! Getting ready for the pulpit!*
>
> *If you haven't yet been into one of the huge railroad terminals & you can make it, go into one – more wonders. Marvelous, stupendous, wonderful & then repeat, is about the only way one can describe things in N.Y.*

My sister, May, was living in Los Angeles at that time. She painted a picture of that city in a letter she wrote to me in February, 1933:

> *You are right about a big city. It's such a heartless place; and it costs so much to do the nice things one wants to do. Only a place for the "idle rich." I never saw so many poor in my life as I have here. On the streets I see such poor devils, and so many beggars. Thousands of people have migrated to Southern California and then have been unable to get work and are down and out. The County has men working 15 days a month at 40¢ an hour, and the City has men working only 10 days a month. All*

the jobs (good ones) are filled by "pull" and friends and the bum jobs don't pay living wages. Fortunately, living is cheap, which helps a lot. Up in S.F. most of the people look prosperous, but here you only see the well-dressed people driving by in limousines, never walking on the street. Sounds funny, but it makes you think the whole scheme of living is wrong somewhere, for some one person to have one hundred million and thousands, not a dollar.

It was a bit of a financial strain to live in New York, but the Company paid me two dollars a day extra and the room only came to fifteen dollars a week for the two of us. I was paid off from the old ship with forty dollars and picked up ten more in a poker game that came in very handy. With my pay, that gave me plenty of money to get by on.

I paid a visit to the dentist while I was in New York, to have a wisdom tooth pulled. I went to the Marine Hospital and expected to be just short of tortured to death. However, the young fellow who did the work was as nice as anyone could be. The first needle hurt a wee bit but after that, it was all in the mind. The sensation was not pleasant as he worked but there was really no pain. Well, he got the tooth that showed out, and then found another one hidden down below and behind the one that he first pulled. It had to come too. I swear there was a wicked gleam in his eye as he started after it. I thought that he would tear my face or head to pieces but after a while, out it came. My surprise at the lack of pain amounted to astonishment. Of course I couldn't eat on that side of my face, but it wasn't even stiff the next day and I was tickled pink about it as I expected to be half dead.

Chapter 11. SS *Santa Lucia*

IN EARLY FEBRUARY 1933, I moved onto my new ship, the SS *Santa Lucia*. It was a brand new passenger ship, much larger than either the *Colombia* or the *Santa Elisa*, and I made the maiden voyage on her. My quarters were new and clean with a nice soft bunk and hot and cold running water in the room. It was an extra fine ship, brand spanking new.

The weather was cold in New York when we sailed, with snow about a foot deep along the decks and ice on everything. It made for some interesting scenes – blocks of ice floating down the river, white streets, and snow piled high on the automobiles and roofs. Fortunately, I was dressed for it and the cold didn't bother me.

They started us out working 16 to 18 hours each day, often working until midnight or later. I slept six hours a night and then got up and went to work again. This went on for months and we were all beginning to feel the strain. At that time the *Santa Lucia* was the largest of Grace Line's new cargo ships, and it was fully loaded much of the time. It took us two days, prior to arriving in New York, to get the paperwork ready to enter there.

We stopped in Havana then went through the Canal and up to San Francisco. We arrived there on March 15 and left on the 16th, back to New York again. As we were sailing toward New York on the evening of April 4, 1933, the *Akron*, a Navy dirigible, went down in a storm not twenty miles from us, but we didn't know about it so we steamed right on. If we had picked up her message we might have been some help.

The whole history of the lighter-than-air craft was a saga of horror. We should have weighed carefully the merits of that type of craft against the possibility of continued and greater losses of life before we went on constructing them. Of course, to become discouraged by adversity and to throw away all the data and experience that those men had sacrificed their lives to furnish us with, was foolish IF the experience had advanced us far enough in the construction of dirigibles to make it reasonably certain that the future craft would be far more airworthy.

With Roosevelt's election, in November 1932, an anti-Prohibition majority in Congress, known as "the wets," passed a law that increased the amount of alcohol allowed in beverages from 0.5 percent to 3.2 percent. On April 7, 1933, the new "three-point-two" was flowing freely and in great demand. Though it was only a drop in the ocean, it helped cut down the income of the underworld in some of the large cities. But until the Prohibition amendment was repealed, the underworld still had as its source of income one of the biggest trades in the country.

The banking system at that time was a mess. People were driven into hoarding, thereby aggravating the situation because they had no confidence in the banking institutions. That lack of confidence did more to put business in the bad shape that it was in than any single factor. Of course with world trade where it was, things were bound to be bad, but I think we would have been in far better straits if it weren't for the breakdown of our financial system. Roosevelt seemed to be working toward improving the situation and I thought that if he accomplished that, he would have done more for this country than any president since Washington. Then on June 16, 1933, the Banking Act of 1933 established the Federal Deposit Insurance Corporation (FDIC), which stabilized banking and helped put the country back on its feet.

I only made two round trips on the *Santa Lucia* and was discharged that May in San Francisco. I went into the Marine Hospital in San Francisco for a couple of weeks. I was quite tired and had lost weight, so they got me straightened around, then they let me out. I went down to San Carlos and stayed with my mother for about a month before they called me up for another job.

Chapter 12. SS *Santa Cecilia*

IN JUNE 1933, I TRANSFERRED to the SS *Santa Cecilia* as Freight Clerk. It was a smaller ship and I liked it better though the work was long and hard. I started work a little after seven-thirty each morning and quit around nine at night, but often worked later.

I became more and more confident about my work, tried hard and did my job properly. There was a certain satisfaction in meeting problems and difficulties and in solving them and getting the best of them, instead of letting them get the best of you.

Though work was hard and exhausting at times, the sea sort of got into my bones. Sometimes I missed everybody at home very much and wished that I was on land somewhere. But when we were in port, I wanted to get underway again. It was a funny thing.

It was on that ship that I met Smitty, Ed Smith. He was the first mate and was in charge of the ship's cargo and deck crew. He had been sailing a long time and was about ten years my senior. He had a room next door to mine and we became pretty good friends. We sailed on a couple of ships together. Many years later, I worked for him at Lake Tahoe on quite a different venture.

About this time Duge started calling me the Ancient Mariner. He had a nickname for everyone and my many years at sea fostered mine. Up until his death, he called me "Ancient."

He and Mom always enjoyed having me home, if only for a couple of days between voyages. The kids, Donnabeth and Bill, especially looked forward to my visits and I tried to be there for fireworks on the Fourth of July, or to go around with them on Hallowe'en and, whenever possible, for Christmas.

When I was on the *Santa Cecilia*, I had a fellow who took care of my room, a China-

Stan at Two Brothers Bar, Havana, Cuba.

man. By that time I was assistant purser, and he took good care of me. He fixed my bunk for me and made it up. Of course he had to, but he used to be particularly fatherly and tell me, "Don't do this, don't do that," and things like that.

We ate with the passengers – there were 65 on each voyage – and there were some very nice people at my table. I enjoyed the enforced lengthy meal hours, as I had to sit there until we had all finished eating. An English couple at my table was very pleasant. He was a great talker and we had a lot of fun listening to him pan the Americans. He did it in such a way that it was impossible to take offense, and we had a lot of fun with him. He was on his way home after a year in China

181

Stan on the *Santa Cecilia*, 1933.

and of course told us a lot of interesting stories about China and the Chinese.

We sailed around to New York and Philadelphia. When we were in Philadelphia I used to stop at Bookbinder's Restaurant. Bookbinder's was one of the most famous restaurants in the world. If you ever go to Philadelphia, you go to Bookbinder's. They served mostly fish, and you could get all kinds of fish there. The chief engineer and the chief officer, Smitty, and I, used to go to dinner there when we went ashore, and we had the best food there. First we had six big oysters on the half shell, then a bowl of clam broth that was the real thing, then some clams, about two dozen apiece. Then we had a broiled lobster, some delicious dinner rolls and we finished up with coffee and smokes. Then back to the ship to listen to the chief engineer's radio for a while.

In February 1934, we made a stop in the Bahamas and I wrote to Mom about it:

> *Dearest,*
> *It is one of those lovely tropical days. The air is like a caress, so soft, so warm. Around us the sea lies smooth and calm and it has taken on that wonderful shade of blue that only tropical waters possess.*
> *Off to the port side, and quite near, is a little island on which stands a lighthouse. At the foot of the lighthouse are two little huts. My, but they are a forlorn sight! All alone on this little island in the middle of this vast expanse of sky and sea. Sky and sea, for here the sky and sea seem one. They seem to melt into one another somewhere on the far-off horizon.*
> *The island itself is beautiful. It is a low hill that runs down to the water in a gentle slope and is covered with the dark green*

foliage of the tropics. This ends at the glistening white sandy beach which runs out into the water. The water nearest the shore is pale green and as it gets deeper the green grows darker and darker until it is lost in the deep blue of the sea.

Far off on the horizon the billowy white clouds form all sorts of fantastic shapes and forms. If you look closely and let your imagination help you a bit, you can see all the animals of the field and some of those that we only see in our dreams and such times as this. The clouds are beautiful, piled bank on bank against the sky and the sea.

All of this is far different from the weather that we had all the way down the coast. The wind blew and blew. Not so hard but so very consistently. It would whip the spray from the waves up and across the decks and the ship would rock and bob about in little short rocks and bobs that got very tiresome. The air itself became saturated with the dampness from the flying spray and everything was kind of damp and sticky. Very unpleasant weather.

Now that we are down in the Bahamas, Cuba is our next landfall, we will sight it at dusk...

Coffee was one of the commodities that we often carried. On one trip we picked up over fifteen thousand sacks in all. That trip we had a lot of cargo going out of Los Angeles so we were very well loaded sailing down the coast. In fact, at times we had to stow flour and coffee on deck. That was very, very seldom done for had it rained, it would have been just too bad. But it didn't rain.

The captain seemed to like my work as he was very nice to me all trip. He and I went to the broker to clear and enter the ship when we got into New York, and all the time we were there he referred to me as the Purser, which was very nice of him as it gave me a little more pres-

Loading cargo off the coast of Mexico.

tige. Everything went along very smoothly while we were there except that the broker asked for the articles, which I did not have with me. He started to fly off the handle, but I told him, in as nice a way as possible, that it was not necessary for us to have the articles in order to clear coast-wise. When he stopped to think about it, he realized that that was so. From then on, everything went without a hitch. It gave me a boost with the captain when he found that I did know something about the necessary papers to enter and clear a ship.

While in New York, I went to the Metropolitan Opera House to see *Salome*. I enjoyed the old-fashioned grandeur of the place with its red walls, red ceiling, red carpets, red seats, red red everywhere, with its gilt decorations and borders and fixtures. Even the names in gilt around the stage of Wagner, Beethoven, Mozart and Gluck, Verdi and Gounod, stood out on a background of red.

> *The bright colored gowns of the ladies sitting in the orchestra were more or less evenly spaced by the black of an evening suit. While around the huge horseshoe-shaped balcony, just over their heads, was a ring of bright color, the gowns of the ladies sitting in their boxes: green, black, red, white, orange and purple. Here and there the sparkle of rhinestones or the flash of jewels. While just behind them, the white fronts of the dinner shirts and the quite frequent shining pate.[51] The squeaks, squeals and squalls from the orchestra pit suddenly cease, the seats are almost filled but for a few stragglers that are hurrying before the lights go out. Then everything in darkness except for the dim lights on the music racks in the pit. The baton is raised. It flashes down and the beautiful strains of the opening overture fill the whole place. The opera has begun.*

I sailed on the SS *Santa Cecilia* until May 1934. I enjoyed it over all, but in May they let me off in New York. They wanted me to work in the accounting department and then to go on the South America run on the East Coast. But I wanted to be closer to home, so I told them that I wanted to return to San Francisco and enter the hospital there for treatment for chronic indigestion. They granted me a leave of absence.

---

51 a bald head

Chapter 13. Cross Country Trip

I DECIDED TO DRIVE ACROSS THE COUNTRY with Mel Whitman. I had met him and his mother on the *Santa Cecilia*, and he was interested in traveling across the country with me. We went out to visit Chick, who I had met in Jamaica, and he fixed us up with a car that he said would give us no trouble. It was a Ford two-door, Model T with a back seat that you could open up. So I bought the car from him and we headed for St. Joseph, Missouri.

First we set out for Boston and, as the car had just been overhauled, we could only do 30 mph, so it was a long, slow drive. When we did get there we spent almost every minute doing Harvard and the historical spots. Such a lot to see! Beautiful trip all the way. We stayed overnight and then were on our way again at 30 mph for another 250 miles. We drove from Boston out to Williamstown, Massachusetts, and past Utica where we stopped for the night.

It was a beautiful trip thru the New England towns – the most lovely towns that I had ever seen. Williamstown was a gem! Good roads and the car ran smoothly. In order to make many miles each

Stan at the Grand Canyon, 1934.

day it meant a lot of driving, but by switching off now and then, it was not too hard a trip.

We slept a few hours in Utica, and then on again through Syracuse up to Buffalo and then down to Warren, Ohio, where John Bruce lived. We stopped for a few hours while Mel slept and John and I talked till breakfast. I pretty well convinced him that he better come back to the West Coast. He was tickled to death to see me – almost cried when I left. He was a good kid, John.

Then we were on our way again and, since we could then hold the car at 40 mph, we went on into Chicago. We arrived there tired and dirty. After a good hot bath and twelve hours sleep, we went out to the fair grounds to see the Chicago World's Fair and look the place over. We went back again to see the lights at night and then went on our way. The Fair was not so hot and I was glad that I didn't drive all the way out just to see it, for I would have been disappointed.

And so on to St. Joseph, Missouri. When we arrived there, we went looking for the house of a girl Mel had met on the ship. She was a particular friend of his during the voyage. We passed the house and went on down the street looking for the number we had been given, but we couldn't find it. So we went back to the house that had to be that number, but it was a mansion! So I said, "Well, let's go in and ask him, what the heck." So we drove in and sure enough it was the right place.

The girl was there and we met her father, I can't remember his name, and they just gave us a wonderful time. He took us out to the country club, introduced us, and said anything we wanted we could have. We could eat whatever we wanted and just sign our name. We got free lunches and everything else, because we couldn't pay for anything – he wouldn't take our money. We stayed at his house, which was a big, big place, for about two weeks.

There were parties almost every night, then we'd sleep till noon the next day. I remember one party out at his aunt's place. She had a big estate with a swimming pool and a big room where we danced. I guess there must have been about 50 couples and that was a big, big party. It was really going into another world. We had a lot to drink at those parties. Everybody drank in those days, and if you were the Gotrocks at all, you drank. By that time, we were getting worried because neither of us had any money. So we left them and came on home, and that was the last I ever saw of them.

186

After we left Saint Joseph we got caught in a storm that was so bad that we had to stop the car. The clouds were low and the rain was coming down so hard that we couldn't see where we were going. We stopped maybe 15 minutes, a half an hour, then it let up and we could see again.

We drove up to Yellowstone. We saw the falls and the hot springs and a herd of elk who were quite close to us. Then we drove down to the Grand Canyon, to the south rim. It was a big canyon, but hazy even in those days. We saw the Indian View Watchtower, which was brand new at the time, and enjoyed a nice view of the canyon from there.

We came on home, back to the West Coast, arriving in California on June 9, 1934. I think we got back with less than a dollar. We had a great time.

Chapter 14. South America on the SS *Cuzco*

IN LATE DECEMBER 1934, I SHIPPED OUT as a Freight Clerk on the SS *Cuzco* headed down the West coast for South America. It was a good crew, skippered by Captain Gilbert.

My quarters were a lot better than when I was a checker but not quite as nice as those on the *Santa Cecilia*. It was a comfortable room and I had a very nice young fellow for a room-mate, the cadet. The boat had a dandy spirit with a decided air of camaraderie about it. The skipper dropped into the office now and again for a little chat, just as if he were one of the boys – real friendly.

The tempo of the work day was so much better. There was a sensible pace to it – we just kept plugging away with none of that mad pounding and rushing that gets you very little but a case of nerves.

The steward was a nice old German though quite American in speech. He did everything he could to make things as nice as possible. The food was good and, though not as fancy as some of the passenger ships, we always had a choice of two dishes at meals – nice.

We had eight passengers and they all ate with us in the salon where there were two tables – the captain's and the chief engineer's. There was no formality about the place and the officers were a bunch of fine fellows. The purser and I worked in harmony. He was a nice young fellow my own age, and since I knew the work, there was no

187

necessity for him to boss me and we got along fine. Yes, everything was quite comfortable – nice room, warm bunk, good food and fine crew with the best skipper in the fleet on the bridge.

The ship traveled along at a nice easy speed making at her best 240 miles per day. We were loaded to the mark and the ship looked like a floating lumber yard with a million feet of lumber on deck and about as much more below decks. She was very comfortable and rode as steady as a rock with such a big deck load, though it made her a bit tender. We made the usual stops going down the coast as far as Panama. Most of the lumber was due to go off in Callao, Peru, so we planned to be there about a week.

We also had three cows on deck aft. Now and then the gentle lowing of the kine could be heard above the noise of the ship, as the breeze carried the sound over the stacks of lumber from the stern. Then too, the faint cackle of the chickens sometimes drifted foreword, as we had a crate of them aboard also.

The first week out, the purser and I worked about sixteen hours a day but after we finished up all the bulk work, we just had a few little odds and ends to clean up before we made each port. I was tired as the deuce when we made Manzanillo, but the next couple of days we were at sea, which was much more restful. The sailors had to make everything fast on deck in preparation for sailing across the Gulf of Fonseca, between El Salvador and Nicaragua, where it was very often rough. We were loaded so heavily that it wouldn't take much of a sea for us to ship a lot of water.

The morning we made Champerico, Guatemala, I got up about 5:30 as we had made port during the night and had to receive the officials at six o'clock. It was dark but soon a faint glow in the East got brighter and the range of volcanoes that rise as a backdrop for the plains along the sea were silhouetted against the golden copper color of the dawn. The group of three huge peaks, Tres Marias, had a faint column of smoke like a bloom rising over the southernmost peak and in the distance you could see about twelve other equally large and beautiful ones. Some of the peaks had craters far below the top and their smoke wreathed their summits in a soft grey mantle. All of this made up a beautiful panorama over a hundred miles in length.

A passenger who was a missionary was interesting to talk to having spent about seventeen years in the interior of Guatemala with the Indians. He was kind of a simple soul and in a manner that was both naive and entertaining described the Indians and the ruins and their life, giving it a different slant from how the average tourist portrayed it. He told of the tribe that he called the Tribe of Kings. The tall (for these people) stately men with their erect bearing and noble features, dressed in bright clothes with head-dresses of red and bright green with tassels hanging down on either side of their faces, looked more like a band of pirates out of *Treasure Island* than anything else. Those kingly men were a proud, fierce lot.

He even gave the market place a different color as he described the big market day when all the weavers of the district brought their wares to the town and stacked them about the plaza displaying them everywhere until the plaza was a mass of color. The buyers and sellers milled about laughing, arguing, gossiping, spreading the news in the only way that it was spread in the mountain districts. The hubbub and orderly confusion made the place both colorful and gay. A native would refuse to sell his entire stock at the edge of town for a good profit if by doing so he would be deprived of his day at the market.

The missionary was on his way to the mountains back up to To-tonicapan, which is about ten thousand feet above the sea. He could hardly wait to get back there. He had found what he liked to do and was content.

When we arrived in Callao, I decided to go to the horse races and they were very colorful. I met a nice young Englishman who took me in tow and showed me how to bet and so forth. He took me up into the steward's stand where he introduced me to his father and mother, which was very nice of him.

These happened to be some special races and the President of Peru and all the ministers were there. In fact, the President was only a few paces away from me. I didn't envy him a bit as the day before someone had tried to bomb him at the palace. In spite of the heavy cordon of police that surrounded us, me and the President, I had an uneasy feeling and was kind of glad when I got out of the stand. I did a little betting but not very successfully. Lost three dollars in fact.

THE BLUE SEA JOURNAL
Exclusive Circulation Ltd.

The Grand Presidential Race: Took in the races today, or to be more specific, was taken at the races today. Not knowing any more about the Peruvian brand of horseflesh than the domestic brand of same, left the track on foot. I arrived in a taxi. It was some special national race in honor of the fourth century of Spanish rule in S.A. The President was there and all the ministers, so of course I could not absent myself. When I arrived at the track the thing had already begun and as another race was about to begin and wishing to hazard a few soles, the national monetary unit of Peru, on some one or another of the beasties, sooo in my best Spanish I approached one of the nearby citizenry and sprang the all important question of where and how a stranger in this fair land went about making a wager, placing a small bet on a particular animal. The gentleman, however, wasn't well acquainted with the particular brand of Spanish that I was using that day so failed to understand just what I was driving at. He started to look around with a look that passed when a friendly voice behind me interrupted the little drama that was about to take place with, "I say old Top, may I be of help to you?" Well the way I greeted him, you would have thought that we had gone to Oxford or someplace together. After a few explanations and much bowing by all parties we sort of backed into the crowd and just let it swallow us up. He offered to introduce me to the intricacies of Peruvian horse racing. The unfortunate part of it all being that he didn't understand all that he knew about the sport of kings. Anyway after placing the required number of soles in deposit at the window that was doing business for the particular entry that we, he, had selected as a likely winner, we wended our way aloft to the steward's stand. It seemed that his father owned a piece of the track. The foreigners own a piece of most everything down here anyway. Well, we got into the stand, which was all cluttered up with the elite, and no sooner had we secured a place of vantage when into the gates of the place rides the President accompanied by his guard, which is all decked out in fancy dress. They all wear high black boots topped by red pants with bright yellow stripes down the sides, a black coat with red trimmings and much gold braid with a wide belt hanging from which was a large saber. To top the outfit off, each wore a bright nickel helmet with chin-strap and at the top of the helmet stuck a spike like that on those of the knights of old. From this spike flowed a long black horse's tail that flapped out behind as the gentlemen marched up to the stand. Here the man whose pleasure (not really) it is to head this country left them and ascended the stairs to take up his place. Here he is surrounded by all the ministers who cluster about him to stop any stray bullets that might be addressed to him personally. All this time the band is playing national airs etc., overhead the national air force is turned out in full, all twenty planes which are dipping and swirling about. The planes, by the bye, are doing the nags a lot of no good fast as they are all out in the track while all this is going on and don't seem to take to this sort of thing, not being air-minded. Finally the President gets into position where he can't see anything because of all the ministers and so forth which have got him just about hid, and the race begins. Well the horse that I am betting on is still watching the aeroplanes when the tape goes up, and fails to notice that there is a race taking place. He did trot in before the next race started as it was getting late anyhow. And so ended the feature race of the day. In the remaining races, with the help of my friend, I picked as pretty a bunch of also-rans as was ever sold to a glue factory. Therefore foregoing the taxi. But walking is good exercise, so they say . . . SCH

Lima was a very pretty place in those days. The electric train service was the best I had ridden on anywhere outside of New York. The cars ran every five minutes between Callao, the seaport, and Lima, which is about ten miles inland. They were fast and very comfortable, and I think they traveled better than 45 or 50 mph.

I played a little bridge one night with the Bolivian Consul, his wife and the cadet. We had a nice evening and they were very charming people. He and the captain went to the bull fights and it was very funny to hear them tell about it when they got back. I had hoped to go but I couldn't because of my health: touch of dysentery.

I was lucky to be in Callao when I got the dysentery, as the doctor at the British American Hospital was one of the best on the coast and knew his stuff. They gave me eight kinds of pills to take so, even though I was feeling fine and dandy, I took pills for about a month afterwards. He told me that if these things are not completely cured they were apt to bother one again, therefore all the pills. I also got vaccinated while I was there, but as usual it didn't take.

1935, February 10 At Sea, aboard the Cuzco
Dearest,
. . . The coast of Peru and Chile is very uninteresting, though in the evening with the soft light of sunset playing upon the rugged shore, which rises in rocky cliffs from the sea, tinting every-

thing in soft colors trimmed with gold, it has a beauty all its own. A beauty that is only found in the desert and the high mountains above the timber line where things are barren and big and rugged. It is scenes such as these that contemplated, start a train of thought that makes men wonder: wonder at vastness of earth and sky; at the beauty of it all. Do you follow me? For as I watch the shoreline a thousand thoughts; a thousand unanswered questions flick across my mind and then strangely enough, I find myself thinking of home and of you: yet not so strangely! . . .

From a tourist's standpoint, the South American run was not nearly as interesting as the Central American run. Of course, there were a number of towns and cities along the coast that were interesting but they lacked the setting: the huge volcano with a little native village nestled at its base, with its thatched huts, its palm and banana trees, and its color: the smiling, picturesque natives with their happy-faced, naked little children playing about the littered streets. There were no trees along the coast, though in some of the towns there were a few, but the streets of the native villages were treeless, sandy, dirty lanes.

In Talara, Peru, there was a native village that had about four thousand people and it was nothing but row after row of barrack-like buildings just swarming with people, and children as thick as fleas about the place. At the end of each lane, between two rows of houses was the public water supply where each housewife went to fill her jar with water from a slow running tap. All the water for baths, for laundry and general washing came from there, and as a consequence, they skipped most of the washing.

The people seemed less happy though they seemed a stronger, healthier lot than the Central Americans. The men who worked on the ships, of course, were the worst class to be found in all those countries. Even by their own country people they were considered little better than dogs, but since they had sort of a loose organization in each country, they were somewhat respected for their voting power, which was important.

When we sailed out of Callao, we left the second cook behind. He failed to join us at sailing time. He went ashore the day before for a few hours and was last seen staggering down the street rip-roaring drunk. He had to wait until one of the other Grace Line ships picked

192

him up and if the connections went right, then we would get him back at one of the other ports. We also left a mess boy in Puntarenas, Costa Rica. He was picked up by the first northbound ship and shipped back to the States.

Having delivered most of our cargo, we picked up 350 tons of ore at Mollendo, Peru, for the Tacoma Smelter.[52] That helped a little as ballast, for we were very light after Callao having only a little over 100 tons of cargo left in the ship. Leaving San Pedro we had over 8000 tons with a draft of nearly 25 feet. Leaving Peru, we had only about 12 feet so of course we rolled a good deal. It was a nice easy roll and I enjoyed it.

After we left Valparaíso we went on south to San Antonio, both in Chile, where we loaded a lot of barley for San Diego, Cal. Our next port was Coquimbo, Chile. The third mate and I went ashore there and took in a native nightclub that was patronized by the cowboys, or *huasos*, of the district. It was pretty much a dive, but then one didn't see places like that every day. The *huasos* were a friendly bunch, but were not very high class. The beer was less than two pesos per bottle and, as the peso was changing at 22 to one, we could just about buy the joint. Well, we stayed until the place closed and danced with all the maids, then went back to the ship, much to the disgust of the maidens. There was a four-piece orchestra that made up for what it lacked in harmony by playing as loud as it could. The time was perfect though. Could have danced for hours more.

Our next port was Caldera, Chile. It was one of the nicest little ports we made, and the people were as friendly as they could be. There were no public places of entertainment such as cabarets, and just one or two bars where the working man could quench his thirst. However, the people invited us right into their homes and were tickled to death to have us come.

The first night we were there they had a public dance, admission free, and the whole town turned out. Sparks and I went ashore at about ten o'clock that night but found we were about an hour too early. We didn't have anything to do so we explored the town, which was very pretty in the moonlight. The streets were of sand and there were no trees or gardens or street lights. It was really a desolate place but in the moonlight it had a charm.

---

52 The Asarco Company operated a copper smelter in Tacoma.

We got back to the dance and stayed until it was over, a little after three. While there, we met a woman who was the leading social figure in the town, which itself boasted of only eight hundred to a thousand. We got along fine, and she invited us to play bridge the next night. So, the next evening we went on over and found a number of people there. We played bridge for a while then wound up dancing.

But the best part was that her two nieces from Santiago were there. They were American citizens, their father having been an American by the name of Learn. They spoke English in that cute way that so many foreigners do, and it was fun just to listen to them talk. One of the girls was about nineteen and the other a bit younger. They were very, very good looking. I kind of fell for the older one and the cadet did fall for the younger in a big way.

The high spot of the night was when the hostess and I were dancing a waltz – we were dancing pretty well – and the others stopped dancing and we put on an exhibition dance. We got quite a hand at the end and I was in a lather no less. It was a fine evening.

The next day, the washer women came out to the ship and they were the most friendly people. There was one woman who had her little girls with her and I gave them each a piece of candy. Later I bought a chance on a lottery for twenty centavos. Well, I won and I think I could have told you who would win when I bought the chance. I got a little hand-made cloth. The oldest girl thought I was pretty fine, which was funny. Oh well, it was a nice port and I would like to stop there again sometime.

The night of the dance, was Saturday and there was no work Sunday so at 5 a.m. the skipper and the third mate and I went out fishing with a couple of the stevedores. We caught about twenty large fish that were about three feet long – sort of a Spanish mackerel. Everything went along beautifully until about 11 a.m. I landed one, and he slipped off the hook as I hit him with a club. He was still very active and as he jumped up, his teeth, which were quite long and very sharp, happened to hit my hand. I had on a pair of gloves but he bit right through and one tooth sank into my thumb giving me a rather bad cut. It healed up nicely, but it was nasty at the time.

On the way north, the mate and I went ashore in Callao and took in Lima. They were celebrating a carnival, something like the one in New Orleans. It was a water carnival that they put on every four years so it was quite a gay time to be in Lima. On the streets they sold little bottles of ether that were scented with rose. They had a little nozzle

194

on them and there was some kind of O-pressure on them that made the ether squirt out in a fine stream. Well, everyone had one of those little bottles and the thing to do was to squirt the stuff on the ladies in the crowd before the ladies squirted you. All very interesting. In the eyes, it burned like the deuce and the smell was kind of bad. Everybody was doing it though, so the mate and I each got one and joined in the fun. We walked up and down the streets for quite a while and then decided to go someplace where we could dance, so we did.

We found a nightclub where everyone was making merry and the crowd was very jolly, so we had a good time. When it was time to go back to the ship the streetcars had stopped running, so we took a taxi, a ride of over ten miles. It cost only five soles, which was a little more than a dollar, and he even took us right up to the gangway. The whole evening was very inexpensive. We went to one of the best nightclubs and with taxi fares, dancing partners and all, it only cost us about three dollars apiece.

Talara, Peru, 1932.

As we made our way northward we loaded gold and copper bulk ore. We had about four thousand tons aboard when we left Chile. We stopped at Callao and then Talara where we loaded case oil and drums for the coast of Central America. We had such a large load on board that the mark was underwater and we had two more loading ports to make, Buenaventura and Balboa. "By the time we get out of Balboa there won't be anything but the house above water." That was putting it a bit strong, but we were down. She rode nicely when she was that way though. We made all the Central American ports and a couple of Mexican ports. On that trip, from San Francisco to Chile and back to San Francisco, we made over thirty ports.

On another trip we were set to sail from Panama City at 11 p.m., and as the hour rolled around we checked over the crew list and found that three men were ashore. The captain gave the order to take in the lines and the crew just walked off the forecastle head and picked up a ladder that was lying on deck and so over the side onto the dock. They said that they wouldn't do anything until the other three men showed up even if they had to hold the ship for two hours. Well, we stayed until the men showed up, which was about twenty minutes. The skipper was wild but it didn't do him a bit of good. That was one nice thing about the union crew; they looked out for each other. The owners had had the upper hand for a long while and once the men had it, they used it to suit themselves. Whoever had the reins used the lash in that game.

It looked like we would get in to San Francisco about the tenth of March 1935. That would make us only a week late, which wasn't so bad considering the load we had on board. Some of the fellows had us as late as the fifteenth but I was putting it at the tenth. That, by the way, was one of the pastimes on board, guessing where we would be on a certain date. It gave the men something to argue about anyway. Almost every conversation turned into an argument and some of them were funny too. In fact we didn't like to get to the table late for fear we would miss the first of some important argument. Some of them were: How much should be spent on the SS *Corinto*? What is wrong with the country, distribution etc. or what have you?

After dinner there was the card game and nightly argument. You would think that their lives depended on the outcome of the game each night. They fought after each hand, got real mad, but came back night after night to fight and play again. Oh hum.

I did a lot of reading aboard ship. I enjoyed *Today and Tomorrow* by Henry Ford, as it gave a new slant on Ford. According to him, the idea behind Ford Industries was more of an opportunity to serve than a means of gaining a large fortune. If he believed as he said, I felt that he would be recognized as one of the outstanding men of the era, not because of the money that he amassed, but for the good that he did to better industry. The success he attained seemed to prove it.

I got a letter from John Bruce in March 1935, in which he told me about how he and Jim Chesnutt, who both worked for the *San Francisco Call-Bulletin*, were out to lunch when the biggest news story of the year came in over the wire. He and Jim had just gone to lunch and, as luck would have it, they decided to try a new place to eat. When the story broke they sent a couple of copy boys out to round up both John and Jim, they being the two men on rewrite that day. The boys, of course, couldn't find them. After lunch, John decided to get a hair-cut, and Jim went on down to Breen's, which was a hangout for all the newspaper men from the *Examiner* and the *Call*. The place was strangely quiet, so Jim thought he would have himself a glass of beer and pass the time away until the hour for lunch was past. After a while, one of the INS[53] men came in for a bite to eat as there were several hours of work ahead getting the news on the wire.

As he dashed in and hollered for a sandwich, he saw Jim and said, "Swell yarn eh?"

"What?" pipes Jim, not too interested.

"A half-dozen convicts kidnap the warden, the whole parole board, and a couple of guards and escape." The way the fellow said it, it sounded like a setup for a story.

So Jim said, "Yea, swell yarn," and then the guy realized that Jim was in the dark and tried to convince him that he was telling the truth and not just setting up a story. The more he talked, the more it sounded like just a plot. Jim finally tumbled that the guy was telling the truth so he dashed on up to the office and plunged into the pandemonium of the San Quentin break. Later, John walked in. He couldn't imagine what had happened, everything was in such an uproar, but he was soon in the midst of it all. And so it goes . . . The way Johnny put it, it did have its funny side.

J. Campbell Bruce, 1936.

---

53 International News Service.

197

Friends on pier at Corinto, Nicaragua, 1935.

I picked up a box of half-dimes for my collection one time, I think it was in Panama.[54] I could have had as many as fifteen dollars worth, but I didn't want to invest that much in them. I kept them in an old cigar box for years.

Sailing northward, the countryside was not nearly as green as when we sailed down. It was the dry season, March, and the hills were quite brown. They also burned the brush on the plantations at that season and cleared the land, so the whole atmosphere was sort of hot and hazy.

In Corinto, Nicaragua, my friend the washer woman brought me a big basket of fruit: nice juicy mangoes, grapefruit, tangerines, and a couple of avocados. She was a big fat native who was as jolly as Mrs. St. Nicholas (Mrs. Santa Claus). When she took my laundry, she charged me an awful price and sold me a pineapple for 25¢ when it should have been no more than 15¢. But being my friend, we didn't quibble over the price too much. It was a laugh but it cost me about a dollar each trip.

After we left Manzanillo, we got a wire ordering us into San Jose del Cabo, on the tip of Baja California. It was my first time there and there was no port there – just a place to anchor while the natives rowed the cargo out to the ship in dug-outs. We picked up a hundred and twenty tons of bones for the U.S. It seemed funny to be bringing old bones into the country from so far away.

On that trip, we sailed up the coast all the way to Vancouver. That was in April 1935, and when we had finished discharging in Seattle,

---

54 The half dime was a silver coin valued at five cents, formerly minted in the United States.

we went into dry dock for two days. I went ashore in Seattle and liked the place very much. When we got off dry dock the purser quit and I was appointed in his place, but only as acting purser to San Francisco with no raise in pay.

That made me mad, but I was glad that I had the chance to show them that I could handle the work. It was mostly all new to me and kept me very busy, but I got along fine with the work.

We went into Greys Harbor and docked in the town of Aberdeen, Washington. There we loaded a million and a half feet of lumber and since nearly a million feet were on deck we rolled quite a lot, a slow and easy roll, as we sailed down the coast. We carried that lumber all the way to Peru where we discharged it, and we sailed out of there very light, rolling quite a lot in a different way.

I had a couple of romances on that trip. A pretty girl came aboard in Manzanillo, and before I knew what had happened, I had fallen in love with her, and thought maybe I had found "her." She got off in Puntarenas and boy, I hated to say good-bye. I thought a lot about her, but never heard from her again.

On July 7, 1935, I wrote to my Mother:

> *In a few days I will be twenty-nine. Yet, I feel so very young, that I have so much to learn – about life and about myself. My birthday brings to mind how much I owe you. The tolerance, the patience you have shown me; the countless things you have always done for me make me feel humble as I think of the lack of appreciation that I have shown. You dear, have been so much more than just plain Mother. You have been a Mother and Mom too! And that means so much that just can't be put into words.*
> *I send you all my love Mom, the dearest Mother,*
> *Your son.*

Chapter 15: Grounding of the SS *Cuzco*

THREE OF US ARE SITTING AROUND the radio in Spark's shack, the wireless room, listening to the lovely strains of a Chicago dance orchestra. Outside, though it is only half past six in the evening, it is pitch black, and the decks are still wet from the last of the many rain squalls we have just sailed through. The ship seems to roll as if it too were mindful of the music that we are listening to.

Deep in the ship, the engine room telegraph split the air with its harsh note and, as we looked up at one another inquisitively, but before anyone could speak, our unanswered question had already been answered.

The ship gave a sudden sickening lurch as though struck by some mighty and sinister unseen hand. At the same time a low rumble, like a groan of pain, told us too plainly that we were aground. Gaining our feet from the awkward positions that we had been thrown into, we rushed out on deck. In the gloom, as we hurried along the deck to our boat stations without waiting for the alarm bell, we could see the white foam of the breakers boiling along the ship's side. As we came around the wheelhouse, a smother of water and spray washed us up against the rail. Cursing in order to fight down the panic that for a second seemed to drain all the strength out of our bodies, we fought our way to the boat deck.

Standing by our boats we realized that it was impossible to launch a lifeboat in such a sea. Just standing there doing nothing, as the ship listed further and further over, each minute seemed like years. My thoughts turned to the days when I was a boy going to a country school and how the blossoms, when the orchards were in bloom, used to smell so sweet. I wondered, too, how the family would take the news. That was the most bothersome part of it all. I hated to cause them the grief that I knew news of my death would bring. All these thoughts were punctuated by the sickening lurches that the ship would take now and again.

We had run aground on a shoal at the mouth of the Lempa River in El Salvador. This shoal reaches out into the sea for about three or four miles. The night was dark and the current had put us inside our course so that we ran aground on the edge of the shoal. The fireman on watch said we had 205 pounds of steam and all of a sudden water shot out of the deep tank vents in the fire room! He didn't know what to make of it. Then the floor plates wrenched and a big shudder shook the ship. He then cut all fires and just as the telegraph sounded full astern, the first threw her astern with no time lost, leaving us fast on amidships under the fire room.

We had too much headway to stop and before the engines could do any good to check us, we had come to a stop in the soft mud at the mouth of the Lempa River, between La Libertad and La Unión. There was no big bump or crash or anything. We just stopped.

Each succeeding wave worked us in toward the beach a little further until we were in about a quarter of a mile on the shoal. The hull was not making any water to speak of.

By 8 p.m. things were looking worse. The men on watch were stripping the lifeboats, getting them ready for use. Sparks had contacted a freighter, which was about 7 hours away, steaming toward us in hopes of getting in on the salvage. The ship shuddered and quaked, listing at better than 10 degrees to starboard. It was a nasty

Heavy seas aboard SS *Cuzco*, 1935.

feeling as it lurched every few seconds, pounded by the waves which splashed angrily along our side. The night was black without a star showing, but the air was warm.

Our deck load was about 22 feet high, which made the ship very tender. Everyone was calm, but the captain looked terribly worried, and I felt very sorry for him. There was little fuss and the passengers didn't know that anything was wrong until about 9 p.m. when the Old Man told them. Four had gone to bed by that time and they knew nothing about it until the next day. He warned all the passengers to be ready to leave the ship at a moment's notice. No one seemed afraid but the feeling was much like speeding around a curve: what will time bring. I figured things were at their worst – but that was only the beginning.

After being shut down for an hour, the engine started up again, trying to work us loose. A gang was forward getting ready for a tow if one came along. Just then there was another bad shudder – it's hard to describe the funny feeling it gave me. My stomach sort of flipped when the ship lurched that way.

By 11 p.m. the tide was turning. The beach was just a couple of hundred feet off to port. The captain told me to get the ship's papers together and be ready to get off, so I knew it was bad. I gathered up all the papers and money and was ready to go any time.

The captain was anxious about the passengers. He wanted to put them off as soon as possible – probably at dawn. The dynamite in our hold made it bad. We had 3500 cases on board. It looked like we might have to slip the deck load but that would make the lifeboats useless, so we held on to it until the lifeboats were clear.

I took a look at my belongings to see what I should take with me, and was surprised, and a little shocked, to find so little – camera, razor, pocketbook, coat.

At midnight, things looked even worse. The third engineer reported that #1 hold was leaking, and the bilge pump was pumping salt water. That was bad.

We were just waiting for daylight so that we could get the passengers off. One woman traveling alone with three babies – one in arms to one four years old – was asleep and didn't know that we were aground. "Ignorance is bliss." She would have been terrified if she knew. But with the dawn she was in for a thrill.

October 27th.

Through the night we played the searchlight in the sky as a beacon for the freighter coming to our aid. The ship was a bit quieter but far from steady. I was curious to know if we could get out by our own power when the tide came in in the morning. I finally decided to take a little nap and dozed off about 2 a.m. I got a couple hours of sleep but was awakened by long blasts of the whistle trying to let the arriving ship know our position, as the visibility was very poor. Then that urge not to miss any of it got me up on deck again. We were continually working up onto the beach, lurching and pounding our way. I was convinced that the *Cuzco* was finished.

About 4 a.m. we put two lifeboats over the side and held them in readiness. I helped get the baggage out of the cabins, and was sweating like a horse by the time we were done. We piled it on top of #3 hatch along with a stack of life preservers. By then it was 5:15 a.m. and dawn was breaking!

With the morning light, we started helping the passengers into the lifeboats. I got one leg wet standing at the foot of the ladder and passing kids aboard. The mother of the little kids was a bit hysterical, and I felt sorry for her. We launched the first boat about 6 a.m. with Collins, the third mate and safety officer, in charge. They rowed away from shore to await the freighter, which still hadn't arrived.

The ship seemed to be in danger of going over, but we were hoping that it would withstand the ebbing of the tide. As the tide went out it was listing a bit more, but seemed a little more steady. The crew was very quiet, waiting for developments. And I was tired.

At 7:30 a.m. there was still no sign of the rescue ship. Waves were breaking across the deck and one drenched the 2nd and 3rd engineers who were standing on the starboard deck near the galley. We all got a laugh out of it, as much to relieve the tension as anything. The ship was listing at about 15 degrees, which made for a damned uncomfortable footing on the deck. The deck load might shift at any time, and the fireworks would pop if it did!

Breakfast was rather sketchy: a big bowl of boiled eggs and some slices of cold meat and cheese. The galley was on too much of an angle to cook. After breakfast I took a shower, which made me feel cleaner, though the water ran across the shower room at a queer angle.

By 9 a.m. we could see the *Point Ancha* about an hour off. There was a big swell running that made it difficult to discharge the first boatload of passengers' baggage, as the boat bobbed like a cork in the foamy water. We started discharging some of the mail about 10 a.m. while the *Point Ancha* stood by picking up passengers. An hour later the oil tanker *Charlie Watson* arrived and was cruising in circles waiting to see how they could help.

The starboard rail aft was down to the water but, as the ship was on the bottom, it made no difference. It was hot as the devil by midday. The ship was being pounded by the waves and the cargo was beginning to shift in #3 hold. It felt like the *Cuzco* might start to break up at any time.

Laying in the breakers like that, if a storm came up, the ship would be awash and therefore dangerous, so the captain had us all move over to the *Point Ancha* for the night. As he said, "One life is worth more than the whole damned boat."

So about 3 p.m. the crew boarded the lifeboats for the *Point Ancha*. It took an hour to row over to her and we all took turns at the oars. Everyone was dog tired by the time we boarded her. The captain had all the crew solidly in back of him and we would all have returned that night if he had given the word. The lack of adverse demonstration and willing cooperation by everyone made it a nice day, as far as that was possible. The Old Man was in a bad spot, but we were all behind him.

The *Cuzco* looked very forlorn as she faded into the darkness when the sun went down. She was abandoned but I figured that if she didn't blow up in the night we still had a chance to get her back.

The *Point Ancha* was almost the same size as the *Cuzco*, and the decks were crowded with all of us on board. It had been a hot day and it was a hot night as I made my bed atop the booby hatch,[55] which looked pretty good to me. The crew gradually quieted down during the next hour and we all got some well-earned rest.

October 28th.

The crew coming to life awakened me at 5:40 a.m., and I could see a faint streak of light along the horizon, which was the sign for dawn in those parts. In a few minutes it would be daylight, and with daylight came the sun which fairly burst into the sky like a rocket, and another day was in the passing.

---

55 Booby hatch: a raised covering over a small hatchway.

Sparks went up to the captain's quarters with two long messages. We all remarked about it and speculated on the contents as we sat or stood about the deck in small groups, smoking and talking more or less quietly.

In a little while the skipper came down and after a few minutes talk with the chief engineer, he told us that he was taking the chief, first, fireman, oiler, 2nd mate, 3rd mate and boat crew over for a look see. They brought one of our two boats and the men climbed down into it. The skipper told us that if they found her fit to board, he would send the boat right back and we would all go over bag and baggage, with the exception of passengers, of course. They shoved off and we followed their movement across the two miles of water. Finally, they disappeared under the counter.[56]

We waited the usual period of time for them to get the fires started, but no smoke came out of the stack. Still we waited, all eyes trained on that green and white stack waiting for the plume of smoke that would be our signal that the *Cuzco* still held her own in this battle for her life against the sea over which she had proudly ridden since she slid down the ways in Oakland in 1918.

Something was wrong. Was she full of water? We could only guess what it might be, for by that time they should have gotten things underway. Then we saw them.

"There's the boat!" someone shouted, "She's coming out around the counter! Too far away to see who's in it. She's making for the bow – must be taking soundings." They spent nearly a half hour along the length of the ship, and then finally started back.

It was time for a bite of chow so we all left the rail long enough to find some food, for it would be some time before the boys got back.

They pulled alongside at 8:30 a.m. – all of them had returned. They climbed the ladder and the word was passed that she was laying over so badly that it was unsafe on board. We could not go back until she settled. During the night she had pounded further on and had only two fathoms of water on the port side by that time.

Though the ship had listed over, she was coming back to an even keel, for the mooring line caused the ship to dig a hollow for itself,

---

56 Counter: The part of the stern above the waterline that extends beyond the rudder stock culminating in a small transom.

SS *Cuzco* aground on Lempa Shoals, October 1935.

In the lifeboat.

and being flat bottomed she just sat there like a shoe box on a shelf. There was nothing to do but wait. We understood that a salvage tug was hurrying up from the Canal and would arrive in two days. I figured that if the weather held, we could be salvaged, but a storm would be the end of the *Cuzco*.

In the afternoon a wire came through with orders to have the *Point Ancha* carry the mail on to Balboa. Doelker and I sorted the bags and worked up quite a sweat.

We had supper early and sat around until 9 p.m. waiting for the Grace Line ship, the *Sekstant*, to arrive. We decided to transfer to the *Sekstant* in the morning, so I settled down atop the hatch. I wrote a letter to Mom letting her know that I was in no peril and might be living aboard the *Sekstant* for as long as a month, anchored off the beach, until the salvage crew was finished with the *Cuzco*. As the coast was uninhabited along there, that was my last chance to write her for a while.

I dozed off and was sleeping peacefully when it started to rain, and the fellows seeking shelter awakened me. My bunk was in the lee of the midship house and under the boat deck so I only got a little moist wind. Finally the noise stopped and I went back to sleep.

October 29th.

All hands roused early, at 4:20 a.m., and got their gear together to take to the boats again, bag and baggage, and row over to the *Sekstant* where we were to stay until the salvage was finished. I washed up and had two cups of black coffee to start the day off in high. Everyone had been so nice to us aboard the *Point Ancha*. They had given us what they could without hurting themselves, and the mess boy had been as gracious as an Indian Prince.

At 5 a.m. the lifeboats came alongside and the guys started throwing their gear into them. We shoved off from the *Point Ancha* and pulled for the *Sekstant*. Forty-five minutes later, we climbed aboard the *Sekstant*, a little boat with none of the modern conveniences. There was no refrigeration so the meat was all salt meat and unless we could get some supplies off the *Cuzco*, things were going to be a bit tough. The *Point Ancha* sailed at 7 a.m., as I watched the cook aboard the *Sekstant* taking some beautiful green bacon into the galley. Breakfast would be a treat!

The coast was beautiful down there. The shoreline was a green strip with a white line border, and rising out of the low lands were a half dozen volcanoes whose steep sides were covered with various shades of green. Plumes of smoke rose from many of the peaks. Soon the haze caused by the heat would blot out most of it, but for a couple of hours in the morning it was beautiful in that colorful tropical way.

After a fine breakfast, two boats put off to the *Cuzco* to get blankets and food. We all wanted to board but there was only room for the boat crews. The first boat returned with food and supplies from the *Cuzco*, so we could eat anyway! When the second boat returned, the boarding party reported that the ship had come back two degrees to about 23 degrees. There were about three feet of water in #1 hold but she was not filling up much elsewhere. The Old Man stayed aboard as did the first assistant.

Nothing was doing all afternoon. I dozed for a bit, fished, and tried to keep cool. We were crowded on that little ship, but I figured that if that was the worst hardship I ever endured, I'd be satisfied.

The *Sekstant* was a funny little boat. It was rather quaint, very different from ours. They didn't even have little things like radios, but the skipper had a phonograph that he brought out in our honor and proudly played. He was a nice old chap – even offered me his settee to sleep on.

The next morning the first tug was due and operations would begin. It would give us something to do.

October 30th.

The gang came to life all along the deck about 5:30 a.m. Talk gradually increased from a few monosyllables to a babble, and another day had begun. I had a good sleep on top of #2 hatch and was feeling fine.

At 7 a.m. all hands of the *Cuzco* took to the boats. All but the mess boys and coolies headed for the *Cuzco* as the tug was coming in. It took almost an hour to row over and Captain Gilbert and Andy seemed glad to see us. The ship was over about 22 degrees and sitting hard on the bottom. They said that she was working hard during the night but was not making water.

By 8:00 a.m. the gang was out on deck chopping up dunnage[57] for

---

57 Dunnage is inexpensive or waste material used to protect and immobilize cargo during transportation.

the fires, in order to get steam for the feed pumps. We planned to start jettisoning the deck load as soon as we got lines to the tug or a mooring anchor.

About 9:20 a.m. the tug sent a cable over to be tied astern, and 15 of us hauled it aboard by hand, up onto the poop deck, stopping three times to catch our breath before we got it aboard. They almost swamped the boat before the line was passed – luckily the sea was calm.

I helped out chopping dunnage for the boilers for a while and we got up steam about 11:00. The fans and lights were running again and the ship lost some of its ghastly quietude as the auxiliaries got underway one by one.

I suggested to the skipper that since none of the stewards were aboard, I could get grub ready for the outfit – about 40 of us, and thereby save the time of moving from ship to ship. He thought it was a good idea, so I prepared food and coffee for 40 men in about an hour. I checked the ice boxes and pulled out a bucket of eggs, some butter and cheese, oranges and apples, crackers, what bread I could find, some canned apricots and pineapple, and made a pot of coffee. It was a good meal, everybody had enough, and the coffee was a success – strong.

After lunch Doelker and I cleaned up. I mopped the salon and pantry, which was one hot job. Everyone was pretty dirty-looking but we were all happy and the work was welcome.

About 2 p.m. the jettisoning began. At first we just threw the loose beams and dunnage overboard, and no cargo was jettisoned at that time.

October 31st.

The next morning began the long, drawn-out job of trying to free the *Cuzco*. At 8 a.m., a large naval tugboat, US *Favorite*, dropped hook and put out a motor boat with two U.S. Engineers. Collins took soundings later in the morning and found that the ship was in about 15 feet of water on the bow, 12 feet amidships, and 15 feet aft. In the afternoon, the tug anchored a cable buoy about 300 yards away, which was about where we first hit. He made ready to lay his hooks, and then the anchors were put down, waiting high water.

The first fleet of cable was taken in mid-afternoon. It was a 2-inch steel cable hooked to an anchor 300 yards off. This in turn was rigged to a set of multiple blocks running 8 strands of cable being taken over the niggerhead, or capstan, of the mooring winch. A fleet takes up about 20 feet of cable. At each fleet the set of stops work this way: while there is a strain on the winch the after stopper is running free, but when the strain on the winch is loosed the after stopper holds the cable and the forward stopper, having no strain, is run back to the aft bit and another strain put on it.

All this strain gave the ship a tender feeling. If she was going to break up, she'd break while that was going on. As soon as the strain became great enough, an effort would be made to move her but, as far as I was concerned, she would not move.

We had been living aboard the *Cuzco* all day and had gotten so used to the list that we hardly noticed it until Collins and I were talking and glanced at the water bottle, "We're over better than 20 degrees!"

November 1st.

I was up and about at 5:45 after a good night's sleep in my own bunk. My bunk was a bit on the bias but it surely was an improvement over a hatch cover.

Out on deck the salvage crew and deck gang were pulling a line onto the bow preparing to haul aboard a towing cable from the *Favorite*. The ship was working a good deal. The salvage master told me that there had been a change of plans. Due to a shift in the soundings, he decided to try and tow the bow off first instead of the stern.

At 7 a.m. the tug *Favorite* took a strain but we didn't move other than to shiver. A little while later the tug took a jerk and the starboard chock let go ripping out the fore rail. 1300 feet of 2-inch cable whipped like a skip rope. Fortunately, everyone was clear. We all knocked off for breakfast and decided to run the cable through the hawser pipe.

A dugout came alongside, with five men in it from the shore, but the captain shooed them away.

After breakfast the gang on the forecastle head and the crew began jettisoning the cargo aft. I helped them for a while and that was one hot job. Then at 9:30 six of us were sent off to the *Sekstant* to pick up the crew's effects. We left the *Cuzco* in the *Favorite* motor launch and plowed through the breakers. It was no mean feat getting into the boat and quite a thrill going through the breakers! We made it around the bow as the hull loomed large overhead.

After we completed our mission, we left the *Sekstant* with one lifeboat in tow and motored back to the *Favorite* for lunch aboard. Around noon we left the *Favorite* for the *Cuzco*. Another ride through the breakers — always a thrill, but that launch was a whale boat type and could go most anywhere. The sea around the *Cuzco* was covered with lumber as our deck load was slowly going over the side. It was quite a trick getting aboard the gangway in those swells, but we all made it.

Stan (left) and Sparks (center) jettisoning deck load.

We arrived on the *Cuzco* to find 22 men from the salvage tug working on lumber on the foredeck while the ship's crew worked aft. The day got hotter and hotter.

I went back to work on the deck load with about 20 men aft and we jettisoned about 300 thousand feet of lumber. That was a lot of lumber — between 500 and 600 tons. We worked hard. There was a crew of 20 nigger on the foredeck and they moved not more than 150 thousand feet of lumber.

There was one time when a huge piece swung across the deck and I thought it was curtains, but luckily there were no accidents. It was hot! I was baking out there and the sweat kept me sopping wet. I couldn't seem to drink enough water.

A little past 3 p.m. the tug started to take a strain on the cable and at 4:45 they signaled to pull all they could. The ship worked hard and

Jettisoning the deck load of lumber, SS *Cuzco*.

an hour later had swung 10 degrees and come back on the list about 10 degrees.

Meanwhile, the *Sekstant* had sailed off at 4 p.m. and on it was a letter to my mother.

I felt a lot better after supper – felt like the original "Little Man You've had a Busy Day." I washed everything that I had on and took a good shower and was ready for the hay! We were all dog tired. That was the hottest day's work I had ever done.

November 2nd.

I awoke at 5:45 and was surprised to find that I was not stiff and sore after my labors. "Guess I'm younger than I thought," I told the cadet.

The tug put on a full strain at 5 a.m. and by 1 p.m. we had moved, but that was about all. However, we still had high hopes of coming clear that night.

It was another day of jettisoning the lumber, and we made good time with it in spite of the heat. We threw another 150 thousand feet of lumber off the aft deck that morning. The sea about the ship was covered with lumber and we all knocked off for lunch to await high tide. The ship was still listed over to about 20 degrees, it having fallen back during the night.

At 7 p.m. the tug was full speed ahead but we only swung the bow 12 degrees. The list came back to about 8 degrees but was gradually settling back. We were still living on the bias and were fed up with it. It was like living on the side of a hill with nothing level – no tables, no chairs, nothing.

November 3rd.

They took a full strain on the cable forward at 6 a.m. and the ship began to work back and forth. Gradually she came up onto a more even keel coming as high as 4 degrees on a roll. The bow started to swing out, and we swung a total of 24 degrees that morning and took in at least 50 feet of cable on the ground tackle. Soundings indicated a little more than 21 feet all over the bottom at high water, and things were looking very favorable for getting off on the next high tide.

We began to lighten the ship by pumping our fresh water after which came oil, both diesel oil and fuel oil.

At 10 a.m. the salvage ship, *Killerig*, was in sight. We expected her to take over all the operations and send the *Favorite* away, as the *Killerig* was sent by the underwriters with the responsibility of re-floating us. She came all the way from Kingston, Jamaica, while the *Favorite* was a U.S. tug from Balboa, 700 miles to the south of us. The *Killerig* arrived at 11 a.m. and put off a motor launch that came alongside the *Cuzco*. The wrecking master came aboard with two assistants and they began taking soundings immediately.

About 1 p.m. the *Killerig* took up a position abreast of the *Favorite* and abeam of us. Her tender came over with gear, and her crew set to work on the forecastle head, rigging a cable from the foremast. The wrecker crew rigged an 8-strand tackle from the jumbo boom around the forward mast leading forward to a 1-5/8-inch touring cable leading out through the starboard bow to a ground anchor, 1500 feet out.

So we had an anchor out 60 fathoms on which to haul with our windless; a two-inch cable to the *Favorite*; a 1-5/8-inch cable to the forward ground anchor, to be hauled on by a 10-strand rig to #2 starboard winch; and a 12-inch manila towing hawser to the *Killerig* all forward. Aft was the 2-inch ground anchor cable to the mooring winch.

"When they start to haul this evening, something will have to give – we will float or else!!"

At 6 p.m. it was full ahead with both tugs. As the tugs hauled the ship out, a steady strain was kept on the ground tackle and any slack

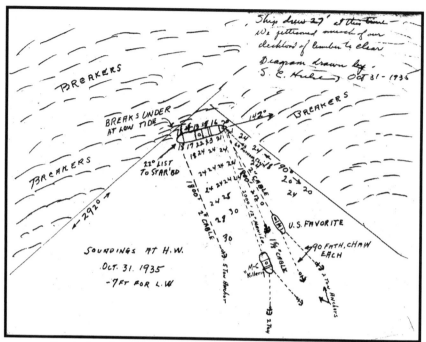

Stan's drawing of the *Cuzco* and the ships trying to free her.

was taken up with the anchor. During the evening, about four fleets were taken in the forward gear, and the ship swung 9 degrees but that was all she would move. We had gone ahead about 5 fathoms.

It looked very much like we would have to work more of the deck load off the next day. Also we hadn't pumped any oil as yet, which might have helped a lot toward getting us off. It had been just a week since we ran aground and a pretty full week at that.

November 4th.

We started towing full ahead at 6 a.m. The ship lay very heavily working only a little, and the morning towing netted very little.

At 8 a.m. our crew turned to on the deck load and jettisoned about 50 thousand feet in 40 minutes, in order to clear the way to run the leads to two ground tackles back from the forecastle head to the Samson posts port and starboard #3 hatch. This was in order to take a longer fleet each time. The forty minutes was a real workout as it was a very tropical day and the tropics is no place for labor such as that or any other kind for that matter.

They were pumping the bilges and found that there was diesel oil in #4 hold. That meant that the ceiling had given under the strain, and there was no way to tell how badly we were damaged but the engineers seemed to think it was pretty bad.

I helped Mr. Collins take soundings, which showed us still hard on the port side while the starboard was almost afloat. It gave me a funny feeling to be standing on the forecastle head amid all the cables while the soundings were being taken. It was necessary to get right up alongside of them in order to get the soundings. The cables were as tight as bow strings and fairly sang from the terrific strain that was on them. If one of them should let go, chances were that it would leave a shambles forward.

The ground tackle was rigged to #3 port Samson post and a strain was taken. The rig used the Samson post to haul against and led forward to the cable which payed out through the bow-port on the port side. It was rigged so that #2 port winch took the pull through a set of 4 sheave blocks and two snatch blocks. A fleet ran the length of the forward well deck which made the second ground tackle forward. One ground anchor is equal to four tugs and by nightfall we would have three out forward, as well as the two tugs, making a total strain equal to 14 tugs forward and 4 aft, due to the gear rigged there, equal to 18 in total. Part of the hull was in 3 to 5 feet of sand though, and it would take tremendous power to move us at all.

In the afternoon we pumped diesel oil over the side to lighten the ship for the night's try. The US *Favorite* had to leave the next morning, so our best chance was at high tide that evening.

The sunset was beautiful. The horizon was a line of pink fading into a pale yellow and against it, like black paper cutouts, stood the two tugs. The water was as calm as a millpond, too calm for our purposes.

We had pumped 700 barrels of diesel oil overboard that afternoon. And the gang from the *Killerig* had rigged a third ground tackle back to the Samson post at #3 starboard leading forward and out through the after chock on the starboard side.

At 6:15 p.m. we were all clear of the decks at #3 waiting for them to take a strain. No one was allowed forward of the midships house because of the danger, should any of the gear give way, with the strain on each cable being in the neighborhood of 25 tons.

By 9:30 p.m. there had been a full strain on the gear forward since 6:30 and we had swung the bow outward about 10 degrees more. It was high slack water and if she didn't come free very soon we stood a good chance of staying there for another week because of the high tides at that time. We had a strain forward of better than 150 tons. I didn't think she'd come off. We were on an even keel and seemed to be resting pretty evenly on the bottom with the port side a couple of feet in the sand.

November 5th.

About 7 a.m. they started taking up on the ground tackle and the tugs went full ahead. At 8 a.m. we were still pumping oil overboard but now it was fuel oil. The *Favorite* was still with us and with her help we were inching through the mud and sand. The ship felt a little more lively as the tide came in and, as it was almost two hours until high tide, we had a good chance to come free.

By 9 a.m. we had swung out to 224 degrees and were headed the same as the *Favorite*. We still had an hour of flow on that tide, and I was very hopeful that we would come off. The ship was beginning to groan as she worked and she sounded terrible, as though she were being wrenched by a terrific unseen power that threatened to tear her to pieces. The smell of diesel oil hung in the air – enveloping the ship as the pumps continued their work.

How great the damage to the bottom was only a guess, but I was afraid that it would prove to be a good deal.

Then at 9:40 a.m. we were afloat! She came off easily after she got started – just slid out. We let go all the ground tackle, and were towed out to anchorage by the *Favorite*. We were one happy crew.

About noon they sent a diver over the side to find the extent of the damage. He went over the entire hull and reported that the damage was not very heavy. The keel was badly bent throughout most of its length and a rib was sticking through #1 hold starboard. We figured we could probably make our Central American ports of call and dry dock in Balboa for temporary repairs.

The *Killerig*, by the way, was just up from Jamaica where she was based. I was talking to the diver aboard her and he told me that he knew Willie Wilson, the husband of my late grandmother, Harriet. He had seen him at the fights quite often for it seemed that Willie was a fight fan.

The *Favorite* sailed southbound at 4:40 p.m. and as we lined the rail it was like waving good-bye to an old friend. She picked up her ground tackle and transferred her gear and sailed off to gas a light off Panama, resuming her regular duties as a lighthouse tender.

November 6th.

After a survey by the masters and chief engineer of the tugs, they granted us a seaworthy certificate and at 3:30 a.m. we sailed for La Unión and other ports of call in Central America as though nothing had happened. We could carry passengers, etc. if any were offered, for other than a few weeps in #1 hold we were as good as ever. But we took it easy until further inspection in Balboa.

And so ended the chapter of the grounding of the *Cuzco* on Lempa Shoals.

Chapter 16: Adventures in South America

WE ARRIVED IN PANAMA without further incident. In Balboa we went into dry dock and I went down to the floor to have a look. It was a huge dock, over a thousand feet long and better than a hundred feet wide. I prowled all about under the ship and saw that the damage was slight. A couple of rivets out and a few dents. It was like being in a low ceilinged cave. The underside of the ship was as flat as a pancake, and looking from end to end of the ship between the chocks that were set in rows to hold the ship off the bottom of the dock, was like looking down a long tunnel. I took a few pictures of the works. We were in dry dock for 30 days repairing the damage from the grounding. That gave

Stan underneath the SS *Cuzco* in dry dock in Panama.

217

me a chance to explore Panama.

I went for a nice long ride around Old Panama and out to the ruins with a girl who had been a passenger on our last trip. I had a lovely time just riding and talking and poking about the ruins for a while. It had rained a lot, but a tropical rain is not wet in the same way that rain is up north. Everything was very, very green at that season and very lovely. In fact, it was more lovely than I had ever seen it.

As soon as the rain stopped I went ashore to the Balboa Club where I sat on the veranda and watched the people and the busses pass by. Traffic in the Zone moved very slowly, and so did the people. Panama City was different. The busses hit it up to a lively clip in the crowded narrow streets, and the first few times I swerved around a sharp, blind curve on the left hand side of the road, it gave me quite a thrill. But somehow the expected crash never materialized, and after a while I relaxed and took it easy.

Balboa was quite a port for the old night life. Those nights had a quality found only in the tropics. A quality that appealed to the nocturnal beast in me. The warm, heavy air had a dank musty odor with now and again a blast of sweet that was so strong that to breathe was difficult. Through this all was the steady hum of a myriad of bugs and insects hunting, feeding, fighting and lovemaking, that gave the nights a living, vibrant tone. They were really wonderful!

After the *Cuzco* was repaired, we sailed to Callao, Peru, to deliver the dynamite that we had on board. It came time to unload it and we needed the dock certificate to do that. The guys came down to inspect it and they wouldn't okay it. The long delay, due to salvaging the ship and dry dock repair in Panama, had made the cargo of dynamite too dangerous to handle in the port. The nitro has a tendency to separate and the dynamite becomes very unstable when subject to prolonged heat. We, therefore, had to go out to sea and very carefully unload the stuff onto a barge from whence it was carefully lowered into the sea. We just had to dump it.

From there we sailed on down the coast to Antofagasta, Chile. From the sea it looked like nothing at all, but ashore one found little plazas, flower-filled and lovely, and a few attractive statues under many different kinds of trees. The trees along the coast had all been planted, as there was absolutely no vegetation in that region. The green of the plazas was striking in contrast to the dull landscape, and there were some nice little shops, a few good-looking buildings and paved streets that were quite clean, well-policed and well-ordered. It was a nice little place but only for a week, no more.

While in Antofagasta I took a ride out to the airport to receive the mail. It was about eight miles out of town atop a mountain that rose directly behind the town to about four or five thousand feet. The field was on the edge of a huge natural plateau. There was not a blade of grass or a stick of vegetation anywhere, just red and grey rock, jagged and rough. The wind that swept off that barren plateau was cold and clean and, for a change, it felt good.

At the field there was a hangar, a little office and waiting room, and a little house for the caretaker and the few attendants that stayed at the field all the time. That was all.

After a while, and on schedule, a little dot appeared in the sky. A moment later, in she came, a fourteen passenger job. It made a perfect landing and taxied onto the apron. A few minutes of activity, while the passengers stretched and did their dos. Soon it was all over. She taxied to the far side of the field, took a run and was in the air. A moment later and she was a fast disappearing speck.

We climbed aboard the station wagon with a small sack of mail and started back to Antofagasta. Looking back as we hit the road, there was nothing but the wind-swept field, the little station house, now locked, and the empty hangar. Not a human being in sight, just the little group of buildings that looked so forlorn and lonely in that

Antofagasta, Chile, was a nitrate port.

vast, windswept expanse, that a few minutes before was the scene of so much activity. Looking again for the speck, it had disappeared toward Valparaíso where the passengers had their dinner that night. We left a few hours later for Valparaíso and it took us sixty hours to make the trip. Quite a contrast!

From Antofagasta we sailed on down to Valparaíso. It was bigger than Antofagasta, more business-like, with better shops, more statues and bigger plazas. The percentage of good-looking women was surprisingly high, and the glances at the *gringos* were quite friendly. A friendly smile to a lonely visitor in a foreign land is apt to add a good deal of charm to any town.

While there, I decided to have dinner ashore, and I had one of the best lobsters that I have ever eaten. Just delicious! I had a glass of *vino blanco*, which still makes my mouth water at the thought, along with the lobster followed by a dandy steak. It would have made a good ad for a butcher, it was that good. It was the best meal on many a voyage.

We sailed, however, with twelve of the crew ashore. They stayed for the night life. The women proved too seductive for them, I guess; anyway they missed the ship and caught up to us along the coast somewhere. I kind of envied them their shore excursion, but I didn't ever want to miss a boat.

We spent Christmas in Tocopilla, Chile. There was a package waiting for me and it was from the girl who I took out in Panama. It had a little Christmas tree with all the trimmings, which made it quite Christmasy aboard. Everyone went ashore that day except the skipper, the chief engineer and me. I just didn't feel like making the rounds of the bars. I wasn't in a drinking mood I guess, so I stayed aboard and read and had a very quiet day.

A few days later, in Huasco, Chile, I had an interesting experience. I met a couple of natives that took a shine to me and invited Doelker and myself up to their place. We took them up on it and were surprised to find that they were some of the richest people in Chile. They had discovered a gold mine a few years before that kept getting richer and richer as they went further into the hill. We allowed that the pictures of the mine looked interesting and he insisted on dragging us about forty miles across the desert and up into the Andes to his mine. It was a most interesting ride. We went out across the desert in the cool of the morning, saw the sunrise in the mountains and a myriad of desert flowers blending into one exquisite panorama of color. The beauty of the desert at sunrise is stirring. The cool mountain air felt so clean and refreshing that it was was almost heady. I just couldn't seem to take in enough. My, but it was good!

Then we drove on up to the mine. There were in the neighborhood of 400 men working there, and all their families lived just around the opening to the mine. It was a native village hanging on the side of a huge mountain peak – one of many peaks in the center of that vast desert. But it was a lone village and, with everything under construction, the place had that exciting atmosphere of a boomtown. Everything seemed to be hubbub and bustle, with a spirit of people striving for expression. It was fascinating.

Then into the mine itself. We followed a tunnel that ran into the hillside for 1800 feet. The tunnel of course followed the vein and wound itself into the heart of the mountain. The owner pointed with pride to all that they had done in the way of opening it up, and as we went along he showed us where the cross veins could be worked at a profit at some future time. They were just skimming the cream, with all the work being done by hand, until they could put in a modern plant and machinery.

He showed us how they had discovered gold and how they got it out. Then he took some ore out and washed it in a pan. Sure enough, when he got through washing, there was a streak of gold in the pan. I suppose 50 years later that same gold would probably be worth $10, maybe more. That was in 1935 when gold was $35 an ounce and in 1985 it was $350 an ounce.

Friends in Chile.

221

He told us that the mine had been worked centuries ago. When the Spaniards arrived and demanded that they produce gold, the people who were running the mine, several hundred of them, dug in the mine and ran out of gold. Actually, the gold was all up in the ceiling of the mine. What they were getting was nothing but rock so they abandoned the mine. That's the way they got out of supplying gold to the conquistadors.

We came to a shaft that led down to another level but by then the air in the tunnel was pretty bad and after a thorough inspection of the hoisting rig, which used a Ford engine for power, our host's suggestion that perhaps we had gone far enough met with instant agreement. We turned back along the tunnel but about halfway out, a mine car came plunging out of the darkness and try as I might, I couldn't think of a place to push myself into to get out of its way. It was much like the old nightmare where the train keeps coming down on you and you can't get out of its way. Well, the car stopped and by flattening myself alongside the wall the thing passed quite easily.

On the way out we took a look at the original diggings that were supposedly worked out by the Incas. These mines being the same that supplied some of the gold to the Inca kings and later the Spaniards. Then back into the open air and daylight. The daylight looked particularly good after being so far under the ground where the air was heavy and hard to breathe and the darkness seemed to press round you like a living thing.

He took us to breakfast just as I was about to perish from hunger, then showed us the water supply and after good-byes to all concerned we were driven back over the still beautiful desert. Some beautiful vistas whose grandeur and coloring defy description lay before us as we came down out of the mountains. Then on down to the ship, and so ended a very interesting and enjoyable shore excursion.

The ship stayed there for about a week loading. We would load a lighter[58] full of gold ore one day, then we'd wait for a day and another lighter of gold ore would come out. It was a terribly slow, monotonous job, because all I had to do was check the lighter and make sure it was loaded on board. We finally received the full shipment and got underway.

---

58 A lighter is a type of flat-bottomed barge used to transfer goods to and from moored ships using long oars.

On New Year's Eve we were at sea, after we pulled out of Samanco, Peru, about nine o'clock that night. The agent brought out a bottle of native firewater and we had a drink with him before he left. It was some of the strongest liquor that it has been my pleasure to taste. The purser and the third mate and I got quite happy about the change of the year. It was fun . . . almost like being ashore at a party.

We arrived in San Francisco in early February 1936, and after a short stay, I shipped out on the SS *Bolivar*, once again for South America. At last I was appointed Purser with a salary of $125.00 per month. I had thought at times that I would never make the grade, but I finally did. I wasn't concerned about being able to handle the work, as I had done it all for someone else a number of times, and there was nothing new about it. As Purser, my job was to do the paperwork necessary each time the ship entered a port, prepare customs declarations, and handle the government mail. I also assigned staterooms to the passengers, stored their valuables and assisted them whenever necessary.

Cargo lighters, 1931.

Golden Gate Bridge under construction, 1936.

It was much nicer being my own boss than doing it for someone else. I was the only one aboard who knew the West Coast very well, and it was up to me to look out for things in general including Grace Line's interests. Even the skipper came to me for advice about this and that at the different ports.

The *Bolivar* was only a little ship, about half as big as the *Cuzco*. She was very comfortable and the officers and crew were a nice lot. The skipper and I got along just dandy.

My quarters were rather small and there was no office, so I had to make a little bench to serve as a desk in my room. It worked out quite well.

When we sailed out of San Francisco that trip, I was quite blue. It usually didn't affect me that way but that time it did. We had fine weather down the coast and the ship rode like a cradle and my spirits improved.

We had a crew of 26 on board, which was ten less than on the *Cuzco*. The food was dandy with more fresh produce, and the change in cooks helped a lot. The bread on the *Cuzco* looked almost like a meat-loaf it was so full of weevils toward the end of the voyage. So was the cereal and other flours on board, full of weevils. But then four months was a long time to keep things fresh, especially going through the tropics the way we did.

We had to lay over in La Libertad for two days awaiting the arrival of a shipment of coffee. One of the mates, the radio operator and myself decided to visit the capital, San Salvador.

The ship lay at anchor about a mile out and the only communication with shore was a little launch owned by the port agent for the shipping company. To signal for the launch we would blow three long blasts on the ship's whistle and out would come the launch. The *Bolivar* had a beautiful whistle, a deep vibrant note that would have done justice to the *Leviathan*. The only trouble was that every time we blew this wonderful whistle it just about took all the steam in the boilers of the little *Bolivar*, which was originally built for service on the Great Lakes and had somehow found herself sailing the big oceans.

We boarded the launch and headed for shore. The pier stuck out just beyond the line of breakers that washed the sandy beach in the sparkling tropical sunlight. Just back of the beach, and seeming to crowd it, was the thick green of the tropics with its stately palms reaching so gracefully skyward.

Because of the swells, it was impossible to mount a ladder and the only way we could reach the pier was to be hoisted up in a chair by the cargo boom. The chair was lowered into the cockpit of the launch and Sparks was seated while the mate and I stood on the rungs on either side. We went soaring into the air and the swinging boom deposited us gently on the pier.

We told the agent of our desire to go up to San Salvador. He took us over to the port captain, a rotund individual of great importance. The captain spent quite some time telling us how difficult it would be for him to make the necessary arrangements. Then he got the brilliant idea that if the agent would guarantee our return on the morning train, he, the captain, would allow us to enter the country for the night. Whereupon the documents were drawn up and duly signed by the port captain, the agent and ourselves as well as by the clerk and a couple of other individuals whose connection with the affair was unexplained.

Soon the train came in: one coach and a couple of flat cars loaded with sacks of green coffee. The freight cars were shunted aside and a couple more coaches hooked on and we slowly left the little village of La Libertad. This only after we had shown our very official documents to all concerned, even the conductor.

As we left the village we passed through a lush green banana plantation. The growth was so thick and heavy that it seemed to press in on the tracks. Many of the trees were laden with big stalks of the green fruit, for they never allow the fruit to ripen on the tree. The trees were only a little taller than the cars on which we were riding, and we could only see a few feet into the dense tangle of their stalks.

We climbed a short way and were suddenly out in more or less open country, a swampy terrain, sparsely studded with scrubby tropical trees and tangled underbrush. Standing motionless at the edge of a glass-like pool stood a pure white crane who seemed to be staring at a perfect reflection of itself. Much of the vegetation was of the parasitic variety and covered most of the fallen and rotting trees. We were not able to spot but a few of the orchids that grow in great numbers there. Now and then the puffing engine would startle a brilliantly colored bird and its flash of color would betray it as it took wing, or we would not have spotted it in the tangle of brush. . . .

In February we encountered an adventuresome couple, Dan and Ginger Lamb. They were traveling in a homemade canoe down the coast of Central America and we picked them up. But they wanted to continue on their journey, and I witnessed their request:

1936, February 18 Aboard S/S *Bolivar*
I, Dan Lamb, herewith request the Captain of the S/S *Bolivar* to allow me to put to sea in my own boat the *Vagabundo*, entirely at my own risk and responsibility, thoroughly believing that my craft is absolutely safe and seaworthy under the existing weather conditions.

Signed: Dan Lamb[59]

S.C. Hulse, Witness

I kept touch with them for many years. Even received a Christmas card from them in 1943.

Dan and Ginger Lamb, 1936.

When the *Bolivar* returned to San Francisco in April 1936, that ended my sailing for a time. I was given a job in the office at W.R. Grace in San Francisco.

---

59 Dana Upton Lamb and Ginger Bishop married February 19, 1933. In August, they embarked on what became a 3-year, 16,000 mile voyage in their homemade, 16-foot canoe, the *Vagabunda*, from So. California down the Pacific coasts of Mexico, Guatemala, and Costa Rica, and culminated in their crossing of the Panama Canal in September 1936. They chronicled their adventures in a book, *Enchanted Vagabonds* (1938).

Then after Christmas 1937, I was "detached from duty in the office" and assigned as Purser on the SS *Curaca*, at a salary of $135.00 per month. On January 3, 1938, I sailed on the *Cuzco*, but I was directed to transfer to the SS *Curaca* at Corinto, Nicaragua, as Purser on that ship.

Sailing, itself, seemed like old times – standing on the deck watching the dock slip away and become part of the panorama of the waterfront. Then Alcatraz quite close at hand; the huge bridge overhead, and out into the open sea. Outside the Gate there was a brief pause as the trim little pilot boat slipped alongside and dropped her dory in our lee and started to circle us in order to pick up the dory which was taking off our pilot. As she cleared our bow a big one caught her and her decks were washed in a white foam. She soon completed her task and with a final salute turned her bow back toward the Golden Gate.

As if the blowing of the whistle had awakened her again, the old ship gradually came to life and slowly regained her course. The weather was clear and the checkerboard of the Sunset District stood out in sharp relief.

At first, the roll of the ship was quite noticeable but by suppertime, I had found my sea legs and was rolling with the ship once again. The fresh salt air gave me a good appetite and a big plate of baked ham for supper disappeared quickly.

By nine o'clock, I was sleepy and so to bed and lost till morning. Seven o'clock found me watching a beautiful sunrise – all soft pink and gold with the silhouette of the mountains in the foreground. The faint finger of dawn tinting the eastern sky with the pastel shades of a coming day. A most lovely way to start the day.

We stopped in Manzanillo, Mexico, and at Puerto Ángel, and we loaded practically a full cargo of coffee as we made our way down the coast. Manzanillo was very interesting. It had changed some in the two years since I had been there: more houses, more people, more dogs and more donkeys. The smells were not nearly as bad as they had been, and I enjoyed walking around the town. Much of it was quaint and picturesque, but the marketplace was still a source of wonder – a wonder that they were not all dead. However, it had been cleaned up a great deal even though the meat still hung in the open where the prospective customer was invited to judge for himself, by the simple expedient of pinching and prodding and hefting several pieces before selecting one. Yes, beauty was local custom.

Loading coffee at Puerto Ángel, Mexico, 1936.

We shipped a new crew that trip and I liked the skipper. The only fly in the ointment was that he liked to play bridge so I had to sit in on a bridge game every evening. I had to learn the game whether I liked it or not. I didn't get the fun out of bridge that I did out of poker. Maybe because we didn't play bridge for stakes. Thank goodness!

I went ashore in the little port of San José del Cabo, on the tip of Baja California. There wasn't much to see but I did go through a sugar mill – just a small mill – and they showed me how they made the cane into sugar. They brought the cane in from the fields right alongside of the mill and ran it through a set of rollers to squeeze the juice out of the cane. In fact the rollers would squeeze the juice out of most anything that got in the way. There must have been a lot of little bugs that went into the sugar, but by the time they got squeezed you wouldn't know them so it didn't matter. Anyway, the juice of the cane, which tasted like sweet water, ran down a trough and into a series of heating tanks, which were each hotter than the last one. Then it went into a tank and was boiled and skimmed off and then boiled down some more and finally into a large caldron where it was cooked like candy. When it was done it was poured into a large trough where it was swished back and forth, to keep the sugar from hardening in glass-like bricks rather than in the granular bricks that you buy brown sugar in. When it started to harden, it was poured into moulds.

The unions had taken over the running of the mill on a share basis and forced the owners out entirely. As a consequence, there was no boss and everyone did just about as they pleased, and the production had fallen off about 50%. The product was not as good as formerly and the men were not making as much money as they were before they took the thing into their own hands. Labor without capital to direct it is like a mighty river: allowed to overflow its banks, it destroys all that it comes into contact with, even silting its own channel and creating swamps and stagnation.

We had picked up a shipment of dynamite coming down the coast. The ship was loaded at the time so they brought the cases in, and the only place they could put them where it was safe was in the purser's office, which was a large room right next to my room. They brought it in and loaded every space around me with dynamite.

We went into La Libertad, El Salvador, and dropped off the load of dynamite. After we sailed the doggone dynamite blew up. We had put it into a lighter and sent it to shore, then they picked it up off the lighter and put it on a railroad car and moved it out of the dock. While it was on the railroad car it blew up. We had left the port by then and heard of it out at sea.

La Libertad, El Salvador, after dynamite exploded.

We stayed in Puntarenas, Costa Rica, for two nights. The first night we didn't get ashore but just lay at anchor. The next night was Good Friday and we went ashore and saw a very interesting procession.

The procession was a mixture of baby parade and funeral. First came the queen of the parade and she was a most beautiful young girl. She was accompanied by the ladies in waiting who were also very beautiful. Next came some youngsters dressed like padres carrying banners and things aloft. Then a troupe of Roman guards followed by a number of little girls with angel wings, each sitting in the center of a flower-like float borne aloft on the shoulders of four men. Some of them were darling and all were quite lovely. Following the little girls, came a bier.

On the bier was a life-like image of Christ. This bier was borne aloft by a number of men and around it were more men. Following behind was a throng of women all inching their way along to the strains of a band that was bringing up the rear playing funeral music – a rather good band too.

We saw the procession later in the evening as it was returning to the church for the grand finale. Some of the tikes were falling asleep and did look so very funny: tiaras awry, wings askew, and that sleepy look that gave them the appearance of all being out on a glorious binge. It was all very entertaining.

We spent two nights in Corinto, and I had a nice time there too. I danced with some of the local pulchritude[60] and did a bit of flirting. The money was six to one, where it had been at a par with ours a few months before, so we splurged. One round of refreshments for twelve in our party cost less than 50¢. It was nice to be rich once in a while. After all, wealth is relative.

Chapter 17: Working in San Francisco

ABOUT THAT TIME, I WAS THINKING about ending my sailing career, and I learned that Mom and Don were making plans to move to the East Coast with the kids, Donnabeth and Bill.

---

60 Beauties.

1938, April 1st, Mazatlán Bound

Have thought so much about you all and the prospect of
your going east. It has more than shaken me. It has bought
home to me, so forcefully, how very lucky I have been to have
such a lovely home to go home to all these years. Truly, I have
been more than fortunate. I feel somewhat like Don felt at the
thought of meeting a change, but I know that whatever change
is made will be for the best.

Love,
Stan

By mid-May, Mom, Donnabeth and Bill were on their way to New Jersey. Duge was plant engineer for Metals & Thermit Company, where he had worked since graduating from Stanford in 1919, with a degree in Mechanical Engineering. The company sent him back east to build a detinning plant for them in Carteret, New Jersey. He had moved out there some months before.

The company bought tin scrap from old tin cans – took the tin off with caustic soda solution. Then the tin went into a slurry and the slurry was run through a cascading plating division: 50 feet of plates. When electricity was applied, the tin came out of the solution and was plated onto the steel tanks. Then they dipped the tanks into a big pot and melted it into pure tin. Duge said that if they could get the tin out of the crimp in the cans, it would be worth a fortune. But they were never able to figure out how to uncrimp the cans.

Mom and the kids took the train across the country. I think it was on the *City of San Francisco*, a streamlined passenger train that took them from the Oakland Mole[61] to Chicago, then they went on to Pennsylvania and New York.

One time they were at a table in the dining car. "A black fellow came to take our order," Bill recalled years later. "We were discussing the menu and he was standing there rocking, as porters will do, and I asked him, 'Would you like to sit down while we're figuring it out?'

"Well, word got around the kitchen, and I ate strawberries and cream all the way across the country.

"In Chicago we got a cab and Mom was looking for a drug store

---

61 The Oakland Mole was a railroad terminal halfway out Oakland's Long Wharf, a massive railroad wharf and ferry pier, where passengers from San Francisco transferred onto cross-country trains.

to get me something to calm my stomach. (Too many strawberries with cream!) The cabby was a nice fellow and he took us to the Chicago Zoo. He just took his cab off line and gave us a tour through the zoo. Then he took us back to the station to catch the train to Philly. We ended our trip in Roselle, New Jersey, about ten miles from where Dad worked."

The family enjoyed their time in New Jersey. Mom said that everything was clean, green and fresh-looking and she enjoyed the storms, thunder-and-lightning and all. They were close to shopping and shows and she just loved it. Duge liked his work but found his leisure trying with nothing to fiddle with. They paid him well and gave him extra money for rent and expenses as well as a Ford to drive around in.

I stayed on the SS *Curaca* until June 1938, when it arrived in San Francisco. Though I enjoyed my job as purser, it came to where I was taking a drink every day. I'd finish my work and sit down and have a drink. It was a good past time. Then one day I got to thinking, my gosh, I've had a drink every day for seven months now. This has got to stop. So when I got into port in San Francisco, I quit the ship. I told them I wasn't going back. I said, "The heck with it. I'm not going to become a bum." Lots of guys did, because it was so easy. We got good liquor real cheap, without any taxes. I think a fifth of liquor then was a dollar or a dollar and a half, and that was pretty cheap. I was making good wages and it was an easy habit to fall into.

Outside of working for Grace Line, I didn't know where to look for a job. But they offered me a job in the Claims Department in their San Francisco office, so I took it.

At that time no one in the office knew anything about claims. The guy who had been handling the claims was a big shot in the office, but he had died and left all of his papers on his desk when he passed away. So I kept his papers and put them out every morning, and months went by, and nobody asked to see any of them. So finally, I just got rid of them, and I took over the claims department.

The guy who died didn't know a darn thing about claims because he hadn't worked on the ships. I found some old claim files from years back, that had to do with the gold ore that we had picked up in South America. I became very much interested in them because I had been down to those ports and I had complained about the way the gold ores came down to the ship. I was able to write a letter telling the people at the American Smelting Company that we were refusing their claim because when the ores had come down to the ship, they were not packaged right. Some of them actually caught on fire because of the acid in them.

I told them that we were in no way responsible for that kind of shipment, and I disclaimed any liability. Well, they immediately sent a representative over to see what was going on. I told the representative that was the way it was, and there was nothing we could do because the ores had been faulty when they had come down to the ships. And I showed him the bills of lading where we had noted that the ores had been damaged when they came on board. He was very much impressed, and he took my claims as correct back to the American Smelting Company. And that's the way we cleaned up several years of claims against Grace Line. I received quite a compliment from that guy. He was glad that I had been there and I had seen it and I knew what I was talking about. He hated to lose the money, but that's the way it was.

I enjoyed that summer, had a lot of fun and didn't have to work too hard. I was making about $75 a month, and was always quite broke toward payday, but I got by. At that time I was working at the office at the dock where the claims department was. I think it was Pier 35 at the foot of Montgomery Street. But in September we moved to the uptown office at 2 Pine Street. The work gave me a lot of responsibility and much of the work was in an executive capacity. I found that the time I had spent at sea gave me a wide knowledge of conditions and circumstances that enabled me to tackle some tough problems. Some of the claims ran as high as three to five thousand dollars and had been in controversy since 1935.

Working that way, the whole thing took on the aspect of a game, a big game that was very absorbing. Like any other game you have to put a lot into it but the pleasure is worth it. So much of the job was patient prodding, but that prodding put me on the threshold of a great theater. That theater was playing the craziest, nuttiest, most exciting drama in history: "Modern Business." In this great show, money pulled with unseen wires the millions of puppets through their various roles – comic, tragic, dashing, brilliant and drab.

At that time I was living with the Winfreys, friends of the family, paying them seven dollars a week. I didn't spend much time there but spent a lot of time with friends – Fred Franck, Johnny Bruce, Jim and

Ruth Chesnutt. My days at sea had given me an ability to make myself at home anywhere. There was always the possibility that I might even get married! Lots of gals seemed to like my company, and one of them might catch me at a weak moment and take me out of circulation. I thought that maybe I should start a family of my own. . . But I was on the go a lot.

Now and then I'd stop to appreciate the autumn crispness and the smell of the damp earth, or to enjoy a movie like *Moonlight Sonata* – with Paderewski playing Beethoven's *Moonlight Sonata* – reminding me of boyhood days listening to my mother play the piano.

The Second Sino-Japanese War was raging in November 1938, and I could see that it was going to change the world.

"Japan's conquest of China conjures a mental cartoon of a Japanese opening a huge Pandora's Box: China. The rest of the world will, I'm afraid, also regret this Oriental version of Pandora.

"War is opening up China! It has rudely awakened the largest country in the world and brought them face to face with a modern world, after centuries of self-sufficiency and aloofness.

"Roads for war are being built. People who for generations have not moved from one spot – excepting in the famine districts – suddenly find themselves fleeing a dreaded monster – the Japanese army – only to be caught up in the mad vortex of war.

"That war is breeding hatred that throughout the rest of history will spawn the seeds of war which will, as the harvest is ready, be harvested by war.

"China awakened! A vast nation modernized, and there is nothing that modernizes a nation like war – centuries of progress in a few short hell-ridden months.

"Out of it all will rise a leader – one always does – and then the tide of empire will change – flow west for a while – and what of the superior white races?

"For what we are witnessing thru our newspapers today is, I believe, the turn of the tide. How much that tide will carry with it!!"

In January, 1939, I went to night school to investigate a course in photography. It seemed funny that I would be interested in that subject after all the time away from it, but there was a young fellow in Palo Alto who wanted to go into the business, and I was thinking about being his partner. So I took a class in photography that winter, but nothing ever came of our business venture.

I drove up to Clear Lake one weekend in January to see my dad, G.C. I knew that he had been ill with both his heart and gallstones, so I decided to drop in on him and say hello. He and Maude owned the Will-O-Point Campground in Lakeport. I left San Jose late, and took it easy – lovely drive, perfect weather – and I got there about 3 p.m. He was raking leaves in the yard – just an old man in a brown flannel shirt and cap – much as he looked in San Jose, only older. His hair was white and his skin was loose on his neck and jowls. The sight of him gave me a powerful lump in my throat. I'd never been filled with greater pity for anyone than for G.C. Just the thought of the poor man – and how utterly poor he was – was enough to make me want to cry.

When I walked into the yard he just thought I was someone stopping to ask a question. He sort of pleasantly glanced up and started to ask what I wanted. When he saw who it was, a sort of confused, happy expression came over his face. Well, we made small talk and then sat on the steps of the cabin and just talked about the season past and prospects for next season. I told him that I wasn't there on business but had heard that he had not been so well and thought I'd run up and say hello.

Maude came out and was pleasant. Then G.C. and I went into the house while Maude went to shop. We watched the lake, Clear Lake, which was beautiful in the winter; admired the view and watched the colors change in the sunset. We talked about some of my friends that he had met and some of Mabel's. He told me about not making any money – losses in the flood – and all the time there was something else so much more important but it just didn't get said. Why? I don't know.

Poor chap. I could read him like a book. Money – avarice – had robbed the poor man of everything in life worthwhile: friends and loved ones – he had no one in the true sense of the word.

One minute I was feeling so very sorry for him, and then he had to tell me about how he had pulled a fast one over on an old guy around town. He sold the fellow his old trailer for $50 while the old fellow was full of whiskey. The old guy didn't have a car and had given G.C. ten dollars to seal the bargain, but a few days later he came around for his money back. G.C. held on to it and the old fellow, in order not to lose the ten, bought the trailer. It was all very clever! Damn G.C.'s hide anyway. It made me mad just to think about it. What can you do with a man like that?

He asked me if I wanted a drink and when I refused that, having already refused a cigarette, he remarked to Maude, "What do you know, he doesn't drink or smoke."

He was really proud of me though – I could tell. It was there some way or other. He was pleased too, that I had come to see him.

Well, to make a long story short, it came time for dinner and Maude called from the store to see if I was staying, and G.C. then had to ask me. I told him I would be on my way as it was a long way back, and I took my leave. I really think that he had not thought to ask me sooner, but as long as I had stayed until the supper hour and nothing had been said, I couldn't stay. It was a fine point – maybe I was right – maybe not.

Years later, when I was down at Camp Roberts in '44, I wrote to G.C. and told him that as far as I was concerned I felt no bitterness over the San Jose affair, but did regret the fact that he and I were so far apart. In thinking it over I was sure that he felt as I did, that each had disappointed the other. I said that if he were willing, I was offering the first step toward a renewed understanding.

I got a nice little note back saying he would like to see me and thought that propinquity would do a lot to erase any misunderstanding. It was the right thing to do as G.C. had gotten nothing out of life and the very tragic evening of life that he faced seemed to be so terrible that I felt if I could, I must offer to relieve the tragic situation.

When I got back, I took a drive around Santa Clara Valley just to look the place over and reminisce. Past scenes and places brought back many memories and made me miss my family a lot. It was beautiful weather – springlike with warmth in the air, and the valley in the early spring was something to see.

It was in 1939, that I met Lu Kemp. My friend Curly Hausam had arranged a blind date for me. I arrived at the apartment on South 6th Street in San Jose and was introduced to three girls: Virginia, Lu and Barbara. Barbara had been going with the same young man since grammar school and Virginia and Lu thought she needed a change. They both worked for the telephone company, affectionally known as Ma Bell, and so did Curly, so they had asked him to find Barbara a date. I came in and met the gals. Lu was ironing clothes in the kitchen and Virginia said, "Lu, why don't you show the fellows how you climb up the door?"

So she performed her trick of climbing up the door jamb, which we all enjoyed. Then Curly and I took Virginia and Barbara out for the evening. Well, it wasn't much of a deal. Barbara wasn't interested in anyone except her man. But the next week I asked Curly if he could get me a date with "the one who climbs doors." So that's how we started dating. We'd go over to Santa Cruz and enjoy the boardwalk. We had a lot of good times together. But with the war coming on, we sort of drifted apart.

Lu Kemp and Stan. The only photograph he had of her before the War.

Chapter 18: Golden Gate International Exposition

"WE ARE HAVING A FAIR, AND WHAT A FAIR! It is beautiful, beautiful, beautiful." But first we had a fiesta – and what a fiesta! A week before the opening the big town started to get a little dizzy. Sort of a fever. It might have been caused by the approach of spring – the weather had been that way. Whiskers sprouted on bank clerks, streetcar motormen, postmen, barmen, salesmen and doormen. Some of the Babbitts about town even let their beards grow. It was a sight. Streets became gulches, and bars (the name was banned) became saloons. False fronts on many of the shops carried all sorts of legends that probably would have made little sense to the pioneers but were a lot of fun anyway.

Stenographers were cowgirls and salesgirls donned bright shirts and short skirts and ten-gallon hats, and little Mary had her day in the sun and so it went. The town was all in festive garb – its citizens all dressed up, parades parading up Market Street – Market Street with her lamp posts freshly gilded, bedecked with flags and bunting, her sidewalks thronged with gayly garbed merry makers. The old street was a gay way. Business slowed to a walk, but old Joe Public was out for a good time. The streets each vied for publicity with decorations and deeds worthy of renown. The hoosegow[62] was erected and if a backward citizen was so lacking as to fail to have something in the way of color about his person, he was apt to find himself incarcerated amid much noise and many gibes. It was all in fun, even the time they hanged the fellow up on Polk Gulch. They had the rope arranged to take the strain on a belt and the noose was just for looks. The belt broke though, so they had to get out the fire department laddies to get the air back in him as he was turning bluish when they noticed the belt was not doing its part. It was a mad carnival week. I never thought that I would see San Francisco take down her hair and have a real romp for herself.

On Friday night there was a dandy parade. There were more horses than San Francisco had seen since the auto. There were lovely lighted floats and a big Chinese dragon doing some of its best evil spirit chasing. Both Chinese and Japanese, in separate groups of course, glided along in lovely lantern-carrying arrangements. There were drum corps and bands, drill teams and people in uniforms and costumes. It was a great party the old City put on, and the whole city was there.

Saturday, February 18, the 1939 World's Fair opened on Treasure Island, celebrating the City's two newly built bridges. Fred and I went over in the afternoon. We tried to get around it but walked until we were dead tired and felt as though we had not even scratched the sur-

---

62 A prison.

face. It was such a beautifully arranged affair: the buildings with bass reliefs on the walls, the statues, groves of olive trees and gardens, lovely fountains, and paintings on some of the walls. Everywhere color and beauty – beauty of design, beauty of architecture, natural beauty of the trees and gardens – all on a beautiful isle in the center of a beautiful bay!

And then nighttime, and the beautiful poem of the day became a symphony of color. Were I writing with a rainbow, I couldn't describe it. When Kipling spoke of "painting on a ten league canvass" he gave some idea of the way I would like to be able to describe that "Arabian Nights Tale" that sparkled like a gem in the jewel box of the West.

Chapter 19: War Years – Fort Ord

WHEN THE SELECTIVE SERVICE ACT was passed in October 1940, I decided to volunteer for the one-year service. I left Grace Line and went into the Army on January 27, 1941. I was one of the first 100 who volunteered at the local board in Redwood City. I was appointed leader of the contingent of men from Redwood City during the journey to the Armory in San Francisco where we were inducted.

There they gave me a physical examination. I weighed 125 pounds and stood 5 foot 7½ inches tall. After the induction, we had a nice trip down to Monterey on the train – 107 of us. They gave us a good box lunch on the way and we arrived there about 7 p.m. As soon as we arrived, they loaded us into trucks and up to the Presidio we went. We were lined up, the roll was called, and they checked our papers by 8:00. Then another line and they drove us into the dispensary in bunches and before we had time to know what was happening, we had been shot in the arm and vaccinated and inspected for lice.

Stan at Fort Ord, 1941.

Then into another line and another and another until we had been fitted with shoes, measured for uniforms, etc. and issued our clothing and gear. It was 11 p.m. before we were through and then up to our quarters and a cup of coffee. We were then assigned to tents and issued bedding. We got to bed about 1 a.m., dog tired but so many of the boys were full of pep that sleep was hard to get amid the noise and hubbub, as another bunch came in about 1:30 and were hours getting settled.

Five forty-five came around real quick and then more lines for rolls and breakfast. Then I.Q. tests and classification interviews to find out what work we were equipped to do. Then drills and instruction and so the day went. At chow time there was another line, and we ate out of mess kits with everything on one plate.

In a few days I was assigned to the field artillery. We had nice quarters in a clean, new building with hot water and warm rooms. We ate in a big mess hall with dishes, which was an improvement over the mess kit. I was a corporal in the Headquarters and Headquarters Battery, 31st Field Artillery Battalion, Seventh Division.

The next four or five weeks were spent learning how to be a soldier – drilling, drilling and drilling and learning the use of equipment. The officers and noncoms were a good lot and were very patient with us "green peas." There were no crude bawling outs, and it was a pretty decent lot of young men who really gave it their best out there on the field. It was really reassuring to see and feel such a fine spirit. It convinced me that the good old U.S. was here to stay, safe in its own democracy, possibly changing to meet a changing world but none the less, secure.

This cute letter came to me from Mom:

1941, February 3
Salute, Private 39000950
   I must say our Paternal Government keeps Moms posted – in 5 days 3 official notifications as to your whereabouts and well-being, so Dear small Love, I knew where you were even if you didn't.
   Letters always welcome but don't write because you feel you must – if tired, relax. The War Dept. will keep me posted!
                   Love dear – always —
                        Mom

The weather, for the most part, was pleasant. I hadn't been outdoors so much in years and I enjoyed it. One time when we were on a cross country hike, we got caught out in the rain. We were about a mile from quarters when a shower broke out, and we were soaking wet by the time we got back. We all had raincoats so the ordinary rains didn't interfere with drills, but on that hike we didn't take them along.

My feet were pretty sore, as I wasn't used to heavy shoes, and I was pretty tired after a full day. But it wasn't what one could call "killing" work, and I spent most of my off-hours on my bunk, as it felt plenty good to stretch out and to get off my poor feet.

The 31st Field Artillery Battalion was composed of Headquarters and Headquarters Battery, Batteries A, B, C and D and Supply and Ammunition Battery. The different batteries had various guns, 4 to 6 guns to the battery, the heaviest being 155mm or a little less than 6-inch guns. These were the howitzer type or short barreled guns used to fire a high trajectory in order to drop shells over hills, etc. Then we had the famous French 75s, 3-inch calibre guns, and anti-tank guns, about 37mm.

I was very happy in the Army – happier than I had been since I was up at Bloomquist's in La Honda. The freedom from responsibility was really a remarkable feeling. I was in better health and ate better than I had in years and found that I could eat most anything without the aid of soda. Maybe if I ever had kids, they wouldn't have to call me Soda Pop!

I took up photography again while I was at Fort Ord. This fellow and I built a darkroom so I could help him with some picture work. An hour or two in the evening was gone before I knew it just piddling around in the darkroom. Some of the stuff we did was pretty good too. The sergeant and I turned out over $20 worth of work one week for the fellows in the battery, just in our spare time.

One night when I was doing guard duty, I was picked as the best soldier by the Officer of the Day and as a reward was made the colonel's orderly the next day, which relieved me from "walking a post" and allowed me to go back to my barracks and spend the night in my own bunk.

The camp was situated in a very beautiful spot. It overlooked the bay and the water was beautiful. Spring was just lovely there on the Monterey coast. The wildflowers were a delight – so many, many kinds and colors. Certain sectors of the reservation were charming little woodland settings with stunted oak trees, Spanish moss hanging from their gnarled branches, and on the ground a green carpet interwoven with so many beautiful and delicately colored wildflowers. Spring is really Spring when you're right out in it and can watch it unfold.

With the beautiful spring weather, it was nice to be outdoors in the brush and field all day. I was in an antitank platoon, and we went out on the reservation most every morning and practiced taking up positions. I saw more of nature and California's wildflowers than I had for many a year. I had almost forgotten that there were so many different kinds of flowers.

Sometimes I wondered if I would ever be able to go back into the office and just sit day after day. I liked it out of doors so much that I didn't even mind a little rain. Of course if the novelty wore off, I might be glad to get behind a desk again.

On March 15, 1941, we had a big inspection day. Every man had to be dressed in his cleanest and best with his shoes and equipment shined. Then we fell out and were inspected by the battery commander. The 130 men in my battery all lined up and the commanding officer looked us over very carefully. When he got to me he looked long and closely – making me feel very uneasy and self conscious.

Anti-tank gun, Fort Ord, 1941

When he finished inspection, he commended me on my appearance and said that I was the best appearing man in the outfit, and being a new man in the outfit, he thought I deserved all the credit. (Didn't mention what credit it was.) Anyway, it was nice to be number one man.

We did a lot of shooting at Fort Ord. One day I worked hard setting up a moving target. We strung out 1500 feet of cable and towed the target over a course by truck. By night I was plenty tired.

We spent a lot of time working on problems. One time we had an all-night problem that involved the whole 7th Division. Long caravans of trucks and columns of troops moved in the pitch dark and took up their positions. We moved our command post about 8 miles, and the ride through the dark and the locating of our new position was all intensely interesting. Through the darkness we heard the infantry march up and the horse drawn outfits go into position near us. Then we set up and established communications between the batteries and battalion headquarters. I enjoyed it, though I got pretty cold.

Along about April 1, we went up to Yosemite. They got us up at 3:30 a.m. and we pulled out about 5:00. It was a long ride (208 miles) in the back of an Army truck. We got there and made camp about 6 p.m. Then I walked around the floor of the canyon for a couple of

Stan at Yosemite on maneuvers, April 1941.

243

Bivouac in Yosemite, 1941.

hours with some buddies and about 9 p.m. we went to bed. I was very tired so I slept pretty well. The sleeping bag was well worth the six bucks I had to pay for it.

We got up the next morning at six o'clock and after breakfast the whole battery hiked up to Vernal Falls. It was a lovely hike and really bracing in the cold mountain air. The snow on the mountain peaks made the park even more beautiful. When we got back we were ready for lunch and ate like we were starved, and indeed we felt like it.

In the afternoon we had nothing scheduled so another fellow and I walked around the floor of the valley and marveled at the beauty and mighty mightiness of the place. We visited the museum and several of the lodges and enjoyed ourselves in spite of the fact that it rained a little now and then. We must have walked more than a dozen miles!

That night we had a lecture on the valley and its fauna and flora, etc. and then to bed. During the night it snowed, and again I was glad that I was in a sleeping bag. We weathered the snow and rain very well, but of course some of the fellows got wet. Their tents were not properly put up or beds not properly made. I slept warm and pretty well except for the showers of rain falling on the tent that woke me now and again.

The next morning the valley was all snow-covered. It was pretty cold getting out at 5 a.m. and getting breakfast in the snow and rain, which was still falling. After breakfast we struck camp and went back to Fort Ord. It was a beautiful trip! Well worth the effort and an experience too – a little more of living, as it were.

They sent me to a special gas school to learn about chemical warfare defense. It was a 30-hour course, three hours a day and required considerable studying. The class walked a long mile down to the beach where we had demonstrations. I learned that with a gas mask, protective clothing, and a knowledge of the agents themselves, a person had little to fear from gas. I was lucky to be picked to attend the school, as there were only two men in the battery attending, and it was up to us to instruct the others.

Another problem we constructed was a tank trap. We built – or rather dug – the trap one night in the dark without lights. We finished about one in the morning and then got an hour's sleep before being awakened to stand guard so that none of our own vehicles would fall in. Later, I got two more hours of sleep before breakfast.

Every night for a week we pulled out and marched in the dark. There were long columns of trucks churning along the roads with their lights off, and the doughboys marching in long lines beside the roads. Then came the horse artillery with all the clanking of harness, the snorting of horses, and the bang and rattle of the ordinance. It made me feel alive and a part of something big and powerful. I got a real kick out of those problems.

But I missed seeing my family and wanted to go home for a visit. It was different than being at sea, for then there was no possible way to get home, but at Fort Ord, it was only circumstances that kept me away: one Sunday I was a table waiter, the week before a dining room orderly, before that measles quarantine, or some darn thing. I did finally get home for a weekend in June.

In the Army I picked up a lot of information and knowledge about the game. It really is quite a game! I'm glad that I didn't make a career out of it though! I was a good soldier and a couple of the sergeants were after me to transfer to their sections, but I elected to stand pat. Also the officers at headquarters had their eye on me for a clerk's job! I didn't want that under any circumstances, and kept my fingers crossed hoping that they would let me stay in the anti-tank section.

245

Corporal Hulse and his gun crew: top picture, standing;
below: in center, sitting before the gun.

In June we began firing real ammunition and preparing for a big maneuver. On the day it began, we were up at 3:45 a.m. for chow and at 5:00 we started to roll. Made our first camp on the Hunter-Liggett Reservation where 65,000 of us stayed for the weekend.

It was a very pleasant camp, though on a rather steep hillside slope overlooking the valley. The days were very warm, almost hot but the nights rather cold. It was nice lying about the camp resting, reading, playing cards and listening to the radio, which brought the surprising news that Hitler had invaded Russia. What did that mean? My guess was that it was a desperate move to allay the rising tide of U.S. intervention and to secure the full cooperation of Japan to keep the U.S. occupied in the Pacific, thereby reducing our aid to Britain.

During the hot afternoon we walked down the road about three-quarters of a mile and had a nice bath in the stream and a pint of ice cream. The stream was lined with soldiers for several miles.

In the evening I enjoyed being out in the open, sitting on the hillside in the gathering dusk. The noises of an army getting ready for the night drifted up, noises that you don't hear anywhere else. It wasn't like any other kind of a camp, but yet it was pleasant. Some laughter, now and then a command, here and there a call to some friend, or someone trying to locate a particular person by calling his name, and always in the background the growling, mumbling noise of the Army vehicles – trucks, cars, jeeps and motorcycles.

The third night we lined up at 8 p.m. and stood by until 10:00 when we decided to take a nap. In about half an hour word came down that we were to proceed to the base camp, which site had been reconnoitered the day before.

The dry, dusty roads were like driving through talcum powder and, though the vehicle in front only traveled about 7 mph, the dust was so thick that the cars following could not keep up. In an effort to follow the red tail lights of the car ahead, to keep from losing the way, the drivers would gun ahead until they had closed the space or were utterly lost in the blinding cloud boiling around them. It was therefore inevitable that many of the vehicles crashed.

Shortly after we started, my driver missed the turn and we were almost over on our side when we stopped. The left wheel had climbed an embankment. We got back on the road and dashed ahead until we picked up the lights on the gun ahead and then slid to a stop to keep from running into it. From then on it was a series of mad dashes forward and frantic stops in order to keep the light in front of us in view.

We soon passed the first of our trucks over on her side, its driver pressing the horn button to attract aid. The column was moving and, though it gave me a sickly feeling, it was impossible to stop and give the boys a hand. You see, we were on our way uphill, but the maintenance truck was close behind and would take over. Needless to say, the first casualty so soon after our start put me in a hell of a state of mind. As we groped forward we passed more and more smashed vehicles: some on their sides, one in the river, others upside-down, a couple horribly smashed over an embankment, one on top of the other. It was a hell of a ride, and when the second truck ahead of me got two wheels over the edge and the car ahead of me called back, "Quick a tow rope! Finch is over the bank," I felt like a sick dog, as limp as a dish rag.

Thank God when I got up there with the rope it was only two wheels and not the horrible mess that I pictured in the black maw of the canyon. In minutes we had him back on the road.

We spent a week there, from Sunday till Friday. During that time we just got snatches of sleep, spending most of our time on the march from 10 or 11 p.m. till dawn. There were over seven thousand vehicles driving over the roads on the reservation, and they just sprayed dust all the time. It was a dirty, exhausting week.

In mid-August we went up to Washington. It was an easy and pleasant trip north, though the early rising each morning was not so good. We got up at 2:30 a.m. and rolled around 4 to 4:30. We made around 250 miles each day and, as the road speed was about 30 to 45 mph, it was easy going. I switched off with my driver every two hours so it made driving a pleasure.

On the way, we went through Willits. It was hot there! But then as we drove through the forests we put down the windshield and, as we had no top on the truck, the cool mountain air with all the delicious odor of the Douglas-fir forest was exhilarating. The unobstructed view of the tall, tall redwoods and firs towering into the sky lifted my spirits until, I'm afraid, I was contributing the only sour note to an otherwise most beautiful ride by my loud but not so beautiful singing.

One place we went through was a very lovely grove named Dungan Grove. I was surprised to see it, as Dungan is not a common name. The name was spelled correctly too.

On that trip, the problem we were working on was principally one of moving most of the Fourth Army about in a given area, and believe me it was a big problem. That whole section of the state was the maneuver area. There were about a hundred thousand troops being used as pawns in the game, and that many men with all their equipment and ordinance being moved daily – and some of them more often – presented a real problem in transport and communications.

Most of the territory was backwoods like the Pescadero district, and to keep a rendezvous that had been given by direction some hundreds of miles away, was sometimes a real problem and of course many strange and funny situations arose.

For instance: one night each sergeant was told to put his two guns into position en route to our new regimental position to protect the march. The positions I was to occupy were given to me, and I started out some 30 odd miles up the highway. It was pouring rain most of the night, and when I arrived in the vicinity of one of the little towns I was to occupy, there was no such town. I got hold of the town marshall of the next nearest town and we got out a map of the area, but could not locate any such place as designated. There I was in an open truck out in the rain looking for a spot on the map that didn't exist! The next morning, by the light of day, I was able to locate the ruins of a couple of old shacks, long fallen apart, that were the town that showed so distinctly on the military map that night. All of the crews had the same difficulty, so the night was interesting. Looking back, it was kind of fun.

We spent most of the nights traveling or occupying some position where we stopped all traffic during the night as a precaution against the enemy getting through. But one night we pulled a lulu!

We were in position about 12 miles from Winlock, Washington, up in the mountains. We went into town to the gasoline dump to fill our three trucks and had a swell hell-for-leather ride! We got to town and gassed up and started back, but the road we came out on had a long convoy on it going past us, so we had to wait a few minutes. There was a break in the convoy so we slipped into it and when we got to where we needed to turn off to go back up into the hills, we ducked down the road and hightailed for our position. When we got there and the dust of our trail settled, we found that the convoy we had cut into had followed us up into the hills and the outfits following them had tagged along. There we were with over a hundred trucks right up there on the front lines jammed up like sardines in a can. After much cussing and no little sweat on the part of some of the drivers of the larger truck and trailer jobs, I finally got them all headed back to town. And so it went.

A portable stove, which we smuggled along with us, helped a lot to compensate for a very lousy kitchen. It was real fun augmenting our regular meals through our own efforts: hot coffee, pancakes, eggs, sometimes picking wild berries or swiping fruit or getting a handout from the farmer on or near whose land we were in position.

We were all a little short on sleep, depending mostly on cat naps throughout the day and night. But aside from that, I was tops. We washed if and when we could and sometimes we got pretty dirty, wet and tired, but our spirits were never down and my crew gave me their best. A dandy bunch. We were up there for a couple of weeks, then headed back to Ord.

To sum it all up, I wouldn't have missed the maneuvers for a whole lot. It was great. Some work, some fun and intently interesting. The trip itself was an experience long to be remembered, and living in the open appealed to me in spite of the rain. It must be that drop of Boone blood.

When we got back, I was assigned to drill the battery in handling a rifle. I was considered an expert rifle instructor, so that was my job.

One day the battery commander called me in and asked me if I wanted to go to Officer School. I was quite surprised, as it was the first time that anyone in any of the outfits I had been in had had the opportunity to go. I told him that, since I did not figure on making a career of the Army, I would not elect to go unless we were at war, as it would mean at least a year and a half more – too long to be out of the swim of things.

At that time I was thinking about going up to Tahoe. My friend Smitty, Ed Smith, an old friend from my sailing days, was up there, and Bill, my younger brother, had gone up for the summer to work with him. I thought that Tahoe offered many things that made life worthwhile: independence, leisure, the great outdoors and three months of rather hectic contact with the good old American public on vacation. It sounded pretty good to me at that time.

In October 1941, my time in the Army came to an end. In many ways I hated to leave the Army. Much of the life was really on a grand scale, full of action – individual and mass – the coordinated existence of the Army. My work as a sergeant was not altogether an

Maneuvers

easy job, but was always interesting. It was really nice to be a leader and have the respect of both my officers and the men under me. One of the lieutenants told me that I would be leaving many friends who both liked and respected me. I guess they had me pretty well puffed up around there, but I knew I had many many shortcomings. It was nice though to look back and say, "I made a success in the Army – I was a good soldier."

I was offered every inducement to stay on – send me to Officer School, make me a staff sergeant where I would be promoted to first sergeant in the near future, etc. But I decided to take up the white man's burden again, or sumpin'.

I got out of the Army on October 24, 1941, and was transferred to Enlisted Reserve as a sergeant. Captain Redden wrote me quite a nice letter of recommendation:

```
HQ. & HQ. BATTERY, 31st F. A. BATTALION
        Fort Ord, California

                                October 24, 1941.

To Whom It May Concern:

        This is to signify that Standish C. Hulse has
been in my organization for nearly a year. During
this time, his service has been honest and faithful.
Standish Hulse was just recently promoted to Sergeant
for his excellent service in the Anti-tank Battalion
of 7th Division. Sergeant Hulse is a trustworthy,
sensible and thoroughly dependable young man. He
possesses initiative, force, good judgment, common
sense and a high devotion to his duty. He has many
qualities which tend to make leadership; among which
are outstanding intelligence, tolerance and good
humor. I feel that Sergeant Hulse can at any time
fill a position of trust, and by both his knowledge
and his example, command respect and obedience from
those who serve under him.

                        FREDERICK R. REDDEN
                        Captain, 31st F. A. Bn.
                        Cmd. Hq. & Hq. Btry.
```

Then I went to work. I didn't go back to Grace Line, though Grace Line wanted me. I went to the shipyard, because I knew that a war was coming on. People who knew, knew there was going to be a war.

First of all, I tried to get into the Canadian Army, but they wouldn't take me because I was too old for my class. If I had been younger and gone up there, I could have become a Canadian and they would have taken me. I just wanted to get into the war; I knew it was coming, and the Canadians were going to get into it before we were.

The Germans were no good. Under Hitler they were terrible. They had to be stopped. I was all alone and I just felt that I should join some campaign against the Germans. I wouldn't give you a dime for all the Germans in the country, in the world. I think they're a lousy bunch of people. They would be just as bad today as they were then. So anyway, I never had any love for the Germans. And I don't have any love today for the Germans.

I didn't know exactly what they were doing, but I knew that it was wrong. They had already started to fight England. They were dropping bombs and blowing up ships and all that sort of thing. I just couldn't sit home and read the papers about them. I just had to get in if I could.

Well, Canada turned me down, they didn't want me. The guy was very nice. He said, "Sergeant, you'll be in before long. Believe me, it's just a short while and you'll be in."

So I thanked him and I left the Canadian post there in San Francisco. I went down to Bethlehem Steel and told them that I wanted to join their outfit, and they said, "Fine." So they took me on and they made me a coordinator.

Chapter 20: Bethlehem Steel

I WAS THERE ABOUT A MONTH when the war broke out, when the Japs bombed Pearl Harbor, December 7, 1941. I was staying with my mother and Duge in San Carlos. It was Sunday morning and I had had a late breakfast and was puttering around in the backyard piling up some scrap pieces of lumber and cleaning out weeds. It was nearing noon and though it was December, it was nice and warm in the yard and the puttering was going very satisfactorily.

Our home was built on the side of a rather steep hill and faced the street on the upper end of the lot. The principal floor plan was on this level, which left space for two rooms on a lower level at the back of the house. On the upper floor level was a porch that ran to the back of the house and formed a sort of a balcony over the backyard, which was terraced in three levels some four feet below each other. It was on this porch that my mother appeared calling, "Stan, Stan," not loudly but with such urgency in her voice that the very tone of it startled me, and as I turned questioningly toward her, she made the statement, "The Japs are bombing Pearl Harbor." At the blank and apparently incredulous expression with which this statement was met, she repeated, "The Japs are bombing Pearl Harbor," in that same tense voice that sounded as though she were repeating something so horrible that though she knew it was true, she still could not believe it.

When the impact of what she was saying hit me, it was as though I had received a blow to the solar plexus. I felt weak and sick. I felt as though all the decency of civilization had suddenly been violated and it left me there in a sense panicked and afraid. I wasn't afraid for myself. I had been expecting this thing for so long that all those subconscious thoughts of the awfulness of war seemed to suddenly crystalize and bring me face to face with what we, the little people of the world, were up against.

My mother then went on to relate that most of the stations were repeating the broadcast from Pearl Harbor, which told of the raid and reported that the fleet had been sunk. I dashed into the house and heard the announcer repeating the Honolulu report and announcing that there had been no further details. Throughout the day we waited for further details but heard nothing except confirmation that the Japs had raided Pearl Harbor and that there had been casualties. We were all shaken by the news, and the censorship of the news from Honolulu caused much anxiety and speculation as to the actual losses we had suffered.

No matter what the losses were, we knew that ultimately we would win this war. It was with something of a feeling akin to pity that we felt toward the Jap, to have been so stupid and misguided as to have attacked us. As one of the boys on the *Call-Bulletin* put it, "The Japs won the toss and elected to kick off! Now we must wait for the final score."

Monday morning I called Jim Chesnutt on the *Call-Bulletin*. He had been against war and was an isolationist when we had last talked things over, but I believe he felt as I did, that we were being drawn closer and closer into the vortex of war. There was no question as to what course we were to follow. Japan had violated her place among the nations of the world. She had become a base and horrible thing: a nation without honor. And what was worse, it was a yellow-skinned people who had done this infamous, treacherous act, and had thereby fanned the fire of racial hatred to a white heat, thus destroying in a few minutes all of the efforts of those many, many good and sincere people, both Japanese and American as well as other foreigners, who had labored so hard since the turn of the century to promote mutual respect and understanding between the two countries. A race war!

Jim had been in touch with 9th Corps Area Headquarters by the time I called him and informed me that the reserves had been instructed to continue at their present jobs and to await orders to report to duty, which orders would come through in due time. There was nothing for me to do but wait.

So I got ready to go back to my outfit. In January 1942, I was notified by the Draft Board that I should expect to be recalled into the

Army. I was working in the Shipbuilding Division in the San Francisco yard at Bethlehem Steel Company, down at the end of 20th Street, and was Supervisor of Outfitting.

I told the captain who was in charge of the building of the ships, "Well, I won't see you Captain. I'm going to go back to join the Army."

"You what?" he said.

"Yea, I'm going back in the Army."

"I don't think so. We need you here."

"Well, I'm a sergeant in the Army. I finished my basic training, and I'm going back in."

"Well, we'll see about that. Don't quit today, I'll let you know."

The next day he nailed me on the dock and said, "Stan, don't worry, you're not going back in the Army, you're going to be right here at Bethlehem Steel as long as they need you."

"Well if that's the way…" I answered, because at that time we were building destroyers. Our country had no destroyers – it had all old-fashioned destroyers – and I was right in the midst of building them.

When I told the boss that I wanted to go back in the Army, he got very excited. He sent a memo to management:

FOR INTER-OFFICE CORRESPONDENCE
SUBSIDIARY COMPANIES OF BETHLEHEM STEEL CORPORATION
SAN FRANCISCO, CAL.

26 February 1942

From   H.P. Chaney
To   J.F. Arntz

Mr. Stanley Hulse, AB-119, has been notified by his Draft Board that he may expect to be recalled to the Army. Mr. Hulse has already served some time and was discharged a few months ago because he was over twenty-eight years of age.

In this particular case, I am asking you to take all possible steps to keep Mr. Hulse in this plant. Mr. Hulse's duties are in connection with the outfitting or the completion of the Naval vessels under construction. At the present time he is in charge of this work on Hull 5367 as my principal assistant on that ship. This work requires a man who has the patience and perseverance to attend to a large number of small details, as well as the personality and

255

ability to coordinate the efforts of the various
crafts involved in the completion of a ship.

While Mr. Hulse is comparatively a new employee,
he has displayed a natural aptitude for this work and
has forged ahead of other men in my department. This
is evidenced by the record which shows that starting
here November 18, 1941, I have seen fit to increase
his pay, first on December 28, 1941 and again on February 1, 1942. I can truthfully say that he is the
most promising man I have on my staff and his loss
would seriously handicap me in my work.

I trust you will put this request in the hands of
the Draft Board and if it will be of any help I will
be glad to appear personally before the Draft Board
in order to keep Mr. Hulse with me.

H.P. Chaney
Superintendent of Outfitting

Then Arntz wrote a letter to the Draft Board requesting my de-
ferment, claiming that I had to stay on with them "in the interests of
National Defense." He outlined my duties as a supervisor of outfitting. My work involved coordinating the work of the various depart-
ments engaged in Navy ship construction. This included electrical
wiring and hook up, the installation of ammunition stowage maga-
zines, lifeboat davits, chocks, bitts, bulkheads for cabins, galley
equipment, all of the interior communication systems and operating
controls, mounting of guns, and the inside and outside painting. Of
course, we had to build to strict Navy specifications, and any mistakes
were costly and could hold up delivery dates of the ships.
Arntz wrote the following:

"In view of the fact that Mr. Hulse has been especially proficient and adaptable to the work now in
progress, we would greatly appreciate retaining his
services as an essential national defense worker. The
success of our construction program depends largely
on the effectiveness of men in supervisory capaci-
ties, and he has clearly demonstrated the ability to
direct other employees in capably carrying out the
outfitting procedures."

Since I had had ten years' experience working on steamships, my services were very valuable to them and they didn't want to let me go.

As coordinator, I had to know everything that went into a destroyer, everything: how many cups, how many spoons, how many knives, how many guns, what kind of an aerial they had, what kind of propellers they had. I had to know everything, and I knew it. At that time I knew everything that went into a destroyer. I knew the weak spots on the frame, even. I knew where they cut part of the keel out. I knew where the ammunition was stored and how it was stored. I knew those ships right down to a gnat's eyebrow.

It didn't take me long to learn everything. I just got on the ship and went over it, and over it, and over it, and over it. I would take a plan like the electrical plan and I'd look at it. "I have wires in here. All right, I need to have the wires go through there."

Then the next guy would say, "Where's this go, Stan?"

And I'd say, "It goes in there," and show him where to run the wires.

He'd take out his plan and show it to me, and we'd agree that's where the wires went.

Then something was changed. Every day there'd be a change. I had to know where the changes went and whether we could incorporate them and still finish the ship on time. If the change was too big, I'd tell them that it couldn't be done.

"All right, delay the delivery of the ship but make the change."

"Okay," I'd say, "we'll make the change and set the delivery date ahead a week."

We had a big shipbuilding operation going on there. During 1942 we turned over nine destroyers to the Navy. Our production rate steadily increased and by the end of July 1943, we were delivering one ship per month.

During that production expansion my duties and responsibilities increased, and I was promoted to Supervisor of Outfitting Coordinators working on destroyers.

One day the big boss came down, he was the big shot for Bethlehem Steel, and gee the place looked like a wreck. "God," he said, "you'll never get this ready for the trial board in the morning."

"Oh, yes," I said, "we'll have it ready for the trial board."

And he looked at me, "Nah, you're crazy."

"Give me time. I'll have it ready." I knew the trial board was coming and I had been shooting for the date for several days.

That night I think I had something like 700 painters on that ship, because I worked all night long. At a certain time I told all the crews to be finished. Then I had the crews taking out the hoses, the lines, just dozens of lines for everything, for welding all over the ship. They took all those lines out and rolled them up. Then I had the painters come in and I turned them loose. They went over the whole ship; they painted and painted and painted. They put some driers in the paint so it wouldn't be wet paint the next day. I think the trial board was eleven o'clock that next morning. They finished painting, cleaned up and picked up the papers and everything and the big boss came down to see it. He didn't think we could deliver the ship on time. He came on board; he looked.

"My God," he said, "You've done it!"

And after that I was a fair-haired boy, I must admit.

I wanted very much to get back in the Army, but I was well aware that it would take time to train a man to replace me, so I wrote to Selective Service the end of July asking them to give my employer three to six months notice of my return to service.

My life-long friend, Col. Jim Chesnutt, handed me this note after a long discussion:

> "You are in fact a member of the U.S. Army now, loaned by the Army to the construction department of the U.S. Navy for special duty. That is what the present situation amounts to.
>
> "The Navy, through Capt. Kell, now requests the Army to extend the period of your loan to them. The Army and Navy are equal factors in the war. If the Navy sees fit to ask, and the Army sees fit to agree, then you should abide by their decision.
>
> "You are now and will continue to be a member of the Army reserve assigned to special duty for the Navy."

I had no desire to avoid combat by taking a defense job. But at that juncture, I had to decide where best to serve. Finally, when it came time for me to join the Army, I wrote to Army headquarters. I told them that I had asked for a review of my Army record, and that now I had completed the work that I had been assigned, and would they please take me in? I got back a nice letter from them saying that they would, and that they were going to call me back on a certain date. They recalled me to active duty in April 1944, and I got into combat in late 1944.

Chapter 21: Camp Roberts

THEY TOLD ME TO GO HOME and get ready, and report down to Monterey. So I packed my bags and said goodbye to the family. It was very hard to say goodbye. To leave home was always hard, but to know that Mom would worry in spite of anything I could say, made it doubly hard. Everyone at home had always been so nice to me, and I just couldn't begin to tell them how much I had appreciated it and how much it had all meant to me.

It was all part of that something that made me get back into uniform. You know "a thing worth having is worth fighting for," and if I could do my part on the team, then I would help to assure for all of us those things that had meant so much to me.

I took the train down to the Presidio in Monterey the end of May 1944. Once there, I felt like a great load had been lifted from my conscience. That feeling of not doing one's part was not a good feeling and being back in the Army, I felt that I could better live with myself.

It felt good to be back in Monterey. My sergeant stripes helped me a lot, and everyone was very nice to the "Sarg." I was sort of in charge of my barracks and took the men over to the mess hall, fell them out to police up the area in the vicinity of the barracks, and saw that the place was ready for inspection and that the lights were out at nine. Nothing hard about it, and it was a bit of fun for me.

In about a week they took us down to Camp Roberts. It's about half-way down the coast, around Paso Robles. Much to my surprise, they put me right through basic training. That was rough in those days, but I did everything just as though I were a rookie. I never made any reference to my position as a sergeant.

There was an hour of physical drill in the mornings. It was the hardest part but strangely enough, when the final whistle blew, I was still conscious, though short of breath and weak-kneed.

It was hot down there, but the nights were cool and the heat didn't bother me, though when it went above 100 degrees, the sweat under my pack flowed quite freely. I discovered many muscles that I had long forgotten, or never knew I had, but I felt good and looked forward to the next 16 weeks, at the end of which I would be in the best physical shape possible.

We had a very nice bunch of men in that outfit. Many of them were married and most of them were willing and tried to absorb the training. But there were always a few who nodded at the classes, and failed to hear what was being said or to take notes. They would be on the casualty lists before the war was over. They were the ones who took little shortcuts: held their breath when allowed to smell the various gasses and climbed over fences rather than wriggled under them. So when the time came, and they got that first faint whiff of a poison gas, they would not know just what it was and might not mask in time. Or when they crossed a field and came to a fence, they would not be proficient in wriggling under it so would take a chance and go over it – another casualty. The more I saw of the Army and its training and the number of men in even a well-trained outfit who didn't go entirely by the book, the more I was convinced that it was the soldier who committed a blunder that got hurt in about nine times out of ten, and the odd time was solely the chance of war.

We spent a week at the rifle range. Rifle practice required a lot of getting into cramped and uncomfortable positions again and again, until those positions became the natural position for you to get into. In rapid fire it meant hitting the dirt quickly and hard. So after a week out there, I was a little stiff and discovered yet a few more new muscles. But with it all I felt pretty darn good as I qualified as an Expert Rifleman. Better than that, I learned to really handle the rifle, for at the end of the qualifying course, I was shooting with the ease of a true expert – at 500 yards I made six bull's eyes, four of which were dead center and the two shots that didn't find the bull were just on the edge of it. It's a great feeling to have mastered yourself to the extent that you can control your muscles and your mind to the point where you can get off shot after shot without flinching and with perfect coordination of eye, breathing and muscles.

We also trained at bazooka practice and spent one afternoon at bayonet practice. That 9-pound rifle with its 2-pound bayonet sure got heavy as the afternoon wore on. We ran one of those courses that you see in the movies. It pulled my cork all right, but it too had its element of fun.

I pulled guard duty one Friday night. My tour of guard wasn't so bad but as Sergeant of the Guard I had to go around to the different posts and see that the sentinels challenged correctly. As all the sentinels were trainees, it gave me a peculiar feeling to be walking through the darkness until challenged. I was, of course, plenty alert for the "Halt!" so that I would be sure to hear it on the first challenge. Otherwise those green peas might take a pot shot at me.

That summer I got a glimpse of one of the new rocket planes as it flew near the range. They seemed to have terrific speed and I was a bit awed by it – my first glimpse of a new era in flying.[63] We were truly living in a fantastic age.

Bivouac is the big point in every trainee's career – two weeks in the field! There we put into practice the many things we were taught during the cycle. We were bivouacked in country with steep hills, and by the end of our stay I felt like I should walk with one foot on the curb when I got into town.

I enjoyed the outdoor life and was perfectly comfortable sitting or lying on the ground under one of those little live oak trees. We were given a canteen of water to shave and wash with daily. It really felt good to dunk the dogs in a few inches of cool water in the bottom of my helmet. The new style of helmet was really a great improvement over the old one. The helmet itself was just strapped over the liner by the chin-strap and could be readily lifted off to use as a bucket, shovel, pail, wash basin, stool, backrest, etc.

We marched out to one site where we stayed for a week, then we packed up at midnight and moved 18 miles to another site where we dug foxholes. We were on C rations – two cans per meal. One had coffee, candy, biscuits and sugar, and the other had hash, beans, or stew. I got a big kick out of making a little fire, heating the can of stew, and making coffee.

We stayed there until the following Friday. That night we went to bed, and at midnight they called us up and told us to get going. We then took a 25-mile march across country in the dark back to the barracks. They put me at the head of the column of about a thousand guys to set the pace, and boy that was something. We would march for 50 minutes and rest for 10. At the hourly break of ten minutes, it was increasingly difficult to rise and get underway again. Once underway, it wasn't so bad, and then there was always the next halt to look forward to. I was 38 years old at that time, and that 25-mile march in the dark took about 8 hours. We arrived back at the camp in the morning. It was a doozy.

I was at the training center for seventeen weeks, from the beginning of June till the end of September. They gave me special training

---

63 July 5, 1944 - MX324, the first U.S. military rocket-powered plane built by Northrup, was flown at Harper Dry Lake, Calif. in the Mojave Desert.

as an infantryman of a rifle company and I became an Expert M1 Rifleman.

After I finished Camp Roberts, I went home on a three-day weekend, and from there I caught a train to Camp Fort George G. Meade in Maryland, out of Washington, D.C. We arrived there November 4, 1944.

I met John Bruce back in Washington. He was working for a newspaper and he introduced me to some of his newspaper chaps.

Then I went up to New York to Camp Shanks, which was the jumping-off point for Europe, and stayed there for a few days until I got orders to move out.

In the meantime, they tried to stop me and keep me in Washington, they wanted me there. But I told them, "No, I want to go where the action is." I had a very special pass, as it were, because I had been in the Army as a volunteer before the war and that carried an awful lot of weight. It gave me access; I could go either east or west, but I wanted to go to Germany because that's where I figured the fighting was, and it was. The other choice was to go west and get stuck on an island and stay there, but I went to Germany. I went to France, actually, and stayed in France for a while.

I felt very strongly the words written by Daniel Webster in 1850:

> I was born an American; I live an American; I shall die an American; and I intend to perform the duties incumbent upon me in that character to the end of my career. I mean to do this with absolute disregard of personal consequences. What are the personal consequences? What is the individual man, with all the good or evil that may betide him, in comparison with the good or evil which may befall a great country, and in the midst of great transactions which concern that country's fate? Let the consequences be what they will, I am careless. No man can suffer too much, and no man can fall too soon, if he suffer, or if he fall, in the defense of the liberties and constitution of his country.

Chapter 22: You're In the Army Now

```
THE WHITE HOUSE
WASHINGTON
```

```
TO MEMBERS OF THE UNITED STATES ARMY
EXPEDITIONARY FORCES:
    You are a soldier of the United States Army.
    You have embarked for distant places where the
war is being fought.
    Upon the outcome depends the freedom of your
lives: the freedom of the lives of those you
love — your fellow-citizens — your people.
    Never were the enemies of freedom more
tyrannical, more arrogant, more brutal.
    Yours is a God-fearing, proud, courageous
people, which, throughout its history, has put
its freedom under God before all other purposes.
    We who stay at home have our duties to perform
— duties owed in many parts to you. You will be
supported by the whole force and power of this
Nation. The victory you win will be a victory of
all the people — common to them all.
    You bear with you the hope, the confidence,
the gratitude and the prayers of your family,
your fellow-citizens, and your President.
```

— Franklin D. Roosevelt

The last letter I received from my mother, when I told her that I was sailing overseas, had this loving message:

> *I want you to know that I deeply appreciate all you have done for me, and tried to do, and I thank you dear. Deep down in my heart I love you most – that is, while not loving my other children any less because of it, there is a certain bond and you are very dear to my old heart, Standish, my Son. God bless and keep you safe!*

I shipped out from Boston on 23 November 1944, on the SS *Brazil*. That was one busy harbor. San Francisco was not the only port who found her harbor full. It was hard to realize that so many ships could possibly have been constructed. They looked like they must have been "growed," there were so many of them. One variety in particular must have grown wild, thanks to Bethlehem Steel and a few others.

The ship I was on was an ex-passenger ship, and owing to her speed, had been used for other purposes before her role as a troop transport.

Though as a supercargo I had seen to the stowage of many a cargo in the hold of a ship, it was my first experience traveling that way. I think there were about 4,000 men on that ship. The ventilation, however, was surprisingly good and the company the best. Though we lived just about as close to one another as was humanly possible, a couple of days out our hold was quarantined, so we all got pretty well acquainted, and being quarantined was somewhat of a break as none of us had to pull guard duty or KP.

KP was a pretty tough job, too. Though we only got two meals a day, the mess hall had a continuous line of men streaming through it from early morning until after nine o'clock at night. The PX was well stocked so, in spite of only two meals, we were never hungry. To keep the record straight, the Army saw fit to give us shots while on the way over, as if just plain seasickness wasn't bad enough for a lot of the poor guys. My saltwater days held me in good stead, however, and by the time we hit our first heavy weather my sea legs were under me.

We arrived in Cherbourg, France, on December 6. From there we rode through Normandy, seeing the devastation of Le Havre and the ruins of Rouen on the Seine River. Like many French coastal towns, the port of Le Havre fell under German occupation in the early 1940s. The Allied forces made an assault to liberate the city from the Germans, which they did on September 12, 1944, and the city was nothing but mud and ruins when we saw it.

I didn't get to see a great deal of France, but I was fortunate enough to see some of the Vosges as well as Normandy. In traveling through the country it was easy to distinguish where the Jerries had put up resistance.[64] Fortunately, from the coast on inland, the Jerries were pretty much on the run until they were almost to the border, so much of France escaped severe damage. Many of her factories were idle only because of lack of transportation, which could not be spared from the war effort.

With the coming of peace, I felt sure that France's industry would

---

64 A German, especially a German soldier.

swing into full production and, as the people were in need of most every type of consumer good, there was sure to follow a period of great prosperity. Lest I give the impression that the war had not caused damage, I hasten to add that it caused a great deal. But the damage, on the whole, was not so great as to be irreparable. The reconstruction was sure to be a great stimulus to trade. The prospect of a prosperous France would do much to stabilize the rest of Europe in the difficult period immediately following the war.

I was transferred to a Reinforcement (or Replacement) Depot near Épinal, France. We were quartered in bunks made of wood, in tiers of three. We had to be back in the area by 8:30 at night and the snack bar closed by 9:30, so by 10:00 the men had usually quieted down except for little groups that huddled here and there, usually over an improvised spirit lamp. Some used impregnate,[65] which gave off a heavy black smoke and an unpleasant odor, and others had the regular GI fire cubes, which were sometimes issued to the men on the lines to heat their C rations. Every once in a while, a more enterprising GI would produce a gasoline burner unit stolen somewhere along the line.

These groups around the fires were usually busy eating either C or K rations or cooking up something that one of them had stolen during the day while on KP or from some other detail he was on.

Sometimes there were other groups. These were usually formed by the arrival of a lone GI who quite obviously had been celebrating and had carefully brought some of the celebration back with him. It was invariably a beer bottle filled with schnapps, which was really high powered tanglefoot.[66]

Old man winter was pretty tough. It was bitter cold and our canteens would freeze overnight. But I liked my billet and it was much better than spending the winter in a foxhole, which would have been pretty rough. As it was, the winter was uncomfortable but nothing worse. My feet were so sore from the cold, to begin with, that I was almost a cinch to have become a victim of trench foot if I had had to stand in the snow for any length of time. Several of the boys who came over with me told me that it got them – laid them up for a

---

65 Probably refers to coal-tar creosote oil.

66 Tanglefoot is an American slang term for illegal liquor, typically whiskey.

Sergeant Stan Hulse, 1944.

while. I did keep catching cold, however, and had three in six weeks.

It was a cold December with plenty of ice and snow. Christmas was not too gay, but when I heard "Silent Night," it brought tears to my eyes. Half a world away, my mother wrote: "I just didn't try to listen to 'Silent Night' nor to any other Carols. One of those 'tears from the eyelids start' emotions and they don't stop 'easy'." I think that Christmas is in the heart and we have to sort of find it there.

I spent the winter in the little town of Épinal, not far from Strasbourg. I was a long way from the front and the front kept getting further away. Once the bitter cold had passed, living was not nearly so uncomfortable. I slept warmly in my bunk, so it wasn't too bad.

We had to stand in the mess line and stood at high wooden benches while eating, as it wasn't practical to have a regular mess hall. During the day, however, I often ducked into the office and sat down for a few minutes before the Colonel's fire. We also had a little hut-like place we called the "Shack" which had a stove and was a spot the Colonel let us fix up for ourselves. There we made ourselves at home, heated water for shaving and had a C ration café.

I kept busy working at the Depot, which was kind of like running a big store, and I was happiest that way. There was lots to do and my fellow workers were very pleasant. More and more, my friends on the post filled up my time at the Depot with requests for food or extras of some kind. Though we had plenty to eat, there was always some movement afoot to get something different. It all made life less monotonous. But I looked forward to it all being over and done with. Such a crazy business!

As winter gave way to spring, the countryside blossomed. It was a relief to shed some of the sweaters and coats we had to bundle up in, in a vain effort to keep warm through the winter. And when the sun came out I could see formations of countless bombers droning high across the deep blue sky on their way to Germany. Things looked a lot brighter.

My guess for the end of the war in Germany was not later than April. I thought it might be sooner but the German government had disregarded, apparently, the welfare of the German people and proposed to hang on for its own selfish ends, until Germany was beaten down by the mace of war to utter defeat. In the spring of 1945, the war was at the stage where, in the boxing ring, the fighter's manager would throw in the towel.

I had a nice time in Épinal. One Sunday in February, I took a walk into town with a fellow soldier. We had a nice stroll but found a great shortage of schnapps there. While we were in a little shop purchasing some cards, I remarked on this sad state of affairs from the GI standpoint, and the woman directed us to the rear of a certain café. On arrival, we found an MP captain having a schnapps. And so started a beautiful friendship, as we each bought a round.

The captain and I then took a stroll and he showed me what little there was to see in the town. However, in the course of our stroll I confided that I had not had any French fried potatoes. He decided that this should be remedied as soon as possible, so on parting he told me he would get in touch with me. Sure enough, the next day he sent word for me to meet him, and we would have dinner in town at the place where he roomed and boarded. It was a delicious dinner! The *monsieur* was a butcher and an excellent cook.

First, we had French fried potatoes and they were delicious. Then we had cold boiled tongue sliced very thin with finely cut onions and a French dressing. It was different but very good. Next we were served the most delicious roast veal, and we topped the whole thing off with a French pastry. My, but it was a treat! I made a pig of myself, but my host would not have it otherwise. He made it a bit of a celebration and produced not only a bottle of very good claret but some nice white wine as well. That was really something as there was practically no wine left in the country. It took some two hours to stow this repast away, and it was the most pleasant two hours since my arrival in France.

We sat around the table and, though I could not converse in the language, I managed to follow much of the conversation. They were great people for poking good-natured fun at one another, and the spirit was very gay. I had a lot of fun.

A week later, my friend, the captain, had me up for dinner again. The conversation was all very French, and I understood only a little of what was said, but the captain kept me posted and I managed to follow the thoughts pretty well. It was a lot of fun and there was a good deal of kidding. The French fried potatoes were so very good, and I enjoyed them so much that my host seemed to get a big kick out of seeing me put them away.

The French people seemed so very natural that, in order to have a good time, all one had to do was to be natural. Food, love, and the state of one's health seemed to be the important things in life – and aren't they, tho?

One day, the madame and a neighbor and I took a promenade – *une bonne marche* – about 10 kilometers round trip, to visit madam's mother. We visited a quaint little village: manure piled in the front of each home; the usual plumbing on the outside; and the little church in the middle of the town. The place looked more like a movie set than anything else.

There were three other women present and a French soldier who was home on leave. No one spoke English so I didn't add much to the conversation, but I believe I was the subject of a good deal of it. I did enjoy two lovely babies. Nice and clean they were. I held one for quite a while and it was very dear. Its petite mama was a young girl, the wife of the soldier. My mother would have loved her complexion! It had a satin smoothness that was very, very lovely – but her husband was present!

We sipped coffee and had cake and there was a lot of chatter and much making over the children. All this took place in the kitchen. And the French kitchen is *the* room. There the sewing is done, the babies are tended, the meals are eaten, the cooking is done and the entertaining takes place. The French live in the kitchen. To a Frenchman, his home was very close to his heart, and his enthusiasm over food and drink was something to see. We had a delightful day of it.

Of course, the poverty of the people was manifest in many ways. In the background was always the tragedy of war. It made me wish that I could do something – share in some way the many luxuries of life that to us are so commonplace, like coffee, soap, fuel, sugar, bread and things we used so freely. They had so little!

The people there knew nothing of many of the good things of life that we took for granted. For instance, only the "better" class people had anything that approached a modern bathroom. Central heating, even in that cold climate, was seldom found, and cars, before the disappearance of civilian gasoline, were only owned by the better classes. We Americans were indeed fortunate.

Where a people were so quick to enjoy the lovely weather, and everyone took advantage of a sunny day to be outdoors, I noticed the lack of little babies. There were the usual percentage of little children 5 years and up, but the comparatively few babies was noticeable. I was told, however, that the spring and summer crop would be the best in years! Yes, the French had really made our boys welcome, and the GI's knew how to take advantage of any opening.

I had dinner a couple of times a week with my French townspeople. I had *beaucoup* French fried potatoes. My, but they tasted good! I had a lot of fun on those evenings though we often misunderstood each other. We had to refer to the dictionary and backtrack and start all over again before we knew what the other was talking about. They made me very welcome, and it was nice to get away from GI's for an evening. I very much enjoyed a look into a little of French home life.

A few weeks later my captain friend left and we had a *bon fête* at the French couple's place one evening – a lot of laughter and good eats.

The French people liked us, as individuals, I am sure. Our waste must have looked very silly to them, but they were realists and accepted it. *"C'est la guerre."* That's war.

As GI's we made out all right. Candy was the only thing that I sometimes ran a bit short of, but most of the time I had too much of it. For instance, one day I might have two candy bars and two fresh doughnuts as well as pudding for dessert at lunch and an apricot cobbler for supper. So I was doing all right.

At times we traveled some miles distant and saw the surrounding countryside, much of it interesting! Traveling in the wake of the machines of war, over a rather large section of the country, certainly gave one something to think about: the bustle and excitement of the long lines of communication and supply, the air power, the dumps, abandoned fortifications, and road blocks that had been cleared hastily. We traveled over some of the roads that, no doubt, Napoleon's soldiers trod! It was really an experience!

War news sounded good for our side in February 1945. The Japs were catching hell. That was a great tragedy, as is all war, but to be led into it by a small group of zealots who had secured control of the government and who had seized the bear by the tail and could not let go, that was the tragedy we saw being enacted on both war fronts. The German people did elect Hitler, but the Japs, poor things, had their religion backfire. What a mess! I hoped the end wasn't too far away, so people could start living again.

In a letter from my mother, she admonished me to never allow myself to hate. That was one thing that I did my best to avoid, to avoid hatred. I had no hatred against the Japs as a race. I met a number of them in the Depot, and they were just another GI, as far as I was concerned. They were just like any other soldier, just part of the Army, and certainly did not rate nor deserve any discrimination. Those of our boys who had fought with the Japanese boys had a great admiration for their bravery and their uncomplaining attitude towards hardship. It was hard to understand the agitation against them on the West Coast. It was a great pity that it existed, and it was an ugly thing, as is all bigotry. I was glad I was serving in Europe so that I could express myself freely in any discussion in which bigotry reared its ugly head.

Japanese nationalism was, however, another question. While we were very remote from the Pacific war, we GI's felt that the Jap Army had to be crushed. The Japs had shown the world that they were incapable of intelligently handling the great power that, through modern productive methods, they were capable of producing. In other words, it seemed that the minds of the ruling class were geared to a feudal outlook that had no place in a modern world.

The great pity of it was that the people, who were deeply religious, had been led into war on the grounds of religion. But a people who were so far out of step with the times were not capable of holding a place among the world powers, and would have to be reduced to the point where they would not be able to commit the crime of war again.

Man with all his blunders has never created anything more stupid than war. Men being what they are, the war was inevitable. The development of science had put so much power in the hands of those who were able to gain control of the reins of government, that it was only a matter of time before that power would be misused. Throughout history there has always been someone who wanted to test the might of the developments of their time. The latest was Hitler. And Japan, feeling the might of her new industrial strength, also put it to the test.

But war brings with it change, and that same science that makes war possible accelerates scientific development a thousandfold. Queer, isn't it? But the period of peace which follows one of these big wars always seems to bring a fuller life to humanity in the long run. I was sure this war would too. It had already shrunk the globe by a greater percentage than all the time between Hannibal and Napoleon, two great experimenters with the power of their times.

The whole thing was a tragedy so great, so overpowering, that it defied any description of magnitude. I had a growing conviction that this war might really be the last in the long history of warfare. All the conferences and the unity of the three great powers were certainly hopeful signs. Out of it had to come a better world.

While the German soldier was my enemy, I could not but have great pity for the individual who had been drawn into the vortex of war. The mother who, amid the ruins of her home, had to listen to the crying of her hungry children, be she German, Jap, Russian or any other nationality, was still tragedy personified.

I'm very glad that I was a part of the war, not for any reason of personal glory, if there is any such in war – I'm not speaking of valor – but because it was such a crucial point in the entire history of man. The war itself was so big that its impact on history, on civilization, was to alter the entire course of it. There would be reevaluation in our lives – the lives of all of us who were alive during and after the war – that would make our lives fuller and richer. Greed would find it more and more difficult to thrive, and there would be a more even distribution of the necessities of life and also of the good things of life.

You could look at the percentage of our people who had traveled the length and breadth of our land from war plant to war plant – the people they had seen and the contacts they had made! Then there were the soldiers – men who for years lived on a common footing regardless of background. They too traveled and learned from their buddies about other parts of the country – some of the local problems peculiar to a certain district. The farmer, the mechanic, the clerk

271

and the businessman were all reduced to a common level, facing daily the same tasks, the same hardships, the same rations. They learned to somewhat think alike.

All of this – and much more too – made possible the development of our own country along certain lines of democratic thought that would never have been possible, if it were not for the war. And these same things had their effect in other countries as well, and on the relations between countries, and it led to a better understanding between people.

Chapter 23: Marching Through Germany

ABOUT THE MIDDLE OF MARCH 1945, I left Épinal and started advancing toward Germany. I was with the infantry at that time, part of the 91st Cavalry.

Then about March 20th, I got a rather lucky break as I was transferred from the infantry to the field artillery. It seemed like a good thing to get out of the infantry and was indeed a piece of luck.

It was good to be out in the field again. I really enjoyed living out in the open. Sometimes I'd just lie in the grass and watch the planes droning overhead on their way to shorten the war. I got a lot of comfort out of them.

The rolling green fields of France and the countryside with its winding roads was very lovely. Here and there were clusters of houses and the usual barnyards with their small flocks of geese – big white ones. It was really very charming and I enjoyed it all so much.

They sent me up to the front, as it were, and I was given a tank. Why, I don't know, but I was made commander of an M7 tank.[67] As commander it was my job to direct the movement of the tank. I sat up in the turret, and the driver of the tank sat below me. To move forward, I used my foot to tap on the driver's back between his shoulder blades. Tapping faster told the driver to go faster. If I wanted him to turn to the left, I pushed his left shoulder with my foot. To stop I pressed steadily on the driver's shoulder blades until

---

67 The 105 mm Howitzer Motor Carriage M7 was an American self-propelled artillery vehicle named the Priest, due to the pulpit-like machine gun ring.

the tank stopped, and to back up, I'd tap on the driver's helmet. And that's the way I commanded the tank.

We traveled through Sarrebourg, France, through the beautiful Vosges Mountains with their rolling, forest-covered hills. In a few days we had passed into Germany and were advancing toward Worms on the Rhine.

The front moved so fast that I didn't know when I would reach my outfit, so we just took it easy back in the rear. We got some training and played a little ball, but that was about all there was to do because, of course, we were not allowed to fraternize with the German people.

When we came into Worms, the town had been heavily bombed and there was gas, not gas, but cinders and dust trapped in the air. It didn't smell good. It wasn't bad, but it was just dusty to smell. Worms had been heavily bombed by the Allies on March 18. They spared the important bridges over the Rhine so that the Allied forces could use them. But as the Nazis retreated, they blew up the bridges, and we had just arrived there when the bridge over the Rhine was blown up. They had just blown it.

Engineers from the 7th Army constructed two pontoon bridges near Worms, and the 12th crossed the Rhine on March 28, 1945. We had to wait until the pontoons got all lined up, and then we made our way across the river on one of the pontoon bridges, and got to the other side.

So, there was a town that had just been bombed. And to come into a town immediately afterwards with the dust still in the air gave me a very funny feeling. I imagine they killed, oh maybe about 2000 or 3000 people that time. But we were soldiers and we didn't worry about civilians. If a civilian got killed that was too bad, we didn't worry about it. It was nothing to us. We were listening for orders to do what we had to do.

After we crossed the Rhine at Worms, my outfit was then in the 7th Army's spearhead headed for the Main River. By April 9th, I was transferred to the 101st Cavalry from the 92nd, which we had been attached to previously. At that point we had caught up with our outfit, the 342nd Armored Field Artillery Battalion. I was in Battery C and I remained with them till the end of the war. I liked it very much. The officers and men were a fine lot and things were very pleasant.

In early April we were constantly on the move and were in the front of the 7th Army most of the time. Of course, we represented

The M7 Priest running through a French village.

only a small portion of the lead elements but took an important part in much of the advance. Life in the open made it very difficult to find the time or the place to write. We had both miserable and delightful weather, and the country through which we traveled was perfectly beautiful with rolling hills and little towns tucked into hollows here and there.

Some of the towns would put up resistance, and then the little town folded up and we went on again until we encountered some more resistance.

We pulled into the little town of Helmstadt, near Würzburg, after bombarding it three times – each time the cavalry could not hold, so we shelled the place and then reoccupied it. We finally got some infantry up and called on the Air Force and leveled the town. When we went in, the place was a heap of rubble – dead cattle strewn among the wreckage and here and there fires burning. The people were dazed, poking around the ruins. One man showed me a pitiful cart-load of bedding and remarked, *"Das ist alles."* And he was fortunate to have even that little. The great tragedy of it all!!

Another place we set up a machine gun in an old mill – 1814-15 – and the bombers came over and dropped a stick of bombs nearby. It shook the place like jelly. My throat was dry, and we were all scared. But we liked the idea of beds so well that we stayed three nights more in the mill, then moved to a new position. Bombers came over every night but they didn't hit in our vicinity. When we moved on there was one place where a couple of kids standing by the road and said, *"Heil Hitler!"* when we passed.

One evening two Jerry planes came over but we kept them too high to strafe or bomb. It was a lovely sight, all the 50 cal tracers in the air.[68] When he would attempt to come in, it gave me a naked feeling.

On April 12, Roosevelt died. Out in the field it was a startling bit of news, but it created no particular stir among the men. It was just the passing of an outstanding figure. It was not taken as the loss of our leader — we just changed the hand at the helm. I guess that was much the way it was at home. I believed that the course of destiny of our country was set with the tide of the time, and there was little that one man could do to alter that course. But I felt that we had lost the man best equipped to deal with the other powers at the peace table.

That night there was a chow line and we crowded in to receive our first hot meal in four days.

As we pushed on through Germany, many of the people seemed glad to see us but others quite naturally looked very unhappy. Little, if any, arrogant looks: some sullen, many scared. The dead horses were the most pitiful sights. Dead soldiers seemed somehow expected.

Village after village was wrecked. Groups of soldiers gave up, and all we did was search them. I had no stomach for entering and searching houses, but it had to be done. In one place, the troops were trying to give themselves up. Their officer got them back, but the white flags had given away their location.

The countryside we passed through was beautiful. People lived in little villages each with its tall clock tower and well cultivated fields surrounding them. The rolling country reminded me of Uvas Canyon and the Almaden areas of the Santa Cruz Mountains. Bells sounded lovely as their ring carried over the clear air.

We threw a track one night after coming down a mountainside. As we waited to get it repaired, we saw three burning towns below us,

---

68 The fourth shell in each .50 caliber machine gun was a tracer for observation of fire, according to Chuck Baker.

275

and prisoners on jeeps and light tanks trickled past us. That night there was aircraft overhead and we could hear the heavy cannonading ahead of us.

April 15 was the date I had picked for the end of the war. It should have been over long before then. The senseless resistance and the consequential destruction of village after village really bothered me. Hitler's men wanted to give up, but their officers wouldn't let them.

On that day I saw a Jerry buried in his foxhole beside the road – tank tracks running over it!! I also saw a big Tiger tank alongside the road. We got it the day before!

As we were approaching a little town, a lieutenant came along and said, "Sergeant, I'm going to take your tank," and he climbed on board saying, "We're going down to meet the enemy."

We went over a bridge entering a town and the bridge collapsed. The M7 fell 10 feet and just the tip of the front end was sticking up. I was shaken up a bit, but he got off the tank and left. So I got another tank to pull me out later. The other tank backed up and put a big cable on me and pulled me out. It sounds like an easy job, but it took about three hours to get me out of there.

I stood in my tank, however, and looked out and saw the Germans running in the town ahead of us and the guys shooting at them. And then, while I was down there in the tank, there was a place on the hill about a mile away where they had encountered the Germans. There was a big fight going on up on that hill. The artillery was going in and bombs were being dropped. The hill was erupting with smoke. Bright flashes of red flames leaped up. I didn't see how they could take it. The losses must have been terrific. The Krauts[69] were giving up, the geese were squawking loudly in the town, and I was just standing there watching it waiting to be pulled out. It was quite something.

That evening we pulled into a position where there was a beautiful castle-like building about 800 yards away on a bluff. The Krauts had put a machine gun up in the place and could look right down on us. The doughs advanced on the castle, across the fields and up the bluff – men in the artillery always referred to the infantry men as "doughs." Even though the Jerrys could see all of our guns at point-

---

69 Kraut is a disparaging term for a person of German birth or descent.

blank range, they fired on the doughs that went up to take the place. The result, of course, was that we sent a dozen rounds of H.E. [high explosive] into the place.

When we shot at the castle, our bullets went right through the darn thing, but they didn't explode until they got inside the castle. They were designed to penetrate and then explode. We didn't have quick-exploding shells because we were after armored cars and tanks, and we wanted the shells to penetrate them and then explode inside, so we used strike and delay explosives. We shot into the castle and the walls were so light that the shells went into the next room and then blew up. We finally drove the Germans out and took nine prisoners. My tank didn't take any of them but some of the tanks did. Net gain to the Krauts, one wrecked lovely building. But we didn't think about that at all. We didn't worry about blowing anything up, we just blew it. That was the way it was. When the time came to act we acted. That's the way it was.

We dug deep that night. Five miles west of us there were tremendous explosions. It must have been an arms dump. Jerry artillery holes were around our gun and in the night there was a five-plane dogfight with much shooting and wild circling overhead. There were three Kraut planes and two of ours. It was quite a show the boys put on, but it wasn't in our vicinity until the end. They got one of the Kraut planes.

A Battery was shelling a town ahead; they were behind us and the shells whistled overhead like a high wind in the pines during a thunderstorm. The town sent up a cloud of smoke. We could tell that it would soon be "liberated." There was a lot of small arms fire in the woods around us that night, which lessened as the morning drew on, but the town only burned brighter.

We had one position where they had dumped a number of dead cattle in a draw nearby. Not very pleasant! And speaking of smells, we often set up our kitchen in a barnyard, and those barnyards were something!!

The countryside was perfectly beautiful. I wish I could have sketched some of the lovely scenes: little picturesque villages dotting the land and beautiful green meadows. The grass was thick like a luxurious lawn, studded with wildflowers – golden dandelions, a lovely little purple mustard flower, deep purple violets, and buttercups were just a few of them. There was the rich smell of clover and pine. The forest had a very "cultivated" appearance while the trees were much smaller than those in the Sierras. They looked more like the groves around Monterey. Under happier circumstances, a trip through that country would have been most delightful, but I enjoyed it just the same.

When we pulled into a position – it might be in a field, as there were no fences over there, a meadow, the edge of a town or most any place where the battery could deploy – we would lay our guns and, if there were no missions, we set shifts. Those not on shift washed and shaved and cleaned their equipment or wrote or caught up on a little sleep. I enjoyed looking at Bill Mauldin's "Willie and Joe" cartoons in the *Stars and Stripes* newspaper. There we were, washing our clothes while waiting to level a village.

We made our home on the gun. Life on one of those M7 tanks was like setting up housekeeping on a tractor – no more convenient. We carried water in cans and we had a couple of single burner gasoline stoves, so if we wanted to do a little cooking – fried potatoes or some "liberated" eggs, etc. – we could do so.

The kitchen truck was always with us, and it set up a chow line nearby. Unless the day's movements interfered, we got three hot meals a day.

We slept near the gun, and usually found some straw to lay our bedrolls on. Unless a heavy mission came through, we took turns in shifts, much like the watches aboard ship. If a heavy mission came through, we all had to hop to it and tote amo and serve the gun. But that didn't happen very often.

We didn't travel in any one direction. We were a corp unit and as such, moved wherever we were needed. The guns were self-propelled so we were highly mobile and moved very often – sometimes short hops and sometimes long ones. I liked it that way. We got a chance to see so much.

I took one day off, as it were, and went back to a dental unit. I got a fine dentist who filled a couple of cavities. I was lucky on that score, as all Army dentists were not as particular about their work or as sympathetic as they might be!

"On the way to Linden, the firing batteries were attacked by Germans who had hidden in a woods near the road we were taking. As we approached the area, the hidden Germans had been taken

278

Stan's trek from Épinal, France, through Germany to Salzburg, Austria.

under fire by a small group of cavalrymen and with our appearance the fire thickened considerably." [70]

The cavalry was lined up alongside the road with their rifles pointed into the woods, thus covering us as we drove through, and we passed through unharmed. Late in the afternoon we moved forward, following the reconnaissance tanks through a couple of towns. The people were all astir. I saw one dead Kraut alongside the road and a lot of equipment cast aside by retreating Krauts.

That night was a bad night. The Krauts were over as soon as it was dark. They strafed positions around us and dropped bombs. There was heavy cannonading by batteries to the east of us and at sunup a Kraut came over, circled and dropped a bomb in B Battery. Shrapnel wounded one man.

We took two positions that day. Just after supper some big stuff came in on the right of our position. It was big, too. It was a terrifying spectacle to see the huge explosion and a geyser of smoke and dirt shoot hundreds of feet into the air. We were all scared and the boys nearest to where the stuff landed hit the dirt in a hurry. It must have been a huge bomb dropped by two Jerry planes overhead. We moved out and took up a new position. We settled in about 10:30 p.m. and turned in to sleep until 3:00, but at 12:30 the Krauts came

70 "On the Way," A Record of the 342nd Armored Field Artillery Battalion, Oct. 1944-July 1945, page 22.

out of the woods and got into B Battery area, but were chased off. They took two prisoners. We didn't see any but it stirred us up. Planes flew over but dropped no bombs. There were three towns burning ahead of us.

April 19 – What a day! Reconnaissance stayed in town and we went into position outside of it. Mid-morning, 120mm stuff began to come over us onto B Battery. There were no direct hits but it looked like a slaughter. B Battery pulled out in a cloud of smoke and dust. Shortly after, it began to come in on us. We broke up position fast and got out with hell popping all around us. No one was hit though – what luck! We moved to a new position and all of a sudden it started to rain in on us. We hooked up the trailer, with rounds dropping all around us, and pulled out – shaken but not hurt. Later we pulled back four miles through a beautiful country on a beautiful evening – a tired, lucky gang.

One time, when we were in Germany, we came into a small town. Those little towns were built on both sides of a main street with very few side streets, and they were narrow streets. We went in to clear this town and we got caught about half-way through, which would be a

Stan standing beside an M7 tank.

block or a block and a half or so into the town. I was leading a column of six tanks – I was driving the head tank – and there was a German Panzer coming toward us. I didn't know what to do, and the German didn't know what to do. So I turned to the left and went down a street because if he started firing, he'd shoot at me. I didn't know what he would do if I shot at him. So I pulled out into a big field out in back of a house and turned around so I could get a sight on him. And he turned around down at his end, and was getting the hell out of town. We had pushed the tanks clear back to this town, and he evidently knew that we were blowing them all up. That's the reason he evidently got out. He just didn't want to be blown up.

So when I was trying to turn around, the tank behind me came around and got stuck, because there was a little creek there. I had to put out a cable to pull him out of the water, but as I was pulling him out of the water I had to keep aware of where this Panzer tank was. Finally I got him out and went up on the road and the German tank had decided to go back. How many tanks were in his column? I never knew. I was too busy to count! But they never let one tank out. Tanks always went in groups. He got out and we got out, and that was that. But it was an exciting bit.

We went through Ansbach and past Dinkelsbuhl on April 21, heading for the Danube. Along the way we passed dead horses and some equipment. Planes continued to fly overhead and it was scary. There was snow in the rain and sometimes it hailed. It was miserable and cold and the road was deep with mud.

Then suddenly, a bunch of Krauts came out of the woods and stumbled into our post. We got two of them and the rest ran back into woods. That night the outpost guard saw one Kraut and called, "Halt!" A second Kraut clicked the bolt on his Burp gun[71] and the guard shot him in chest. He was only wounded so he shot him again two times.

As we moved on toward the Danube we travelled through some beautiful country. We passed the ruins of some ancient castles and I imagined the shades of the old knights must have stood in awe as they saw the long columns of armor of this day pass by: I know the people did.

---

71 The German Submachine Gun, the MP40, made a firing sound that provided a nickname, the "Burp gun."

We saw many liberated French soldiers as well as others. The French greeted us with the greatest delight; the poor fellows had been at forced labor for five years and at last were on their way home.

The 7th Army moved considerably during the month of April and we were right in the van [the front of an army] most of the time. Of course, we represented only a small portion of the lead elements but we were an important part in much of the advance.

As we pushed on through Bavaria the resistance became stronger. I awoke one morning about 5 a.m. to the sound of incoming 88mm shells from anti-aircraft guns – I was too sleepy to care.

But the next night was real bad. The Krauts were all around. Artillery was coming over and a mortar was fired into the town in back of our position. B Battery got shelled and snipers shot two men and killed one of them. About 2 a.m. some doughs got through to us, and I felt a little easier. Planes flew overhead and it was a noisy, uneasy night. I was so tired that I slept pretty soundly from 3 a.m. on.

We were some of the first troops to reach the Danube and crossed it on April 26 at Dillingen. As we were marching down the road to the bridge, our battalion was strafed and one man in A Battery was killed. "The next day or two were given over to long marches, for contact with the enemy had been lost."[72]

One night we marched 45 miles. We saw a group of buildings burning to our left and the 12th Armored Division shelling woods to our right. TAC boys [Tactical Air Command] were bombing and strafing from overhead, and prisoners were giving up as we came through the woods, so we took several hundred prisoners. Coming down the mountain we saw five towns burning. The next morning we could see the Alps in the distance.

The people greeted us most enthusiastically as we entered many little towns. They gave us beer and bread and cake. One town in particular, we entered it so rapidly that the people had not had time to dispose of all the Nazi flags and to hang out their white banners. The *Bürgermeister* must have put in some anxious minutes, but we didn't pay much attention to the color of the flags.

We saw a number of GI's who had been prisoners. They were certainly glad to see us and were high in their praise of the way the Red Cross had taken care of them.

---

72 "On the Way," pg. 23.

Many of the other liberated people took off as soon as we entered a town, and they started for home. I wondered what many of them would find, poor things? I was told that the pay – if and when – was 8 marks a week – about 80¢.

Considering the miles we traveled, it was little short of a miracle the way supplies kept up with us. The food was much better than one might expect. We also got good medical care, dental service and even shots in the arm!

For a few nights, we were lucky enough to be near either a barn or a house so that we could sleep where it was at least dry. One night I was in a house that had a nice little stove that did a good job of keeping us warm.

Another time we had just finished eating three ducks we had liberated and sat down to a game of poker. The first pot was being dealt – stud – when a couple of rounds came in. Shovels took the place of cards at once. And suddenly towns were smoking right in front of us.

We moved into a new position where we watched nine MEs [Messerschmitts] and eight P-47s [a USAAF fighter] tumble about in the air above us spitting death at one another amid the clatter of their guns. One P-47 showed an orange flash on its motor, rolled over and plummeted to earth to disappear in a huge red and black mushroom of smoke and flame. Then another P-47 started to tumble down and at the last moment the welcome sight of a chute appeared, while the plane landing nearby became another huge ball of fire. Then an ME started to smoke and, losing altitude rapidly, swerved low over the town to crash land. The other MEs disappeared, while the P-47s roared low over their fallen comrade's funeral pyre as a last salute. One of the other MEs was downed but I didn't see it. It all was over so fast!

Though it was spring, the rains continued and some days it was cold and miserable. One morning we played poker under a tarp stretched over the breech of the gun. In the afternoon we moved out and it took us nine hours to go eight kilometers. We crossed the Lech River at Landsberg on a broken railroad bridge. Half of our tracks were over the edge of the bridge, and it shook like the dickens.

I remember liberating one of the concentration camps, but I don't remember just where it was. It might have been near Landsberg. Bob Gray, one of the guys in my Battalion described it this way: "We liberated a prison camp. Some of them had already died, some couldn't get up and some were in pretty good shape. They were pushing these artillery guns and horse carts. When we busted the gates down and let those guys out, they started cutting the horses and eating the flesh raw. They were starved! We cleared out of that town."[73]

We took a new position in the grounds of the *Luftwaffe* [the air force.] We passed elements of three German armies and the towns were a confusion of Germans surrendering and armored troops. The Alps were just ahead of us about 20 miles.

Snow and rain continued and sleep was hard to get. I was so tired!! I only got 2 ½ hours sleep that night in the rain and cold, as I went on guard at 3:00 a.m.

We swung around Munich and I didn't get to see it at all. But one night I slept in a house filled with refugees from bombed Munich. We passed Weilheim, southwest of Munich near the Ammersee, and took up a position overnight. It was snowing heavily and the trees and the landscape were beautiful. Soft white snow came down like feathers, covering the ground with three inches of fresh powder. The Alps were to the right of us a few miles distant.

We were seeing thousands of prisoners by then. We passed two very large air fields where hundreds of planes sat, many of them destroyed. We traveled 35 miles one day and it was cold. We slept in a barn for two nights and procured some wine from some GI's. We found a reconnaissance plane hidden behind a barn and burned it.

We moved into our next position in the black of night in rain and snow. Then we moved on to Rosenheim, in the foothills of the Bavarian Alps, and saw many wrecked vehicles on our way to Salzburg. The countryside through Bavaria was very lovely. It was still cold though, and we got our last snowstorm around the first of May.

As we neared Salzburg the weather became real spring weather and it was delightful. The days were warm and the evenings lovely. We sat around outside in shirt sleeves until dark, which came after 9:00 p.m. and it was very comfortable.

Spring, of course, brought forth lovely wildflowers, and the meadows and fields were covered with them. Apple blossoms were bursting forth and dandelions carpeted the fields. A short distance from our position, the Alps rose to snow-capped peaks that reminded me a great deal of the mountains around Tahoe.

---

73 From a phone conversation Jenny Watts had with Bob Gray on Feb. 25, 2003.

Chapter 24: End of the War

"On 8 May 1945, when VE day was finally proclaimed, we were in Nieder-Aschau, situated in a beautiful valley which wound its way through the steep, imposing Bavarian Alps."[74]

The war ended much as I thought it would. I won't say "expected" for in war anything can be expected. I was off, as far as the date was concerned, a couple of weeks, but the drive didn't get underway as soon as I thought it would. When it did get underway, I was surprised that the Germans continued to put up such ineffective resistance in the face of our advance, in a delaying action that was without purpose as there was no line of resistance being organized in the rear. The net result was the destruction of little village after little village. When we finally did overtake the army we were opposed to, we just overran it and that was the end. The other Allied armies had much the same experience.

The end of the war did not come as a great climax, but instead it sort of petered out. One day we were in pursuit of a fleeing enemy, then he began to surrender in such numbers that it was evident that the great German Army had begun to disintegrate. After that, we began to pass long lines of smashed and broken vehicles and equipment, and it became increasingly clear that the army we were overtaking had met with disaster. We, of course, bypassed much of the enemy but their supply lines and communications were completely severed and any pockets of resistance were quickly overcome by our wide use of armor.

During the last few days of the war, we were in support of a cavalry unit that carried a Nazi general around to contact the little groups of SS troops holed up in the mountains. The mission was to seek out small groups of German soldiers who had retreated into the foothills of the Bavarian Alps. Upon being contacted, these groups invariably surrendered without a fight, and in a short while we had accomplished our mission. The German 7th was the last German Army to put up any organized resistance. When we repaired to our assembly area, it was only a short time later that this army too surrendered and the war was over.

---

74 "On The Way"; VE Day meant "Victory in Europe" Day.

The great last ditch stand that Germany was to make in the Austrian Alps was a fizzle – we beat them to the punch and never gave them a chance to get set. We out "blitzed" 'em!

As far as the *Volkssturm*[75] was concerned, it played a very feeble part. When you consider that according to Nazi propaganda, we as invaders were going to rape, pillage and murder on an unprecedented scale, it was surprising that the *Volkssturm* did not constitute a real force. But it didn't. A couple of times we ran into the *Volkssturm* but both times they had an SS fanatic leading them and when the going got too hot, they gave up.

The strange part was being greeted, as we entered town after town on the heels of the fleeing defenders of the Reich, as "liberators." People actually cheered and waved and in some places proffered eggs and wine and schnapps. It was hard to understand, for in the wreckage of the town – the only parts wrecked were those where some soldier had holed up and offered resistance – were soldiers who had died defending these people against us.

The only explanation seemed to be that they knew, within themselves, all along that Germany was not going to win the war. They knew that the Reich was wrong (no pun intended) and they had been living in dread of the day of reckoning. That day having arrived, and no dreadful tales of horror having preceded us, it must have been a great relief to at last find us actually on the ground. We were there. We had not ridden in and machine-gunned the town. We hadn't set the place on fire. The soldiers we captured were not shot, not mistreated or beaten, but had been taken on vehicles and sent back to the States or had been scooped up and carried along as time and the situation permitted. That must have been a relief! Then, too, we were not the Russians. That, in itself, was a great relief.

There was another thing: under Nazism the people had come to have a great respect for force. While there was Nazism, the German mind seemed to be able to only follow the winner – "might makes right" with them. Once Nazism had fallen, the people had no use for it, with some exceptions, of course. And it did bring them a lot of grief!!

They put up a bold front, but when they were whipped, they were

---

75 The *Volkssturm*, or People's Army, was a German National Militia organized in the last months of World War II, designed to supplement the defense of the homeland.

very quick to bow and scrape. "The hand that holds the whip is the hand to lick." They sank so low that there was hardly anything they wouldn't do to show us that they were friends – America is Good; America is Big; America is Powerful; America is Rich. We held the whip!

I had to admire the individuals, of whom there were very few, who saw us as we really were: invaders. The rest played ball with the winning team.

So it was that the Nazis got their power and kept it. Those who had the guts to oppose them, they bent to their will or were disposed of. The result: a people noticeably lacking in self-respect and integrity.

It was not good to find these things. And it made me wonder how these people felt when they found a political clique had begun to tell them how long they should work, and for how much, and how much they must pay for each commodity, and how much of that commodity they could buy or sell. And if a man didn't agree or refused to cooperate, he was thrown out and his business seized and he had no recourse or redress. The party in power grew in power and crept into every phase of the people's lives. And lo, there was National Socialism!

May all the thinking Americans consider Germany and, regardless of political ties, look ahead unbiased and unopinionated by those ties, at the road we are following. Too much has been spent in blood and tears and sweat in the name of freedom for us to allow any man, or any group of men, to abridge or filch from us one particle of that freedom.

It is not enough to recognize danger when it approaches, but one must warn those threatened and, if they be asleep and insensible to the danger, they must be awakened to it.

"Eternal Vigilance is the price of freedom," takes on a new meaning when we suddenly realize that we have not been exercising that vigilance and that our freedom has been taken from us, a little at a time, so that we didn't notice it. It is not yet too late but the time grows short.

The Germans destroyed the Jews – millions of them by gas, shots, and machine guns. They even castrated impure Germans, trying to build a perfect state. The camps were brutal. It was so terrible – their cruelties were hard to understand. I don't know how human beings can do the things that they did, but they do! We can all understand how people can hate, but so many of the worst cruelties are

287

practiced against defenseless people who have given no cause for retaliation and have done nothing to provoke much that has been done to them.

The Germans' treatment of the Jews was something that prior to the war, the world would have thought impossible. At least I was naive enough to think so. Yet the things that were done to those people defied the imagination. I couldn't understand it. It seemed that there was room to doubt that the forces of good were gaining over the forces of evil in that eternal struggle. But you can't entertain an idea such as that any more than you can contemplate the vastness of the ocean when your boat springs a leak. You have to confine yourself to bailing, bucket by bucket.

I spent a lot of time thinking about the uselessness of war and loathing it. Our boys were no angels – they were poking about in Germans' homes, getting drunk and terrorizing people. They had to search the houses, and they liberated liquor and eggs and ham as they did so. They drank freely of people's stores, and it was hard to keep them away from the German girls. There was no rape by our men, but three French soldiers took a crack at a German girl on the autobahn.

Thousands of German soldiers were giving up; long columns of them marching back home. They looked poorly. GI's would shake them down, and take anything they wanted. The Germans said we would fight the Russians with them someday. They said they only lost because of lack of materiel: weapons and munitions. They received no discharge pay from the German Army, and for days after the war ended, men came straggling by. But a week later, things were quieting down.

The German people seemed to have plenty to eat, but they were not robust-looking. They had very little meat in their diets and meals were simply feeding time. One man brought a large dog to us to shoot it for his food.

I first saw girls wearing GI shoes in France, but by the end of the war, many women were wearing men's shoes in Germany. Most of the women on the farms went barefoot to do chores in the house and the barn. They took care of the cows, which were kept in stalls, and brought grass to them. The stalls were kept clean, but the handling of milk was way behind the times.

The German people were poor. I watched them gather twigs, by trimming trees, and haul the sticks home. Then they piled them in the attic to dry. Most houses did not have running water and their furniture was cheap furniture. They had very little, but they were clean. They aired their bedding often and did the laundry regularly.

As we rolled through the Bavarian Alps, I was impressed by the many houses in the little villages that were very ornately painted with religious scenes or pictures from tales. Many had a balcony over which the roof extended. The balconies were painted red, blue and white with red predominating – a brick red. The men wore an odd dress of leather pants and a hat with feathers.

The church played a big part in their lives and was the central feature of every town. The beautiful churches that covered the Bavarian countryside came in all shapes and sizes and were prized and well-maintained by the people who lived and worshiped at them. They had a culture but it was not a "high" culture: a force for moral and political good. It was more of a popular or mass culture, and the church played a large roll in it.

Chapter 25: Salzburg

WE ARRIVED IN SALZBURG the middle of May 1945. The old castle high on the hill was large and imposing and seemed to be keeping watch over the city.

One night I was Sergeant of the Guard, and though the night passed without incident, I couldn't help but be thankful for the peaceful night as I made my rounds of the guard posts. It was late, but here and there a light shown in a window and though a plane droned past, there was no alarm and the warmth of the light looked good. There was no sense of danger lurking in the shadows, and there was peace.

We were stationed there for about a month. I put out guards around the town one time, then a couple of hours later I had to go around and pick them all up. I started out to pick these guys up and I got lost; I didn't know where the devil I was. So I went around the doggone town and finally I found some of the guys. I don't know how the heck I got out of that. I found some of the guys, and the rest of them came back to where the station was. But I was sure unhappy for a while. I never got called on the deal, but oh boy, I was unhappy. It's a pretty good-sized town, with a maze of cobbled streets. Years later, when we were there as a family in 1962, we also got lost and couldn't find our hotel. I told them how I had gotten lost there after the war. So it goes with Salzburg.

There was another time when my tank was pulling another tank through the city using a long cable. We rounded a corner into a narrow street, and the cable cut right through the corner of the building! That wasn't so good, but that was what happened.

I spent several weeks as part of the occupation living in a little village outside of Salzburg. It was called Viehausen. When we had been there for two weeks, things were quieting down and I could finally relax. I could go to bed and get a good night's sleep and not have to get up until time for breakfast at 7:30. Our duties were very light, and I was rested and in fine health.

Our battery of about a hundred men was located in a little group of farmhouses, some two dozen, that almost made a village but didn't quite. There was a *Gasthaus* [guest house] there but it and a wee church were the only buildings other than the farmhouses and their sheds. Each of the houses included a large barn and cow-shed all under one roof.

We made the *Gasthaus* our headquarters and kitchen, and took over a room in each of the farmhouses for the men. Though the families were all large and the loss of a room crowded them considerably, they were quite anxious that we remain.

That may sound odd, but as occupying troops we behaved very well, much to the surprise of those people who expected the worst. Also, there was the fear that if we left, the Russians would come. The very thought of them coming was simply terrifying to those people.

In the rear of the *Gasthaus* were several large chestnut trees, under which were tables and benches where we dined. The climate was so mild at that time, that it was quite comfortable out of doors from sunup to dark and sitting under the trees was very nice.

The non-fraternization policy made living that way a bit awkward but not too bad. We didn't fraternize to any extent — that is where we would be seen. But some of the many kids were always around and the GI's slipped them a candy bar or a stick of gum every now and then. How can one enjoy a candy bar with a little tow-headed kid watching you eat it with that hunger in his eyes that comes of a deficient diet?

Of course, the situation with the women was something else again. Boys will be boys, and there was a big shortage of men in those parts so the women were lonely. Non-fraternization became increasingly difficult to enforce.

Most, if not all, of the women had lost a father, brother, husband or sweetheart and yet there was such little feeling of resentment that it often made me stop and wonder. It seemed that people just didn't really have such a deep feeling of hatred.

There was one young woman whose husband was killed. She was of the age that came in for Hitler's youth movement and must have been thoroughly indoctrinated. She had a cute little baby. When we first arrived, she would not look at any of us. Though her duties brought her into close contact with us when we were at meals at the *Gasthaus*, she maintained a very unapproachable attitude, and while most everyone else acted friendly and nodded or spoke, she would not unbend. But one day, as she wheeled the baby indoors past a group of three of us, she looked up with a little smile. And so it goes. If the flame of hate is not fanned, it seems to die very quickly. It's strange in a sense.

Since I couldn't speak or understand the language of those around me, I think I took a much closer look at them. It's not that there were such great differences, but we were forced to learn from observation, rather than from conversation.

One day I visited Berchtesgaden.[76] The setting was beautiful. A good highway led to the foot of the mountains where it was situated, and a fine paved roadway ran up to the town. It was hardly a town though. It was more like a resort built on the side of a rather steep mountain. The buildings were of heavy masonry with smooth plaster exterior and broad, rather flat roofs for such a climate. The whole installation was spread out over a couple of kilometers. Its accommodations were not as nice as any first class hotel in the U.S., and the finer resort hotels at Yosemite were much better.

Of course, it was not at its best appearance, from the standpoint of tidiness. There were altercations toward the end of the war, but it was not as badly smashed as we had imagined. It seemed queer to me but there was nothing to suggest relaxation or scenes of happy vacationers that you sometimes sense, with a bit of a nostalgic feeling,

---

76 He was probably in the district of Berchtesgaden, at the mountain retreat of Obersalzberg, where there were chalets and mountain lodges belonging to the Nazi Party elite, including Adolf Hitler's famous mountain retreat, the *Berghof*.

when you look over an abandoned pleasure place. There was none of that. The swimming pool had that same cold attitude about it that you sometimes find at a pool on some fine estate that is perfectly appointed and perfectly kept but unused.

The ballroom, not large, had no warmth. It reminded me of a dancing school rather than a place of music and laughter. The view from the huge windows at the end, however, was very beautiful: looking out over a heavily wooded slope that ran downward to the base of the wall of huge mountains that are the Alps, the eye swept up to lofty, snow-covered peaks above which the white clouds swirled in the deep blue sky.

I soon tired of poking about the rubble and looking over the wreckage, but there was none of that feeling of loss that I experienced when I viewed the wreckage of some of the fine and beautiful things that we had passed in the last few months. The lovely bridge across the Rhine at Worms seemed a tragic wreck by comparison.

While there, I gave lessons to a little girl on how to jump rope! Those people were country people and to see men playing ball and able to jump rope quite amazed them. The kids jumped all right but in a lumbering manner and to skip lightly became the ambition of some of them. "Got to watch this non-fraternization!"

One morning the end of May, another GI and I walked to a little village a couple of kilometers away. There was a church celebration and procession going on – Corpus Christi, I believe it was called.

The church itself was much like all the others, and there were so many of them: the altar, ornate and splendid in its gold; the lovely altar cloth; candles in their golden candlesticks, which may have been brass but matched the gold of the altar; around the walls religious paintings in their heavy, gilt frames; the sun against the stained glass windows; the solemn intoning of the priest; the toll of the bell, the incense!

The place was crowded. We stood along the back wall and enjoyed the lovely music: a good organ intelligently played, and a choir that sang to make music, not just for the exercise.

Everyone was dressed in his or her Sunday best and, as this was a country parish and all were farmers and their families, their dress was anything but up to the minute. Most of it seemed to refer back to the turn of the century.

Some of the women had on narrow-brimmed straw hats, either black or tan, with a large, rather high, flat crown. These were adorned with a wide black or dark-colored ribbon fastened at the back that hung down to the knees. The hat was worn squarely on the head.

Some of the old women, in widow's weeds, had a voluminous black head-dress of the stuff hair ribbons are made. It was shaped like two huge "buns" at each side of the head and fastened at the back to hang down over the shoulders to the waist.

Corpus Christi celebration.

Many of the women wore old-fashioned shirtwaists with flowing skirts, no doubt billowed with the help of a couple of petticoats. (I'm not sure of this last – no fraternization, you know.)

The men, in their stuffy dark suits, could have been attending the coronation of Kaiser Wilhelm, as far as style of clothing was concerned. The material, for the most part, was a heavy, rather stiff boiled wool of dark color. Some of the dark grey coats were piped with small, dark green piping that gave a lift to the otherwise sombre clothing. Some of the suits had elk-horn buttons. They were good, stout, substantial suits that were built to last a lifetime and would probably be used as long.

The hats matched the suits and were a type often seen in that locality. It was a narrow-brimmed felt hat with a somewhat conical crown, which was not very high. It was adorned with a little feather or brush sticking jauntily out of the narrow band around the crown and held in place by an ornamental pin or clasp, often made of carved bone.

The little girls were dressed in white: white dress, white stockings, and a small white wreath of artificial flowers on their heads. All were very conscious of their splendor.

The little boys looked particularly stiff in their Sunday finest. Sober little country bumpkins, scrubbed to a polish.

Then, lest it seem that we overlooked them, there were the *Mädchen*. Most of them were in their first finery since their white dresses. There was nothing unusual about their costumes, just soft colored, darker toned dresses. They all seemed most pleased with their appearance and did look lovely. Clear complexions and unassisted coloring – simple food and hard work in the fields gave them a delightful freshness. Of course, the shy smile and the giggle that seemed always about to escape, as well as the soft curves and some not so soft, all made them worthy of at least a second look.

The bell tolled; the banners were raised; the priest, under a beautiful canopy brocaded with gold, came down the aisle and the procession had started. It wound its way out of the church and through and around the wee bit of a village; over a path lined with laurel branches; past the farmhouses, each with its little altar and flower-decked religious pictures decorating the front of the house. They stopped before a crucifix under which a temporary altar had been set, while the priest offered prayers and asked for blessing on the land; then on again to eventually re-enter the church.

In early June I had a comfortable billet and was enjoying the leisure and the nice climate. One night it rained, one of those hard summer rains. The roofs of the houses were large, covering house and barn, so of course, they shed a great deal of water. The water running off the eaves – there were no downspouts – almost played a tune as it was whipped about by little gusts of wind or was suddenly augmented by a heavy sheet of rain. It seemed to splash almost in symphonic rhythm.

Then the lightning and thunder – which I always like – started with all its brilliance and crashing din. We were right up against the mountains and the roar of the thunder would roll back into them, flung from peak to peak like a plaything of the gods. I fell asleep listening to it!

The next day there was little to do as the rain continued. I played the radio awhile and tried to converse in German with the family in whose house we lived. But I'm not much of a linguist.

I looked in on the cows – there were ten of them. The barn part of the house was quite up to date – nice cement floor and concrete feed trough. The cows just ate and slept and gave milk. All of their food was brought to them and they never left the stall, except for a short time at extended intervals to visit a very handsome bull who lived but a short distance down the road. He was the only bull in the village and, I believe, was taking care of some hundred odd cows.

The women in the little community were hard working *Hausfraus*. They milked the cows, cut the hay, cleaned the barn, worked the fields, cut the wood, washed the barn, and scrubbed the floors. They did little cooking, eating being a pause between jobs only. They were big husky babes, nice but not too bright in the sense of being worldly.

There was a Polish girl, about 19 years old, who tended the cows and milked them three times a day. She was a character: husky, solidly built, nice light brown hair and small but laughing blue eyes. Her grin – and she always seemed to be grinning, rather than smiling – was broad and displayed a nice set of strong white teeth. She seemed to have taken a shine to yours truly and I liked to kid her. It was kind of like kidding a bear though, as she was plenty stout. One day she gave me a playful shove that landed me halfway across the barn.

A couple of Poles got married one morning and she left that afternoon for the celebration. My, but she was in high spirits as she described the fête! To us, who have always had so much of the good things of life, her joy was pathetic. They were going to have fresh meat! And good bread! And something to drink, good schnapps and wine! There would be dancing, dancing too! Everyone would be happy, eating and dancing! Off she went, her gay spirits undampened by the pouring rain. I'm sure it was a great day.

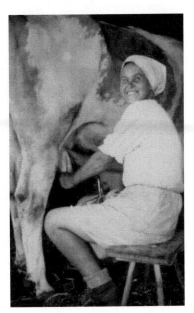

One day, I was going to wash my fatigue clothes, which were pretty dirty as I had been working in the grease on the M7 (our gun). I built a fire and started to boil them in a bucket of water when the woman from the house in back of the one where I was staying came over and insisted that she do the washing.

The next day she brought back my clothes to iron them and we chat-

Polish girl milking a cow.

ted. One of the boys who spoke a little German was there to keep me on the conversational track. She told me many things about the war. It was interesting. Her brother-in-law had listened to an American broadcast over the radio, and the *Gestapo* and SS took him away. For that seemingly trivial offense he paid a terrible price. The point I make though, is this: it seems incredible that in our time people could allow themselves to fall into such complete subjugation by a minority group. But they did, and that same danger is faced by all democracies.

I could not join in the hymn of hate that was so painstakingly sold in so many quarters. With reservations, it appears something like this was the set-up: The German people knew of the terrible treatment of prisoners in the concentrations camps. They all knew of someone who had suffered at the hands of the *Gestapo*. But these people, not being used to democracy, being trained in that thorough German manner with its emphasis on system and organization, could not conceive of an organized group that could buck the almost perfect organization of the party in power. There were exceptions, but when they were brought to light by some word or act, the *Gestapo* took immediate action and the little flicker from the flame of liberty was quickly quenched.

It was quite conceivable that had the Germans won the war, they would have indicted the Democratic party for the "barbaric bombing" of German cities. They were fighting the same war we were fighting, but they looked at it through one end of the binoculars and we saw it through the other end.

I know that we were right. We had to win. But many of those people thought that they were right. They had to be taught that they were wrong, and the degree of success with which we taught that lesson would largely determine the future peace of Central Europe.

In early June 1945, the peace in Europe seemed a fragile thing. Only by a rapid recovery to some sort of economic stability could it be nourished into something that would endure. I thought we lost the one great opportunity to fashion a perpetual peace when we did not stipulate what our demands would be when we doled out Lend-Lease with such lavish hand in 1941.[77]

---

77 The Lend-Lease Act allowed the U.S. to lend the Allies war materials in return for repayment after the war.

296

But I was very encouraged by the news that Russia had agreed to concede to the opinion of the other nations' representatives regarding the veto rights at the San Francisco Conference – the United Nations Conference on International Organization which drew up the United Nations Charter. On first reading, the preamble to the proposed world organization charter failed to make much of an impression on me, as far as eloquence was concerned. I had hoped for something couched in terms of greater grace and beauty. It was fine, but it was such a tremendous step, if successful, that I would have liked to have been struck by its eloquence as well as by its lofty ideals.

That the Germans had shown a capacity for cruelty, which was for me almost beyond understanding, was true. But they were likewise a nation of strong, industrious, self-possessed and stubborn people. We, as guardians of the future, had to give them the opportunity to develop along democratic principles of thought and government. We had to not only point the way but chart the course, at least until their ship of state was well out of danger of the hidden shoals of intrigue and away from the rocks of economic depression.

If this were intelligently done, there was no reason why the peace could not become a lasting one. So

Germans after the War.

297

much depended upon the leaders of our times!! "May God guide and direct them in this critical hour. The future peace of the world lies within their hands."

As I set down these poor words, I realized that I only attempted to present a layman's point of view, and it might be wide of the mark. My opportunity to study the German people was limited, due largely to my inability to converse with them.

But it was evening and the rain had stopped and it looked as though the skies were clearing. Tomorrow could be a lovely day.

One morning twenty of us went to a nearby airport, and our two liaison pilots gave each of us a ride. The little Cub planes were almost like being up in a kite! It was just swell! We rode in a large circle around Salzburg, circled the old castle, swung out across some lakes and back to the field, all too soon.

Even the sudden change in atmosphere was thrilling. It was like leaving the valley and driving to a high peak and stepping out of your car and filling your lungs with the fresh cool air. Well, it was something like that anyway, only much, much better.

The beautiful color of the woods and the fields seemed somehow intensified. And the city seemed to float past under you, as though you were watching a miniature on a revolving stage. The river and the canal that flowed thru the city seemed to cut it into segments and to provide points of focus to add to one's enjoyment. And then, in the distance behind the city, providing a perfect background, stood the Alps, peak after snow-capped peak into the distance.

One day I saw this same plane attacked by seven Me 109's.[78] I was talking to the pilot about it and he admitted that on that occasion he had simply given up. He started down but was just waiting for the end. Somehow, they missed him – the difference in the speed of the two planes probably accounted for the almost unaccountable.

We got a few shots at the 109's that day with our 50 caliber guns and I think maybe a few hits on one of them that was diving down on the observer as he landed. All of which may have been one of the reasons why he was around to take us up.

---

78 The Messerschmitt Bf 109, sometimes incorrectly called the Me 109 (most often by Allied pilots and aircrew), was a German World War II fighter aircraft.

The war was over, but it was too early to find out what was to be done with us: home, the C.B.I. [China-Burma-India Theater], or occupation, so we just had to wait for time and the Army to tell us what our next move would be.

I was so very glad that I did get in on the fighting. To be in combat is an experience that tells a man more about himself than, I believe, does anything else. There was an excitement about it that was fascinating. How it felt to be under a plane that was going to bomb or strafe you or both. No, it wasn't horrible. When it's over and you're unhurt, you come out laughing and cussing and greatly stimulated! And probably shaking a little, too.

War is big. Men get hurt. Men die. Things happen close to you but they don't touch you. There are other things that are so much more real – a shared ration or a drink, and countless little things that make a buddy or a comrade. These are the things you live with and they make impressions. The other things happen fast as a rule. Tragedy strikes – all hell busts loose and you are hit or you're not hit. If it takes place a hundred yards away, it's some other guy's. When it's all over, you're not sure just what happened. And you forget rapidly. And that is what usually happens in combat. There are exceptions, many of them, but they are still the exceptions. And too, the biggest percentage by far never actually see combat, though they are in a combat zone!!

As far as a man wanting to get out of the Army, that is most natural. It's not the fighting, it's not the training, it's not the long marches or the bitter cold that gets to a man, but it is the petty little minds of the men who give the commands. You can't do this. You can't do that. You must do this. You must do that. Those are the things that drive many a good man over the hill, if it's just to get good and drunk. Our outfit wasn't too bad. But there we were, just through a tough winter. It was summer and the order was out that ties should be worn at all times. Most of the men hadn't had a shirt buttoned at the collar since they got over there and then to look good in front of a lot of Krauts, we had to fall over backwards on spit and polish: button our collars and wear a tie, so that the summer became, for us, just as unpleasant in its way as the winter was in its.

I sure hated the prospect of being a garrison soldier. Combat ruins a man for garrison duty. It did me anyway. The thought of keeping spruced up all the time got me down. I'd take combat to what's known as "Chicken" any day!!

Chapter 26: The Riviera

HERE I AM IN NICE – taking a little vacation on the Riviera! They drew twelve names out of a hat and the lucky ones got a week in Nice, plus traveling time.

It was with a real pang that I left Viehausen, the little spot we stayed in in Austria. Had I stayed a few more weeks, the parting would have been really difficult. No woman trouble, but a couple of the little youngsters found their way into my heart. Little Freddie, 5, who'd jabber away at me in Kraut and be so pleased when I understood something that he said, which was rarely. And there was a little girl, 10, who adopted me. And the families of these kids, and the *Bauer* and *Bäuerin* of the house in which I stayed, all regarded me with so much respect and treated me with such consideration that I could not help but be impressed. It really paid to be a gentleman.

We left Salzburg by truck and came down thru the Brenner Pass via Innsbruck, Trento, Verona, Milan, Pavia and Genova. The ride itself was extremely beautiful – scenic beyond description. It would be well worth spending many days in travel but we did it all in two – too damn fast!

The Army set up a rest center in Nice and took over the hotels for the GI's. The very beautiful ones were headquarters and such things like the Red Cross – which was ensconced in the Nice Casino. I heard Jascha Heifetz play his violin there one night – beautifully!

I stayed in a small hotel a block from the heart of the vacation center of Nice. Nice is several towns in one – vacation land, business district, residential and Old Nice. When I first stepped into it – and you descend a flight of stairs to get to the old town – I just stood there for a moment, fascinated. I almost expected to have the diva step from the wings and cross to center stage, it was so very like a set from grand opera. The buildings, several stories high, formed a perfect "U." The people leaned from windows or lolled about the buildings just exactly as though they were the chorus. Though, of course, it was all much more real and dirty and smelly. Toward the back of the "stage" and leading into the "wings" ran an alley. We went to the right and, though it was broad day, the light had lost its brightness by the time it reached the narrow street, and we walked in sort of a gloom. The streets were so narrow that they were not wide enough to permit an auto to pass through them.

It was warm down there, but not too hot. I so often wished that my mother might have shared all the enjoyable parts of that great adventure I was living! There were so many things that I saw: some beautiful tea roses – red and yellow – at the stalls along the edge of the park in the morning; the music at night; the beautiful Alps, wooded mountains with bare, snow-streaked peaks plumed with mist; the pastel shades of the houses – towns so rich in color; the chimney pots, a myriad of designs; the olive groves, their silver-green leaves shimmering in the sun; the rock terraces, old and moss-grown; the

Stan at Brenner Pass, 1945.

ever picturesque ruins of castles perched atop mountain peaks – always a reminder of the past; a glimpse of the Coliseum at Verona.

While I was there I took a tour of the Côte d'Azur. First to Monaco, where we saw the lovely gambling Casino de Monte-Carlo from the hilltop above it, but did not get into the place. Monaco, as you probably know, is just a little country, having a standing army of 90 men and three officers. Her people pay no taxes, as the Casino takes care of the country's revenue requirements, but her citizens are forbidden to gamble at the Casino.

On the way we passed the fine old hotels of Nice situated on the hill back of the town: the Majestic Palace, Europe's finest hotel at one time, and the Regina, the favorite haunt of Queen Victoria. A lovely statue group – a tableau with Queen Victoria seated upon a throne and four maidens arranged about her, representing the Queen and the four lovely cities she enjoyed: Nice, Grasse, Antibes and Cannes –

is in front of the Regina. The Germans, however, had decapitated the Queen. It was most disgusting. What fools men are! For some smart American will certainly do something equally asinine, but so far the German holds all records I am sure.

The road to Monaco lies along the route the Romans took on their way to and from Spain, and it is rich in lore and landmarks that seem to mark the pages of history. There is the Chapelle Notre Dame de la Garoupe [in Antibes] built, I believe, about 400 A.D. It was later destroyed and the new and more modern church was built in its place about the year 900. The old garden, however, was still producing its figs and olives.

We also passed an old Roman-built arena that in its time seated about 7,000. I wonder what the spectators witnessed in the hollow of those crumbling walls? Have we come so very far?

Let's be on our way. The road is hewn from the rocky side of the steep mountain that runs up from the narrow shore. The blue Mediterranean stretches out below. The terraced hillsides below the road are covered with olive groves.

We went over the Devil's Bridge – a beautiful piece of masonry. Tall, slender arches rising from the deep canyon give it an especial air of grace. One arch, however, had been destroyed – the Germans again, following the dictates of the strategy of war. We passed the castle, or more correctly the fort, at Eze. It was the latest design in forts in its time, as it did away with the high walls and introduced the low thick walls, brought about by the use of cannon.

We saw the beautiful villa of Gloria Vanderbilt and another of Leopold II, in fact two of his lovely places: one high on the mountainside and the other closer to the sea, overlooking it.

On our trip the scars of war were noticeably few, but the history of the route is punctuated by wars. Old Europe and her old hates and animosities!

Well, the tour ended, as tours have a habit of doing, and we each went our separate ways to tell or write as many versions of what we saw as there were passengers.

The rest of my stay was pleasant tho I didn't do a great deal. I met a few nice women at the clubs, but funds and a not too keen appetite for the liquor kept me out of them for the most part.

It was real summer weather there, and it was indeed a pleasure to sit at a table in a sidewalk café or on a bench along the promenade and watch the throngs of pretty gals go past, especially those on bicycles. The fashion there was a tight-waisted, rather full, short skirt; gay wooden-soled 'wedges'; and snug shirtwaists – which gave a very accurate, though sometimes exaggerated, view of their womanly charms. Sometimes the shirtwaist was so short as to leave a little gap between skirt and shirt and a little bit of the bare mid-rift showed. And as the girls rode by on their bikes, their full skirts fluttering gayly, they displayed a most generous portion of an oft times shapely leg. Their modesty was preserved by a pair of little swimming shorts, like panties. The GI's found the passing parade very entertaining and they would sit for hours watching it.

It was surprising the way the girls and women turned themselves out – blonds with brown eyes and décolleté necklines. They certainly had the imagination and the 'know how' to make themselves attractive. They must have spent a lot of time fixing themselves up, but the results were well worth the effort because they did look cute. Some of them were so petite and had such lovely figures and they took full advantage of their attributes when they dressed – I mentally took my hat off to them as they passed. They knew how to employ their charms charmingly.

Some of the things we saw there would seem strange and a bit fantastic elsewhere, but there it looked 'chic'. For instance, many of the girls had pompadours 6 and 8 inches high; hair colored purple, lavender, blue, black, silver, red, pink or most any color that hair can possibly be dyed. Some of it coal black on top and the lower half of a long bob, platinum blond – it was attractive, too! Many of the high pompadours had an inch wide streak of blond or grey or silver in them, and in the black hair it was very effective. But some of the

Sergeant Hulse, 1945.

303

Stan Hulse, in Nice, France, 1945.

brighter shades were a bit startling.

There were a few, of course, who displayed their charms for commercial reasons but the ones I speak of were just being feminine and enjoying their femininity.

There were some stunning and very fascinating women at the nightclubs. Their looks were their stock-in-trade, or part of it anyhow. And they were part of the picture of Nice and far from the least charming part too. But that was Nice!

Evenings were particularly delightful. The bare-bellied bartender uncorked some delightful Nice wine while a GI strummed on the old battered piano in the smashed bunker that was serving as a café, the music becoming more sentimental as the dawn drew closer. A midnight snack was a sandwich of dark French bread, tomatoes, onions, spicy dressing with radish, washed down with a delicious glass of Nice wine, a delightful drink.

I took a walk by the sea. The moon through the palm fronds made a straight silver path on the slate black of the sea. The Mediterranean seemed to lap its shores like a cat, compared to the voracious roar of the waves pounding the Atlantic Coast.

The tinkle of the harness bells and the clop-clop of the horses' hooves were soothing as the cab rolled through the warm, moonlight night. With the soft air like a caress, you settle back against the carriage seat and wrap yourself in the splendor of the night.

Well, to sum it all up, I just poked about the city (some 400,000 pop.) and looked. I'd sit on a bench and look some more, or spend a bit of the morning among the stalls of the open marketplace. Sometimes I enjoyed an hour or two in the company of another GI, and we'd fight the war over a couple of glasses of beer. There were GI's all over the place, fighting the war in every bar and sort of rehearsing some of the tall ones they'd tell back in the States! Surprising how many hero's this man's army has! But all the stories wound up with, "I was plenty scared," which was about the only truth to most of them.

I planned to meet my outfit in Northern France when I left Nice. Then we might be redeployed, and if so would be back in the U.S.A. within the next couple of months. I was due to get a 30-day furlough if that happened. I didn't expect to stay in Europe as I had elected to stay with the outfit and when it moved, I would too.

Chapter 27: Heading Home

OUR TRIP HOME WAS VIA AIX-EN-PROVENCE near Marseille, through southern France to Dijon, then through the Champagne region to Camp Brooklyn, which was not far from Rheims. I didn't see a great deal of that city, but the old cathedral was still there, scarred by war. I did enjoy the Champagne region, which is in a lovely section of the country, covered with vineyards.

As we travelled through France, the scars of war were not particularly noticeable, except for the hundreds of German vehicles that lay beside the road – nothing but twisted and rusting wrecks giving mute testimony to the first of the crushing defeats to Hitler's armies on the Continent.

All in all, I was fortunate to have gotten around as much as I did. I saw a pretty good slice of Europe, parts of which were most beautiful and charming, but I still prefer the good old U.S.A.

I stopped at a public scale to see what my weight was. It printed out a ticket that said, "The weight indicated on the back was yours as of the date of 28/6/45 (June 28, 1945) You weigh 61 kilos (135 lbs.)"

On my birthday I was still in France at Camp Brooklyn, one of the redeployment camps near Suippes, southeast of Rheims. I was soon transferred by train to Camp Top Hat in Belgium, right outside of Antwerp. Our trip was interesting though the train poked along with exaggerated slowness.

The next week was an easy one. There was no training and no duties to perform so we just took it easy, playing cards, reading and enjoying the sun. The climate was very mild – a little on the warm side but very pleasant. It was a nice, easy, quiet week. It looked like we would be on our way before long, headed back to the States.

We finally got away, headed for home on the SS *Claymont Victory*, one of the Victory ships, which were a type of cargo ship that was mass-produced during the war. We sailed out of Antwerp on July 19, 1945, and arrived in Boston to lots of cheering and flag waving on July 29. It was good to be home.

I sent this Western Union Telegram to my mother when we arrived in the States:

CAMP MYLES STANDISH MASS JULY 29 1945

MRS D K DUNGAN
501 SYCAMORE ST SAN CARLOS CAL

ARRIVED TODAY. GOOD CROSSING. LEAVING
FOR CAMP BEALE WITHIN FEW DAYS AND
THEN WILL BE HOME ON FURLOUGH.
HEAPS LOVE,
STAN

I had a very enjoyable furlough that terminated on the 6th of September. Then I went up to Camp Beale, near Marysville, California. One week later I was discharged from the Army on September 12, 1945, with an Honorable Discharge. I returned to San Carlos, no longer at the beck and call of the Beard (Uncle Sam). It was time for me once again to take my place as a gainful member of society. Yes, back to work I must go, ah me!

As the golden orb sinks slowly in the West,
Don't say another day is gone –
Rejoice and say another day has been added to the annals,
Another thread in the tapestry of life.
Tomorrow's deeds will add new luster to the beauty that is there.

Dwell more on the lovely colors some threads did add –
the blues, the golds, the whites, the reds
blending to enrich the whole.
Pass over lightly, here and there,
the sordid splotches that time alone will fade away.

Stan

PART THREE:

When My Ship Comes In

Chapter 1: Civilian Life

After I was discharged from the Army, I went down to San Carlos and stayed with my mother and Duge. Then I got in touch with Holly Winfrey who was in the construction business.

Holly and his wife had been friends of my mother for many years. He and his brother Vic were good carpenters and builders. They had built some nice houses in the San Mateo area. Holly, whose full name was Holman E. Winfrey, served in World War I and married a Jewish girl named Rae on the East Coast. I went to work for him as a carpenter.

He let me cover the jobs he was doing and told me that someday I'd be able to do it alone. And he said the quicker the better, as he wanted to take a long rest.

It meant turning down a nice offer from the head man at Bethlehem Steel to come work for them, but Holly's proposition looked good to me. Bethlehem's offer meant a nice desk and was very flattering, but this other was out of doors, and Holly hadn't done so badly. I was surprised and very pleased when he invited me in to learn his business.

I had dinner with Ed Smith, Smitty, one night in San Francisco. He had been first mate on the *Santa Cecilia* when I sailed on her back in the '30s. He was going to go to sea for one more year but still wanted me to go into some kind of business with him. I told him we'd see what developed when he returned.

I was still having girl trouble: trouble finding the right one. I figured I'd just have to keep on looking, but looking was not so bad. In fact, it was kind of fun. Then in February, I received a Valentine from Lu Kemp – just a friendly card. So on Valentine's Day I called her mother in San Francisco to find out where she was. She told me that she was visiting Win Simmons in Palo Alto, so I dropped by Win's house and there was Lu and Win and Win's mother.

So we started dating. She was working in San Francisco at Western Airlines, and I was taking a course there on building contracting so I could get my license. I'd pick her up after work and we'd go out to dinner together. This went on for several months, then in May 1946, I proposed. We drove out to the beach and parked where we could see the ocean. Then I said, "Open your mouth and close your eyes," and I slipped a ring on her finger, and that was that.

We were married June 8, 1946, at Portalhurst Community Church in San Francisco. My mother and Duge were there and brother Bill, but Donnabeth and Chuck were up in Spokane so they couldn't make it. All of Lu's family was there: her mother and father, Eva and James

Wedding party, left to right: Marilyn, Robert Sr., Robert Jr., Eldamarie Kemp; Stan and Lu; Bernice and Philip Condit; Don, Bessie and Bill Dungan; Eva and Murray Kemp. Dan Condit, photographer

Murray Kemp; her sister, Bernice, with her husband, Daniel Condit, and son, Philip; and her brother, Robert, with his wife, Eldamarie, and children, Robert and Marilyn. So it was quite something. It was a short ceremony then there was a reception of some kind. I think we cut the cake and then left and went over to my friends' Jim and Ruth Chesnutt's house, where we celebrated with champagne. Ruth described it years later: "I can see you and Lu on our doorstep – radiant – to share your happiness over champagne and sandwiches. Then sending you on to your honeymoon. So right then – as now. Here's to you and the always lovely Lu."

We wanted to take a honeymoon but I was working for Winfrey and Winfrey said, "No, you don't go anyplace. You stay here." So there I was. He was a bum.

We went up to Blue Lakes and spent a couple of days up there. It was just beautiful out on the lake. Then we went over to visit my dad and Maude, who were living in

Lucile and Standish Hulse.

Lu Hulse at Blue Lakes.

311

Lakeport. He was not well at that time and he called Lu in by herself and he said, "You take good care of him." And she said she would. He died there just a few years later, in 1951.

On my birthday, July 10, 1946, I received this poem from my mother:

> *Count your garden by the flowers, never by the leaves that fall –*
> *Count your days by golden hours, don't remember clouds at all –*
> *Count your night by stars, not shadows,*
> *Count your life with smiles, not tears.*
> *And with joy on this your birthday,*
> *Count your age by friends, not years!*
> > *With love to my dearest son,*
> > *Mom*

Chapter 2: Newlyweds

RIGHT AFTER THE WAR it was very hard to find housing. There had been very little new construction during the war, and with so many soldiers coming back and looking for a place to live, houses were few and far between. So we were lucky to find a place to stay on Paloma Avenue in Burlingame. The place was owned by one of Winfrey's employees who went on a two-month vacation, and he said we could use his house.

His name was Tuck[79] and he had a dog and a cat. The dog became very fond of me and knew when I was coming home. How the dog would know, I don't know. But I could be two blocks away from the house and the dog would run to the front door and whine, and Lu knew that I was coming up the street. It was really surprising.

When Tuck came back, we moved to 865 Bayshore in Burlingame, where Winfrey lived. He was gone a month, so when he returned we stayed at my mother's for a couple of weeks until we found an apartment at 1507 Newlands Avenue, Burlingame, owned by a woman named Mrs. Rossi. I was doing some remodeling work for her in Hillsborough, converting a five-car garage into a residence with Winfrey's help.

---

[79] The Burlingame City Directory of 1949 lists Ernest Tuck, carp contr, at 1016 Paloma Ave., Burlingame.

Winfrey set me up in the contracting business and he said, "Now, I'll be around to help you and get you started, so don't worry about it, I'll always be there." Then he sold me the business, and he went off to Sebastopol and we never saw him again. He was a tough one. He left me high and dry.

We had very little furniture and for a while we ate our meals off of a low coffee table in the kitchen. The coffee table was about 24 inches wide and that's all we had. So we were living on a shoestring. Lu and I each had about a thousand dollars saved up when we were married that we put into the business, and we had to wait for job completions before we could buy anything. We never bought on credit, always paid cash. So we didn't have very much for a little while.

Smitty looked me up when he got back from sea. He had some property up at Lake Tahoe and he said, "Why don't you come up and build me a cabin." So in the summer of 1947, Chuck Baker, who was working with his dad in the construction business, and I agreed to spend the summer at Tahoe and build a cabin for Smitty. Chuck and Donnabeth and Lu and I all went up there and camped on his land and built him a cabin.

Chuck Baker, Smitty and Stan at Lake Tahoe, Summer 1947.

313

Donnabeth and Chuck slept in a tent and Lu and I threw a mattress on the ground outside. Each morning we were awakened by cows bawling in the next meadow. It was very loud.

It was a great summer. We cooked over an open fire and sat around the campfire at night thinking up various ways to become rich. We had a good idea too: a card that you could use instead of cash for buying things. But we didn't act on it and by 1950, the credit card was beginning to appear.

Once a month we'd drive down to Burlingame in the truck and Lu would see the doctor. Our first baby was due in December and, since we didn't know if it would be a boy or a girl, we referred to him as Oscar.

We fished in Lake Tahoe with Smitty for mackinaw trout. He knew exactly where to find them. He'd tell us to row out to where we could see that point over there and this point over here, then stop. We'd have our line out and he'd tell us when to expect a bite and by golly it would happen. He'd tell us to reel in, and we'd have a fish! We had to pull the trout up very slowly otherwise they'd bloat, they were so deep in the lake. He got some big trout – 3 feet long.

Duge and Lu with mackinaw trout and a young helper.

314

Sometimes we fished off the pier for rainbow trout. We'd cook the fresh trout over the fire and my, it was good. It almost convinced us to stay up there and live at Tahoe.

Smitty had made the first tourist map of Lake Tahoe and put the maps in shops around the lake. He would go around and pick up his money and gamble at State Line at the dollar machines. He would win $10 or $20 then go shoot craps and lose it all.

In September the cabin was finished, and the baby was soon to arrive, so we went back to Burlingame. I hung out my shingle as Stan Hulse Builder and went to work.

I built quite a number of houses in Burlingame and Hillsborough, mostly in Hillsborough. There were some nice ones. On one lot I built three houses, including one with an indoor swimming pool.

Timothy James was born while we were living on Newlands Avenue, December 7, 1947, and he had his first Christmas there. Then we moved to 865 Bayshore, after Winfrey left and moved to Sebastopol. We lived upstairs in a nice little apartment above Bayshore Plumbing, which was on the ground floor. It was just one bedroom and as the family grew larger, we just kept putting more beds into that one bedroom. We looked right out on Bayshore Freeway, and I used to judge how the economy was doing by the number of cars on the freeway.

Jennifer Jane was born July 8, 1949, while we still lived at 865 Bayshore. Lu's dad advanced us money to buy a lot at 1376 Vancouver Avenue, Burlingame, for around $4000. We chose the neighborhood because it was a safe place for the kids to play, and Burlingame had good schools, with the grammar school just two blocks away. I designed a nice two-story house for us and started building our home there. It took quite a while to build the house because I would only send carpenters up to work on it when I didn't have any other jobs for them.

Timmy with Grandma Dungan, 1949.

315

Stan with Jenny and Timmy, 1950.

Otherwise, I needed the money, so I had to keep the guys on the job.

Geraldine was born November 9, 1951, and our little family of five moved into the Vancouver house over Memorial Day, 1952.

The house had three bedrooms and a bathroom situated over the two-car garage. Downstairs was the living room, dining room, kitchen and dinette. The living room had a fireplace at the far end, and a hallway led past the dining room to the kitchen. The kitchen window looked out on the backyard so Lu could keep an eye on the kids, and the window in the dinette let the morning sun shine in. We had radiant heat throughout the house, which was very pleasant. Lu especially liked the warmth of the bathroom floor.

A flight of stairs went from the front door to the upstairs. The bathroom was all tiled with two sinks, one lower than the other for the kids. A tub, a shower and a toilet completed the room. The master bedroom looked out on the backyard and the two smaller bedrooms faced the street. Jenny and Geri shared the larger one and Tim had the smaller room, which had a big closet in it where we kept things that you might store in your attic. It was not a large house, but was adequate for our little family.

316

Then in 1955, we heard about a motel in Fresno that was for sale. It was the Fresno Motor Inn and was called 55 Cottages. I liked the place and thought we should try it, so we moved to Fresno that year. We were there for about six months, until we realized that the owner had misrepresented the amount of business he was doing. Meanwhile, we had asked my mother to try to sell the house on Vancouver Avenue, but it hadn't sold, so we moved back to Burlingame and settled in there.

Chapter 3: Toastmasters and Lions

I JOINED THE BURLINGAME TOASTMASTER CLUB in the early 1950s so I could improve my public speaking skills. We met once a week in the evening and gave speeches that we had written, to each other. On November 27, 1956, I was part of a debate on "Should the U.N. form an organized police force?" Fred Rice and I took the affirmative and two other guys argued the negative. It was very interesting.

I made a lot of good friends there. I remember Abe Miller, Sherrill Brown and Carlos Montandon. Sometimes I was a speaker and sometimes I was a critic.

This is a speech I gave entitled, "Let's Look at our Army."

Do any of you know how many men we have in our Army? If you do, I assure you, you are in the minority. We have 1,170,000 men.

Senator Humphrey said the other day that, in view of the world situation, it is nonsense to cut our military strength. This was in response to President Eisenhower's suggestion that the Army be reduced by 140,000 men.

First, I submit that President Eisenhower knows a heck of a lot more about the Army than the Senator. He knows a lot more about the world situation and its threat to peace than does the Senator. And he has a great deal better understanding of the Russian political mind.

For in the face of this criticism as nonsense, our Seventh Fleet evacuated the Tachen Islands, off the coast of China, without a shot being fired, while the Red Chinese guns spoke only silence just eight miles away. The evacuation was a calculated risk, but to me it proves that the Administration knows what it is talking about.

But I am not here to discuss the changing tensions of the international situation; I am concerned about the size of our Army.

In 1917-1918 the Army had a high of 4 million after the war; in 1920-1930, our Army was 130-odd thousand. World tensions caused an increase to 267,000 in 1940, and then a high of over 8 million in 1945.

In 1950 it shrunk to one-half million, then with Korea, up to an estimated 1.5 million. Our present Army is close to 1,170,000 and the President suggested that from this vast peace-time Army we should drop some 140,000 men.

Now, I maintain that if the critics want to make a case for putting the country on a total war footing, let them do so, but to argue that the President is emasculating our Army by this reduction is in itself nonsense. We must not be goaded into trying to compete man for man with the two most populated countries in the world.

Mao Tse Tong's remark that "the Imperialists will be wiped clean from the surface of the globe" is another attempt to create tensions and force us to spend and spend and spend on arms, and so to exhaust ourselves. We must above all keep a cool head. And it is my opinion that in these times, this nation is divinely blessed by having a man who can correctly appraise the enemy, who will not be goaded into a fight, and who knows war so thoroughly that he will go to any honorable lengths to avert a war. The world will soon realize that our position is not one of cowardice, but of strength. And that is the only way we can hope to win this cold war without it becoming a shooting war.

Our present base of a million men is a broad enough base on which to build any wartime fighting force. Technological advancement and the introduction of atomic weapons has made the 4 or 8 million man Army as obsolete as the horse cavalry.

And speaking of the technological advancements, I would like you to note that it has practically done away with horse stealing in this country!

Another speech I gave was entitled "Review Your Thinking."

The other day I was asked to go down to the site of the shooting range on the city's land at the dump at the foot of Broadway. I found a half a dozen men or more working like the proverbial beaver cutting, sawing and putting together the structure that was to house the affair. A great deal of work had been done, a great deal of material had been used, and a great deal of money had been

318

spent. Much of the work, much of the material, and much of the money had been wasted.

Why? Because someone had not given the project the proper thought. The building was 88 feet wide but the sum of all the intermediate spaces only totaled 84 feet on the plan. The way out was clear. The project needed new thought, new plans to build by. And these are now in the making.

Most of us are having just as much trouble with our lives as those men were having with their building and for the same reason: we have not given our lives the proper thought – our plans, our thoughts are not right.

Marcus Aurelius, some 2,000 years ago said, "The happiness of our life depends upon the quality of our thoughts." That statement is just as true today. Our own thinking is a habit. It can either be a good habit or a bad habit and it is up to us to improve the quality of our thoughts.

Undirected thoughts are the result of bad thinking habits. These are the mental and emotional termites that destroy our happiness as surely as termites can destroy our house. These termites are worry, greed, hate, lust, self pity, vain glory. One can spend all their time dwelling on such thoughts and reap a bumper crop: a bumper crop of frustration, fear and misery.

But with just a little effort we can direct our thoughts through new channels: the channels of controlled thinking, the channels that lead to a fuller, more abundant life.

I also drew on some of my experience from the war to talk about the horror that I saw in Germany, and "Man's inhumanity to man." With that in mind, I gave this speech on Nazism:

From the beginning of time, man has wanted to belong. We see how important it is to teenagers of today to belong by being as much like their contemporaries as they possibly can. A girl in the eighth grade must have saddle oxfords. A boy about this age must have a certain type of jacket.

And a funny thing about man: from the beginning of time – aside from disease and hunger – man has been man's greatest enemy.

Just in the six years of World War II, we people of the earth managed to kill in battle about 15 million people, and another 10 million through bombing, starvation and as a direct result of hostilities. 25 million man-made deaths in six years. And to produce this huge casualty list, there were 100 million men under arms. How was it possible that these men were engaged in trying to do away with one another and succeeding in some 15 million cases?

Time does not permit going into all the underlying causes of World War II, but suffice it to say that this fundamental urge to belong coupled with the innate cruelty of man, made it possible for one man to motivate these fundamental urges under the sign of the swastika and unleash upon the world this fantastic blood bath.

We have all seen pictures of the poor, miserable, starving creatures that survived the barbed wire hell from which we liberated them. There were six or seven million who did not come out of those camps.

It is not my purpose to try to turn your stomach by describing all the brutality and bestiality that went on, even to the fashioning of lamp shades from the skin of these poor unfortunates.

But what I have described did take place. And the German people did listen to Hitler and his doctrine of hate. And these atrocities were committed by Germans, under the sign of the swastika. All because a little group of men were willing to listen to an obscure house painter with a great talent for oratory that took the place of brains.

We here have knowledge of that great war – we who saw the pictures or were there will never be taken in by a silly man in a brown shirt.

But a whole new generation throughout the world is growing to manhood. They have the same fundamental desire to belong. The same innate capacity for cruelty that is man's heritage. They too can make that same mistake that culminated in the bomb-torn rubble of Europe.

This must not happen.

This cannot happen.

We cannot break faith with those who gave their lives that you and I might be sitting here tonight as free men.

Today in our land are thousands of youth who need leadership. There is something about youth that cries out to belong. To be a member of a group. This desire is deep-seated, it goes back to the beginning of time when man with his stone hatchet learned to slay the mammoth and loudly howl so that the clan would come trouping in to enjoy the crimson feast.

This world has moved on in the lathe of time, but man still clings to that prehistoric urge to join his fellows at the kill. Civilization and learning has helped man to rise above these crude impulses. But the young, and those who have not found the companionship and release from basic impulses, have a need. And this need will be filled.

In our modern civilization who is left out of the feast? Those who, because of economic reasons, don't have enough money to make them one of the circle, to put them a little higher on the scale of living. This breeds resentment! And a focal point for this resentment must be found.

In Germany we saw a great economic collapse in which all men suffered. This made a situation that was ideal for the growth of this primal urge to belong. To strike back at a society that was failing to supply the needs of its people.

It was easy to instill hate, to draw men together that they might point the finger at the one – anyone – responsible for their misery.

So they stirred up the prejudice that lay concealed beneath the surface. And in that way were able to commit the horrible atrocities of which I speak.

It is to guarantee that this never happens again that we must dedicate ourselves to inculcating in the minds of our growing generations the abolishment of racial prejudice.

By May 1957, I was the area governor of our area and in 1958-59, I was lieutenant governor for all of District 4. Every spring there was a big district meeting at Asilomar, on the Monterey Peninsula. Lu and I took the kids and spent the weekend there. There were meetings and such then there was a speech contest in the evening. In 1959, I was the chairman of the contest, so that was quite something. I was a member for about five or six years.

I also joined the Burlingame Lions Club and there made a number of good friends. Let's see, there was Clarence Rusch,

Lions Paul Lechich and Stan Hulse, 1960.

Gil Larish, Art Preston, Frank Conti, who I became business partners with, Paul Lechich, the city librarian, Wayne Guthrie, and Herm Schmidt. In April 1957, I became first vice president. Paul Lechich was secretary-treasurer of our club for years and years and years. Everybody else turned over once a year, but Paul stayed the same. I was friends with him for a long time.

We met at Bobs on Broadway for luncheon meetings. We had a White Cane Drive every year, which raised money to help the blind, and I would stand on a street corner on Broadway with the kids selling little white canes. We had a big Easter egg hunt every year in Washington Park

Stan with Jenny, Geri and Tim at Lion's Convention in New York, 1959.

Stan with Geri, Tim, Jenny and new 1959 Star Chief Pontiac at 1376 Vancouver Ave., Burlingame.

on Easter morning. It was fun to help out with that.

In 1959, I was installed as President of the Burlingame Lions Club. We had 98 members. That was pretty good. That summer they sent me to the Lion's International Convention in New York City. So we took the family and made a trip out of it. We went to New York and Washington, then up to Niagara Falls and across Lake Erie to Pontiac, Michigan, where we picked up a brand new Pontiac Star Chief, white with a dark blue roof, and drove it home.

In May 1960, the Lions held their district convention at Hoberg's Resort in Lake County. It had a big lodge and cabins, a swimming pool, dance hall and a big dining hall and was located on Cobb Mountain in the pines near Clear Lake. We had a good time there with the family.

Sometimes we would have a family night and one time we put on a variety show and I dressed up in red long johns. That was quite something.

Chapter 4: Family and Friends

MY FAMILY LIVED IN THE BAY AREA. My mother and Duge lived in San Carlos, Donnabeth and Chuck lived in Los Altos, Mabel lived in Menlo Park, and Bill lived in Belmont. My sister Jane lived on Summit Road in the Santa Cruz Mountains, but I seldom saw her. The rest of the family I would see from time to time.

Every year around Christmastime we'd all get together for a chop suey dinner. That tradition began a long time ago. Mimi, who was brought to this country from Japan as a little girl and raised by J. R. Whitney and his wife, my great-grandparents, was about my mother's age and they were life-long friends. She'd cook up a big pot of meat and vegetables and serve it over rice. Then I became the cook and we continued that tradition the rest of my life. I guess we did it for almost fifty years. We had a lot of fun at those dinners.

In November 1957, my mother died from a stroke at her home in San Carlos. She was 74. We had always been so close that it left a big hole, as it were. It was just two days before Thanksgiving. I remember I sat on the couch with Lu and wept.

The kids went to Roosevelt School just two long blocks away on Vancouver Avenue. Lu was very active in the P.T.A. and I helped out with the school carnival. I would often man the booth where kids tried to hammer a nail into a 2x4 with the fewest swings of the hammer. I would teach them how to hold the hammer and how hard to swing it, keeping their eyes on the nail. I got a big kick out of it. They had the annual Halloween parade and folk dance festival and I tried to get there when I could.

Sunday mornings were a special time when the kids were little. They would come pile into the bed with me, while Lu began her

Jenny and Stan with blue jay in backyard of 1376 Vancouver Ave., Burlingame, 1955.

morning ablutions, and we'd talk and play games. Lu and I made Geri a stuffed bear and I made him come to life for her – his big loose ears wagging back and forth. One time the girls put my hair up in pink sponge rollers. Then I was dolled up!

I enjoyed the backyard and my garden. One summer I tamed a young blue jay and got him to land on my head and eat the peanuts I put there for him. I liked to grow giant dahlias and beautiful gladiolas. In the summer I often had the baseball game on. The kids enjoyed playing in the backyard while I gardened, and rooting for the San Francisco Giants was something we shared.

Geri recalled, "We had a small suburban lot on the Peninsula but Dad put his dreams into it. I remember the planting of the apricot tree as if it contained the promise of the sublime. And in just a few years it delivered juicy fruit that he would deftly tear asunder, smile at its golden meat and devour half by half. He seemed to love to garden and I loved to be a satellite to his happiness. He grew huge pink and yellow dinner-plate dahlias and a rainbow of gladiolas. He taught me to water the roots not the faces of the flowers. But we rarely planted together. I think the garden was his personal restorative time. He kept a large strawberry patch and would proudly deliver a brimming bowlful of berries to Mom so she could make strawberry shortcake. I often overheard the radio voice of Lon Simmons crying out 'And that's bye, bye baby!' as probably Willie Mays or one of the Alou brothers hit a home run, while I was playing in the dirt crafting mud pies. He built a patio house that took years to complete, and we played in it in all its phases of construction. If the cobbler's kids have to wait for shoes, I guess the carpenter's kids have to wait too. I was so delighted when he built me a simple swing, two lengths of rope knotted below a horizontal board attached to the header of the doorway."

Lu and I went to the San Francisco Giants' opening game in Candlestick Park on April 12, 1960. That was quite exciting. Jenny remembered another baseball game that I took her and Tim to see: "When I was about 12, Dad took us to a Giant's baseball game at Candlestick Park. We sat high in that huge amphitheater, enjoying not only the game but also the men selling peanuts and popcorn. Dad had a transistor radio with him so he could listen to the game on the radio as we watched it in the park. Then, about the middle of the 8th inning, we left. Yep, we didn't wait for the end of the game, because then we would have to fight everybody getting out of there and, which was worse, all the cars trying to leave the huge parking lot at

once. So we never saw the end of the game, but we could hear the crowd cheering, so I guess it turned out all right."

Lu and I played ping-pong when I came home for lunch. She was pretty good and a hard one to beat. She tried to keep me active and was always up for a lively game.

We always had dinner at 6 o'clock sharp. Lu and I had decided that consistency was important for the kids. It was something I never had as a child. We bought our first television in the early 1950s. When the kids were a little older, we let them watch it for one hour a day, from 5:00 to 6:00 p.m. They usually watched *The Mickey Mouse Club* and cartoons. Then after dinner I'd watch the news and cowboy movies with the kids, and sometimes boxing matches. I also enjoyed *Victory at Sea*, a documentary series about naval warfare during World War II, and some other programs that showed footage of actual battles. You see, while I was in the war, we didn't really know what was happening in other theaters – in the Pacific, for example. So that was how I learned about the war.

Some evenings the kids and I would take a brisk walk around a block or two just to get some exercise. I showed them how to take big strides in order to walk faster.

Aunt Hattie, Lu's aunt, lived in Burlingame, and she came over for dinner frequently when the kids were little. She had a very sharp mind, was a pleasure to talk to, and was a very admirable person. We always enjoyed having her over. Lu's mother and dad often came down from San Francisco on Sunday evenings. After dinner we played bridge. I generally was Eva's partner and Lu played with her dad, Murray.

Eva was fond of me, and she wrote this nice letter to my mother:

Jan. 4, 1950

Dear Betty:

I appreciated your letter so very much. It was nice of you to tell me that Stan enjoyed "our folks." He is such a dear boy and the longer we know him, the more we love him. He is a Prince of a fellow, so good to Lucile and the babies, and so thoughtful, loving and courteous to me. I am <u>so proud</u> to have such a dear son-in-law.

Here's hoping this finds you much improved in health and when you are strong and well again, we will drive down to see you . . .

Give our best regards to Mr. Dungan and Bill, and with loads of love to you, Betty, and best wishes for your return to good health and for happiness and prosperity in the New Year.

I am as ever,
Lovingly,
Eva H. Kemp

Murray liked to take the family to dinner at the Villa Chartier in San Mateo. One time he took us together with Bernice, Dan and Philip; and Bob, Eldamarie, young Bob, and Marilyn. I sat next to

Tim, Geri, Stan and Jenny in 1956.

327

young Bob, and he was served a plate of ground sirloin with mashed potatoes and lima beans. He didn't want to eat the lima beans, so I discretely removed the beans from his plate one at a time. When there was only one left, I smiled at Bob and, pointing to the lone bean, I said, "That one is yours." He recalled that dinner many years later.

Tommy and Evelyn Freeman lived down the street on Vancouver Avenue and we became good friends. Their daughter, Molly, was about Jenny's age and both the girls enjoyed playing with her. We got together now and then to play bridge. We often had New Year's Eve together with a big crab dinner. Afterwards, the girls entertained themselves upstairs in their bedroom while we played bridge in the living room. We stayed in touch for many years.

In July 1960, Lu's father, Murray, died at the age of 77. He was a fine man with a quick mind and a big heart. He had loaned me some money, at one time, and said, "Stan, you use this money in your business." So I invested it in my business and paid him dividends, as it were. When he died they had to decide what to do with his business, the Kemp Agency, an employment agency. I expressed an interest in it and Bernice said, "But Stan owes Murray money. How can he buy the Agency when he is in debt already?" That wasn't the point. Murray had given me the money as an investment, not as charity. So I paid back the loan in full and made an offer on the business. But they told Mr. Hubner, who had worked for him for a long time, what my offer was, and he made a better offer, so they sold it to him. I was really put out, especially with Bernice who was handling matters for Eva. So we cut off relations with Bernice. Didn't see her until Eva's funeral, I guess. That was too bad.

Chapter 5: Construction Business

IN 1956, AFTER WE RETURNED FROM FRESNO, I sold 30 shares of Penn Dixie Corporation stock for about $3600 and invested it in my business, Stan Hulse Builder. Those were the boom days for construction after the war. As Veterans found jobs and took out Veteran's Administration loans to buy houses under the GI Bill, there was a big demand for new houses, and I was right in the midst of it.

Builder Stan Hulse in lath house he built, 1954.

I did a lot of work for Harry Shanzer in Hillsborough. I worked for him for quite a while. Then I did some work for Tommy Harris. He owned Tommy's Joynt on Van Ness Avenue in San Francisco. He had made his name as a radio singer and was known for his voice and his sharp wit. Then there was another fellow right on the corner, and across the street from them another job. I built a beautiful home there. So my reputation spread by word of mouth.

I also worked for Fred Noonan who was the president of Waterman Steamship Company. He had a wonderful collection of ivory carvings, some of them were three feet tall. That was long before ivory was banned. I did some remodeling for him on his house in Hillsborough.

Jerry Ratcliffe was a colored boy who worked for me. He lived with his wife in San Mateo, and I think they had a couple of kids. He was a laborer, but he was very conscientious. He always looked out for my interests on any job and he was very good. He was with me for quite a long time. He worked on a lot of my jobs in Hillsborough.

I worked out of our house and the dining room was my office. Lu answered calls when I was away, but she didn't work for me. She just answered the phone. Geri described it like this:

"Dad's office was in the home. His business papers were sprawled out over the entire dining room table all year long and were only cleaned up for holidays or company dinners. His hand-cranked adding machine produce long spirals of white paper with little black numbers weakly imprinted on it. He had some kind of a time card machine too, and a big black manual Underwood typewriter. I played with them all when he wasn't around. With endless fascination I jammed the letter-arms together on the typewriter and loved to pull down the big handle of the adding machine that made such a profound clunk with each addition.

"We had a dull black telephone that could travel to all ends of the house. Its receiver rested in a cradle that forced down the disconnect buttons positioned above the rotating dial. When the long black cord led to the dining room it served as Dad's work phone. It was our only phone. One of Mom's jobs was to protect Dad from phone calls at dinnertime. She would politely say, 'Stan, isn't in,' and we children would exchange glances at this carefully crafted circumvention of the truth."

I used to enjoy taking the kids to work with me. We'd ride in the truck together, talking and telling stories. I was fortunate to be able to take them with me now and then.

Geri recalled those times: "My favorite times were during the summers, when I think Mom negotiated with him to take at least one kid off her hands for the day. And so he did. He took us, one by one, to work. Work fascinated me. It was an industrious world of men and materials and equipment. His work in the building trade meant that I got to go to the hardware stores and lumber yards and handle the tools on the pegboard racks and watch him as he purchased materials for his jobs. I loved the smell of fresh lumber and of sawdust. I remember arriving at half-built houses, two-by-fours framing a stick house you could see through, and watching strong muscled men saw quickly through a board with a simple handsaw. I remember I loved the drill that they grabbed with two hands, one on top to steady it, and one below that produced the winding action that drove that spiraled steel into the wood. He commanded authority with his workers and he was respected if not a little feared.

"I remember the long drives to Pacifica where he built the first tract homes. I even remember the first trip when it was still an artichoke farm and watching him look over the land with eyes that were beyond the vision of a 7-year old. I remember the even longer trips to Livermore on hot summer days and the picturesque barn that he would always point out to me silhouetted on the top of a hill. We would often stop at fruit stands in that then-rural region and purchase a paper bag crammed full of cherries, plums or apricots to savor on the way home. I learned from him to roll the window down, polish the fruit on my pants and savor its slurpy juices as they ran down my chin. We'd wipe our chins with the backs of our hands and then spit the seeds out the window as the warm summer air sped by. He seemed less in his element when the tract home business really got going and he was busy furnishing the models with sleek wall-to-wall carpets and long luxurious couches, colonial bedroom sets and gaudy glass lamps. I think he was more of an outdoor man."

"I remember," Jenny added, "going over to Livermore with him when it was still a tomato farm: Wagoner Farms. He'd walk out into the field, choose a ripe, juicy red tomato and lean over as he bit into it, the warm red juice dripping down his chin, and a big smile erupting on his face, his pure blue eyes twinkling at me."

Then I got to know Frank Conti. He was a fellow Lion and he said let's go ahead and build a tract. So he and I became Hulse Associates and we went into business together. He was the promotional guy and I was the contractor.

In June 1958, we bought 20 acres of land to develop in Pacifica, north of Half Moon Bay. I paid, I think it was $140,000 for the land in the heart of Linda Mar, a section of Pacifica. That was the first housing development that I did, and I built about 50 three- and four-bedroom houses on the land. They sold for around $14,000 each.[80] Frank and I named the streets, so there's a Standish Road and a Standish Court and a Lisa Court, named after Frank's daughter.

---

[80] San Mateo Times, June 18, 1958, page 4.

One night I got a phone call from one of the homeowners. He said there were beetles flying around his house and they were coming out of the floor, leaving holes in the hardwood floors! He was alarmed and wanted to know what I was going to do about it. The next day, I went over there and sure enough, the beetles were coming right out of the wood floors. I called the lumber store and talked to the manager. It turned out that the wood had the larvae of some kind of beetle in it and when they were ready, they just chewed their way out of the wood, leaving little holes behind. Fortunately, once they came out they just flew away and that was that. So I had to send in a man to putty up the holes left by the beetles, and that took care of it. But boy, it sure gave me a scare. I thought I might have to replace all the hardwood floors. That was something.

Actually, I did replace the floors if the homeowner asked me to. Bill Meyerhoff was one of those, and I replaced his floor for him. We also added a couple of rooms on the back of his house for his large family. Years later he remembered the incident and said, "Stan was a real gentleman."

In 1960-61, I built some houses in Belmont. They were all on the side of the hill. They were nice homes with three- and four-bedrooms, a family room, all-electric, built-in kitchens, and a big picture window with a nice view. The new hillside design had a sun deck on the rear of the house on the main floor that left a space for a patio underneath it, since it was on the side of the hill. They were very good-looking homes.

In 1961, I had several jobs in Burlingame and Hillsborough. I bought an old house on the corner of Carmelita Avenue and El Camino Real in Burlingame, and built an apartment building there. I remember taking the kids into the old house before we tore it down. It was a very old place and in disrepair, so we checked under the carpeting and linoleum and tore it up looking for money or treasurers. Tim found $30 in our search, under the linoleum in the hallway.

So I built an apartment building there. It was three stories high with the garages on the ground floor and eight units on the two floors above. It was just one long block from Broadway, so it was quite a good location. I think we named them the Capri Apartments. That year my income was $27,750, so I was doing pretty well.[81]

---

[81] That's equivalent to about $200,000 in 2010 purchasing power.

In March 1961, I applied for a building permit to build a house on Vancouver Avenue near Roosevelt School. There was a lot there on the west side that was quite deep and there was room to build two houses on it. I thought I'd build one for us to live in and one to sell. I estimated the value of the house for us at $25,000.

The house at 1376 Vancouver Avenue was a little small for us. The girls had to be in the same bedroom and Tim had a very small bedroom, so we thought we should build a bigger house. But the more we got to thinking about it, the more we realized that time goes so fast, and about the time we would get it all built everybody would be off and running. At that time Tim was 13 and we could see that it wasn't such a good idea after all. So I never built on that lot, and in a couple of years we were glad that we hadn't gone that way.

My biggest project was in Livermore. On December 10, 1962, we broke ground on what had been Wagoner Farms. It was a large development, 310 acres, and Conti and I were partners on the deal. I remember Lu and I signed a note for a million-dollar loan to buy the property and start the project. We went down and talked to the bank president and he gave us the loan. My, that seemed like a lot of money at the time.

It was designed to be a $20 million residential/commercial/ industrial complex located off East Avenue in Livermore, between Vasco Road and Jefferson. It would have been a small city with a shopping center, schools, parks and apartment houses along with the single-family homes. The first unit included about 125 single-family homes in the $18,000 to $25,000 price range. There were six designs and six model homes. Eventually, it was to have 1300 homes, a commercial area, including a shopping center and a small industrial park.

The homes were 3 and 4 bedrooms ranging in size from 1300-2300 square feet on 8000 square-foot lots. They had two-car garages, and brick, wood-burning fireplaces. We opened six model homes in August 1963, and had sold 21 houses at that time. But I was unhappy with the way things were going. We took a trip to Europe in the summer of 1962, and while we were away, Conti reduced the size of the lots so he could fit more houses on the land. I had laid out nice spacious lots so people could put in swimming pools and that kind of thing in the backyard. Livermore is very hot in the summer and that seemed to me the way to do it.

But there we were, stuck with these smaller lots and I was disappointed in the whole thing. The winter of 1962-63 had been very wet

so we had gotten way behind in building the houses and I was getting into trouble financially. I owed Conti money, since he had put up a lot of the financing, so I gave him the Jaguar that we had bought in London. But I still owed him money. It was a bad time and I didn't get a good night's sleep for months. I built 23 houses there between 1962 and 1964. Then we sold our interest to Conti and we bought Lake Pillsbury Resort.

When we were camping up at Lake Pillsbury Resort in the summer of 1964, we heard that Tanner and Tarvin, the owners who had been there for eleven years, were going to sell the business. They were asking $125,000.00 for it. And we said, "Gee, it'd be nice to be up here all the time," because we really liked it. Then we thought about the kids and their schooling, so we had a family council and we said, "Now this would mean a change in your school and you will have to go to Potter Valley for high school. What do you want to do? Do you want to stay in Burlingame? If you want to stay in Burlingame, we'll stay in Burlingame, if you want to go up to the lake, then we'll do it." The girls said, "Yeah," and Tim abstained. But Tim was only a year from graduation, so we decided to give it a go.

We thought that it would be best if we went into the resort business with a partner. Phil Butterfield was my foreman over in Livermore and he was a hard-working, pleasant young man – I think he was about 26 – so I asked him if he would be interested. He talked it over with his wife and he was all hot for it. So they moved up there that winter with their two little kids.

Chapter 6: Vacations

WHEN WE LIVED IN BURLINGAME, we took short vacations because I couldn't leave my business for long. We often we went to Half Moon Bay for a picnic or down to Pescadero.

Jenny recalled, "Sometimes we'd go to Half Moon Bay on Sunday for a picnic. We'd drive down the long road from the town to the beach, then we'd play in the sand and the water. Once in a while we'd be there when the smelt were running. Dad probably knew it and had brought along a burlap sack. There would be several fishermen throwing big nets into the water and hauling out thousands of little fish. He'd go ask the fishermen if we could have some and they always said we could. When they hauled in the nets there were thousands of wiggling 6-inch fish dumped up on the beach and we'd all grab them and throw them into the burlap bag. It was very exciting and the fish dinner that night was delicious."

We took an occasional long weekend for camping and fishing at Lake Pillsbury. It took about five hours to drive up there in those days, so we would stop at Asti, near Cloverdale, at the Italian Swiss Colony tasting room on the way. We all went in and sat on the bar stools and the kids ate cookies from a big cookie bowl while Lu and I sipped the wine.

Once we took the kids to the Pinnacles, south of Hollister, and they had a lot of fun climbing on the rocks. We also visited the mission at San Juan Baptiste. We went up to Angel's Camp one time and camped by the river there where the kids and I fished for crawdads in the river.

Jenny said of those trips: "Dad seemed to usually be in a hurry. When we were going someplace for a drive, he would walk out and get in the car and wait for Mom to get us kids collected and out of the house and into the car. He never honked the horn, but just waited, listening to the radio until we were all aboard. He liked to drive pretty fast and had no fear of passing cars. In those days, many of the roads were just two lanes, and when you got behind a slow car or truck, you waited for an opportunity, then 'put your foot on the gas' and passed him. It was very exciting to me as we pulled in front of the car we had just passed with only seconds to spare before the oncoming car passed by us. I was often standing up in the back seat with my brother Tim and sister Geri watching the action. Driving was never boring. Dad liked to sing, though he was the first to admit that 'he couldn't carry a tune in a bucket,' and we often sang in the car: 'California Here I Come,' or 'I've Been Working on the Railroad,' or 'Ninety-nine bottles of beer on the wall,' or something equally as challenging. He would often point things out as we were traveling. 'Look at the new-born lambs over there,' or 'Do you see the smoke? I wonder what that's from?' Driving was a happy time and I think my dad enjoyed being the Master of Ceremonies in that close but warm environment."

I don't think Geri felt the same way about the trips. On the road to Pillsbury, anyway, she found the windy mountain roads that fell off to the Eel River far below, to be a hair-raising adventure. But years later, she was driving that road like she owned it.

We took the family to Disneyland in January 1960, shortly after it opened. That was quite something. We went on lots of rides: the Jungle Cruise, the Matterhorn, the Mad Hatter teacups, the Dumbo Flying Elephants, Mr. Toad's Wild Ride, and Autopia. The kids were pretty tired by the end of the day. We also visited Knott's Berry Farm. It wasn't an amusement park in those days, just a place with an old "ghost town" there. I got a kick out of Sad Eye Joe, a carved-wooden mannequin who talked to me from the Ghost Town Jail.

Jenny, Tim, Stan and Geri at the Lair of the Golden Bear.

336

In the summer of 1960, we went to the Lair of the Golden Bear in the Sierra foothills. It was a family camp organized by the U.C. Berkeley Alumni, and since Lu had gone to Berkeley, we were able to participate. It was a week packed full of activities for the whole family. The kids had a good time and so did we.

In December 1961, we took the family down to Guaymas, Mexico, on the Gulf of California, for Christmas vacation. We stayed in a nice motel with brand new bungalows right on the beach. It was called La Posada de San Carlos, and was ten miles outside of Guaymas. We ate outdoors at the cabaña and did some swimming and sightseeing. The kids collected hermit crabs on the beach and brought them back to the room. We woke up the next morning to the sound of each one crashing to the floor as they walked off the table. It was very pleasant and we had a relaxing time there. That was before it became a tourist destination. I guess it's pretty crowded now, but back then I think it was the only motel around.

In the summer of 1962, we took the family to Europe. Lu's dad had taken Bob and Bernice and their families to Europe several years earlier, but our kids were too little. So he put aside some money for us to take a trip later on. We added some of our own money and took a nice, ten-week vacation.

We left home on May 5 and flew to Jamaica. When we arrived there, we discovered that our travel agent had made reservations for us in a hotel that hadn't been completed yet. So we found a charming old hotel in Kingston instead, the Abbey Court Hotel. There were arbors and gardens and we ate ripe tropical papayas every morning. We went to the markets filled with colorful fruits, and saw colored women with their localized English accents selling produce, clothing and bags.

While in Jamaica, we saw a number of things that I remembered from the time I spent there as a kid. We went out to Port Royal and saw the fort, the cannonballs and a plaque to Horatio Nelson. We visited the Crafts Market, took a drive through the lush Fern Gully, and swam in the warm water of the bay. Then we boarded the SS *Orsova* and sailed to Haiti and Bermuda on our way to England.

When we got to England, we bought a Jaguar in London, and toured Europe for eight weeks. The Jaguar was a beautiful car, white with red leather interior. We needed a big car to fit the three kids in the back seat, so that's what we bought. We saw Stonehenge and

Tim, Stan, Jenny and Geri at Stonehenge.

London then took an overnight ferry to the Hook of Holland. We drove through Germany, seeing some of the country I had marched through during the war, then into Austria. It was quite a thrill to drive on the Autobahn. I think we hit 100 mph one time.

We stayed a couple of days in Salzburg, Austria, and I was reminded of the last time I was there, during the war. We checked in to a hotel and then set out to explore the castle on a hill above the city. When we headed back to the hotel it was raining and we couldn't find our way back. We couldn't even remember the name of the hotel or the street it was on. We were lost! I had to drive back toward Munich and turn around and come in again, retracing our route. So I told the family about the time I had set out the patrol around Salzburg when we were there after the war. But when it came time to collect the men, I got lost and I spent two hours gathering them up. Anyway, we eventually found our way back to the hotel.

We left Salzburg, heading for the pass into Italy. But it was snowing heavily and the passes were all closed. So we put our car on a railroad flatcar that took us through a tunnel into Italy. There we visited Pisa, Venice, Rome and Naples. We had a wonderful guide who marched us through the Roman Forum and when we went to the ruins at Pompeii, our guide showed us all sorts of out-of-the-way places, and beautiful wall paintings and frescos in bright colors, some of which they would only let the men see.

Then we drove up to Nice for the Lions International Convention. We had a lot of fun at the convention. We picked up a number of trading pins that were given out by each state and country, and watched the big Lion's parade. It was almost a Mardi Gras with women in fancy clothing and high heels. The waiter told the kids to smile vertically, in other words, to keep their mouths closed or someone might come up behind them and hold confetti to their mouth until they had to inhale it. The next morning we watched as brigades of men with brooms made of twigs, swept the streets and sidewalks until the city was clean again.

We were all pretty tired by then, so we drove into Spain and stopped in Sitges, south of Barcelona, where we spent several days just relaxing. It was a cute native town with a lovely beach and we enjoyed our time there.

Then down the coast to Valencia and up through Madrid. We slowed down as we drove by some *braceros* who were riding on donkeys, and they yelled, *"Ricos Americanos!"* at us. I guess we looked pretty wealthy in our Jaguar. We drove through southern France where we visited the Lascaux Cave. The cave paintings were really something to see. I guess they closed the cave to the public a few years later, so we were lucky to see them.

Then to Paris where I took the family to the Folies Bergère. We saw dancers, acrobats, strong men, and bare-breasted women swinging back and forth on decorated swings – a memorable spectacle for a 14-year-old boy. We visited the Louvre Museum and saw the *Mona Lisa*, whose eyes would follow you as you walked back and forth in front of her.

We drove up to Le Havre, where we had booked passage on the brand new SS *France* sailing to New York. At that time she was the longest passenger ship ever built and one of the fastest in service. I was looking forward to sailing on her.

While there we went out to Normandy and saw the American Military Cemetery overlooking Omaha Beach, the site of the D-Day landings. I told the kids how thousands of men in the Allied forces had sacrificed their lives on the beaches below on June 6, 1944. I was overcome by the sadness of that "longest day" as I looked at the rows and rows of white crosses stretching out before us and I recalled the poem – I may have recited it – *In Flanders Fields*.

Geri, Stan, Jenny and Tim overlooking Omaha Beach.

In Flanders fields the poppies blow
   Between the crosses, row on row,
  That mark our place; and in the sky
  The larks, still bravely singing, fly
Scarce heard amid the guns below.

We are the Dead. Short days ago
We lived, felt dawn, saw sunset glow,
  Loved and were loved, and now we lie
    In Flanders fields.

Take up our quarrel with the foe:
To you from failing hands we throw
  The torch; be yours to hold it high.
  If ye break faith with us who die
We shall not sleep, though poppies grow
    In Flanders fields.[82]

We arrived to board the SS *France* only to learn that there was a strike on, so the voyage was cancelled. We drove back to Paris and took an Air France flight to New York, and then home to San Francisco. The plane was so loaded down with baggage that we weren't

---

[82] Written during the First World War by Canadian physician Lieutenant Colonel John McCrae.

sure it was going to get off the ground. I held Lu's hand and thought it was the end for a minute or two. Then finally, the plane lifted off right at the end of the runway. That was something. We saw a great deal in those ten weeks and came home with lots of good memories.

We went to Yosemite during Easter week in 1963. We hiked up to the top of Vernal Falls and saw Yosemite Falls and Bridalveil Falls. They were beautiful that spring. It brought back memories of the spring of 1941, when I had hiked up to Vernal Falls when I was in the Army. It was every bit as majestic as I remembered it.

That spring Mari Takaichi, the daughter of Fuji and Leroy Takaichi, got married and we had quite a nice party at Fuji's house. Mari married a Japanese man, but it didn't last. Too bad. It was a lovely wedding, though, and was the last time that my whole family got together, including my sister Jane, that is.

In December 1963, we took a Christmas cruise to Hawaii on the newly christened SS *Lurline*, of the Matson Line. We sailed out of San Francisco with serpentine flying after a wonderful bon voyage party that many of our friends came to. It was a 15-day trip and we visited

At Mari Takaichi's wedding: Leslie Dungan (Bill's wife), Duge, Stan, Donnabeth, Jane, Mabel and Bill.

341

five islands and slept on the ship every night. The ship travelled between islands at night and we enjoyed sightseeing during the day. It was such a good trip, that we did it again three years later! We had a lot of fun.

Dinner on the SS *Lurline*, 1963: Geri, Jenny, Stan, Lu and Tim.

Chapter 7: Lake Pillsbury Resort

WE BOUGHT LAKE PILLSBURY RESORT in the fall of 1964. It was a rustic resort with seven little cabins and thirty-odd campsites. There was a boat house and a dock where we kept a number of fishing boats that we rented out, and another dock where customers could berth their motor boats. A snack bar was next to the boat house. The store was in the main building, which was situated between the campground and the cabin area, and our home was attached to the store. The campground was made up of four areas: the main area near the store, Pine Grove just beyond that, Loafer's Point on the next point over, and Lazy Acres beyond that, where the boat ramp was.

In December 1964, there was a big flood that that took out many of the bridges on the Eel River. Highway 20 was closed due to a bridge washout and the Hopland Grade was closed due to slides, so we had to drive from Hopland over Highland Springs Road to Lakeport to get into Lake County, then through Upper Lake and over Elk Mountain to get to Lake Pillsbury. That was a long trip.

Phil Butterfield and his wife and little kids moved up there that spring and his wife was just terrible. She hated it. They would go down to Ukiah and tell everybody that they had bought Lake Pillsbury Resort. But they didn't put any money in it, he was just a working partner. She liked the idea of being big time stuff and then when we came along to move in, it demoralized her. She missed her coffee klatches that she had with the women on the block, and going to the movies on Friday night. She resented Lu and wanted to do things her own way if she was going to do it. I think they quit by Fourth of July.

We spent a nice summer up at the lake. The whole family pitched in. Lu ran the store from 7 in the morning till 10 at night. The girls cleaned the cabins and helped out in the store. Later, they ran the snack bar, getting up at 5 a.m. to serve coffee to the fishermen. Tim cleaned the bathrooms and raked the campsites when people moved out, and he did the garbage runs with the hired help. They'd load the garbage cans into the old World War II weapons carrier that we named "Harriet." Then kids from the camps would climb on board and we'd take them all to the dump and back.

The store at Lake Pillsbury Resort, 1965.

Bill, Dennis, Jenny, Larry, Geri and Tim with "Harriet," Summer 1964.

There were some other people working for us – they sort of came with the place. Bertha ran the snack bar and Dick and Dolores helped out with various things. Dick knew how to work on the generator and he worked real well but had to be told or he didn't see things. Dolores cleaned the cabins and helped out in the store sometimes. We also hired a boat man, whose job it was to keep the fishing boats clean and the outboard motors running.

Then there was Dennis, a kid out of high school who needed some work and a place to be. He strummed on his guitar most any time he had the opportunity – a strange kid. He was also quite an artist. He helped out but often did something stupid and got hurt. He was a nice kid. Bill, on the other hand, kept busy. He was the son of one of the cabin regulars and he did accomplish quite a bit. But they were a couple of prize examples of kids wanting to face the world long before they were ready for it and deluding themselves into believing that they had it made. They would be lucky to make wages, let alone any money! or a life!

Joe Canet was an old-timer there. He was a retired policeman from Mill Valley and was about ten years older than me. He had been coming to the resort for years and had permanently rented Camp 1, right next to the snack bar. He had that camp all fixed up with bamboo screens around it for privacy. It was his home away from home. His wife, Dorothy, who was called "The West Coast Betty Crocker," would come up from time to time. But I think he was happier at the resort with a little distance between them. Joe was a big help actually, as he knew how the place was run, so he helped me out on many occasions.

We decided that it would be best if the kids spent one more year in Burlingame, so that Tim could graduate there. So when the summer was over, Lu went back to Burlingame with the family. That was pretty rough.

My Love and all my Dear Ones ––
You left me with quite a lump in my throat. I hated so having you leave –
It is a beautiful morning, but quiet, so very quiet. The deer have decided to ignore us as we go about our business and they look so pretty.
Yesterday almost no one came to the Resort tho we now have two campers for a few days.
Yesterday when I was talking to you, Bertha came running to the phone and, all in excitement, said Bill had almost cut his thumb off. So I had to end our conversation in such a hurry that I didn't really say all the things I wanted to say – mainly that I love you!!
After supper I went down to the dock and fished for about an hour – no luck but all was quiet and beautiful.
Bill pulled the plug on the double bottom of the Fire Boat and we must have drained off at least 1500 lbs. of water – no wonder it was so dead in the water! We will patch the leaks in the hull before we take it to get the clutch fixed. We are going to finish cleaning the roofs of the cabins today. There are so many things to do!
Was real sorry to hear your Mother was in such bad shape. Do hope she has a speedy recovery – The car should have ridden better with the new shocks. Did it?
School – How was it, getting back to the routine? And Geri, the first day at High! Jen, I expect was all set. How did Tim make out with the "conflict?"
Time rushes on and I must get organized!
Hope that each of you are happy in your courses at school and that you, my Dear, are taking care of your dear self and that the kids are helping to take care of you –
My love to all ––
Pop.

There were always things happening up there.

345

Geri, Stan and Jenny, October 1965.

Mrs. Smith pulled out at noon, took the road to Lazy Acres for the road out – pulled out their transmission and had to get the car towed out at about 2:00 PM. It is now after six and she and the kids are just leaving with some campers – riding in the back of a camper!

Her husband left with the tow truck and is waiting for them in Ukiah – a long, long wait!!

This is an unmentionable – but I found a dead squirrel in the water tank – ugh. Had to drain the tank and clean it out with Purex [liquid chlorine bleach] and now the water is 100%. Have added a little Purex for good measure but you can't taste it in the water.

I am out on the porch and it is a little cool as the sun sets. The trees across on Loafer's Point, are turning gold and brown and with twilight and a touch of fall in the air, it is beautiful and sad and I am lonesome. Miss all of you terribly –

The end of the fishing season was early November, so all the serious fishermen came up in October when the fish were the largest. Then the last weekend in October we had a big barbecue with everyone who was there. Joe Canet took charge of the cooking and everyone had a good time. That year the whole family was there for the barbecue, but then Lu left with the kids again.

October barbecue. Stan on the left.

October, 1965

My Love,
It was so good having all my dear family with me up here.
I'll come down Friday but will have to come back up after a few
days with some supplies, etc.
This morning Shrouts left as did Vic, Blumers and Mickey &
Jack, so about noon we closed the store!
I've been working on the books with time out for the
garbage to the dump. The lake still goes down but we still get
water. I'm going to get some more pipe tomorrow and hope we
can pump that far.
Has gotten a lot colder since you left – had the furnace on
all day. Bill will wrap the water pipes to the cabins for winter
use. Also we will shut down the big generator. Then it will be
dark at night here.
Well, dearest our first season is over. We grossed over
$38,000.⁰⁰ on the books.[83] *Not bad!*
Well that's about it. I'll mail this on my trip to Ukiah tomor-
row and see you Friday PM. All my love to you dearest and a
kiss to the kids.

Dad

I stayed up there for a while after we closed the resort to make
repairs and put the place to bed. Then I went back to Burlingame for
a couple of months to be with the family.

---

[83] In 2015 dollars, that would be equivalent to $288,000.

That winter there was a lot of political unrest in the country. The campus at Berkeley was alive with those opposed to the war in Vietnam. It was said that our defense spending was far too great. But it was cheap if it kept a free flag over our heads. This country was born in revolution and it is the desire for individual choice that has kept this country free. We are a people among whom were those who were willing to die that we who came after them might live in freedom. Peace is only purchased at a price. History bears this out.

The season began the end of April, so I went back to the resort in the spring to get things ready to open. The family came up over Easter vacation in early April, and everyone worked real hard to help me get the place ready for opening weekend. But it was hard to see them go back home.

My dearest Love,

There is still a little lump in my throat from the goodbyes of yesterday. It was so hard to see you leave.

The kids just overwhelmed me the way they so willingly pitched in and worked so hard. They were <u>wonderful</u>!!

It rained all day after you left and last night it got cold. Mt. Hull is covered with snow – when you catch a glimpse of it through the clouds – for it is a dull O.C. [overcast] day.

Of course the phones are out so can't do much about the generator and worse, I could not call you last nite to hear of your ride home. But the generator bit leaves me with no plan for bringing it down for repairs. If we don't get the phone soon, I'll lug it down either to Ukiah with a chance fixing it or bring it down to S.F. later in the week.

Expect Smalley to bring in the mail and will send this and any checks. It has just started to rain again!

Our talk with Tim has left me with much on my mind. I won't dwell on it but I do hope that they can find in their hearts the love for one another that I know is there. It is such a precious thing and the time will come when they will so need each other for they are all such fine and sensitive people. God bless them!

I hope you can get rested after the hard, hard week of work, work, work – Ask the kids, for me, to give you a hand and get what rest you can. I love you so.

I send my love to each of the kids too, and I miss all of you so very much!

All for now,
Your Love –

The phone lines up to Lake Pillsbury were privately owned and maintained by the folks that lived up there. Glass insulators kept the wires from touching the poles and grounding out, but every winter the phones went out because there were trees that would fall or lean on the lines. In the spring, we got together a work party and drove the whole thirteen miles down to the mill where the line connected to the main phone line. It sometimes took us a day and a half to complete the job. We checked for problems and cut off branches and trimmed trees or whatever needed to be done to get the phones working again. So in the winter, we had no phone. Instead, we used a CB (Citizens' Band) radio to talk to each other around the lake. Sometimes a little sunshine would dry things out and the phone came back in for a little while, but it was generally out all winter. When it did ring, after maybe three months of silence, it was a startling noise that we had to get used to again.

Our phone was a party line that we shared with the other businesses around the lake. If you picked up the phone to use it, there might be someone else using the phone and you could hear their conversation. So you'd hang up and keep checking the line until the other party was done and then you could make a call. We received many of our reservations by phone, so it was very important to have it working. Each party had a different ring. Ours was two long rings and a short one.

In the winter we had mail call once a week at Soda Creek Store on Wednesdays. Ted Smalley was the mailman and we'd all gather at the little store around the pot-bellied stove and wait for Ted to arrive with the mail. It was quite the social event.

That winter there was a guy named Phil who came to work for me. He was a tall, lanky fellow, maybe an Indian, with dark hair and a rather long face. He did odd jobs around the place.

> *Phil is all enthused over fishing – we had some fish for dinner tonight and it was good. Phil has the day off tomorrow and is going fishing. I think he will stay – I hope. People like him, and the kids get along very well with him. Also he cleans out the boats – they are clean for the first time since we took over.*
>
> *Phil just called me from the dock to tell me he had triumphed – he had gotten a stubborn motor to purr like a kitten. He's a character, needs so to have recognition. He's still a big help tho he knows how to do so little. He's willing and that sure counts for a lot.*

It was a hard year to be away from my family. The kids were growing up fast and there were the usual problems. I was sorry that Lu had to handle so much of it on her own.

Was so glad to learn about the girls' recovery. They are both such dear people. We have been blessed, my dear.

About Tim, I know the feelings you experience when you just can't reach him. Just remember that much of this is a natural thing. It is the urge to throw off the parental restraints. It is growing up. In our eyes he never will be fully equipped to cope with the world – but were you? His respect for authority will probably do more to keep him out of trouble, and this is good. I had none and skirted rather close to the brink on occasion. It was good to talk things over with you for I was a little mixed up about him too. And I feel better now, too.

Tim still loves us but right at this point it wouldn't take much to change that. It may be best to keep what we have. We are still away ahead of most people, dear. Many, many have never had the love and respect that we have enjoyed, and will for some time to come. But we have to let them grow, try their wings – and fly away! But be of good cheer, for this is the Divine scheme of things and as parents, we are a success! Does hurt a little, doesn't it? I love you.

I feel much better about the resort since I talked to you, too. Even tho you are not right beside me you are very close and it will only be a little while longer before we can be together.

The resort did real well for us. People seemed to like us and they kept coming back. Many would come up and stay for a couple of weeks then, when they were leaving, they would make reservations for the following summer. Lu kept reservation charts on large sheets of cardboard for all the campsites and cabins and marked people down for the weeks and campsites that they wanted.

In June 1966, Tim graduated from high school and signed up for the Air Force. We thought it would give him some structure and help him find himself.

Jenny took a trip to Wales that summer, and we hired some kids to help out at the resort. It worked pretty well, so we hired three or four kids each summer and they cleaned the cabins and the campsites, picked up the garbage and ran the snack bar. We fixed up a room in the corner of the barn and painted it light blue. That became the "blue room" where the boys bunked. We all ate dinner together and sometimes Lu was cooking for eight or nine every night.

Mike Carlson worked for us in 1968 and 1969. He became good friends with Tim. His family had been coming to the lake for years but he sort of adopted our family too. He was a good kid and stayed in touch with us over the years. He even came up to visit us when we lived in Willits almost 30 years later.

There was a big fire that summer in early August, about five miles south of Lake Pillsbury, and it covered the place with soot and ashes for days. We couldn't even see across the lake. The ground and everything was covered in gray ash! It was just a mess. That was the Elk Mountain Fire.[84]

Tim helped us out that summer, before he left. One time he helped me pull a customer's boat out of the lake. He told it like this: "It happened in mid-September of 1966. The site is the boat ramp in Lazy Acres, at Dad's family-run resort. The scene is a heavily-rainy afternoon and we're trying to pull a big ski boat from the lake. The slipperiness of the cement ramp is one thing, but the torn-up mud driveway is what really put this father-son team to the test.

"The first attempt was not working out at all and I distinctly remember Dad yelling from the pickup's cab, 'Give me the office! Give me the office!' which loosely translates to 'what in hell's goin' on back there?'

"Well, I couldn't shout loud enough to tell him nothing good was going on, so he stopped, got out and came back to size up the operation. I don't recall if we were planning to quit till the rain stopped, but we had to get that boat out! So Pop thought a bit and his solution worked. Boy did it! I ended up playing the part of a freight wagon driver shouting directions to Dad over the noise, and hauling on the big rope tied to the trailer and guiding it as Pop gunned the engine and hauled it up the hill.

"Yup, we made it and I got 5 bucks from the customer."

In the fall he enlisted in the Air Force and went to Amarillo, Texas, for his basic training. He had a good attitude and tried real hard.

Until 23 days from now nothing much will be good except that I'll pass every test, do every push-up and make every bed from now on in. . .

We only have 22 days to go and I'm in there pitchin' all the way. . .

---

[84] It officially became known as the Round Fire.

I just got Dad's and Geri's letters and wow did that make me
happy, 2 letters in one day. That's what I like. Keep 'em coming.
I Love You All So Very Much
I Want To Come back to the Family Hutch
Your Bard In Blue
Tim

Then he was sent over to Spain to the Morón Air Base near
Seville. He was very young in the ways of the world and took up
drinking with the boys. One day they found him asleep on the job
and tried to wake him up but couldn't. So they took him to the hospital and discovered that he was in a diabetic coma. They fixed him up,
shipped him home, and retired him as a Veteran, which was lucky for
him, because they paid all his medical expenses for the rest of his life.

The girls agreed to move up to the lake and go to school, but because the resort was in Lake County, they were supposed to go to
Potter Valley High School. It was a very small school with something
like 60 students and it didn't offer some of the advanced courses that
the girls needed to go to college. So we went to the school board and
got permission for them to go to Ukiah High instead. That first year
Jenny was a Senior, so she drove our 1959 Pontiac the 35 miles into
Ukiah every day. They picked up a couple of the other kids who lived
around the lake and went flying down the road to school each day. I
remember one day when they didn't get home by the usual time. It
was a Friday afternoon and it had been raining hard for several days. I
finally went out looking for them. As Geri and Jenny recalled:

"We proudly took on the task of traveling the 26 miles of dirt
road along the winding Eel River to make our way each day to Ukiah
and back for school. Dad and Mom must have had worried conversations, out of our hearing, but all I remember was his seemly supreme
confidence in us. Jenny drove the great boat of a Pontiac down those
dusty or slippery roads in all kinds of weather and we were often late
to school because of the extra time it took to roll rocks from the road.

"One evening in midwinter during a major storm we tried to get
home via the Logging Road and got stopped not two miles from
home by a large pile of rocks in the road. Jenny turned the big car
around and backtracked back to the mill and headed up the County
Road only to be stopped by a landslide. Quite on our own with no
means of communication and encountering no neighbors, we made
the decision to turn around again and go back up the Logging Road
and try to walk home. It was Friday and we had our gym shoes and

352

pants in the car so when we got there, we put on our gym shoes and headed for home. When we came to the foot of our long driveway, there was a considerable stream flowing across our path, so we waded across it, nearly knee-high in moving water, and walked up the last mile and a half to the resort. Shortly after we got home Dad drove in. He had been out looking for us. He had figured out exactly where we had gone and what we had done. He had arrived to see our tracks on both roads shortly after we had executed our decisions and then spied the car on the other side of the river and followed our tracks home."

Another time Jenny came home in the Chevy truck honking the horn as she pulled in behind the house. Tim jumped out and ran up the back steps yelling, "Dad, get your gun! Some drunks are chasing us!" As the kids tumbled into the house, I went to the back door just as the drunks were heading for the steps. I shot over their heads then yelled, "The next one's for you!" They took off in a hurry, ripping a door off on a post as they backed out of there. I called the sheriff who caught up with them down the road.

We enjoyed the winters at the lake. We became good friends with the Patterson's, Pat and Jackie, who owned the resort across the lake, Lake Pillsbury Pines. We got together sometimes just to share a pumpkin pie – imagine driving five miles in the dark over rutted, muddy roads for pie! But we enjoyed spending a nice evening together. We'd loop about "blowing the dam" and sailing down the Eel River on the big wave. We got along real well.

Christmas 1966, we took the girls on another cruise to Hawaii. It was another fun trip. There was a costume parade and a hat contest that I think I won. I made a great big hat that covered my head and shoulders and I held my arms up inside the hat, then we painted a face on my T-shirt, and Lu attached my suit coat around my waist. It was quite a costume. We also enjoyed shuffleboard and ping-pong and

Stan's winning entry in the hat contest on board the SS *Lurline*.

Jim Chesnutt, Stan and John Bruce on the SS *Lurline*, December 1966.

there was plenty of food and entertainment. At our bon voyage party that time, Jim Chesnutt and Johnny Bruce both came to see us off. I guess that was the last time the three of us were all together.

In the summer of 1967, I taught Geri how to drive. Actually, I taught all the kids to drive. As Geri told it, "It was really Dad who taught me how to drive in the yellow Chevy pickup. In the summer Dad went to Ukiah once a week to get supplies. He got all the food for the week for the family and all the folks who worked there. He got paper supplies and frozen burgers for the snack bar, picked up the paper-wrapped bundles of dry-cleaned sheets at the cleaners, got parts for boat engines, trucks and generators at the auto parts store and office supplies for Mom. The summer I was 15, he decided it was time for me to learn to drive. I wasn't so sure I wanted to learn to drive. I'd seen my sister navigate those tricky roads where oncoming cars could barrel around a corner in a second and greet you in the middle in a cloud of dust, but Dad said it was time to learn to drive.

"Every week that summer he'd say, 'I'm going to town. Come on. You drive.' I would reluctantly get in the driver's seat and the journey would begin. The quickest way to town was the Logging Road. Its path was mostly low along the Eel River with a few climbs over the shoulders of ridges. It was called the Logging Road for a reason. All summer long logging trucks rumbled up and down that road. On their trip up, while we were going down to town, they were running light with their trailers stacked, one atop the other, and moving fast to make time. He would hear them coming before me, perhaps see a wisp of dust in the distance and say, 'Pull over! Pull over!' And I would frantically search for a pullout or broad shoulder where we could take refuge before the impending arrival. On the way home from town it was the same only this time the trucks were leaving the forest and they were running full and heavy, stacked high with huge off-highway loads heading for the mill at the end of the road. The sheer weight bearing down on us almost petrified me but Dad would awaken my good sense and get me to pull off into a tiny sanctum in just the nick of time."

I worked for PG&E while we were up at the lake. I was the "Dam Man." They needed someone to check the dam from time to time and take readings. One night there was a little earthquake so they called me and told me to go over and examine the dam and make sure that it was all right. So I had to go down inside the dam in the middle of the night and look for cracks and seepage. There wasn't any damage but I saw several ring-tailed cats living in there. They ran away from me, but I saw them.

In September 1967, Jenny left for college in Los Angeles, Occidental College. Lu and Geri and I missed her terribly.

Hi Honey – Just a line to greet you and tell you we miss you and love you. We are anxious to hear all about your new surroundings, people, classes, profs, etc., etc. but know you are busy and I hope very happy.

We have been busy – Mom running all the blankets through the washer, etc. and Don and I giving the cabins good cleanings – washing the paint, etc. Also we have cleaned the main camping area until it almost shines!

Then too, Tuesday afternoon the generator stopped running!! Always a crashing silence and the big question, Why? What to do!? Well, I concluded it needed a cleaner radiator so proceeded to give it a good cleaning and, after a dirty job well done, we did get it started again. It's still running!

You know, we missed you so much. Geri said she'd sure forego having a room to herself if you were only back. She's a good kid and seems to be getting along real well at school. . .

Well my dear daughter, that is about it for now. Mom
misses you as do all of us, but we feel sure you will be having a
great experience and we hope a happy one.
We send our love,
Dad

The generator was our only source of electricity. It was a big yellow beast built by Caterpillar – a diesel engine. Geri remembered it not too fondly: "I think the generator was his nemesis. Like the control room where the *Wizard of Oz* was able to produce his spectacles, Dad worked tirelessly to produce the spectacle of electricity that kept the whole place going. In the winter we would only use the generator in the evenings, and every night I would hear that great roaring beast succumb to deep silence after Dad would head out the back door into the night and extinguish its rumbling clamor."

In the summer it ran all the time and made quite a racket, but there was nothing to do for it. It was housed by a building, which dulled the sound some, but we needed it for lights in the house and the cabins and to run all the freezers in the store. We had to have it. We had propane for the stove and all the refrigerators, and a big oil heater in the house.

At the resort, people showed up from time to time looking for work. It was a parade of interesting characters. One time when I was in Ukiah, I gave a dollar to a beggar and when he took it to get something to eat, instead of a drink, I asked him if he wanted a job. That fall I saw some hippies camped at the gravel bar by the dam. I invited them to come work, as they looked pretty hungry. So I had three hippies – really not so hip – helping me clean the boats, wash down the cabins and rake leaves. Lu didn't approve, but to me they were like strays – "There, but for the grace of God go I."

That year the fall colors were most beautiful. I enjoyed the crisp fall weather while raking leaves and hauling them out to the point to burn them. Then I'd take one or two of our helpers down to the river and we'd haul truckloads of gravel back to the campground to gravel the roads. One Sunday afternoon Lu and I took a drive up to the Sanhedrin Lookout Station. We picked some elderberries on the way, and Lu made a pie. It was good but almost too rich.

For Thanksgiving 1967, we met Jenny in San Francisco and we all went to the opera. I had enjoyed seeing operas in my youth and wanted to share that with my family. I believe we heard *Madame Butterfly* and it was just beautiful. In 1969 we saw *La Bohème*. We stayed at the Chancellor Hotel near Union Square and made a nice holiday out of it.

Sometimes in the winter it snowed so hard that we couldn't go anywhere. We might get eight inches of snow, which made it impossible to get out on the steep, muddy roads. On those days, Geri had to stay home because we couldn't get her to school. But it was kinda nice when that happened. Afterwards, we had to remove the trees that came down across the road in order to get out, when the snow melted a bit. The County would plow the road as far as Soda Creek, but we had to maintain our own road from there to the resort, about two miles long.

In January 1968, Jeff and Gary and I drove up to Rattlesnake Creek to liberate some of the form lumber from the bridge that the Forest Service had built up there. The road was frozen and the snow light, so we picked the time as most propitious. And it was, as who was just getting out of his truck ahead of us, but Pat Patterson and his boys. We both got a pretty good load and so down the mountain. Had a lot of fun.

We had a dog up there named Hobie. He was part German shep-

Christmas at Lake Pillsbury Resort, 1967: back row: Jenny, Geri and Robin (Teri's daughter); middle: Mabel, Donnabeth, Stan, Teri (Bill's wife), Bill and Duge; in front: Hobie and Lu.

herd and part mutt, and he was a good old dog. One day I went out to the barn to give Hobie some food and I stuck my hand in the dog food, which we kept in a garbage can, and there was a skunk in the dog food. He didn't squirt me though. He was just down in there eating. So I put the lid on the garbage can and got some guys to pick it up and put it in the truck, and they took it down to Soda Creek and dumped it in the creek!

That was the spring that Tim came down with diabetes while he was in Spain. In May he surprised us with a call from Travis Air Force Base saying that he had a two-week leave. When he arrived at the lake he was doing pretty well, but he had lost 20 pounds since he got sick. He was in good spirits about his illness and was giving himself one shot of insulin a day.

In August 1968, Tim was discharged and returned from Spain. He moved in with the three of us and was angry and difficult to have around. Lu weighed and measured all his food for him, but he had to have an insulin shot every morning. So I'd give him his shot. But he couldn't keep his diabetes under control and he frequently had insulin reactions, when he lost all muscle control. It was very upsetting for all of us.

Stan and Lu, Spring 1968.

1968 was an election year and I was happy when Nixon was elected. He sounded like a pretty good guy, and I thought no one should doubt his sincerity. I just hoped his judgment, and that of his cabinet, would be as good.

358

I am hopeful for a better administration than any in this century. This man has shown real ability to organize and to achieve. There is so much to do! Our cities are obsolete. Central America can be developed as a friendly southern neighbor or it can go Commie. Nixon is aware of these and all the myriad of other problems, including NATO. I am an optimist – it could be that he will show the way.

The day after the election we had the CB on and suddenly we heard Ivan cut in with something like, "Yeah, that's a 10-4. Imagine those 200,000 votes going to the wrong one. Bet that will make Humpy [Humphrey] happy!" Lu and I ran for the radio. We had been so happy that morning when Nixon was declared the winner and we couldn't believe what we heard. The radio soon confirmed that Nixon had really won and all was well. Ivan had been talking to himself on the CB just to stir up the forest – he was a democrat and got a kick out of playing a trick on everyone around the lake.

In late January we always went down to San Francisco to the gift show. It was a huge show held in the Civic Center. We bought souvenirs to sell at the resort, like little wooden plaques or thermometers or little stuffed animals – all kinds of little things. It was a lot of fun, but very tiring. One year we bought Tim an electric guitar, his first of many. When we gave it to him, he asked if it was a Fender Guitar, and I told him, "No, but it's made by the same people that make Fenders!" – which wasn't really right. We bought him a Japanese import as a Fender was pretty expensive for a first guitar. He eventually had a small collection of fine electric guitars, including a Fender Stratocaster and a Rickenbacker.

In February 1969, Tim went down to the City to look for a job. He found one with J. Barth & Co., a stock brokerage firm on Montgomery Street in the heart of the financial district. They were paying him $300/month to put together account books and file I.B.M. cards. He moved into a residence club where he got two meals a day. He had good intentions, but things didn't always work out for Tim. He wrote me this letter:

I know my faults, but so far the only way I've found out is by experience and it's always been "learn the hard way," but I think I'll hold down my job until I can get enough money to go to school, because I couldn't have a job and school, too. Is my first step a good step? Sometimes I think it is a good one and sometimes I think it is a poor step. But I need a cheering section

and coaching. Thanks for the tips. I think I am getting under-
way as a self-supporting being. I hope so, and L.P.R. is my
home; but you are right, the idyllic life is not always the most
feasible. I'm on one track and my eyes are open.

But the good ol' days with you and Mom, J & G and Hobie
are the best part of my life so far. I guess I don't see it until it's
over.

I hope life treats you as good as I am going to try to make
my life.

     Thanks for all and I do love you.
      Your son,
      Tim

But a couple of weeks later he called to say he had lost his job because he had two insulin reactions in a week and they couldn't cope with that. So he came back home for a while. We knew he needed to get out on his own, but he also needed regular meals and regular hours, so we put him to work around the resort again.

In early May I received a phone call from the sports writer at the Oakland Tribune, Andy Morgensen, asking me about the fishing at the lake. Opening weekend had been stormy but the next weekend looked good so I told him, "The action is improving daily. Everyone is getting fish and there are quite a few limits. Most fish run to 15 inches." They were catching them on red salmon eggs in the lagoons and Triple-Teaser lures out in the lake. It was a fun business to be in.

Memorial Day weekend was real busy. The Forest Service reported that there were 11,000 people on the lake that weekend. All the campsites were full and overflowing. The store was bustling all weekend and everybody bought something. It was the beginning of a very busy summer season. I enjoyed the campers and especially some of the little kids. In the warm evenings I liked to sit on the padded bench in the store and play simple games with some of the camper kids.

My old friend John Campbell Bruce came up and read his play to us. It was good to see him again. We reminisced about old times, especially the month we spent together at the Chili Bean Ranch outside of Almaden in the winter of 1931. That adventure created an enduring bond between us.

In June, Geri graduated from Ukiah High School, and in the fall she went off to college. We took her down and put her on the train to Santa Barbara, where she had been accepted to the University of

California. When she left, she made a drawing on our blackboard, the one that we posted messages on, of Pooh and Piglet walking away down the road. At the bottom she wrote, "We say goodbye," a quote from the last chapter of *Winnie the Pooh*. It touched us so much that I don't think we ever did erase it. With her gone, it just wasn't the same at the resort.

> *Well, today Geri took her departure and with it took a big chunk of the happiness that has been ours, Mom's and mine. These have been such wonderful years up here, with you girls being the wonderful, beautiful people that you are. And now there are two.*
> *But enough of this vein or the paper will be all soggy and I won't be able to write! We are proud of you kids, so very proud. You are such darn swell people!*

We had a lot of kids work for us but sometimes they'd leave just when we needed them the most. That week we lost both of our helpers – they both moved on to other opportunities. But Lu and I were determined to make it work. We knew we had a good business with the resort and just had to keep rolling with the punches. It was a rough time, and it was so easy to entertain doubts – they are the unwanted guests that are always at the door of our consciousness waiting to slip inside and confuse and worry us. But I told myself, "You can confidently expect all good things to happen to your life, if you will take the first step and pronounce everything good." And it was good. The resort was a gold mine for us; my ship had finally come in.

But my heart was giving me trouble. Lu said that sometimes in the night it would pause a long time and I would stop breathing, then I'd come back with a great gasp. My ticker just wasn't right and I was tired much of the time. So we decided that it was time to sell the resort and move on. We had just about paid off the place and were in a position to make some real money from it. It was like shooting Santa Claus to leave, but I had no choice.

Geri's drawing, "We say goodbye."

In November we sold the resort and started getting our things together to move out.

We listened to the Apollo 12 space launch on November 14, 1969. Conrad called back in a voice almost in a panic, that some of their instruments had gone out, and they thought they had been hit by lightening. They had left in a downpour of rain and as soon as they gained altitude the rain had frozen on their windows. But five days later, two men again set foot on the moon. I always enjoyed listening to the space launches.

We didn't know where to go after we left the resort. I wanted to stay active and maybe find another business to get into – something not as strenuous as the resort. We kicked around everything from Hawaii to Idaho to Twain Harte or Grass Valley. But we couldn't really figure things out until we locked the door for the last time and headed down the road.

We sold the resort to Ted and Erma Maddock, who had been customers at the resort for many years. Ted came up and stayed with us for a couple of months that fall to learn how to run the place. He was a big help getting the cabins and boats cleaned, the docks moved around, and everything put to bed for the winter. They became the new owners of Lake Pillsbury Resort on January 11, 1970. The Maddocks and the Witsamens came into the house about 10 a.m. and signed the contract of sale. Then Erma wrote out a check for $24,000 and handed it to us. The deed was done, the resort was sold, and a great, great load rolled off my shoulders. We said good-bye to Lake Pillsbury Resort and shoved off.

The drive up to the store at Lake Pillsbury Resort.

Chapter 8: Return to the Santa Clara Valley

We drove down to San Francisco on Saturday, January 17, 1970, and I decided to go out to the V.A. Hospital to see if they could do something about my irregular heartbeat. A doctor checked me out and told me to come back on Monday and go to the heart clinic. I was 63 at that time. After another exam, they admitted me to the hospital for observation. I didn't have any idea how long I would be there – a couple of days, a week. So there I was, sort of stuck, as they tried out different medications on me trying to regulate my heart. They said the problem was a combination of anxiety, nerves, and tension that had built up since I fell and hurt my shoulder. I had six or seven doctors checking on me while I was there.

> *Some of the pills have worked better than others and we all hope they will soon find the right combination and I'll be out of here.*
>
> *I am on a low sodium diet – everything without salt. I sure look forward to a salty meal!*
>
> *The nurses and doctors are all very nice and are making my stay as pleasant as possible. They take really good care of me.*
>
> *I'm waiting for Mom and expect her soon, which will make my day!*

Lu stayed with her mother in San Francisco so that she could come visit me every day. They tried everything on me. Some of the medications made my blood pressure so low that it was scary and others had my heart beating too fast. But I got a lot of rest while I was there. And I was there for six long weeks. They even tried electric shock. They finally let me go, though they hadn't found any medication that worked. But I was feeling a little better. So they told me to get my affairs together and said, "Good luck," and that was that. I was released on February 26, and we moved into brother Bill's house in Belmont while he went on a trip. I was pretty tired for a while.

Lu wrote me this limerick:

> *A gentleman whose name is Standish*
> *Had a pulse beat, really outlandish.*
> *Doctors, nurses they came*
> *And corrected the same*
> *Until soon he was feeling quite dandish!*

Over Easter, we drove down to San Diego and spent a nice week with Jenny and Geri while they were on their spring break from college. We went to the zoo and spent time on the beach. The funny part of San Diego, though, was that the fog was in most of the time and we'd sit on the beach and freeze, but we sat on the beach! After all, we'd gone there to go to the beach.

Lu and Stan on the beach in San Diego, March 1970.

In April, I was feeling better so we took a road trip. We bought a used Chrysler and drove to Fresno, Bakersfield and on to Death Valley looking for desert wildflowers. Then we drove to Santa Barbara to hear Geri's chorus concert, then on to La Jolla and, seeing nothing we liked, went back to the bay area.

After that we traveled around for several weeks looking for a place to land and decided on Cupertino. In May, we rented an apartment at Villa Serra and met a couple of young men in their early twenties, John Haley and Jim, who wanted to start a printing business. They had been working at someplace like Intel, and they wanted to be their own bosses, so we got together with them. One of the boys told us that his father was in the government printing office in Washington D.C., so he felt that he was a master printer and that he could get us lots of government contracts. So we put up some money to get the business started and went into the printing business with them. We called it Industrial Instant Printing.

By the end of June 1970, we had purchased an expensive press, making three presses in all. We were all set to do big business. Lu went through the phone book and mailed out letters of introduction to all the businesses in the area. In just a few days we were receiving orders.

We got some good contracts: one with Ames Research Center at Moffett Field for about $2000 a month, and some other jobs. But the government contracts didn't materialize. So we made a little money at it. But Jim thought he could take two-hour martini lunches and play golf on Wednesdays, since he owned a business. And that was bad. He left in October, by mutual consent, and Lu and I enjoyed the shop a great deal after that. It became fun, once we learned a little about the operation of the press and about papers and such. We were pretty green when we started, but it is fun to tackle new things. I thought we would make a real go of it and it did keep us busy.

Jenny needed some encouragement from time to time. I wrote to her that spring:

Just remember – you are the creator of your own good. Know this and happiness and all of God's good things are yours for the asking – knowing. Remember you are the creator.
I know you are lonely but you must not be lonesome, for God will help but you must let Him. Just ask Him.

And in the fall I wrote again:

Hope you are busy and enjoying life. You must enjoy it, dear, for it is the only one that we can guarantee. – Hope there are others though.

and again:

I'm sure the blow-up [with your boy friend] was for the good. Sometimes our guidance comes in curious ways – not as we think it should come. Know that in your affairs, God is guiding you – you are a child of God. Know that happiness is yours and that you are happy! You and I know that this is true.

Geri took a trip to Finland in September and came back all enthused. She had a wonderful time there with her friend Helena, who had been an exchange student at Ukiah High. She went up to Lapland, overnight on the train, and just loved it.

In November 1970, there was an election. I voted Republican because I had heard nothing that convinced me that there was a single Democrat worthy of a vote. I was fed up with "the followers of the great leadership of the Kennedys." It was high time we had some forward looking leadership!

I was glad Ronald Reagan was re-elected for governor of California. But San Jose did itself a disfavor when it turned down transit bonds. The area needed a mass transportation system so badly. In fact, I thought that the transportation problem throughout the country could be the 'works' that would provide the next period of prosperity. There was so much to be done. The whole concept of movement of the masses had to be reevaluated. The railroad system was in almost the same form at that time, as it was before the automobile came upon the scene. The obvious problems of pollution, and congestion needed to be met and solved.

But enough of the problems. Just be happy that they are there. They make anticipation of the future so exciting!

Tim was living with us at that time. He was pleasant to have around and it was nice to have at least one of our "chicks" at home. He had a job at Macy's and was enjoying it and seemed to be doing quite well with it. He held that job for several months, until he was caught making remarks about somebody, in his rather loud voice. He also had been goofing around – playing mountain lion on the mattresses. So he was called in and fired. That was a big disappointment and he was discouraged.

Then he was in an accident and totaled the truck. It was the old truck we had used up at the lake and it was amazing that he walked away from it without a scratch. Then it was even harder for him to look for a job without his truck.

About a month later, in the middle of the night, Tim had a bad reaction. He had been drinking and went out like a light for five or six hours. We called the ambulance and they put him in the intensive care ward at 3 a.m. Saturday morning, then the doctor sent us home. He called us at 9 a.m. and said that Tim was going to make it. We had some anxious moments waiting for that call. So there he was: no truck and no job. His world just came crashing down around him.

Jenny was in her last year of college at Occidental and having boyfriend problems. I tried to give her some guidance.

February 1, 1971

Your dear letter touched me deeply and brings you ever closer to my heart. You ask some mighty big questions and maybe at this moment in time, there are no easy answers. I think the important thing is to know that there are answers to all questions and knowing this the questions and doubts will be no more. I, like you, have been a sensitive person, and well do I know how it is to be hurt. At the time the hurt was so very real, but the big thing is that time passed and the hurt was no more, possibly a scar, yes, but the hurt gone and the cure complete, absolutely . . .

I was so in love. I had endowed the girl with every possible virtue only to see her have a "shotgun" wedding. I was crushed. I lost track of her sometime before the war – after she had been married a couple more times. I tell you this because at that time I was so sure that I knew the answer to what I wanted in life – and then, Wham!

And time passed and one day I was in love again! More time – more loves – and there were heights and depths – – –

Then your Mother came into my life – slowly at first, but love took on a new dimension – something that two people build together. It has meaning but as for answers, must there be any? I think one word gives a clue – Faith.

With it you can face any situation. You must learn to trust, to have faith. You have demonstrated faith in your own life when you knew that you were happy.

In life there are so many hard decisions, so many goodbyes to be said that can be met only through faith – Know your way now – Be of good cheer – Keep faith. . .

As in my contracting days, so many of the jobs that I did not get were really a blessing – they brought so much grief to the guys who got them.

In April 1971, we sold our interest in Industrial Instant Printing to John who, unfortunately, went broke a couple of years later.

Off we went looking for new worlds to conquer. We had many ideas but we wanted to stay in that general area. We finally decided on the Santa Cruz Mountains. There were small communities there with lots of redwood trees and no smog, and we were ready for a slower pace. We were thinking in terms of a business that we could do on the same property. I enjoyed business. Business has a romance all its own, and if you can find and capture that spirit, it can become most absorbing.

Jenny was studying economics at college and that spurred some interesting discussions. I wrote this letter to her :

367

Jenny dear –

The Corporation idea is what has given to us, and the world, the modern "goodies" that we enjoy – Our corporate strength has enabled us to arm the defenders of the "free world" in two great wars - -

Nader's approach to the car would have delayed its advent (for better or worse) by countless years. And the 'people' would have never had the pleasure of it. Standards that deprive us of the joys of ownership!

The consumer is the jury – the marketplace the judge. Controls won't produce a better mouse trap.

The "Fiscal Constituencies," frightening in a sense, but all part of a changing world – and on and on.

Love, my dear daughter –
your Dad

Chapter 9: Ben Lomond

IN MAY 1971, WE FOUND A CUTE LITTLE HOUSE in Ben Lomond on Highway 9 in the Santa Cruz Mountains and we lived there until 1975. It was right on the San Lorenzo River and our bedroom overlooked the river with a beautiful view of redwood trees.

In June, Lu and I celebrated our 25th anniversary. Donnabeth put on a party for us at their house and it was a nice affair.

25th Anniversary: Tim, Geri, Stan, Lu and Jenny.

My 69th birthday came on July 10th, and both the girls were away. Jenny was in Colombia visiting a friend from college, and Geri was up in the Marble Mountains with friends. But sister May came down and spent the night and after dinner, Bill and his wife, Teri, and her daughter, Robin, and Duge appeared unexpectedly and walked in singing "Happy Birthday" to me. Lu made a strawberry pie and we had a nice visit until about ten o'clock. Then on Sunday, the Freemans arrived and we had a chicken barbecue with corn and salad and cake, then played a game of bridge to round out the evening. It was a delightful day.

Tim was living with us at that time. He still didn't have a job so he took the civil service examination, but nothing ever came of that.

I really enjoyed Ben Lomond. The property was ¾ acre with fruit trees and a garden. I spent most of the day outside planting things and catching gophers. In my garden I got to play God and decide what lived and what died. I put in a nice asparagus bed and connected the drain from the kitchen sink to a pipe that carried the water out to my garden. But the gophers were a big problem. I was using poison bait to kill them, but it was hard to get the bait all the way down into the gopher run.

One day I saw an ad in the paper for "Swift Sword," a device for dispensing the gopher bait. It was a toy plastic sword in a plastic sheath but the end of the sheath was cut-off and the point of the sword was more of a ball. You used the sheath as a funnel to put the gopher bait deep down in the run, then you stuck the sword in the sheath to push the bait into the tunnel. The man who had been selling them lived in Aptos and he wanted to get out of the business, so I bought what he had, maybe 1500 of them, and went into the mail order business. We advertised in Sunset Magazine and it kept us busy filling the orders.

Lu's mother, Eva, passed away October 22, 1972. She just died in her sleep. There was a funeral and all of Lu's family was there. It was the first time we had been together with the Condits since Murray died in 1960, and I guess it was the last time I saw most of them.

For Halloween I carved a beautiful pumpkin and fixed him up with a flashing light and put him on top of a little ladder with a sheet draped over it. Lu baked gingerbread boys and we set the pumpkin on the porch and waited for the trick-or-treaters. Well, a few kids came up to the house and we enjoyed them, but it was nothing like the hoards we had years later in Willits.

In the fall of 1973, we decided to take a trip through Central America. We had a new car, a Mazda with a rotary engine. It was quite a new thing at that time. We decided to take a freighter down to the Canal with our Mazda on board, and then drive home all the way through Central America. It was a most interesting trip.

We sailed out of San Francisco on the MS *Tijuca*, a Norwegian ship, which carried 12 passengers.

Yesterday afternoon we boarded a freighter bound for Panama, and last night I lay in my bunk, listening to the groan of the winches as they labored throughout the night, filling the holds. Fifty years have passed since I, a skinny, tousled-haired kid, lugged a battered suitcase aboard a rusting tanker for my first voyage. My the changes; and yet the eternal sameness of a ship preparing to put out to sea! I still feel much of the same sense of anticipation, the same eagerness to see the land slipping away astern and to explore that ever distant horizon where sea and sky become one.

In the evening we had watched the huge crane swing tons of steel aboard. Hoses had filled our water tanks; oil had been pumped aboard, stores loaded – all part of "sailing."

While it was still early, first one and then another crew member would head up the dock for a night ashore. You could almost feel his anticipation as he half hurried to challenge the night in a foreign port (the crew is Norwegian.)

Grey morning ended a fitful sleep in which kaleidoscopic scenes of other ships and other ports had tumbled through my dreams. A little tug with its line to the bow slowly widened the sliver of water between ship and dock, and the all but silent engines sent a small shiver through the ship. Slowly the sliver became open water as the docks slipped past; with a slow pulsation, the land fell astern. We were on our way!

At last we got to sea! It's been a delightful voyage. The officers and crew are some of the nicest. This hospitality is overwhelming. Most every evening there has been wine at dinner, or champagne. After dinner we gather in a most comfortable lounge for coffee and liqueurs – brandy, Cointreau, Creme de Menthe, scotch, brandy, or what have you. The Captain and Chief Engineer spend the evening seeing that each of us has all they wish. Their English is good and it's no trouble to follow their conversations. A couple of nice guys, about forty. The ship is most comfortable – has a slow roll as it waddles along – makes a little over 400 miles a day, which is good time. Some of the newer container ships are faster but we overtake and pass a number of other ships. Only one has overtaken us.

Tomorrow, Panama! There is a very nice Panamanian aboard, and from what he says, the whole place has changed considerably in the past forty years since I knew it. We will soon see. Will spend a couple of days there at least. Mom wants to go through the Canal so we will do so, if it can be arranged.

When we first left L.A., the fog was quite heavy and, as we got farther and farther out, the air became cleaner and cleaner. The sea blue deepened and the next morning we awoke to a beautiful, clear, sunshiny day. The sea is as calm as Pillsbury. The ship slowly rolls as it spins the ribbon of its wake, and now and then, from the bow wave, flying fish flicker across the water a ways – some surprisingly far – a hundred yards or more – before vanishing into the deep blue from whence they sprang.

So many memories ride along. When we passed Point Tosca at the tip of Baja, the sight of the rocks brought back that night 40 years ago when the "Colombia" ripped herself to pieces – the lifeboats, the dark, the people; my Mom greeting me when, a couple of ships later, I got back to San Francisco –

But memories could fill pages – –

On our way through Mexico we stopped in Guanajuato. It was a delightful little town. One of the most amazing things was that the town was built in a deep canyon. Down the center of the town, at one time, ran creek. This creek cut a rather deep channel so, needing a place for a road, they bridged over the creek, letting the channel run down below, and used the bridge that they made as a thoroughfare. So all the traffic streams up and down the old creek bed on top of the creek.

The surprising thing was the prosperity in the town. All the little houses, which were built on the steep hillsides, had TV antennas, and the place was clean and prosperous-looking.

The market was a busy little place. There was a variety of everything and the prices were right. In that market they didn't haggle over the price like they did in some of the Indian markets further south. Much of it was a fixed price, which was kind of a surprise, but the prices were very low. We bought a pot and two saucers for 40¢. The market was so very colorful, with fruits and vegetables displayed more attractively than at any other market we saw. The people didn't seem hurried, they were very polite and very charming to deal with. We spent $20 there – we got carried away! – but luckily we had a car to bring it home in.

As we drove north from Guanajuato, the flowers along the road were just a mass of beautiful, yellow daisies – just carpets of yellow flowers all through Mexico. We passed a flower garden with poinsettias that were the deepest red that I have seen anywhere. It was just beautiful.

Some of the hills had rugged peaks, but many of them were soft, rolling hills like those that rim the Santa Clara Valley. And the air up there, between 6,000 and 7,000 feet, was just as invigorating and delightful as it could be. It was springtime in that part of the country, and we were riding along in our shirtsleeves – nice and warm without being too hot. Just a beautiful day for traveling. The sky was clear with a few puffy clouds – a beautiful day.

In May 1974, Geri married David Stephens in a little ceremony at the Chapel near Lake Pillsbury Resort. That summer they took a job with the Forest Service as lookouts on Mount Sanhedrin in Lake County. David recalled our first visit to the lookout:

> *You and I were talking, and the subject of Indians' rights came up (probably because of the lookout's view down onto the Round Valley Reservation). You and I were on opposite sides of the question and we debated it for, oh it must have been 20 or 30 minutes. Finally, each of us exhausted all of our arguments.*

Stan and Lu on Mt. Sanhedrin lookout tower, Summer 1974.

We looked at each other in amused silence and then both of us laughed. We had not budged each other's opinion one iota from its original position – you the indefatigable conservative, and I indefatigably liberal. It was fun!

A couple of years later, they decided to buy a house.

to Geri Hulse-Stephens on Mt. Sanhedrin Lookout
Monday, May 30, 1977

Geri dear –

The big Memorial Day weekend will be over by the time you get this. Hope it was a pleasant one. A quick look at your stocks: Mervyn's hangs in at the 28-30 level; McCormick at around 17½. The switch still looks good. Hope you find some good real estate. In the past year it has risen in value some 30% to 60% and even more in some cases.

I think the important thing in financial matters is to make <u>decisions</u>. You can't know all there is to know about everything but you can use your intelligence – investigate – ask questions and reach decisions. Don't just vacillate. Vacillation is the death of progress and the way to lost opportunity. I point this out for at <u>your</u> age you have so much time. Don't squander it!! "Plough deep while sluggards sleep."

This is beginning to sound like a sermon and I have no desire to pontificate so early in the day – it is not yet noon! But please, dear. Think and <u>Act</u> . . .

Lots of love ––
Dad.

They found a house in Sebastopol and I took a look at it with them. David described it some years later:

When we set our sights on a house in Sebastopol, you had me crawling on my face under the house to inspect the plumbing and check the foundation for termite damage, etc., and then up into the hot attic to check for rot and roof leaks.

When we were discouraged by the price, you said to offer what we could afford. When I offered as low as I did, you were surprised, and when the offer was accepted, we were both surprised!

Because of all the inspecting you had me do, we were never surprised by any unforeseen problem with the house. It was a wreck and we knew it! It turned out that buying that house was the best thing we could have done.

Thanks, Stan, you taught us a lot during those times.
David

It needed a lot of work, including a foundation, but it looked solid enough, so they bought it and spent quite a number of years working on it. They spent their summers at the lookout on Mount Sanhedrin and in the winter, they worked on their place in Sebastopol. It was quite nice when it was done.

Chapter 10: The Villages

IN APRIL 1975, WE MOVED TO SAN JOSE, to a senior community called The Villages. We bought a condominium there at 6350 Whaley Drive and I figured that was my last move. We still wanted to stay active so we swam almost every day and took up golf for a while.

One day we were up at the swimming pool and a woman came up to us and said, "We have a little square dance club and we'd like to have you come along."

And we said, "Well, no, no. Thanks anyway, no."

"Oh come on. Just come on down and take a look."

We talked about it and said, "We could just go look at them and see what they're doing."

So we went down and the first thing we knew, we were hooked. So we looked around and we joined another club and that one didn't hold up very well, so we joined another club. I guess we ended up members of three different clubs and then we round-danced with Clark and Maxine.

I wrote to my friend Johnny Bruce on June 1, 1976:

> Lu & I go square dancing 3 evenings a week and also to a folk dance class. It's a lot of fun. Meet a lot of nice people and we are getting so we can dance pretty well. Was pretty confusing at first – me with two left feet.
>
> We are sailing on the Mariposa on June 10 for Honolulu, going to the Lion's convention. We will board at 3:00 PM and she sails at 5:00. If you are in the big city come and see us off. It would be great to see you and Bianca. We'll be at pier 35, Pacific Far East Lines.
>
> Best to you and yours.
> Always
> Stan

On that trip, Donnabeth came with us and we had such a good time together. We got off in Honolulu and then stayed in a condominium on Waikiki. It was a lot of fun to travel together.

Lu and Stan square dancing, July 4, 1976.

The country celebrated its bicentennial on July 4, 1976, and I wrote these thoughts a few days later:

> *The Big 2 has become history and I have had a cold and felt lousy ever since. We had a great celebration here at The Villages – lots of eating, dancing, music, games – fun! Big fireworks up and down the Peninsula and on T.V., much oratory. The President gave something of a history lesson – and about as well received. But then, it's pretty hard to tell, in so many words, what this country is all about. It's kind of like an iceberg: just the tip is visible. The vast invisible bulk – the people's dreams, their*

*hopes, their drives – can't be paraded. But it is these intangibles
that make a man or nation great. His willingness to protect the
commonweal. Some 30 million men have borne arms in the five
great conflicts in our history, from the Civil War to the Korean
conflict, and over a half million gave their lives.*

*And the generosity: the U.S. has contributed millions to
foreign aid, and much of this money in hard dollars that were
worth much much more than today. Our speed in lending aid in
time of disaster – the huge aid to Japan after the 1923 quake;
Nicaragua; Guatemala.*

*Our willingness to invest: the schools this country has built!
Our space program. These are not the acts of little men nor that
of dreamers, but of men with vision. Our judicial system works
– we do not live in fear of imprisonment as does much of the
world.*

We became real good friends with Betty and Tinsley Lee, and Bob
and Jan Caldwell, and Terry and Pat Tussing. The eight of us would
go to the hoedowns and we'd square up together and have ourselves a
great old time. Lu and I got to be pretty good dancers and sometimes
we were dancing five or six nights a week.

In fact in March 1978, a group of us took a Square Dance Cruise
on a ship in the Caribbean. We had several square dancing workshops
on board and just had a delightful time.

July 20, 1978

Dear John,

*We have been enjoying our far from hum-drum existence.
We belong to three dance clubs and usually attend a hoedown
on Saturday nights. It's a lot of fun.*

*The last of this month we will go to Quincy, Cal. to the Oak-
land recreation camp for four days and nights of dancing. A
real nice group meets there every year. Last Sunday we pic-
nicked near Morgan Hill – about a hundred of us – and spent
some time square dancing. Lots of fun – And one of the nice
things about it is that there is practically no drinking. I should
have been introduced to this pastime a long time ago – My mind
might be a lot better...*

*This spring, Lu and I took a week's cruise on board a Rus-
sian ship out of New Orleans with a group of square dancers.
Had a lot of fun. And to be at sea again felt <u>good</u>. And speaking
of feeling good – Lu keeps me popping vitamins and except for
the annoying arrhythmia, once in a while, I'm holding my own.
On the tenth just past, the family took due note of the passage of
72 (gawd, what a number) years since my natal day.*

376

Where has the time gone???
    But the rewards have been many – good times, good friends,
happy memories –

There were other activities at The Villages that we participated in. They had "talent shows," and one time I dressed up like a ballerina with a few of the other men. Another time I was a gopher for a Halloween show. It was pretty silly.

Stan at The Villages talent show, 3rd from left.

About the same time we moved there, Jenny decided to go into the nursery business. She rented some property with a little building on it a few miles from The Villages and opened her business. She asked us if we could help her out, and I told her that we would work for her but she would be the boss. So we helped her start Evergreen Nursery in San Jose. We helped at the nursery a few hours almost every day, and on Sundays we ran the shop for her so she could have a day off. It gave us something to do and we liked it. We also tried to get in a daily swim and that was good for us. It kept us busy.

Then Jenny started doing some landscaping, as there was a lot of new construction in the area, and I helped her out with bidding the jobs and such. She had quite a little business going there.

Around that time, I had a mild stroke. It didn't bother me, but made me confused sometimes. Lu said that I came out of the bathroom and asked her where my razor was. She said it was in the drawer where it always was. But I was looking for my old safety razor, not the electric one I had been using for years. I was still able to work and do things but the kids said it changed my personality, made me more easygoing, I guess. So, that was that.

In July 1978, I received a check from John Bruce. He had borrowed money from me at one time so that he could take a year off from his job in order to write a play. Well, the play never made it big, but he kept paying me off month by month as he was able. Then he had a big break: back in 1963, he had been commissioned to write a book about the convicts who escaped from Alcatraz. The book was called *Escape from Alcatraz*, and it was popular, but not a best seller. As John put it:

McGraw-Hill expected it to be one of their big books of the year, and it would have been, except that the director of the Federal Bureau of Prisons shrewdly closed it, with great TV fanfare, a week ahead of publication – – and suddenly, Alcatraz was past history.

Then in 1978, Hollywood decided to turn it into a movie, so they bought the rights and John got something for it. He sent me a check in the mail, saying:

Well, well, after all these dormant years, the Bruce Gold Mine is finally declaring a dividend!
What a pleasure that is for me!

I wrote back:

Gio, I am so happy for you! Funny – the last few days you have been much on my mind. I had meant to write – even today – to see how you were and how you were getting along. And now this! I am so happy for you. You've had such a terrible lot of discouragement. Lu joins me – We think it is just great. We thank you too, fellow – Not many people would have remembered, Gio. You are the greatest! The money is fine, but the priceless gesture of friendship brings wealth beyond measure –
I am indeed fortunate.

So that gave us a little extra cash, and that fall we decided to take a trip down the Amazon River. I described that wonderful trip to John in a letter:

Oct. 25 '78

Dear Gio, dug this old mill[85] out of the garage and thought it about time I knocked out a few lines to you. Got your card from Big Ben and surroundings. So much that shows man's better nature and achievements and so many reminders of the price that has been paid because of human foible: the beautiful stained glass windows dedicated to those who gave full measure that those surroundings might endure. Even the Beef Eaters[86] in their ridiculous costumes become dignified amid the grandeur of their setting. But for the rest of London – Give me good ole greater San Francisco. Do hope you had a good, good time.

Now the Amazon is something else. The long flight to Lima, Peru (10½ hours) having left L.A. at 8:00 PM. Had a real good dinner. Read, napped and along about the equator watched a fantastic electrical storm play about the sky below – some of Nature's fireworks at their best. During breakfast, dawn outlined the clouds below and lo, from a red pool of cloud the fiery ball of sun majestically took command. We put down in Callao, the seaport on the outskirts of Lima. I put in there in the '30s on a ship carrying a load of dynamite. I remember well because when we got there the tests showed that the stuff was too unstable to transport by rail, so we had to take it out to sea and dump it. They had an electric trolly car that was the first railed vehicle that I ever saw that had rubber-clad wheels. It was high speed, fast and smooth and whisked one into the center of town in about 20 minutes. It's gone now. Stinking autos (low grade gasoline) bump over poorly paved roads fender-to-fender like a flock of sheep being herded by an unseeing devil. On a scale of 1 to 10, the charm of Lima rates about 2. A couple of nights and we are glad to be off to Iquitos.

The snowcapped peaks of the Cordillera Oriental reached toward us from the barren, hostile terrain. On the eastern slope below the snow line, here and there in this vast isolated wilderness you see a little hut. From it traces a hair-like path to a neighbor hut a few hundred yards to a

---

[85] slang for typewriter.
[86] ceremonial guardians of the Tower of London in London, England

379

mile or more away. How they ever eke out an existence is a mystery. (Reminded me of the old gal up on the Chile Bean.) But down here, only a few hundred miles from the Equator it is so danged cold. Man, it's COLD in them there mountains at night! Soon the forbidding landscape takes on a pale green that shortly becomes the lush green of the tropics. We touch down at Tarapoto, an isolated little town way out in the jungle. Its only link with the outside world is the bi-weekly plane from Lima to Iquitos. At the side of the grassy runway is another plane. It is waiting for repair parts for its landing gear, which was wiped out attempting a take-off. A drove of pigs trotted onto the runway at that particular moment.

A handful of letters changed hands and a few packages were passed down and we roared past our crippled sister ship. We came out of a cloud cover, past some rugged peaks that tow-ered above us, and there below lay the mighty Amazon. Half the water of the rivers of the world flow into and down the Amazon to the Atlantic. It lies sprawling like a huge yellow serpent, sometimes twisting back over itself as it takes full command of the dark green jungle in which it lives. We are some 2,300 miles from its mouth and only 320 feet above sea level, yet at flood enough water flows down her in one day to supply the city of New York for eight years! An hour later we circled over the river and made a nice landing at Iquitos.

Iquitos was a principal port during the rubber boom in the late 1800's. It's still quite a thriving place. Busy traffic in the center, tho all roads peter out not many miles from town as there are no roads into the region from outside. Infested with motorcycles – The Nips[87] have done a great job of merchandising, ug! The sun is hot but the openness of its situation along the river allows a nice circulation of air and the warmth is not unpleasant. Forest products, hardwoods, etc. are the main trade that keep the 60,000 inhabitants busy chasing the almighty Sol.[88]

---

[87] slang for Japanese
[88] The sol was the currency of Peru between 1863 and 1985.

Boarded an oversized rowboat equipped with an outboard motor and started up the Nanay to the Jungle Lodge. Found the lodge high on the bank about a half hour from Iquitos. At this time of the year the river is some fifty feet below its flood stage, sometime along the latter part of December. On the way we passed a number of little dugout canoes. They have almost no freeboard and look like they are in imminent danger of swamping. Yet whole families perched precariously around a load of bananas happily wave to us as the disappearing footprints of their oars carried them past.

The main building, thatched-roofed and open on all sides, had an area containing eight tables that was screened and was where we ate. Screened cubicles with two cots provided the sleeping accommodations. Food was sort of camp style, served buffet. The fish caught in the river was delicious. Native fruits and poultry, canned butter from Denmark, jam from England and fresh bread.

Spent two nights at the lodge. During the day we took short excursions visiting some nearby Indian villages. The Yaguas decked themselves in their native costumes and demonstrated the use of the blowgun. In spite of their very primitive living, they seemed to have certain values that were lost by those we later saw living in squalor and poverty in some of the big cities. They are friendly and fun to be among. The Bora village was a little larger: about a dozen thatched huts along the edge of a clearing that was their soccer field, a great sport down here. Some mixture of races here and the children were a friendly, smiling, and noisy group. Had a good time passing out gum and candies. They pointed out a particular bird that had the run of the place. It spent its time looking for and eating snakes. A particularly deadly "Parrot" snake flourishes in these parts.

(I stopped for a moment. I have rambled on and on and don't dare read what I have written or I will surely tear it up. Please don't feel you have to wade through any more. It's just kind of fun to relive what was a delightful trip and to thank you again for your part in it.)

Back at the Lodge: night comes quickly shortly after sunset. The only light we had was kerosene lanterns. Had a noggin of Pisco punch[89] while waiting for the buffet to be spread. In the pool of darkness at my feet I was suddenly grabbed by a kinkajou.[90] Tho startled, I realized that it wanted to play as it attacked my shoe with vigor. The darkness also brought out some of the biggest cockroaches. Harmless things – just a trifle disconcerting tho when you lay down in the darkness and know that they are scurrying about all over the place. On awakening, the night noises gave way to the sounds of a myriad of birds noisily starting their day.

At breakfast a parrot flew onto the table. And a couple of beautiful Macaws made themselves at home looking for a handout. A monkey created some anxiety as he climbed about overhead (they can be pretty nasty, especially when you are eating directly below them). Saw some of the biggest ants imaginable. Big black things that were over an inch long, have a bad sting and can devour a man if they overtake him while he is asleep. The multiple stings would be fatal.

Back to Iquitos, where we boarded the "Adolpho," a funny old relic built in 1905 for the rubber trade and left over from the boom days. Steam has given way to a new diesel engine and the hull has been iron clad. A good thing too as we bumped several hidden bars on the trip and could have been in for trouble if it were not for the iron. The boat, about 100 feet long and 16 feet wide, had an upper deck where its 15 passengers lived. Two bunks to the cabin that was only six feet wide and seven feet long.

Hard to imagine the charm of this voyage. We all ate at two tables on the open upper deck mid-ships. The food was similar to that at the lodge: buffet style. Along the deck were a half-dozen hammocks, lovely to lie in and watch the ever-changing panorama flow past. Sometimes the river would be a half-mile wide and the soft warm air felt good as we rested, shielded from the sun by an overhead tarp. The air was so pure you couldn't even see what you were breathing – particularly hard on a couple that were from Los Angeles. They

---

[89] Pisco punch is an alcoholic beverage made from Peruvian brandy; a noggin is a small cup.

[90] A small primate that is actually related to the raccoon.

wanted to get home so that they could see what they were breathing.

After dinner last night, sitting around the table enjoying the cool of the evening, the engine set up a loud squeal and abruptly stopped. For a while we were swept along by the stream and then at last up against a steep bank. A crew member leapt ashore with a line seeking something that he could tie to. For about a mile he scrambled along the edge of the bank in the blackness as we bumped along, before he found anything suitable. All this time a couple of other crew were struggling with the anchor. At last our aimless bumping and drifting came to a halt. It was past 10:00 PM when a boat was dispatched for Iquitos for parts. We awoke this morning still moored to the bank awaiting those that were swallowed by the black night. It's been a beautiful morning. The rising sun tinted the clouds in pastel shades, silhouetting a little dugout canoe with its three occupants slowly making its way across the wide expanse of the river. An artist could not have wished for a lovelier scene.

We had a pool for the hour when repairs would be com-

Stan enjoying his hammock on the *Adolpho*

383

pleted. I lost by one minute – 180 Soles. A little dugout pulled alongside while we were awaiting repair parts. It had a live turtle. The cook bought it and we had a special treat: soup – fresh turtle, nicely diced and slightly thickened.

The river is truly a wondrous thing. It's the highway through this vast area, with people living along its banks. It provides amusement, communication, their laundry facilities, their food, their water supply and drains their villages. A great system. Glad I had my G.G. shots![91] Was unaware of the state of things – we had bottled water to drink – until I saw them dip a bucket of water out of the river to wash the glasses in. Found we use the river for all our needs, cooking, etc.

The river is full of fish. Huge catfish with heads the size of watermelons – delicious. See a lot of freshwater dolphin, and a big slow fish about 6 feet long. The Indians fish both night and day. We saw some in a dugout with a lantern using spears. Fish plays a big part in their diet.

Made eight stops at Indian villages in the 200-mile trip. The natives were delighted to have us visit. They would deck themselves out in their native trappings and show us their dances. One old gal grabbed me – had me join the dance. We pranced back and forth and had a lot of fun, much to the merriment of all. Here and there, high on the bank and up on stilts, are their little thatched huts. Usually a number of banana trees are nearby and along the bank rice flourishes. It will be harvested just before the flood waters in December. Tapioca bushes flourish; all they have to do is to poke a cutting into the ground. Oops! My typing is something else.

Back to the natives. They also eat yucca root. It tastes pretty good. Faintly resembles a French fried potato. Fish, which is plentiful, is the main source of protein. They have little use or understanding of money and would rather trade goods for their beads and bamboo flutes and poorly made

[91] Gamma globulin shots are usually given in an attempt to temporarily boost a patient's immunity against disease.

blowguns (just for the tourist trade) and some nicely woven basketry. They are pretty sharp traders, too.

Just at dark on the third day we stopped at a leper colony. Was a little apprehensive as we made our way through the unlit streets to the hospital. The poor unfortunates were glad to see us and appreciated our stopping. The place was clean tho rustic by our standards but a far cry from Michener's Molokai.[92] There were about fifteen hundred in the colony, mostly relatives of the inmates – some fifty or so. A friendly, laughing crowd of youngsters accompanied us all the way. There is a natural friendliness about these remote people that is utterly charming.

The next day we arrived at Leticia, Colombia. One would have thought our little 100-footer was the "Leviathan" from the pomposity shown by the immigration and custom officials. After much scanning of passports and stamping of same we entered a motor launch and crossed the river to the town.

We had had a nice and an adventurous voyage. The heat gave us no trouble. The food good, the people nice. The mosquitos all but carried Lucile off but she is mending. I might add that the trip is not for the faint of heart, the weak of stomach nor for the infirm of limb. We enjoyed it thoroughly. On the way home, stopped at Manaus, Brazil; Bogota, Mexico City and back to San Jose via Dallas. It's good to be back home, n'est-ce pas?[93]

Greetings from us both and buss[94] Bianca for me.
        Stan

In March 1979, Jenny married Dave Watts in a small ceremony up at Big Basin in the redwoods. We were all there and I marched Jenny down the aisle, so to speak. We went out for a nice luncheon afterwards. Lu and I hosted a reception for them at The Villages a couple of weeks later.

---

[92] refers to James Michener's novel, *Hawaii.*
[93] isn't it so?
[94] kiss

On December 18, 1979, our first grandchild, Nathan, was born to Geri and David. They were living in Sebastopol at that time. The next summer they went back up to the lookout on Mt. Sanhedrin and took little Nathan along. We went to visit them there, and when we got home I wrote her this letter:

August 20.

Geri dear – where does the time go?? Have taken pen-in-hand a couple of times since our visit but no go. We enjoyed our stay with you and Nathan so very much. You are such a good mommy!

I have thought a lot about our conversation and a remark you made about our seeming to be "looking forward to disaster" re. the course of humanity.

All history is etched with "disaster." From the earliest man, who met "disaster" when he was slapped into oblivion by the swish of the brontosaurus' tail, down through history. The "disaster" that fell to those in the path of Genghis Khan; the wars, the plagues that have swept across Europe and the Mid East since the beginning of time all spelled disaster to those who fell victim. Then there was Japan's thrust through Asia and its hundreds of thousands of victims and the millions that perished at the whim of Hitler. Hiroshima and Nagasaki spelled disaster for many. History is caught up in the chronicle of "unmerciful disaster followed fast and followed faster."[95] So much for the dark side.

Nature took care of the dinosaur. Genghis "abode his destined hour and went his way,"[96] while the Napoleons of the past lie still, their voices stopped with dust. Thanks to Lister et al., the terrible Horseman Disease (Death) sweeps unchecked across the land no more. Japan's dreams of conquest became a nightmare. Hitler chose the coward's way. But in spite of all the havoc wrought down through history to the masses or to the individuals, one thing stands out clearly: man is destined to survive! Those who have not been swept aside by fate, fulfill destiny. What the future holds no one knows. Nor from day one has anyone known. Let's therefore view the future from a different angle.

The future is here. Every new day is yesterday's future.

This, I believe, is the challenge that we face. How we meet the future – "scourged by passions, doubts, and fears"[97] or with

---

[95] from "The Raven" by Edgar Allen Poe
[96] from "The Rubaiyat of Omar Khayyám"
[97] from "At The Banquet To The Chinese Embassy" by Oliver Wendell Holmes

an unfaltering trust that lets "one wrap the drapery of his couch about him and lie down to pleasant dreams."[98]

In this brief discourse I try to give you the gist of what it's all about. Believe in your destiny; Know that it is good. Put your hand in the hand of God and know that life is good (God). Advance, with faith and confidence, toward the fulfillment of your dreams.

I did a lot of writing both when we were living in Ben Lomond and also at The Villages. Here are some of my thoughts:

Since every human being partakes of the Godhead through his own better self, he needs no mortal intermediary for communion with the Almighty!

Though we were not religious in our living, we always had an awareness of our Creator and appreciation of the command to shun evil. This evil was not definitely defined. I never deliberately did an evil thing – often being confused as to just what was evil, I shunned that which appeared evil, tho in the light of time appearances have much changed.

One of the precepts that I tried to apply to my business was not what was in it for me but could I turn out the job the way it should be for the money involved. This was not smart business practice. I gave away much too much of my time, and my easy attitude about extras – my reluctance to charge enough to cover the costs – did little to heighten the appreciation of the job. My attitude was 180° reverse from that of H.E. Winfrey who, in instructing me as to how to bill a job, said, "Always remember: the squeals of the sucker are music to the gondolier's ears."

I sometimes think of the costs of all that we have. It didn't just happen. It took labor – lots and lots of labor – to build this country.

No matter how sophisticated his means of communication, no matter how advanced his modes of transportation, man remains, at bottom, an aggressive and often hostile beast. In like vein, one can take comfort in the conviction that whatever the diplomatic cosmetics, conflict, more than comity, dominates relations between nations. Refer to the solemn grey columns of the news media.

---

[98] from "Thanatopsis" by William Cullen Bryant

On December 2, 1980, Lu's birthday, our second grandchild, Michael Standish, was born, and in January 1981, Jenny and Dave and little Michael moved up to Willits leaving Lu and me to run the nursery until it sold. I was very anxious to move up to Willits and help them out at their new business, Sanhedrin Nursery. We had hoped to move up when Evergreen Nursery sold in April, but deal after deal fell through on the sale of our condominium. We finally got a buyer in June and moved up to Willits. It was a good move to be near our family and out of the smog and traffic of the Bay Area.

Christmas 1980, at The Villages. Jenny, Mikie, Dave, Stan, Lu, David, Nathan, Geri and Tim.

Chapter 11: Willits

WE MOVED INTO THE CREEKSIDE APARTMENTS and started helping out at Sanhedrin Nursery. It wasn't long before Geri and David moved to Willits with Nathan, who was about a year and a half old. A year later, we bought a house on the corner of West Mendocino and Easy Streets, and moved in on April 1, 1982, in a snowstorm. Tim followed us up soon after and moved in with us.

Jenny and Dave hired a contractor to build a nursery sales building attached to their house. When the contractor was done there was still siding to put on and sheetrock to tack up. So I helped Dave wherever I could. I even helped him put on the siding, holding up the boards as he nailed them on. I guess we were 15 feet up in the air to finish that job.

Dave and Stan putting siding on Sanhedrin Nursery building, Nov. 1981.

Whether the project has been large or small, your steady hands, Stan, have helped our dreams come true. So thanks for the memory of many hours working together.

Dave

Stan and Dave holding Mikie, October 1981.

We were very happy in Willits. When Milo was born, March 24, 1983, we arrived at Geri's house just a couple of hours later and she let me hold him when he was just hours old. That was a special moment.

Every morning Lu and I would drive over to the nursery and help out for a couple of

Stan holding Milo, March 24, 1983.

390

hours, then have some lunch, and work for a couple more hours in the afternoon. Lu helped out in the store so Jenny could tend to the babies – Suzanne was born in their house August 29, 1983 – and I helped out with watering and planting. I even helped transplant little seedlings for Jenny:

Stan transplanting at Sanhedrin Nursery, 1987.

> *After we started the nursery, we saw the need and desirability of growing some of our own bedding plants. Dad became my first transplanter. We picked up an old kitchen drainboard sink that we placed on the patio and it became our first potting bench. Dad would fill the cell-packs one at a time: he would reach into the bag and scoop up a pot full of dirt, then dump in onto the flat and press it into the cells. Then, with the watering can, he would pour water on the flat to wet the soil. After that he began planting the little seedlings into the cell-packs. It was a pretty messy process but the seedlings got planted and they grew into decent little vegetable plants.*
>
> *When he was done, Dad would clean his fingernails with his pocket knife. It was an old pocket knife with just one blade, I think. He would struggle a bit to pull the blade out, then set to carefully cleaning the dirt out from under his nails with it. He never cut himself that I can remember.*
>
> *Then he'd adjust his hat. He wore his hair combed straight back (it was rather long if it hung down in his face). When he put on a hat, he would run his left hand back over his hair, then*

put the hat on with his right hand and firm it into place with
both hands. When he was younger, he always wore his hats
rather smartly, cocked a little to one side. But as he got older, he
took to wearing a baseball cap and he always set it too high on
his head so it looked rather funny, but he didn't care.

Dad liked animals, especially dogs. We usually had a dog
and he would always greet her by encouraging her to lie down
on her back so he could rub her stomach with his shoe. He was
very gentle and the dogs enjoyed it. I remember when we had to
put our old dog, Brutus, to sleep. We loaded him into the van
and, before we left for the vet, Dad went over to the van, stroked
his head and said, "Good-bye, old man."

When we worked at the nursery, we'd sit on the front porch with
our lunch and Mikie and Zanny would join us. Then when Mikie was
a little older, we used to go downtown to the Willits Creamery for
lunch and a milkshake, and he came with us almost every day. Later,
they both joined us for lunch and we got a kick out of taking them
along. Sometimes Nathan and Milo would join us too.

Mike recalled it years later:

The horn at the firehouse blew a long steady tone. Across
town at "the nursery" Grandpa and I looked up from the task at
hand. Grandpa held the handle of a long watering wand while I
kneeled in the dirt, fighting a kink in the dirty green hose. The
horn meant it was noon. Lunchtime. One last row of dry potted
plants and our work would be finished.

"Are you two about finished?" Grandma yelled from the
back porch of the store. How she could project her voice so well
from her petite frame was a mystery to most. My five-year-old
self, of course, never gave it a second thought. That's just the
way it was.

I helped Grandpa coil up the hose and we headed towards
the store. My rain boots were better equipped than Grandpa's
soft leather Hush Puppies for plodded through the puddles
forming in our path. His tucked-in, plaid button-down shirt and
brown slacks meant he was the best dressed employee at San-
hedrin Nursery. Since he was never technically paid, he was
more correctly a volunteer.

"What's 4 and 9?" Grandpa asked as we walked. Some-
where along the line I was taught in school that "and" was an-
other term for addition, but I quickly learned that "and" in the
context of watering plants with Grandpa meant we were deal-
ing with multiplication. Whenever I joined him on watering
duty we worked on multiplication. Upon finding the answer he
would say, "That's right. Now, what's 3 and 7?"

We met Grandma inside the nursery and washed up before heading out to their small two-door tan Mazda sedan. My younger sister Suzanne, or Zanny as everyone called her, joined us and we crawled into the back seat while Grandma drove. I don't think we ever questioned why Grandpa didn't drive, but I remember him showing me the scar under his left breast after his pacemaker surgery. At the time I didn't understand what it meant that he'd "had a stroke."

Ever since the Willits Creamery had closed, Grandma and Grandpa had been on a quest to find the next-best chocolate milkshake in town and the shake at McDonald's topped their taste list. As it was summer, a fair number of travelers passing through town were already in line when we arrived. As was typical, a short line formed behind each of the four registers.

The task at hand was simply to choose the shortest line and patiently wait our turn. This philosophy, however, was not shared by all patrons. We could only shake our heads at the groups who, upon finding their line to be moving at a subpar level, would jump lines. This, of course, only caused confusion and the perceived time gains often never materialized.

"May we have two chocolate shakes, one Chicken McNuggets and a small French fries?" Grandma politely asked. The total came out to something in the vicinity of $12.95, so Grandpa reached into his front pocket to find his cash. He carried a wallet in the seat of his slacks, of course, but he always kept some cash in his front pocket. On this occasion a few bills slipped out and fell to the ground.

Ever on the lookout for this eventuality and driven by a moderate fear that some erstwhile convict would rob us, I quickly snatched up these stray bills. I could feel the eyes of everyone in line looking at me and my face went bright red with embarrassment as I noticed the face of Benjamin Franklin on one of the Greenbacks. I slipped them back into Grandpa's pocket.

Our favorite table to eat at was the booth in the corner with a good view of the counter. "There sure are a lot of Japanese," Grandpa noted, as if he were an anthropologist tracking this particular group's travel patterns. As a World War II veteran, I think he was genuinely surprised to see so many people from a country that we had been at war with not that long ago.

Zanny and I split the nuggets evenly. She ate the ones with white meat and I ate the ones with dark meat. Then we split the small fries four ways and Grandpa made sure we ate every last one. By the end, he pushed the last few crispy burnt fries to each of us in turn, one by one.

Back in the car, we headed to Grandma and Grandpa's house on Easy Street, always the same route across town. A young boy on a bicycle swerved out in front of us causing Grandma to hit the brakes. "Damn fool," Grandpa cursed. "Run him over!" To which Grandma quickly "shushed" him.

We pulled into their carport. Grandpa was done with his work at the nursery for the day, but Grandma would take us back after a bit and run the cash register until 4 p.m. We went inside through the back door and walked through the kitchen into the living room. Grandpa took off his coat and trucker hat, which sat just slightly crooked on his head, and sat down in his brown easy chair with a sigh. He turned on the TV and the set-top-box while Zanny and I piled onto the couch just in time to hear the beginning of our favorite jingle, "Flintstones. Meet the Flintstones. They're the modern stone age family . . . "

After The Flintstones, we switched over to one of the "cowboy" channels. "Bang! Bang! Bang! Bang!" introduced the honorable Rifleman, one of Grandpa's favorites. When the commercials came on, Grandma would have Grandpa mute the sound, "Who can stand that racket?"

During one of the breaks, Grandpa shared a short story about his experience in Germany during WWII. "We were driving around some city, I can't remember which. They knew they were beat. But we were driving around and I had my head out the top of the tank telling the pilot where to go. I would tap on his left shoulder or his right shoulder, you see, and he would turn. So we turned down this narrow street and just like that a German tank turned down the same street facing us. We both just froze there for a minute. Then the German tank slowly backed up and went on his way."

I don't think I understood the significance of this story when I first heard it. I was probably far too young. If either tank had fired on the other, they most likely both would have perished. I think he had a level of respect for the German soldiers fighting against him. They were doing what they had to do, just like he was. He would often say he was lucky not to have fought against the Japanese. If the war hadn't ended when it did, however, I think he would have seen combat in the Pacific.

When the Rifleman came back on he finished tracking a group of bandits and finished them all off in a dramatic shootout. "I want to show you something." Grandpa said and took me into his study. From a closet he pulled out an old Army ammo box and opened it up. Inside were a number of collectibles including some old coins. Grandpa pulled out a thick silver 50-cent piece and showed me with a magnifying class where you could find the year it was made and the initial on it corresponding to the mint. Then he had me look up its current value in a great big paperback book with thin newspaper pages.

When we finally found it, I think it was worth $1.50, to which he said, "Don't ever talk to anyone about your money."

Even though I was too young to really understand what he was talking about, I understood that he spoke from experience. "Don't talk to your friends or girlfriends. You never know who you can trust. That's the way it goes."

It was time for Grandpa's nap and time for us to return home. "Goodbye Grandpa!" We gave him big hugs and followed Grandma to the car.

Suzanne remembered the lunch outings also:

The best memories I have of my grandpa were our frequent lunch outings with him, Grandma, and Mikie. Somewhere along the line the "d" was lost, however, and they were always fondly referred to as "Granpa" and "Granma". Lunchtime was always a much anticipated event. On the weekends and during the summer I anxiously waited until Granpa and Granma were through with their morning work at the nursery so we could hop in their car and go to lunch. The location changed over the years. I was told that the first place was the Creamery, but the first location I remember was TNT, with the arcade and lively high school kids running around. Despite their fabulous milk-shakes, I guess TNT became a little too noisy after a while, so we headed south of town to go to the big golden arches of McDonald's! Despite the change in location, the routine was the same. Milkshakes for Granpa and Granma, chicken nuggets for me and Mikie and French fries to share. And share we did, right down to the very last crumb! I'll never forget Granpa divvying up the last tiny, crispy fries on the lunch tray. There was no question that every last bit of food would be eaten. After the last French fry had been eaten, we knew it was time to head back home when we heard Granpa slurp up the last drops of his shake – what a satisfying sound!

Some days we would go to Granpa and Granma's house for lunch instead. Granma would make us Top Ramen noodles with little hotdogs. We would eat our lunch and watch cartoons, Gun Smoke, or if it was Sunday, football. Granpa had his customary chair in the middle of the living room, right in front of the TV. Those football games seemed to drag on for hours! I would always ask, "Granpa, how much longer till the end of the game?" And he would say, "Oh, just 10 more minutes." I quickly learned that 10 football minutes really meant about 30 childhood minutes. The games always eventually ended tho, and we would head back home. Sometimes the short drive home became a little adventure when Granpa would suggest, "Let's take the bumpy road!" That pothole-covered road never got old, and boy was it fun! It was a sad day when the property owner blocked the road and we had to go in search of other pothole-covered roads to make our voices jiggle.

And then there was the shoelace stunt that Milo and I thought was so clever. For years we had our own little tradition during the holidays. Every Thanksgiving and Christmas, we would "sneak" under the table at dinner and untie Granpa and uncle Chucky's shoelaces. We would then cross the laces and tie their right and left shoes together. I think we may have surprised them the first time, but they played along with it for several years at least, providing us with many giggles and much entertainment.

As a little kid, I was drawn to my Granpa's love of collecting. I remember his coin collection and a multitude of Dr. Seuss books. He helped me start my own small coin collection, which then influenced me to start a collection of stamps and baseball cards. Granpa was the one who bought me my first real bike! It was blue and was a special "girls" bike. I spent hours and hours riding up and down the nursery driveway on it and riding around the neighborhood. I have many fond memories of Granpa Stan. More than anything, I'll always remember his loving smile and warm demeanor.

I really enjoyed being Grampa. I always had a special bond with my grandchildren. I was lucky, I guess.

Stan with his grandchildren: Milo, Zanny, Nathan and Mikie, July 1987.

Halloween in Willits was something else again. We lived on the corner of West Mendocino Avenue and Easy Street, about three blocks from the grammar school. It seemed that every family in Willits brought their children to trick-or-treat in our neighborhood. First Geri and Jenny would come over with their little ones in their costumes. Then they'd go trick-or-treating while we handed out candy to the kids that came up

Nathan and Grandpa, Halloween 1982.

to our door. Lu would count them and we often had over 300 trick-or-treaters in an evening. We'd turn out the porch light when we ran out of candy, or when the teenagers started arriving. It was a most entertaining.

After we moved to Willits, I started investing in second mortgages. Just a few at first, with a guy named Barry Simms. He knew people who wanted to build a house or something but couldn't get a bank loan, so he loaned them money – our money – at about 12-15% interest. So we made quite a bit of money at that. But he turned out to be a crook. He had sold several different people "mortgages" on his house, then he got into trouble and couldn't pay any of the loans back. They found his body in the hills off an embankment. I guess he just couldn't face it so killed himself. But in the meantime, we had a nice income from the mortgages. And that gave us some money to take a trip each year.

Stan on a camel in Egypt, 1984.

Stan and Lu in China, 1985.

Chapter 12: World Travelers

WE TOOK A NUMBER OF TRIPS, mostly traveling by ship. For several years we booked passage on freighters: some were cargo ships and a few were container ships. Freighter trips have no exact itinerary. Sometimes they have to wait hours or days to get into a port, and it usually took several days to load or unload the cargo, so that gave us time to explore each port town. It made for a relaxing voyage. I just loved being on the ocean, watching the wake uncurl behind the ship, spotting a flying fish or a school of dolphins, smelling the salt air.

There were usually about twelve passengers aboard and we ate with the officers. We had a small cabin and there was a lounge of some sort. We traveled that way until I turned 80, then we had to take passenger liners because freighters don't have doctors on board so they have an age limit.

In 1983, we went to Japan on a freighter. We hit some heavy weather and a lot of the passengers didn't come up for dinner. I guess the swells were 50 feet high. It was quite exciting.

In 1984, a freighter to Egypt took us to Alexandria and from there we went to Cairo. Egypt is dirty, full of people and cars. The pyramids, of course, stand out

Lu holding Suzanne, Stan and Mikie, October 1984.

in my memory plus a short camel ride. I had my picture taken on the camel and it reminded me that my grandfather, I.R. Burns, had also been to Egypt and had his photograph taken on a camel too. I still have that photograph somewhere.

In 1985, we flew to Hong Kong and went into China for two weeks then returned by freighter to Long Beach.

In 1986, we took a cruise ship to Vancouver, BC, to the World's Fair.

In 1987, we took a freighter from Long Beach to Australia and back to Tacoma, Washington.

In 1988, we took a cruise ship from Miami around South America.

In 1989, we took a South Pacific cruise and we liked it so much that we did it again in 1990.

In 1991, we took a cruise ship from San Francisco to Alaska and back.

In 1992, we flew from Los Angeles to Sydney, Australia, where we stayed with the Robinsons for eight days, and then returned on the Princess ship to San Francisco.

In 1993, we took a roundtrip from Fort Lauderdale to the Caribbean islands for 21 days.

So we've seen a lot of the world. We enjoyed our travels.

Home from the South Pacific, 1989. Donnabeth, Stan and Lu.

Chapter 13: Golden Anniversary

ON JUNE 8, 1996, LUCILE AND I CELEBRATED our 50th wedding anniversary. Donnabeth and Chuck came up and the girls came over with their families. They cooked us a cioppino dinner that was just delicious. We were all decked out in Hawaiian clothes and the girls and their kids did hula dances for us. We just had a wonderful time.

A month later I had my 90th birthday. They put a big "90" on my birthday cake. "My, that's old," I said. I've lived a long time. It's been a good life. I've been lucky.

Lu and Stan on their 50th Anniversary, June 8, 1996

50th Anniversary family photo. Lu, Mike, Suzanne, Geri, Milo, Nathan; Tim next to Geri; Stan and Jenny in front.

Chapter 14: Last Days

CHRISTMAS 1996, WE RECEIVED A CHRISTMAS CARD from Bianca Bruce. She told us that Johnny had passed away back in July. The news shook me greatly. He was the last of my old friends, someone I had known for 70 years. It made me feel like the last leaf on the tree.

During the last weeks of his life I, Geri, was his caretaker. He had had a stroke on February 7th that had taken speech away from him and all of his movement on one side and most on the other. Mom was so dazed by the event, Jenny had a serious flu and it fell to me to care for him round the clock. I consulted with Mom and the doctor and hospice people and did the duties of care that those days required. A week after the stroke, Freckles, their dog had a spontaneous rupture and they had to put him down. It was as though he was getting out of the way for the bigger event that was soon to follow. While I was caring for Dad he would work hard sometimes to express something to me. One time he just wanted me to arrange some flowers I had hastily stuck in a vase but one day, on Valentines Day, he had something earnestly important to get across to me. He pointed and tried to form words that would not come and I was confused but finally I got it that there was something in the bedside cabinet that he wanted me to find. I reached in there and I found a Valentine card for Mom that he had already signed with love and sealed a week or two before. He loved her so.

> "I never thought it possible
>   for there to ever be
>   a person who'd enrich my life
>   the way you have for me.
> I never thought it possible
>   to feel the love I do
>   or know the joy that sharing brings –
>   till God blessed me with you.
> You've filled my heart with happiness,
>   and there is not a day
>   when I don't give my thanks to God
>   for bringing you my way."

> Happy Valentine's Day
> Stan.

Once during that time I said to him, "Thanks for all the things you have done for me." And he responded to that with two syllables that were hard for me to decipher but after much repetition I realized he was saying, "Like what?" I said, "Like the swing in the backyard, and helping me learn geometry and for the white wool coats you bought Jenny and me when we were young teens." But I couldn't really get down to anything else. Sometimes it takes most of a life to make you realize where you came from and who really helped you become who you are. Now I think I would say, "for teaching me self-reliance, for loving poetry and crying over opera, for having the courage and patience to teach me to drive and not yelling at me when I cracked up the car and for so often, pointing out to me the beauty of the world."

Stan, Dad, Grandpa 1991.

Epilogue

February 26, 1997

Dear Geri,

I was saddened to hear of your father's death.

I know it's possible to say, accurately, that he lived a full life, that his life span beat the Biblical three score and ten by a whole other score, and even that he had 27 years on the house after a gloomy prognosis in his 60s.

But there's still the stark fact that an important being is no more. All the wonderful mechanisms, sensitivities, emotions, skills and memories that made up Stan Hulse have ceased, and that's shocking even when one knows a life is ending. I can understand the sense of loss that you feel.

But in the one human purpose we all know Nature intends, he helped create you, Jenny, Tim, Nathan, Milo, Michael, Zanny and the generations to follow, which could not have existed without him. In all his considerable accomplishments, nothing compares with that. Looking at all of you, he must have known he was a success by the only standard that finally counts.

I was touched by the final message you were able to give him with the "We love you" card on Valentine's Day. What a beautiful thought that was to carry him into eternity. He was a lucky man to have such a family around him in his final hours.

Doris and I always think of you fondly, but our thoughts for you are particularly intense just now, and we send you much love.

Steve

by Harrison Stephens, David Hulse-Stephens' father.

405

Afterword

WHEN I WAS A LITTLE GIRL I loved hearing my father tell stories of his past. The fact that he had survived three shipwrecks fascinated me. Always the romantic, I pictured him in great galleons weathering wild storms at sea and just barely escaping with his life. He also told us stories about his family history, his grandparents who traveled the world over and his great-grandfather who had come across the country in a covered wagon. He told us we were related to Daniel Boone and Myles Standish. I was awed and proud to be related to famous men. I savored those stories.

When my family was growing up and Dad was getting older, I realized that my poor memory hadn't retained those wonderful stories, so I decided that I wanted to get them on tape. In 1984, when we were all living in Willits, I sat down with him and Mom and recorded many of his stories. In 1994, I again did some oral history work with him and collected some more bits and pieces about old San Jose and his years at sea. Those recordings, his personal writings and letters make up the bulk of this book. I have compiled it more than written it, letting Dad tell his story in his own words.

After Dad died, February 21, 1997, I realized that I wanted to gather his stories and his writings into a book. As I became the depository for his belongings, I found a vast collection of letters to and from his mother comprising a correspondence that spanned many years. When I also discovered his own writings, I knew that I had enough material. So I began by creating a timeline and then by transcribing his writings, letters and the oral histories. About that time, I realized that Mom probably only had a few years left herself, so I turned to encouraging her to write down her memories. After she died, I spent over a year compiling her story. After I published her book in 2009, I returned to my father's story.

The correspondence between Dad and his mother comprises over 250 typewritten pages. I also transcribed a notebook with the details of the shipwreck of the *Cuzco* on Lempa Shoals, and another that he kept during the war in Germany, a practice that was strictly forbidden by the Army. I came across a bundle of letters that he wrote to Mom during the winter and spring of 1966, when he was at Lake Pillsbury and we were in Burlingame – another 20 pages. And then there were letters that he wrote to Tim, Geri and me after we left home with advice and encouragement. The oral histories comprise over eight hours of material that I also transcribed, and digitized. Parts of all of these have found their way into this book.

This book has been developing in my mind for almost twenty years. My work has certainly not been continuous during these years, as the task has been a large one. But after I was diagnosed with ovarian cancer in October 2010, I decided that finishing this book was my top priority, as I was pretty sure it would not happen if I did not write it. So I spent many hours, when I was unable to work at the nursery, resting on the couch, working on this book.

As I complete this book I feel a great satisfaction knowing that I have preserved Dad's life as best I can. I have tried to present him so that those who knew him will enjoy getting to know him better, and so that the generations to come may have the feeling of being acquainted with him. I hope that I have been successful and that my readers have enjoyed taking this journey through the 20th Century with Stan Hulse.

Poetry

DAD LOVED POETRY. Sometimes he would read poems to us at the dinner table. He loved to read the *Rubaiyat* by Omar Khayyam, "When Earth's Last Picture is Painted" by Rudyard Kipling, and *Evolution* by Langdon Smith. He also loved Edward Lear's *Book of Nonsense,* and poem, "The Owl and the Pussycat."

He could be very touched by poetry. Often when he would read, tears would come to his eyes as he appeared to be quite moved by the text.

I include here some of his favorite poems.

When Earth's Last Picture is Painted
by Rudyard Kipling

When Earth's last picture is painted and the tubes are twisted and dried,
When the oldest colours have faded, and the youngest critic has died,
We shall rest, and, faith, we shall need it -- lie down for an aeon or two,
Till the Master of All Good Workmen shall put us to work anew.
And those that were good shall be happy; they shall sit in a golden chair;
They shall splash at a ten-league canvas with brushes of comets' hair.
They shall find real saints to draw from -- Magdalene, Peter, and Paul;
They shall work for an age at a sitting and never be tired at all!

And only The Master shall praise us, and only The Master shall blame;
And no one shall work for money, and no one shall work for fame,
But each for the joy of the working, and each, in his separate star,
Shall draw the Thing as he sees It for the God of Things as They are!

If
by Rudyard Kipling

If you can keep your head when all
about you
Are losing theirs and blaming it on you;
If you can trust yourself when all men
doubt you,
But make allowance for their doubting
too;
If you can wait and not be tired by
waiting,
Or, being lied about, don't deal in lies,
Or, being hated, don't give way to hat-
ing,
And yet don't look too good, nor talk
too wise;
If you can dream – and not make
dreams your master;
If you can think – and not make
thoughts your aim;
If you can meet with triumph and dis-
aster
And treat those two imposters just the
same;
If you can bear to hear the truth you've
spoken
Twisted by knaves to make a trap for
fools,
Or watch the things you gave your life
to broken,
And stoop and build 'em up with
worn-out tools;
If you can make one heap of all your
winnings
And risk it on one turn of pitch-and-
toss,
And lose, and start again at your begin-
nings
And never breath a word about your
loss;
If you can force your heart and nerve
and sinew

To serve your turn long after they are
gone,
And so hold on when there is nothing
in you
Except the Will which says to them:
"Hold on";
If you can talk with crowds and keep
your virtue,
Or walk with kings – nor lose the
common touch;
If neither foes nor loving friends can
hurt you;
If all men count with you, but none
too much;
If you can fill the unforgiving minute
With sixty seconds' worth of distance
run -
Yours is the Earth and everything that's
in it,
And – which is more – you'll be a Man
my son!

Selections from the **Rubaiyat of Omar Khayyam**, Edward FitzGerald's Translation

Awake! for Morning in the Bowl of
Night
Has flung the Stone that puts the Stars
to Flight:
And Lo! the Hunter of the East has
caught
The Sultan's Turret in a Noose of
Light.

Come, fill the Cup, and in the Fire of
Spring
The Winter Garment of Repentance
fling:
The Bird of Time has but a little way
To fly---and Lo! the Bird is on the
Wing.

Here with a Loaf of Bread beneath the Bough,
A Flask of Wine, a Book of Verse---and Thou
Beside me singing in the Wilderness---
And Wilderness is Paradise enow.

I sometimes think that never so red
The Rose as where some buried Caesar bled;
That every Hyacinth the Garden wears
Dropt in its Lap from some once lovely Head.

Ah, my Beloved, fill the Cup that clears
TO-DAY of past Regrets and future Fears---
To-morrow?---Why, To-morrow I may be
Myself with Yesterday's Sev'n Thousand Years.

Lo! some we loved, the loveliest and best
That Time and Fate of all their Vintage prest,
Have drunk their Cup a Round or two before,
And one by one crept silently to Rest.

Ah, make the most of what we yet may spend,
Before we too into the Dust descend;
Dust into Dust, and under Dust, to lie,
Sans Wine, sans Song, sans Singer, and---sans End!

Into this Universe, and why not knowing,
Nor whence, like Water willy-nilly flowing:

And out of it, as Wind along the Waste,
I know not whither, willy-nilly blowing.

There was a Door to which I found no Key:
There was a Veil past which I could not see:
Some little Talk awhile of ME and THEE
There seemed---and then no more of THEE and ME.

Then to this earthen Bowl did I adjourn
My Lip the secret Well of Life to learn:
And Lip to Lip it murmur'd---"While you live
"Drink!---for once dead you never shall return."

I think the Vessel, that with fugitive
Articulation answer'd, once did live,
And merry-make; and the cold Lip I kiss'd
How many Kisses might it take---and give!

For in the Market-place, one Dusk of Day,
I watch'd the Potter thumping his wet Clay:
And with its all obliterated Tongue
It murmur'd---"Gently, Brother, gently, pray!"

The Moving Finger writes; and, having writ,
Moves on: nor all thy Piety nor Wit
Shall lure it back to cancel half a Line,
Nor all thy Tears wash out a Word of it.

Listen again. One Evening at the Close

Of Ramazan, ere the better Moon
arose,
In that old Potter's Shop I stood alone
With the clay Population round in
Rows.

And, strange to tell, among that
Earthen Lot
Some could articulate, while others
not:
And suddenly one more impatient
cried---
"Who 'is' the Potter, pray, and who the
Pot?"

Then said another---"Surely not in vain
"My Substance from the common
Earth was ta'en,
"That He who subtly wrought me into
Shape
"Should stamp me back to common
Earth again."

Another said---"Why, ne'er a peevish
Boy,
"Would break the Bowl from which he
drank in Joy;
"Shall He that 'made' the Vessel in
pure Love
"And Fancy, in an after Rage destroy?"

None answer'd this; but after Silence
spake
A Vessel of a more ungainly Make:
"They sneer at me for leaning all awry;
"What! did the Hand then of the Pot-
ter shake?"

Said one---"Folk of a surly Tapster tell
"And daub his Visage with the Smoke
of Hell;
"They talk of some strict Testing of
us---Pish!

"He's a Good Fellow, and 'twill all be
well."

Then said another with a long-drawn
Sigh,
"My Clay with long oblivion is gone
dry:
"But, fill me with the old familiar Juice,
"Methinks I might recover by-and-
bye!"

Ah Love! could thou and I with Fate
conspire
To grasp this sorry Scheme of Things
entire,
Would not we shatter it to bits---and
then
Re-mould it nearer to the Heart's Desire!

The Owl and the Pussycat
by Edward Lear

The Owl and the Pussy-cat went to sea
   In a beautiful pea-green boat,
They took some honey, and plenty of
money,
   Wrapped up in a five-pound note.
The Owl looked up to the stars above,
   And sang to a small guitar,
"O lovely Pussy! O Pussy, my love,
   What a beautiful Pussy you are,
      You are,
      You are!
What a beautiful Pussy you are!"

Pussy said to the Owl, "You elegant
fowl!
   How charmingly sweet you sing!
O let us be married! too long we have
tarried:
   But what shall we do for a ring?"

They sailed away, for a year and a day,
  To the land where the Bong-Tree
grows
And there in a wood a Piggy-wig stood
  With a ring at the end of his nose,
        His nose,
        His nose,
  With a ring at the end of his nose.

"Dear Pig, are you willing to sell for
one shilling
  Your ring?" Said the Piggy, "I will."
So they took it away, and were married
next day
  By the Turkey who lives on the hill.
They dined on mince, and slices of
quince,
  Which they ate with a runcible spoon;
And hand in hand, on the edge of the
sand,
  They danced by the light of the
moon,
        The moon,
        The moon,
They danced by the light of the moon.

Evolution
by Langdon Smith
First Edition by L.E. Bassett and Company

When you were a tadpole and I was a fish
  In the Paleozoic time,
And side by side on the ebbing tide
  We sprawled through the ooze and
    slime,
Or skittered with many a caudal flip
  Through the depths of the
    Cambrian fen,
My heart was rife with the joy of life,
  For I loved you even then.

Mindless we lived and mindless we
    loved
  And mindless at last we died;
And deep in the rift of the Caradoc
    drift
  We slumbered side by side.
The world turned on in the lathe of
    time,
  The hot lands heaved amain,
Till we caught our breath from the
    womb of death
  And crept into light again.

We were amphibians, scaled and tailed,
  And drab as a dead man's hand;
We coiled at ease 'neath the dripping
    trees
  Or trailed through the mud and
    sand.
Croaking and blind, with our three-
    clawed feet,
  Writing a language dumb,
With never a spark in the empty dark
  To hint at a life to come.

Yet happy we lived, and happy we
    loved,
  And happy we died once more;
Our forms were rolled in the clinging
    mold
  Of a Neocomian shore.
The eons came, and the eons fled,
  And the sleep that wrapped us fast
Was riven away in a newer day
  And the night of death was past.

Then light and swift through the jungle
    trees
  We swung in our airy flights,
Or breathed in the balms of the
    fronded palms,
  In the hush of the moonless nights.
And, oh! what beautiful years were

these,
When our hearts clung each to each;
When life was filled and our senses
thrilled
In the first faint dawn of speech.

Thus life by life, and love by love,
We passed through the cycles
strange,
And breath by breath, and death by
death,
We followed the chain of change.
Till there came a time in the law of life
When over the nursing sod
The shadows broke, and the soul
awoke
In a strange, dim dream of God.

I was thewed like an Auroch bull,
And tusked like the great Cave Bear;
And you, my sweet, from head to feet,
Were gowned in your glorious hair.
Deep in the gloom of a fireless cave,
When the night fell o'er the plain,
And the moon hung red o'er the river
bed
We mumbled the bones of the slain.

I flaked a flint to a cutting edge
And shaped it with brutish craft;
I broke a shank from the woodland dank,
And fitted it, head and haft;
Then I hid me close to the reedy tarn
Where the mammoth came to drink;
Through the brawn and bone I drave
the stone,
And slew him upon the brink.

Loud I howled through the moonlit
wastes,
Loud answered our kith and kin;
From west to east to the crimson feast
The clan came tramping in.

O'er joint and gristle and padded hoof,
We fought, and clawed and tore,
And cheek by jowl, with many a growl,
We talked the marvel o'er.

I carved the fight on a reindeer bone,
With rude and hairy hand;
I pictured his fall on the cavern wall
That men might understand.
For we lived by blood, and the right of
might,
Ere human laws were drawn,
And the Age of Sin did not begin
Till our brutal tusks were gone.

And that was a million years ago
In a time that no man knows;
Yet here tonight in the mellow light
We sit at Delmonico's;
Your eyes are deep as the Devon
springs,
Your hair is dark as jet,
Your years are few, your life is new,
Your soul untried, and yet –

Our trail is on the Kimmeridge clay,
And the scarp of the Purbeck flags;
We have left our bones in the Bagshot
stones,
And deep in the Coralline crags;
Our love is old, our lives are old,
And death shall come amain;
Should it come today, what man may say
We shall not live again?

God wrought our souls from the
Tremadoc beds
And furnished them wings to fly;
He sowed our spawn in the world's dim
dawn,
And I know that it shall not die;
Though cities have sprung above the
graves

414

Where the crook-boned men made war,
And the oxwain creaks o'er the buried caves,
Where the mummied mammoths are.

Then as we linger at luncheon here,
O'er many a dainty dish,
Let us drink anew to the time when you
Were a Tadpole and I was a Fish.

Thanatopsis
by William Cullen Bryant

TO HIM who in the love of Nature holds
Communion with her visible forms, she speaks
A various language; for his gayer hours
She has a voice of gladness, and a smile
And eloquence of beauty, and she glides
Into his darker musings, with a mild
And healing sympathy, that steals away
Their sharpness, ere he is aware. When thoughts
Of the last bitter hour come like a blight
Over thy spirit, and sad images
Of the stern agony, and shroud, and pall,
And breathless darkness, and the narrow house,
Make thee to shudder, and grow sick at heart;—
Go forth under the open sky, and list
To Nature's teachings, while from all around—
Earth and her waters, and the depths of air—
Comes a still voice—Yet a few days, and thee
The all-beholding sun shall see no more
In all his course; nor yet in the cold ground,
Where thy pale form was laid, with many tears,
Nor in the embrace of ocean, shall exist
Thy image. Earth, that nourished thee, shall claim
Thy growth, to be resolved to earth again,
And, lost each human trace, surrendering up
Thine individual being, shalt thou go
To mix forever with the elements;
To be a brother to the insensible rock,
And to the sluggish clod, which the rude swain
Turns with his share, and treads upon. The oak
Shall send his roots abroad, and pierce thy mould.
Yet not to thine eternal resting-place
Shalt thou retire alone, nor couldst thou wish
Couch more magnificent. Thou shalt lie down
With patriarchs of the infant world,—with kings,
The powerful of the earth,—the wise, the good,
Fair forms, and hoary seers of ages past,
All in one mighty sepulchre. The hills
Rock-ribbed and ancient as the sun; the vales
Stretching in pensive quietness between;
The venerable woods—rivers that move
In majesty, and the complaining brooks

That make the meadows green; and, poured round all,
Old Ocean's gray and melancholy waste,—
Are but the solemn decorations all
Of the great tomb of man! The golden sun,
The planets, all the infinite host of heaven,
Are shining on the sad abodes of death,
Through the still lapse of ages. All that tread
The globe are but a handful to the tribes
That slumber in its bosom.—Take the wings
Of morning, pierce the Barcan wilderness,
Or lose thyself in the continuous woods
Where rolls the Oregon, and hears no sound,
Save his own dashings,—yet the dead are there:
And millions in those solitudes, since first
The flight of years began, have laid them down
In their last sleep—the dead reign there alone.
So shalt thou rest; and what if thou withdraw
In silence from the living, and no friend
Take note of thy departure? All that breathe
Will share thy destiny. The gay will laugh
When thou art gone, the solemn brood of care
Plod on, and each one as before will chase

His favorite phantom; yet all these shall leave
Their mirth and their employments, and shall come
And make their bed with thee. As the long train
Of ages glide away, the sons of men,
The youth in life's green spring, and he who goes
In the full strength of years, matron and maid,
The speechless babe, and the gray-headed man –
Shall one by one be gathered to thy side
By those, who in their turn shall follow them.

So live, that when thy summons comes to join
The innumerable caravan which moves
To that mysterious realm, where each shall take
His chamber in the silent halls of death,
Thou go not, like the quarry-slave at night,
Scourged to his dungeon, but, sustained and soothed
By an unfaltering trust, approach thy grave
Like one who wraps the drapery of his couch
About him, and lies down to pleasant dreams.

The Charge of the Light Brigade
by Alfred, Lord Tennyson

Half a league, half a league,
Half a league onward,
All in the valley of Death
  Rode the six hundred.

"Forward, the Light Brigade!
"Charge for the guns!" he said:
Into the valley of Death
   Rode the six hundred.

"Forward, the Light Brigade!"
Was there a man dismay'd?
Not tho' the soldier knew
   Someone had blunder'd:
Theirs not to make reply,
Theirs not to reason why,
Theirs but to do and die:
Into the valley of Death
   Rode the six hundred.
Cannon to right of them,
Cannon to left of them,
Cannon in front of them
   Volley'd and thunder'd;
Storm'd at with shot and shell,
Boldly they rode and well,
Into the jaws of Death,
Into the mouth of Hell
   Rode the six hundred.

Flash'd all their sabres bare,
Flash'd as they turn'd in air,
Sabring the gunners there,
Charging an army, while
   All the world wonder'd:
Plunged in the battery-smoke
Right thro' the line they broke;
Cossack and Russian
Reel'd from the sabre stroke
   Shatter'd and sunder'd.
Then they rode back, but not
   Not the six hundred.

Cannon to right of them,
Cannon to left of them,
Cannon behind them
   Volley'd and thunder'd;

Storm'd at with shot and shell,
While horse and hero fell,
They that had fought so well
Came thro' the jaws of Death
Back from the mouth of Hell,
All that was left of them,
   Left of six hundred.

When can their glory fade?
O the wild charge they made!
   All the world wondered.
Honour the charge they made,
Honour the Light Brigade,
   Noble six hundred.

Requiem
by Robert Louis Stevenson

UNDER the wide and starry sky
   Dig the grave and let me lie:
Glad did I live and gladly die,
   And I laid me down with a will.

This be the verse you 'grave[99] for me:
   Here he lies where he long'd to be;
Home is the sailor, home from the sea,
   And the hunter home from the hill.

The Prison And The Angel
by Henry Van Dyke

Self is the only prison that can ever
bind the soul;
Love is the only angel who can bid the
gates unroll;
And when he comes to call thee, arise
and follow fast;
His way may lie through darkness, but
it leads to light at last.

---

[99] engrave

Sources and Acknowledgments

When I began this project, I had little idea of the places it would take me, the threads I would follow, the history I would learn. I thought that with the great treasure trove of material that Dad had left me, it would just be a matter of compiling it, much as I did for my mother's book.

But time after time I was drawn into the history that I was recording and found myself digging deeper, verifying factual information, exploring historical figures and events that surrounded my ancestors and even confirming the use of words that were not in my vocabulary. The journey was fascinating for me and the number of times that Dad's facts were correct is a tribute to his excellent memory.

Part I.

I enjoyed reviewing newspaper articles that mentioned J. R. Whitney. Through them I was able to ascertain that he made his fortune as a commission merchant. This was a fact that Dad was never able to turn up. He spent many hours at the Bancroft Library in Berkeley trying to uncover the mystery behind his great-grandfather's wealth, and concluded that he had made his fortune with second mortgages.

I was amazed to come across an account in a newspaper of the time Harriet Whitney Burns gave her chauffeur $6000 to buy an automobile. I hardly believed that story until I read it in the newspaper! I studied the Jamaica Family History website and found an obituary for her that included some information about her interests and noted that she was well liked there.

To cover the Hulse side of the family, I studied the history of both St. Louis, Missouri, and Weston, Missouri, in the 1840s. I wanted to understand why my great-great-grandfather had received a gold-headed cane from Ben Holladay. Through my studies, the family stories, old letters and historical events came together and my family history came alive. I checked census records to learn that George Tuthill Hulse had been a slave owner and that his attitude toward slavery influenced his move to St. Louis in 1865. All of this information I developed into an imaginary conversation between Dad and his Granddad. The connection between Ben Holladay and Buffalo Bill and the fact that Dad had seen Buffalo Bill at the circus – Buffalo Bill's Wild West show – made a nice tie-in.

In relating Dad's stories about Jamaica and Uncle Willie, I stayed true to his words, in spite of the fact that today they are not considered politically correct. My intention was to characterize Uncle Willie as accurately as possible, rather than trying to make him sound like a nicer person than he was. I spent a lot of time trying to track down William Wilson, and finally discovered him in "Massachusetts, Marriages, 1841-1915," with his marriage to Harriet Eliza Whitney, Dad's grandmother, in 1909. From there I was able to determine that he was born in England to a prominent English family and was active in recruiting Jamaican men for His Majesty's Army during World War I.

My father often said that his grandmother, Harriet, lied about her age and it was interesting to read, in her obituary in the Jamaica press, that she was born in Paris, clearly a fabrication.

I wrote the piece about Norman's death after he was burned playing with firecrackers and gasoline. Dad had told me what happened, giving me the outline for the story. But I wanted very much to bring to life this pivotal event that forever changed the lives of the Hulse family members. I wrote it while I was taking a memoir writing class with my mother and when I read it out loud to the class, I looked up after I was done, and there wasn't a dry eye in the room. I knew that I had captured the feeling of the event.

Part II.

Among Dad's possessions was the September 1932 issue of *Scribner's Magazine*. In it I found an account of the shipwreck of the *Colombia* written up in an article entitled "To the Lifeboats!" by Helen Bird. Some information that came from that article included: "The lifeboats were swinging out from the boat deck. The *Colombia's* whistle was crying, the most forsaken, hopeless cry I had ever heard. The passengers were all on deck in various stages of attire from pajamas and negligées to complete street dress. One man had even put on a necktie. The captain appeared. 'Everybody get life-preservers and warm coats. It will be cold out there.'

"Creaking of winches. Grinding of ropes. The first lifeboat was at the rail. The chief steward was supervising the loading of the boat.

I looked at my watch. Twelve forty-five. 'Women and children first,' the captain's order was hoarse and staccato."

The steward helped the women and children into the first boat. It was crowded as they began to lower it toward the water. "The boat was tipping and jerking, sinking down into black emptiness. Then it caught on the side of the listing *Colombia*. The ship's lights went out. The sailors were struggling with the oars trying to pry the boat away from the ship. It swung out and the bow dropped several feet below the stern. They hung there tilted in midair. 'Hold everything! Hold everything!' shrieked a sailor, waving a flashlight. Then somehow the boat touched the water, floated, and was dashed against the black wall of the *Colombia*. The sailors were trying to brace the ends of the oars against the ship." Just at that moment, the second lifeboat began to descend toward the water. A waving flashlight came from the first boat along with the cry, "'Hold that boat! Hold that boat!' A madness of shrieks and screams." Finally the first boat cleared the ship and was safely away.

"Waves battered and buffeted the boat. The sailors were rowing desperately to keep us off the rocks. We were thrown up into the air, then suddenly dropped down into an abyss. Every one was hanging over the side of the boat vomiting agonizingly. The boat bounced up and down as if it were suspended on springs. It tipped, tilted, rocked, dipped, lurched, swayed, pitched, performed every acrobatic feat known to a boat except to capsize." The *Colombia* sent up rockets, one shower of light after another. "A sudden flash of red enveloped the *Colombia*," as they tried to signal a passing ship.

By three o'clock "the sea was calmer. The sailors rested their oars and lit cigarettes.

"The east grew gray and pink and white. Then through the western mists we saw lights, lights in the outline of a ship. It was ten minutes to five. 'Row! Hell, come on! Row! Let's get together, now row!' But our exhausted sailors could make little impression on the distance between us and the ship. And the current was against them.

"Finally, the *San Mateo*, taking soundings as it came, sailed toward us." There were a few discrepancies between her account and Dad's, but I stuck with Dad's story for the book.

From a newspaper clipping dated September 18, 1931: "Worn from their experience and from crowded conditions aboard rescue ships, the 234 passengers and crew of the wrecked liner *Colombia* arrived at Los Angeles harbor. Thus ended their adventure."

I learned from a unnamed newspaper article the "back story" about the Chinese passengers. "The Chinamen were for the most part wealthy merchants banished from Mexico under the new governmental order. They had sold their businesses in Mexico City and elsewhere and had with them close to $100,000 in gold and silver." The *Colombia* was declared a total wreck and abandoned to her underwriters with the gold still aboard. The gold and silver were recovered from the strong box of the sunken ship some six weeks later.

I spent quite some time figuring out where exactly Dad traveled on his cross-country trip in 1934. His letters described his trip up to St. Joseph, Missouri, and his photographs of Yellowstone and the Grand Canyon helped me establish his trip through the western part of the country.

Dad kept an extensive journal of the grounding of the *Cuzco* and the twelve days spent freeing her from Lempa Shoals. I quoted his journal as completely as I could and, though some details may be difficult for the landlubber to follow, I hope they are of interest to some.

It was interesting to come across the letter from Dan Lamb and his request to be "put to sea in my own boat the *Vagabundo*." I read a little about him and his wife, Ginger, and they were quite the adventurers. His book, *Enchanted Vagabonds*, is now in my possession.

On one of my visits to see Uncle Bill, Dad's younger brother, he told me about their trip across the country by train in 1938, and also about Duge's job with Metals & Thermit Company. It seemed ironic to me that they moved east just when Dad quit the ships and moved to San Francisco. But that meant that they continued corresponding by letter and I became the beneficiary of their correspondence.

When Dave and I were in Lakeport one time, we made a point to find the campground that my grandfather, G.C. Hulse, owned: the Will-O-Point Campground. It is still there, along with the big willow tree from which it drew its name. It was a nostalgic moment for me to walk under those same trees where my grandfather raked up the leaves. I could almost picture him there.

I was happy to come across Dad's description of how he learned about the bombing of Pearl Harbor. I didn't remember him telling me that story and was glad I could include it.

From Dad's writings and letters it was impossible to tell where he had landed in Europe, when he shipped out to join the War. But I was lucky to come across the AllExperts website and to contact Richard V. Horrell of WW 2 Connections, who was able to fill in some important gaps for me. Giving him Dad's dates of departure from Boston harbor and arrival in France, he was able to tell me that he had sailed into Cherbourg, France, and gave me a list of possible ships he had sailed on. From Dad's description of his transport ship in a letter he wrote, I was able to conclude that he had sailed on the SS *Brazil*.

He also explained, "Your father was trained as an Infantry Replacement. This is not good nor bad, just a fact of history. He was sent overseas to take the place of a soldier already assigned to an Infantry Division who was a casualty." By giving Mr. Horrell the APO addresses that were on the letters addressed to Dad, he was able to tell me approximately where he was located throughout his war experience. In that way I found out that Dad was stationed near Thaon-les-Vosges, France, from October 20, 1944, through March 21, 1945. And in fact, there were a number of postcards of that town in his belongings. Épinal is about five miles away.

I read a booklet that was in Dad's belongings called "On the Way, A Record of the 342nd Armored Field Artillery Battalion, Oct. 1944 -July 1945." It did not seem to be an exact account of Dad's war experience, but there were a number of stories that were similar to Dad's diary notes. I corresponded with Chall Allred and Bob Gray who were both in the 342 Armored Field Artillery Battalion. I had a very nice talk with Bob Gray on the phone. He confirmed Dad's story about liberating the prisoner camp and remembered a Jeep being hit, that sounded familiar. I did some research on the liberation of the prison camps in Germany and found that the work camp at Landsberg was liberated by the 12th Armored Division on April 27, 1945. Given Dad's path through Germany and the dates when he was at various locations, I concluded that this was the camp they helped liberate. I also took a close look at a pair of sugar tongs that Dad had brought back from Germany. They have "Landsburg" engraved on them and I learned from a man with a website dedicated to such things, that they were from the Luftwaffe Mess in that area.

I studied up about Berchtesgaden, Austria, and concluded that Dad was actually referring to Berchtesgadener Land, a district of Bavaria, Germany. Obersalzberg, where Hitler and the Nazis built a community, is situated in the hills above the town of Berchtesgaden. This is where the ruins were and not the resort town of Berchtesgaden, which was not actually bombed. There were also a number of bus tickets for Obersalzberg in his belongings.

Mr. Horrell also helped me read Dad's discharge papers to glean information about his departure from the European Theater. He also sent me a number of documents showing the tank that Dad commanded with explanations of its parts and operation. He greatly helped me understand Dad's war experience.

Part III.

Dad had kept a journal of his jobs when he was a building contractor in Burlingame. As I went through it I came across familiar names: Shanzer, Tommy Harris, Fred Noonan. I spent some time on the internet learning who these men were and found them to be colorful characters.

Living in Willits, we became friends with Bill Meyerhoff and his wife, Linda. In talking with them one time, I learned that he had bought one of the houses that Dad built in Pacifica. And what's more, he remembered the time when the beetles came up out of the hardwood floors. He felt that Dad had been an honest and conscientious contractor and added, "Stan was a real gentleman."

I learned the details about Dad's subdivision in Livermore from newspaper clippings I found on the internet. I had no idea that it was supposed to be a $20 million residential/commercial/industrial complex. No wonder he didn't sleep at night!

On our European trip in 1962, we were able to see a lot of sights that are no longer open to the public. We were lucky to see the Lascaux Cave in southern France, which was closed to the public in 1963 to preserve its Paleolithic cave paintings. Less than a third of all buildings in Pompeii open in the 1960s, were available for public viewing in 2008, according to a Wikipedia.

Geri helped with some details about Lake Pillsbury days. I went through old letters from Tim to piece together his story after he joined the Air Force. I also used letters that Mom wrote to me to fill in parts of the story during the time I was away at college.

Among the letters that Dad had kept were a number of them from J. Campbell Bruce, an old, old friend of his. As I was reading through them, I came across a comment that John Bruce had made in a letter, "Thanks for that free trip down the Amazon! By way of HEE – – Hulse Exotic Excursions. Your account was so vivid, I was there – – and at times so creepingly vivid, I was just as glad I was here, while there vicariously." Oh, how I wished that I had that letter that Dad had written to John. So I began a hunt. I found J. Campbell

Bruce's obituary and from that found out the names of his children. Then through Facebook, I searched for his son, Anthony, and found such a person living in Berkeley who worked at the Berkeley Architectural Heritage Association. So I contacted him through the Association and when he responded that his father was indeed John Bruce, we began a nice correspondence. On a trip to Berkeley in May 2013, Dave and I met him and spent a couple of hours with him sharing letters and photographs of our fathers. It turned out that he was living in the same house that his dad had lived in for over 50 years, so it was a treat to see the beautiful old home and spend time in John's office where I'm sure the two old friends had passed the time together. In the months that followed, Anthony and I exchanged letters and he at last came across "the letter" and sent it to me. I was glad to get to know Anthony and we had a fun time digging into the past together.

Mike and Suzanne both wrote pieces for me to include about their memories of Grampa. They helped to complete the picture of what it was like for him to be a grandfather. Because Dad and Mom worked at the nursery every day, Mike and Suzanne were lucky to know him in a very special way.

My thanks goes to all of my family who have encouraged me in my long journey writing this book. Thank you to Suzanne, Geri and Linda Wiley for proofreading. You were a tremendous help.

My very special thanks goes to my husband, Dave, for inspiration and help with the dust jacket and book cover, as well as many excellent suggestions along the way. Your continued encouragement and motivation are the reason this book has finally come to fruition.

Finally, I hope that Dad would be pleased with this book. I certainly have enjoyed going along for the ride.

Index